Charles O...

September 17, 1959

COLLECTED ESSAYS

Books by Aldous Huxley

NOVELS
The Genius and the
    Goddess
Ape and Essence
Time Must Have a
    Stop
After Many a Summer
    Dies the Swan

Eyeless in Gaza
Point Counter Point
Those Barren Leaves
Antic Hay
Crome Yellow
Brave New World

**ESSAYS AND
BELLES
LETTRES**
Tomorrow and
    Tomorrow and
    Tomorrow
Heaven and Hell
The Doors of
    Perception
The Devils of Loudun
Themes and Variations
Ends and Means
Texts and Pretexts
The Olive Tree
Music at Night

Vulgarity in Literature
Do What You Will
Proper Studies
Along the Road
On the Margin
Essays New and Old
The Art of Seeing
The Perennial Philosophy
Science, Liberty and
    Peace
Collected Essays

**SHORT
STORIES**
Brief Candles
Two or Three Graces
Limbo.

Little Mexican
Mortal Coils
Collected Short Stories

BIOGRAPHY
Grey Eminence

POETRY
The Cicadas

Leda

TRAVEL
Beyond the Mexique
    Bay

Jesting Pilate

DRAMA
Mortal Coils—A Play
The World of Light

The Discovery,
    Adapted from
    Frances Sheridan

**SELECTED
WORKS**
Rotunda

The World of Aldous
    Huxley

COLLECTED

ESSAYS

by Aldous Huxley

Harper & Brothers Publishers

New York

COLLECTED ESSAYS

Library of Congress catalog card number: 59-10583

"I am a man and alive," wrote D. H. Lawrence. "For this reason I am a novelist. And, being a novelist, I consider myself superior to the saint, the scientist, the philosopher, and the poet, who are all great masters of different bits of man alive, but never get the whole hog. . . . Only in the novel are *all* things given full play."

What is true of the novel is only a little less true of the essay. For, like the novel, the essay is a literary device for saying almost everything about almost anything. By tradition, almost by definition, the essay is a short piece, and it is therefore impossible to give all things full play within the limits of a single essay. But a collection of essays can cover almost as much ground, and cover it almost as thoroughly as can a long novel. Montaigne's Third Book is the equivalent, very nearly, of a good slice of the *Comédie Humaine.*

Essays belong to a literary species whose extreme variability can be studied most effectively within a three-poled frame of reference. There is the pole of the personal and the autobiographical; there is the pole of the objective, the factual, the concrete-particular; and there is the pole of the abstract-universal. Most essayists are at home and at their best in the neighborhood of only one of the essay's three poles, or at the most only in the neighborhood of two of them. There are the predominantly personal essayists, who write fragments of reflective autobiography and who look at the world through the keyhole of anecdote and description. There are the predominantly objective essayists who do not speak directly of them-

selves, but turn their attention outward to some literary or
scientific or political theme. Their art consists in setting forth,
passing judgment upon, and drawing general conclusions
from, the relevant data. In a third group we find those essayists who do their work in the world of high abstractions, who
never condescend to be personal and who hardly deign to take
notice of the particular facts, from which their generalizations
were originally drawn. Each kind of essay has its special merits
and defects. The personal essayists may be as good as Charles
Lamb at his best, or as bad as Mr. X at his cutest and most
self-consciously whimsical. The objective essay may be as
lively, as brassily contentious as a piece by Macaulay; but it
may also, with fatal ease, degenerate into something merely
informative or, if it be critical, into something merely learned
and academic. And how splendid, how truly oracular are the
utterances of the great generalizers! "He that hath wife and
children hath given hostages to fortune; for they are impediments to great enterprises, either of virtue or mischief." And
from Bacon we pass to Emerson. "All men plume themselves
on the improvement of society, and no man improves. Society
never advances. It recedes as fast on one side as it gains on
the other. For everything that is given, something is taken."
Even a Baltasar Gracian, that briefest of essayists who writes
as though he were cabling his wisdom, at two dollars a word,
to the Antipodes, sometimes achieves a certain magnificence.
"Things have their period; even excellences are subject to
fashion. The sage has one advantage: he is immortal. If *this*
is not his century, many others will be." But the medal of
solemn and lapidary generalization has its reverse. The constantly abstract, constantly impersonal essayist is apt to give
us not oracles but algebra. As an example of such algebraic
writing, let me quote a short passage from the English translation of Paul Valéry's *Dialogues*. It is worth remarking that
French literature has a tradition of high and sustained abstraction; English literature has not. Works that in French are not at
all out of the common seem, when translated, strange almost to
the point of absurdity. But even when made acceptable by
tradition and a great talent, the algebraic style strikes us as
being very remote from the living reality of our immediate
experience. Here, in the words of an imaginary Socrates, is
Valéry's description of the kind of language in which (as I
think, unfortunately) he liked to write. "What is more mysterious than clarity? what more capricious than the way in
which light and shade are distributed over the hours and
over men? Certain peoples lose themselves in their thoughts,
but for the Greeks all things are forms. We retain only their
relations and, enclosed, as it were, in the limpid day, Orpheus-

like we build, by means of the word, temples of wisdom and
science that may suffice for all reasonable creatures. This great
art requires of us an admirably exact language. The very word
that signifies language is also the name, with us, for reason
and calculation; the same word says these three things." In
the stratosphere of abstract notions this elegant algebra is all
very well; but a completely bodiless language can never do
justice to the data of immediate experience, nor can it contribute anything to our understanding of the "capricious lights
and shades" in the midst of which, whether we like it or not,
we must perforce live out our lives.

The most richly satisfying essays are those which make the
best not of one, not of two, but of all the three worlds in
which it is possible for the essay to exist. Freely, effortlessly,
thought and feeling move in these consummate works of art,
hither and thither between the essay's three poles—from the
personal to the universal, from the abstract back to the concrete, from the objective datum to the inner experience.

The perfection of any artistic form is rarely achieved by its
first inventor. To this rule Montaigne is the great and marvelous exception. By the time he had written his way into the
Third Book, he had reached the limits of his newly discovered
art. "What are these essays," he had asked at the beginning
of his career, "but grotesque bodies pieced together of different members, without any definite shape, without any order,
coherence, or proportion, except they be accidental." But a
few years later the patchwork grotesques had turned into living organisms, into multiform hybrids like those beautiful
monsters of the old mythologies, the mermaids, the man-
headed bulls with wings, the centaurs, the Anubises, the sera-
phim—impossibilities compounded of incompatibles, but compounded from within, by a process akin to growth, so that
the human trunk seems to spring quite naturally from between
the horse's shoulders, the fish modulates into the full-breasted
Siren as easily and inevitably as a musical theme modulates
from one key to another. Free association artistically controlled—this is the paradoxical secret of Montaigne's best
essays. One damned thing after another—but in a sequence
that in some almost miraculous way develops a central theme
and relates it to the rest of human experience. And how beautifully Montaigne combines the generalization with the anecdote, the homily with the autobiographical reminiscence! How
skilfully he makes use of the concrete particular, the *chose
vue,* to express some universal truth, and to express it more
powerfully and penetratingly than it can be expressed by even
the most oracular of the dealers in generalities! Here, for
example, is what a great oracle, Dr. Johnson, has to say about

the human situation and the uses of adversity. "Affliction is inseparable from our present state; it adheres to all the inhabitants of this world, in different proportions indeed, but with an allotment which seems very little regulated by our own conduct. It has been the boast of some swelling moralists that every man's fortune was in his own power, that prudence supplied the place of all other divinities, and that happiness is the unfailing consequence of virtue. But, surely, the quiver of Omnipotence is stored with arrows, against which the shield of human virtue, however adamantine it has been boasted, is held up in vain; we do not always suffer by our crimes, we are not always protected by our innocence. . . . Nothing confers so much ability to resist the temptations that perpetually surround us, as an habitual consideration of the shortness of life, and the uncertainty of those pleasures that solicit our pursuit; and this consideration can be inculcated only by affliction." This is altogether admirable; but there are other and, I would say, better ways of approaching the subject. *"J'ay veu en mon temps cent artisans, cent laboureurs, plus sages et plus heureux que des Recteurs de l'Universite."* (I have seen in my time hundreds of artisans and laborers, wiser and happier than university presidents.) Again, "Look at poor working people sitting on the ground with drooping heads after their day's toil. They know neither Aristotle nor Cato, neither example nor precept; and yet from them Nature draws effects of constancy and patience purer and more unconquerable than any of those we study so curiously in the schools." Add to one touch of nature one touch of irony, and you have a comment on life more profound, in spite of its casualness, its seeming levity, than the most eloquent rumblings of the oracles. "It is not our follies that make me laugh," says Montaigne, "it is our sapiences." And why should our sapiences provoke a wise man to laughter? Among other reasons, because the professional sages tend to express themselves in a language of highest abstraction and widest generality—a language that, for all its gnomic solemnity is apt, in a tight corner, to reveal itself as ludicrously inappropriate to the facts of life as it is really and tragically lived.

In the course of the last forty years I have written essays of every size and shape and color. Essays almost as short as Gracian's and, on occasion, longer even than Macaulay's. Essays autobiographical. Essays about things seen and places visited. Essays in criticism of all kinds of works of art, literary, plastic, musical. Essays about philosophy and religion, some of them couched in abstract terms, others in the form of an anthology with comments, others again in which general ideas are approached through the concrete facts of history and biography. Essays, finally, in which, following Montaigne, I have tried to make the best of all the essay's three worlds, have tried to say everything at once in as near an approach to contrapuntal simultaneity as the nature of literary art will allow of.

Sometimes, it seems to me, I have succeeded fairly well in doing what, in one field or another, I had set out to do. Sometimes, alas, I know that I have not succeeded. But "please do not shoot the pianist; he is doing his best." Doing his best, *selon ses quelques doigts perclus,* to make his cottage upright say as much as the great orchestra of the novel, doing his best to "give all things full play." For the writer at least, and perhaps also for the reader, it is better to have tried and failed to achieve perfection than never to have tried at all.

ALDOUS HUXLEY

CONTENTS

Preface   v

SECTION I

Nature

Wordsworth in the Tropics   1
The Olive Tree   10
The Desert   19

Travel

The Palio at Siena   29
Sabbioneta   36
Between Peshawar and Lahore   42
Jaipur   46
Atitlan   48
Sololà   49
Copan   51
In a Tunisian Oasis   53
Miracle in Lebanon   62

Love, Sex, and Physical Beauty

Beauty in 1920   67
Fashions in Love   70
Sermons in Cats   77
Appendix   82

SECTION II

Literature

Subject-Matter of Poetry   91
Tragedy and the Whole Truth   96
Vulgarity in Literature   103
D. H. Lawrence   115
Famagusta or Paphos   129

Painting

Breughel   135
Meditation on El Greco   144
Form and Spirit in Art   151
Variations on Goya   157
Landscape Painting as a Vision-Inducing Art   167

Music

Popular Music   173
Music at Night   176
Gesualdo: Variations on a Musical Theme   180

Matters of Taste and Style

Variations on a Baroque Tomb   197
Faith, Taste, and History   206

SECTION III

History

Maine de Biran: The Philosopher in History   217
Usually Destroyed   236

Politics

Words and Behavior   245
Decentralization and Self-Government   255

Politics and Religion   268
The Scientist's Role   286
Tomorrow and Tomorrow and Tomorrow   291

SECTION IV

Psychology

Madness, Badness, Sadness   299
A Case of Voluntary Ignorance   308
The Oddest Science   319

Rx for Sense and Psyche

The Doors of Perception   327
Drugs That Shape Men's Minds   336

Way of Life

Holy Face   347
Pascal   352
Beliefs   361
Knowledge and Understanding   377

NATURE

Wordsworth in the Tropics

In the neighborhood of latitude fifty north, and for the last hundred years or thereabouts, it has been an axiom that Nature is divine and morally uplifting. For good Wordsworthians—and most serious-minded people are now Wordsworthians, either by direct inspiration or at second hand—a walk in the country is the equivalent of going to church, a tour through Westmorland is as good as a pilgrimage to Jerusalem. To commune with the fields and waters, the woodlands and the hills, is to commune, according to our modern and northern ideas, with the visible manifestations of the "Wisdom and Spirit of the Universe."

The Wordsworthian who exports this pantheistic worship of Nature to the tropics is liable to have his religious convictions somewhat rudely disturbed. Nature, under a vertical sun, and nourished by the equatorial rains, is not at all like that chaste, mild deity who presides over the *Gemüthlichkeit,* the prettiness, the cozy sublimities of the Lake District. The worst that Wordsworth's goddess ever did to him was to make him hear

> Low breathings coming after me, and sounds
> Of undistinguishable motion, steps
> Almost as silent as the turf they trod;

was to make him realize, in the shape of "a huge peak, black and huge," the existence of "unknown modes of being." He seems to have imagined that this was the worst Nature *could* do. A few weeks in Malaya or Borneo would have undeceived him. Wandering in the hothouse darkness of the jungle, he

1

would not have felt so serenely certain of those "Presences of Nature," those "Souls of Lonely Places," which he was in the habit of worshipping on the shores of Windermere and Rydal. The sparse inhabitants of the equatorial forest are all believers in devils. When one has visited, in even the most superficial manner, the places where they live, it is difficult not to share their faith. The jungle is marvelous, fantastic, beautiful; but it is also terrifying, it is also profoundly sinister. There is something in what, for lack of a better word, we must call the character of great forests—even in those of temperate lands—which is foreign, appalling, fundamentally and utterly inimical to intruding man. The life of those vast masses of swarming vegetation is alien to the human spirit and hostile to it. Meredith, in his "Woods of Westermaine," has tried reassuringly to persuade us that our terrors are unnecessary, that the hostility of these vegetable forces is more apparent than real, and that if we will but trust Nature we shall find our fears transformed into serenity, joy, and rapture. This may be sound philosophy in the neighborhood of Dorking; but it begins to be dubious even in the forests of Germany—there is too much of them for a human being to feel himself at ease within their enormous glooms; and when the woods of Borneo are substituted for those of Westermaine, Meredith's comforting doctrine becomes frankly ridiculous.

It is not the sense of solitude that distresses the wanderer in equatorial jungles. Loneliness is bearable enough—for a time, at any rate. There is something actually rather stimulating and exciting about being in an empty place where there is no life but one's own. Taken in reasonably small doses, the Sahara exhilarates, like alcohol. Too much of it, however (I speak, at any rate, for myself), has the depressing effect of the second bottle of Burgundy. But in any case it is not loneliness that oppresses the equatorial traveller: it is too much company; it is the uneasy feeling that he is an alien in the midst of an innumerable throng of hostile beings. To us who live beneath a temperate sky and in the age of Henry Ford, the worship of Nature comes almost naturally. It is easy to love a feeble and already conquered enemy. But an enemy with whom one is still at war, an unconquered, unconquerable, ceaselessly active enemy—no; one does not, one should not, love him. One respects him, perhaps; one has a salutary fear of him; and one goes on fighting. In our latitudes the hosts of Nature have mostly been vanquished and enslaved. Some few detachments, it is true, still hold the field against us. There are wild woods and mountains, marshes and heaths, even in England. But they are there only on sufferance, because we have chosen, out of our good pleasure, to leave them their freedom.

It has not been worth our while to reduce them to slavery. We love them because we are the masters, because we know that at any moment we can overcome them as we overcame their fellows. The inhabitants of the tropics have no such comforting reasons for adoring the sinister forces which hem them in on every side. For us, the notion "river" implies (how obviously!) the notion "bridge." When we think of a plain, we think of agriculture, towns, and good roads. The corollary of mountain is tunnel; of swamp, an embankment; of distance, a railway. At latitude zero, however, the obvious is not the same as with us. Rivers imply wading, swimming, alligators. Plains mean swamps, forests, fevers. Mountains are either dangerous or impassable. To travel is to hack one's way laboriously through a tangled, prickly, and venomous darkness. "God made the country," said Cowper, in his rather too blank verse. In New Guinea he would have had his doubts; he would have longed for the man-made town.

The Wordsworthian adoration of Nature has two principal defects. The first, as we have seen, is that it is only possible in a country where Nature has been nearly or quite enslaved to man. The second is that it is only possible for those who are prepared to falsify their immediate intuitions of Nature. For Nature, even in the temperate zone, is always alien and inhuman, and occasionally diabolic. Meredith explicitly invites us to explain any unpleasant experiences away. We are to interpret them, Pangloss fashion, in terms of a preconceived philosophy; after which, all will surely be for the best in the best of all possible Westermaines. Less openly, Wordsworth asks us to make the same falsification of immediate experience. It is only very occasionally that he admits the existence in the world around him of those "unknown modes of being" of which our immediate intuitions of things make us so disquietingly aware. Normally what he does is to pump the dangerous Unknown out of Nature and refill the emptied forms of hills and woods, flowers and waters, with something more reassuringly familiar—with humanity, with Anglicanism. He will not admit that a yellow primrose is simply a yellow primrose—beautiful, but essentially strange, having its own alien life apart. He wants it to possess some sort of soul, to exist humanly, not simply flowerily. He wants the earth to be more than earthy, to be a divine person. But the life of vegetation is radically unlike the life of man: the earth has a mode of being that is certainly not the mode of being of a person. "Let Nature be your teacher," says Wordsworth. The advice is excellent. But how strangely he himself puts it into practice! Instead of listening humbly to what the teacher says, he shuts his ears and himself dictates the lesson he desires to hear.

The pupil knows better than his master; the worshipper substitutes his own oracles for those of the god. Instead of accepting the lesson as it is given to his immediate intuitions, he distorts it rationalistically into the likeness of a parson's sermon or a professorial lecture. Our direct intuitions of Nature tell us that the world is bottomlessly strange: alien, even when it is kind and beautiful; having innumerable modes of being that are not our modes; always mysteriously not personal, not conscious, not moral; often hostile and sinister; sometimes even unimaginably, because inhumanly, evil. In his youth, it would seem, Wordsworth left his direct intuitions of the world unwarped.

> The sounding cataract
> Haunted me like a passion: the tall rock,
> The mountain, and the deep and gloomy wood,
> Their colors and their forms, were then to me
> An appetite; a feeling and a love,
> That had no need of a remoter charm,
> By thought supplied, nor any interest
> Unborrowed from the eye.

As the years passed, however, he began to interpret them in terms of a preconceived philosophy. Procrustes-like, he tortured his feelings and perceptions until they fitted his system. By the time he was thirty,

> The immeasurable height
> Of woods decaying, never to be decayed,
> The stationary blasts of waterfalls—
> The torrents shooting from the clear blue sky,
> The rocks that muttered close upon our ears,
> Black drizzling crags that spake by the wayside
> As if a voice were in them, the sick sight
> And giddy prospect of the raving stream,
> The unfettered clouds and regions of the heavens,
> Tumult and peace, the darkness and the light—
> Were all like workings of one mind, the features
> Of the same face, blossoms upon one tree,
> Characters of the great Apocalypse,
> The types and symbols of eternity,
> Of first, and last, and midst, and without end.

"Something far more deeply interfused" had made its appearance on the Wordsworthian scene. The god of Anglicanism had crept under the skin of things, and all the stimulatingly inhuman strangeness of Nature had become as flatly familiar as a page from a textbook of metaphysics or theology. As familiar and as safely simple. Pantheistically interpreted, our intuitions of Nature's endless varieties of impersonal mysteriousness lose all their exciting and disturbing quality. It makes the world seem delightfully cozy, if you can pretend that all the many alien things about you are really only manifestations of one person. It is fear of the labyrinthine flux and complexity of phenomena that has driven men to philosophy, to science, to theology—fear of the complex reality driving them to invent a simpler, more manageable, and, therefore, consoling fiction. For simple, in comparison with the external reality of which we have direct intuitions, childishly simple is even the most elaborate and subtle system devised by the human mind. Most of the philosophical systems hitherto popular have not been subtle and elaborate even by human standards. Even by human standards they have been crude, bald, preposterously straightforward. Hence their popularity. Their simplicity has rendered them instantly comprehensible. Weary with much wandering in the maze of phenomena, frightened by the inhospitable strangeness of the world, men have rushed into the systems prepared for them by philosophers and founders of religions, as they would rush from a dark jungle into the haven of a well-lit, commodious house. With a sigh of relief and a thankful feeling that here at last is their true home, they settle down in their snug metaphysical villa and go to sleep. And how furious they are when any one comes rudely knocking at the door to tell them that their villa is jerry-built, dilapidated, unfit for human habitation, even non-existent! Men have been burnt at the stake for even venturing to criticize the color of the front door or the shape of the third-floor windows.

That man must build himself some sort of metphysical shelter in the midst of the jungle of immediately apprehended reality is obvious. No practical activity, no scientific research, no speculation is possible without some preliminary hypothesis about the nature and the purpose of things. The human mind cannot deal with the universe directly, nor even with its own immediate intuitions of the universe. Whenever it is a question of thinking about the world or of practically modifying it, men can only work on a symbolic plan of the universe, only a simplified, two-dimensional map of things abstracted by the mind out of the complex and multifarious reality of immediate intuition. History shows that these hypotheses about the nature of things are valuable even when, as later experience reveals, they are false. Man approaches the unattainable truth through a succession of errors. Confronted by the strange complexity of things, he invents, quite arbitrarily, a simple hypothesis to explain and justify the world. Having invented, he proceeds to act and think in terms of this hypothesis, as though it were correct. Experience gradually shows him where his hypothesis is unsatisfactory and how it should be modified. Thus, great scientific discoveries have been made by men seeking to verify quite erroneous theories about the nature of things. The discoveries have necessitated a modification of the original hypotheses, and further discoveries have been made in the effort to verify the modifications—discoveries which, in their turn, have led to yet further modifications. And so on, indefinitely. Philosophical and religious hypotheses, being less susceptible of experimental verification than the hypotheses of science, have undergone far less modification. For example, the pantheistic hypothesis of Wordsworth is an ancient doctrine, which human experience has hardly modified throughout history. And rightly, no doubt. For it is obvious that there must be some sort of unity underlying the diversity of phenomena; for if there were not, the world would be quite unknowable. Indeed, it is precisely in the knowableness of things, in the very fact that they are known, that their fundamental unity consists. The world which we know, and which our minds have fabricated out of goodness knows what mysterious things in themselves, possesses the unity which our minds have imposed upon it. It is part of our thought, hence fundamentally homogeneous. Yes, the world is obviously one. But at the same time it is no less obviously diverse. For if the world were absolutely one, it would no longer be knowable, it would cease to exist. Thought must be divided against itself before it can come to any knowledge of itself. Absolute oneness is absolute nothingness: homogeneous perfection, as the Hindus perceived and courageously recognized, is equivalent to non-existence, is nirvana. The Christian idea of a perfect heaven that is something other than a non-existence is a contradiction in terms. The world in which we live may be fundamentally one, but it is a unity divided up into a great many diverse fragments. A tree, a table, a newspaper, a piece of artificial silk are all made of wood. But they are, none the less, distinct and separate objects. It is the same with the world at large. Our immediate intuitions are of diversity. We have only to open our eyes to recognize a multitude of different phenomena. These intuitions of diversity are as correct, as well justified, as is our intellectual conviction of the fundamental homogeneity of the various parts of the world with one another and with ourselves. Circumstances have led humanity to set an ever-increasing premium on the conscious and intellectual comprehension of things. Modern man's besetting temptation is to sacrifice his direct perceptions and spontaneous feelings to his reasoned reflections; to prefer in all circumstances the verdict of his intellect to that of his immediate intuitions. "L'homme est visiblement fait pour penser," says Pascal; "c'est toute sa dignité et tout son mérite; et tout son devoir est de penser comme il faut." Noble words; but do they happen to be true? Pascal seems to forget that man has something else to do besides think: he must live. Living may not be so dignified or meritorious as thinking (particularly when you happen to be, like Pascal, a chronic invalid); but it is, perhaps unfortunately, a necessary process. If one would live well, one must live completely, with the whole being—with the body and the instincts, as well as with the conscious mind. A life lived, as far as may be, exclusively from the consciousness and in accordance with the considered judgments of the intellect, is a stunted life, a half-dead life. This is a fact that can be confirmed by daily observation. But consciousness, the intellect, the spirit, have acquired an inordinate prestige; and such is men's snobbish respect for authority, such is their pedantic desire to be consistent, that they go on doing their best to lead the exclusively conscious, spiritual, and intellectual life, in spite of its manifest disadvantages. To know is pleasant; it is exciting to be conscious; the intellect is a valuable instrument, and for certain purposes the hypotheses which it fabricates are of great practical value. Quite true. But, therefore, say the moralists and men of science, drawing conclusions only justified by their desire for consistency, therefore *all* life should be lived from the head, consciously, *all* phenomena should at *all* times be interpreted in terms of the intellect's hypotheses. The religious teachers are of a slightly different opinion. All life, according to them, should be lived spiritually, not intellectually. Why? On the grounds, as we discover when we push our analysis far enough, that certain occasional psychological states, currently called spiritual, are extremely agreeable and have valuable consequences in the realm of social behavior. The unprejudiced observer finds it hard to understand why these people should set such store by consistency of thought and action. Because oysters are occasionally pleasant, it does not follow that one should make of oysters one's exclusive diet. Nor should one take castor-oil every day because castor-oil is occasionally good for one. Too much consistency is as bad for the mind as it is for the body. Consistency is contrary to nature, contrary to life. The only completely consistent people are the dead. Consistent intellectualism and spirituality may be socially valuable, up to a point; but they make, gradually, for individual death. And individual death, when the slow murder has been consummated, is finally social death. So that the social utility of pure intellectualism and pure spirituality is only apparent and temporary. What is needed is, as ever, a compromise. Life must be lived in different ways at different moments. The only satisfactory way of existing in the modern, highly specialized world is to live with two personalities. A Dr. Jekyll that does the metaphysical and scientific thinking, that transacts business in the city, adds up figures, designs machines, and so forth. And a natural, spontaneous Mr. Hyde to do the physical, instinctive living in the intervals of work. The two personalities should lead their unconnected lives apart, without poaching on one another's preserves or inquiring too closely into one another's activities. Only by living discreetly and inconsistently can we preserve both the man and the citizen, both the intellectual and the spontaneous animal being, alive within us. The solution may not be very satisfactory; but it is, I believe now (though once I thought differently), the best that, in the modern circumstances, can be devised.

The poet's place, it seems to me, is with the Mr. Hydes of human nature. He should be, as Blake remarked of Milton, "of the devil's party without knowing it"—or preferably with the full consciousness of being of the devil's party. There are so many intellectual and moral angels battling for rationalism, good citizenship, and pure spirituality; so many and such eminent ones, so very vocal and authoritative! The poor devil in man needs all the support and advocacy he can get. The artist is his natural champion. When an artist deserts to the side of the angels, it is the most odious of treasons. How unforgivable, for example, is Tolstoy! Tolstoy, the perfect Mr. Hyde, the complete embodiment, if ever there was one, of non-intellectual, non-moral, instinctive life—Tolstoy, who betrayed his own nature, betrayed his art, betrayed life itself, in order to fight against the devil's party of his earlier allegiances, under the standard of Dr. Jesus-Jekyll. Wordsworth's betrayal was not so spectacular: he was never so wholly of the devil's party as Tolstoy. Still, it was bad enough. It is difficult to forgive him for so utterly repenting his youthful passions and enthusiasms, and becoming, personally as well as politically, the anglican tory. One remembers B. R. Haydon's account of the poet's reactions to that charming classical sculpture of Cupid and Psyche. "The devils!" he said malignantly, after a long-drawn contemplation of their marble embrace. "The devils!" And he was not using the word in the complimentary sense in which I have employed it here: he was expressing his hatred of passion and life, he was damning the young man he had himself been—the young man who had hailed the French Revolution with delight and begotten an illegitimate child. From being an ardent lover of the nymphs, he had become one of those all too numerous

> woodmen who expel
> Love's gentle dryads from the haunts of life,
> And vex the nightingales in every dell.

Yes, even the nightingales he vexed. Even the nightingales, though the poor birds can never, like those all too human dryads, have led him into sexual temptation. Even the innocuous nightingales were moralized, spiritualized, turned into citizens and anglicans—and along with the nightingales, the whole of animate and inanimate Nature.

The change in Wordsworth's attitude toward Nature is symptomatic of his general apostasy. Beginning as what I may call a natural aesthete, he transformed himself, in the course of years, into a moralist, a thinker. He used his intellect to distort his exquisitely acute and subtle intuitions of the world, to explain away their often disquieting strangeness, to simplify them into a comfortable metaphysical unreality. Nature had endowed him with the poet's gift of seeing more than ordinarily far into the brick walls of external reality, of intuitively comprehending the character of the bricks, of feeling the quality of their being, and establishing the appropriate relationship with them. But he preferred to think his gifts away. He preferred, in the interests of a preconceived religious theory, to ignore the disquieting strangeness of things, to interpret the impersonal diversity of Nature in terms of a divine, anglican unity. He chose, in a word, to be a philosopher, comfortably at home with a man-made and, therefore, thoroughly comprehensible system, rather than a poet adventuring for adventure's sake through the mysterious world revealed by his direct and undistorted intuitions.

It is a pity that he never traveled beyond the boundaries of Europe. A voyage through the tropics would have cured him of his too easy and comfortable pantheism. A few months in the jungle would have convinced him that the diversity and utter strangeness of Nature are at least as real and significant as its intellectually discovered unity. Nor would he have felt so certain, in the damp and stifling darkness, among the leeches and the malevolently tangled rattans, of the divinely anglican character of that fundamental unity. He would have learned once more to treat Nature naturally, as he treated it in his youth; to react to it spontaneously, loving where love was the appropriate emotion, fearing, hating, fighting whenever Nature presented itself to his intuition as being, not merely strange, but hostile, inhumanly evil. A voyage would have taught him this. But Wordsworth never left his native continent. Europe is so well gardened that it resembles a work of art, a scientific theory, a neat metaphysical system. Man has re-created Europe in his own image. Its tamed and temperate Nature confirmed Wordsworth in his philosophizings. The poet, the devil's partisan were doomed; the angels triumphed. Alas!

(From *Do What You Will*)

The Olive Tree

The Tree of Life; the Bodhi Tree; Yggdrasil and the Burning Bush:

> Populus Alcidae gratissima, vitis Iaccho,
> formosae myrtus Veneri, sua laurea Phoebo....

Everywhere and, before the world was finally laicized, at all times, trees have been worshiped. It is not to be wondered at. The tree is an intrinsically "numinous" being. Solidified, a great fountain of life rises in the trunk, spreads in the branches, scatters in a spray of leaves and flowers and fruits. With a slow, silent ferocity the roots go burrowing down into the earth. Tender, yet irresistible, life battles with the unliving stones and has the mastery. Half hidden in the darkness, half displayed in the air of heaven, the tree stands there, magnificent, a manifest god. Even today we feel its majesty and beauty—feel in certain circumstances its rather fearful quality of otherness, strangeness, hostility. Trees in the mass can be almost terrible. There are devils in the great pine-woods of the North, in the swarming equatorial jungle. Alone in a forest one sometimes becomes aware of the silence—the thick, clotted, living silence of the trees; one realizes one's isolation in the midst of a vast concourse of alien presences. Herne the Hunter was something more than the ghost of a Windsor gamekeeper. He was probably a survival of Jupiter Cernunnus; a lineal descendant of the Cretan Zeus; a wood god who in some of his aspects was frightening and even malignant.

> He blasts the tree, and takes the cattle,
> And makes milch-kine yield blood, and shakes a chain
> In a most hideous and dreadful manner.

Even in a royal forest and only twenty miles from London, the serried trees can inspire terror. Alone or in small groups, trees are benignly numinous. The alienness of the forest is so much attenuated in the park or the orchard that it changes

its emotional sign and from oppressively sinister becomes
delightful. Tamed and isolated, those leaping fountains of
non-human life bring only refreshment to spirits parched by
the dusty commerce of the world. Poetry is full of groves and
shrubberies. One thinks of Milton, landscape-gardening in
Eden, of Pope, at Twickenham. One remembers Coleridge's
sycamore and Marvell's green thought in a green shade.
Chaucer's love of trees was so great that he had to compile
a whole catalogue in order to express it.

> But, Lorde, so I was glad and wel begoon!
> For over al, where I myn eyen caste,
> Weren trees, claad with levys that ay shal laste,
> Eche in his kynde, with colors fressh and grene
> As emerawde, that joy was for to sene.
> The bylder oke, and eke the hardy asshe,
> The peler (pillar)elme, the cofre unto careyne,
> The box pipe tree, holme to whippes lasshe,
> The saylynge firre, the cipresse deth to pleyne,
> The sheter (shooter) ewe, the aspe for shaftes pleyne,
> The olyve of pes, and eke the drunken vyne
> The victor palme, the laurere, to, devyne.

I like them all, but especially the olive. For what it symbolizes, first of all—peace with its leaves and joy with its
golden oil. True, the crown of olive was originally worn by
Roman conquerors at ovation; the peace it proclaimed was
the peace of victory, the peace which is too often only the
tranquillity of exhaustion or complete annihilation. Rome
and its customs have passed, and we remember of the olive
only the fact that it stood for peace, not the circumstances in
which it did so.

> Incertainties now crown themselves assur'd,
> And peace proclaims olives of endless age.

We are a long way from the imperator riding in triumph
through the streets of Rome.

The association of olive leaves with peace is like the association of the number seven with good luck, or the color green
with hope. It is an arbitrary and, so to say, metaphysical
association. That is why it has survived in the popular imagination down to the present day. Even in countries where
the olive tree does not grow, men understand what is meant
by "the olive branch" and can recognize, in a political car-
toon, its pointed leaves. The association of olive oil with joy
has a pragmatic reason. Applied externally, oil was supposed
to have medicinal properties. In the ancient world those who
could afford it were in the habit of oiling themselves at every

opportunity. A shiny and well lubricated face was thought to be beautiful; it was also a sign of prosperity. To the ancient Mediterranean peoples the association of oil with joy seemed inevitable and obvious. Our habits are not those of the Romans, Greeks and Hebrews. What to them was "natural" is today hardly even imaginable. Patterns of behavior change, and ideas which are associated in virtue of the pattern existing at a given moment of history will cease to be associated when that pattern exists no more. But ideas which are associated arbitrarily, in virtue of some principle, or some absence of principle, unconnected with current behavior patterns, will remain associated through changing circumstances. One must be something of an archeologist to remember the old and once thoroughly reasonable association between olive oil and joy; the equally old, but quite unreasonable and arbitrary association between olive leaves and peace has survived intact into the machine age.

It is surprising, I often think, that our Protestant bibliolaters should have paid so little attention to the oil which played such an important part in the daily lives of the ancient Hebrews. All that was greasy possessed for the Jews a profound religious, social and sensuous significance. Oil was used for anointing kings, priests and sacred edifices. On festal days men's cheeks and noses fairly shone with it; a matt-surfaced face was a sign of mourning. Then there were the animal fats. Fat meat was always a particularly welcome sacrifice. Unlike the modern child, Jehovah reveled in mutton fat. His worshipers shared this taste. "Eat ye that which is good," advises Isaiah, "and let your soul delight itself in fatness." As for the prosperously wicked, "they have more than their heart can wish" and the proof of it is that "their eyes stand out with fatness." The world of the Old Testament, it is evident, was one where fats were scarce and correspondingly esteemed. One of our chief sources of edible fat, the pig, was taboo to the Israelites. Butter and lard depend on a supply of grass long enough for cows to get their tongues round. But the pastures of Palestine are thin, short and precarious. Cows there had no milk to spare, and oxen were too valuable as draught animals to be used for suet. Only the sheep and the olive remained as sources of that physiologically necessary and therefore delicious fatness in which the Hebrew soul took such delight. How intense that delight was is proved by the way in which the Psalmist describes his religious experiences. "Because thy lovingkindness is better than life, my lips shall praise thee. . . . My soul shall be satisfied as with marrow and fatness; and my mouth shall praise thee with joyful lips." In this age of Danish bacon and unlimited margarine it would

never occur to a religious writer to liken the mystical ecstasy
to a good guzzle at the Savoy. If he wanted to describe it in
terms of a sensuous experience, he would probably choose a
sexual metaphor. Square meals are now too common to be
ranked as epoch-making treats.

The "olyve of pes" is, then, a symbol and I love it for what
it stands for. I love it also for what it is in itself, aesthetically;
for what it is in relation to the Mediterranean landscape in
which it beautifully plays its part.

The English are Germans who have partially "gone Latin."
But for William the Conqueror and the Angevins we should
be just another nation of Teutons, speaking some uninteresting
dialect of Dutch or Danish. The Normans gave us the English
language, that beautifully compounded mixture of French and
Saxon; and the English language molded the English mind.
By Latin out of German: such is our pedigree. We are essentially mongrels: that is the whole point of us. To be mongrels
is our mission. If we would fulfill this mission adequately we
must take pains to cultivate our mongrelism. Our Saxon and
Celtic flesh requires to be constantly rewedded to the Latin
spirit. For the most part the English have always realized this
truth and acted upon it. From the time of Chaucer onwards
almost all our writers have turned, by a kind of infallible
instinct, like swallows, toward the South—toward the phantoms of Greece and Rome, toward the living realities of
France and Italy. On the rare occasions when, losing their
orientation, they have turned eastward and northward, the
results have been deplorable. The works of Carlyle are there,
an awful warning, to remind us of what happens when the
English forget that their duty is to be mongrels and go
whoring, within the bounds of consanguinity, after German
gods.

The olive tree is an emblem of the Latinity toward which
our migrant's instinct commands us perpetually to turn. As
well as for peace and for joy, it stands for all that makes
us specifically English rather than Teutonic; for those Mediterranean influences without which Chaucer and Shakespeare
could never have become what they learned from France
and Italy, from Rome and Greece, to be—the most essentially native of our poets. The olive tree is, so to speak, the
complement of the oak; and the bright hard-edged landscapes in which it figures are the necessary correctives of
those gauzy and indeterminate lovelinesses of the English
scene. Under a polished sky the olives state their aesthetic
case without the qualifications of mist, of shifting lights, of
atmospheric perspective, which give to English landscapes
their subtle and melancholy beauty. A perfect beauty in its

way; but, as of all good things, one can have too much of it. The British Constitution is a most admirable invention; but it is good to come back occasionally to fixed first principles and the firm outline of syllogistic argument.

With clarity and definition is associated a certain physical spareness. Most of the great deciduous trees of England give one the impression, at any rate in summer, of being rather obese. In Scandinavian mythology Embla, the elm, was the first woman. Those who have lived much with old elm trees—and I spent a good part of my boyhood under their ponderous shade—will agree that the Scandinavians were men of insight. There is in effect something blowsily female about those vast trees that brood with all their bulging masses of foliage above the meadows of the home counties. In winter they are giant skeletons; and for a moment in the early spring a cloud of transparent emerald vapor floats in the air; but by June they have settled down to an enormous middle age.

By comparison the olive tree seems an athlete in training. It sits lightly on the earth and its foliage is never completely opaque. There is always air between the thin grey and silver leaves of the olive, always the flash of light within its shadows. By the end of summer the foliage of our northern trees is a great clot of dark unmitigated green. In the olive the lump is always leavened.

The landscape of the equator is, as the traveler discovers to his no small surprise, singularly like the landscape of the more luxuriant parts of southern England. He finds the same thick woods and, where man has cleared them, the same park-like expanses of luscious greenery. The whole is illumined by the same cloudy sky, alternately bright and dark, and wetted by precisely those showers of hot water which render yet more oppressive the sultriness of July days in the Thames valley or in Devonshire. The equator is England in summer, but raised, so to speak, to a higher power. Falmouth cubed equals Singapore. Between the equatorial and the temperate zone lies a belt of drought; even Provence is half a desert. The equator is dank, the tropics and the subtropics are predominantly dry. The Sahara and Arabia, the wastes of India and Central Asia and North America are a girdle round the earth of sand and naked rock. The Mediterranean lies on the fringes of this desert belt and the olive is its tree—the tree of a region of sun-lit clarity separating the damps of the equator from the damps of the North. It is the symbol of a classicism enclosed between two romanticisms.

"And where," Sir George Beaumont inquired of Constable, "where do you put your brown tree?" The reply was disquieting: the eccentric fellow didn't put it anywhere. There are no brown trees in Constable's landscapes. Breaking the tradition of more than a century, he boldly insisted on painting his trees bright green. Sir George, who had been brought up to think of English landscape in terms of raw Sienna and ochre, was bewildered. So was Chantrey. His criticism of Constable's style took a practical form. When "Hadleigh Castle" was sent to the Academy he took a pot of bitumen and glazed the whole foreground with a coat of rich brown. Constable had to spend several hours patiently scratching it off again. To paint a bright green tree and make a successful picture of it requires genius of no uncommon order. Nature is embarrassingly brilliant and variegated; only the greatest colorists know how to deal with such a shining profusion. Doubtful of their powers, the more cautious prefer to transpose reality into another and simpler key. The key of brown, for example. The England of the eighteenth-century painters is chronically autumnal.

At all seasons of the year the olive achieves that sober neutrality of tone which the deciduous trees of the North put on only in autumn and winter. "Where do you put your gray tree?" If you are painting in Provence, or Tuscany, you put it everywhere. At every season of the year the landscape is full of gray trees. The olive is essentially a painter's tree. It does not need to be transposed into another key, and it can be rendered completely in terms of pigment that are as old as the art of painting.

Large expanses of the Mediterranean scene are by Nature herself conceived and executed in the earth colors. Your gray tree and its background of bare bone-like hills, red-brown earth and the all but black cypresses and pines are within the range of the most ascetic palette. Derain can render Provence with half a dozen tubes of color. How instructive to compare his olives with those of Renoir! White, black, *terra verde*— Derain's rendering of the gray tree is complete. But it is not the only complete rendering. Renoir was a man with a passion for bright gay colors. To this passion he added an extraordinary virtuosity in combining them. It was not in his nature to be content with a black, white and earth-green olive. His gray trees have shadows of cadmium green, and where they look toward the sun, are suffused with a glow of pink. Now, no olive has ever shown a trace of any color warmer than the faint ochre of withering leaves and summer dusts. Nevertheless these pink trees, which in Renoir's paintings of Cagnes recall the exuberant girls of his latest, rosiest manner, are somehow quite startlingly like the cold gray olives which they apparently misrepresent. The rendering, so different from Derain's, is equally complete and satisfying.

If I could paint and had the necessary time, I should devote myself for a few years to making pictures only of olive trees. What a wealth of variations upon a single theme! Above Pietrasanta, for example, the first slopes of the Apuan Alps rise steeply from the plain in a series of terraces built up, step after step, by generations of patient cultivators. The risers of this great staircase are retaining walls of unmortared lime-stone; the treads, of grass. And on every terrace grow the olives. They are ancient trees; their boles are gnarled, their branches strangely elbowed. Between the sharp narrow leaves one sees the sky; and beneath them in the thin softly tempered light there are sheep grazing. Far off, on a level with the eye, lies the sea. There is one picture, one series of pictures.

But olives will grow on the plain as well as on the hillside. Between Seville and Cordoba the rolling country is covered with what is almost a forest of olive trees. It is a woodland scene. Elsewhere they are planted more sparsely. I think, for example, of that plain at the foot of the Maures in Provence. In spring, beside the road from Toulon to Fréjus, the ploughed earth is a rich Pozzuoli red. Above it hang the olives, gray, with soft black shadows and their highest leaves flashing white against the sky; and, between the olives, peach trees in blossom—burning bushes of shell-pink flame in violent and irreconcilable conflict with the red earth. A problem, there, for the most accomplished painter.

In sunlight Renoir saw a flash of madder breaking out of the gray foliage. Under a clouded sky, with rain impending, the olives glitter with an equal but very different intensity. There is no warmth in them now; the leaves shine white, as though illumined from within by a kind of lunar radiance. The soft black of the shadows is deepened to the extreme of night. In every tree there is simultaneously moonlight and darkness. Under the approaching storm the olives take on another kind of being; they become more conspicuous in the landscape, more significant. Of what? Significant of what? But to that question, when we ask it, nature always stubbornly refuses to return a clear reply. At the sight of those mysterious lunar trees, at once so dark and so brilliant beneath the clouds, we ask, as Zechariah asked of the angel: "What are these two olive trees upon the right side of the candlestick and upon the left side thereof? What be these two olive branches which through the two golden pipes empty the golden oil out of themselves? And he answered me and said, Knowest thou not what these be? And I said, No, my lord. Then said he, These are the two anointed ones, that stand by the Lord of the whole earth." And that, I imagine, is about

as explicit and comprehensible an answer as our Wordsworthian questionings are ever likely to receive.

Provence is a painter's paradise, and its tree, the olive, the
painter's own tree. But there are disquieting signs of change.
During the last few years there has been a steady destruction
of olive orchards. Magnificent old trees are being cut, their
wood sold for firing and the land they occupied planted with
vines. Fifty years from now, it may be, the olive tree will
almost have disappeared from southern France, and Provence
will wear another aspect. It may be, I repeat; it is not certain.
Nothing is certain nowadays except change. Even the majestic
stability of agriculture has been shaken by the progress of
technology. Thirty years ago, for example, the farmers of the
Rhône valley grew rich on silkworms. Then came the invention of viscose. The caterpillars tried to compete with the
machines and failed. The female form is now swathed in
wood-pulp, and between Lyons and Avignon the mulberry
tree and its attendant worm are all but extinct. Vines were
next planted. But North Africa was also planting vines. In a
year of plenty *vin ordinaire* fetches about a penny a quart.
The vines have been rooted up again, and today the prosperity
of the Rhône valley depends on peach trees. A few years from
now, no doubt, the Germans will be making synthetic peaches
out of sawdust or coal tar. And then—what?

The enemy of the olive tree is the peanut. *Arachis hypogaea*
grows like a weed all over the tropics and its seeds are fifty
per cent pure oil. The olive is slow-growing, capricious in its
yield, requires much pruning, and the fruit must be hand
picked. Peanut oil is half the price of olive oil. The Italians,
who wish to keep their olive trees, have almost forbidden
the use of peanut oil. The French, on the other hand, are the
greatest importers of peanuts in Europe. Most of the oil they
make is re-exported; but enough remains in France to imperil
the olives of Provence. Will they go the way of the mulberry
trees? Or will some new invention come rushing up in the
nick of time with a reprieve? It seems that, suitably treated,
olive oil makes an excellent lubricant, capable of standing up
to high temperatures. Thirty years from now, mineral lubri-
cants will be growing scarce. Along with the castor-oil plant,
the olive tree may come again triumphantly into its own.
Perhaps. Or perhaps not. The future of Provençal landscape
is in the hands of the chemists. It is in their power to preserve
it as it is, or to alter it out of all recognition.

It would not be the first time in the course of its history
that the landscape of Provence has changed its face. The
Provence that we know—terraced vineyard and olive orchard
alternating with pine-woods and those deserts of limestone

and prickly bushes which are locally called garrigues—is profoundly unlike the Provence of Roman and medieval times. It was a land, then, of great forests. The hills were covered with a splendid growth of ilex trees and Aleppo pines. The surviving Forêt du Dom allows us to guess what these woods —the last outposts toward the south of the forests of the temperate zone—were like. Today the garrigues, those end products of a long degeneration, have taken their place. The story of Provençal vegetation is a decline and fall, that begins with the ilex wood and ends with the garrigue.

The process of destruction is a familiar one. The trees were cut for firewood and shipbuilding. (The naval arsenal at Toulon devoured the forest for miles around.) The glass industry ate its way from the plain into the mountains, carrying with it irreparable destruction. Meanwhile, the farmers and the shepherds were busy, cutting into the woods in search of more land for the plough, burning them in order to have more pasture for their beasts. The young trees sprouted again —only to be eaten by the sheep and goats. In the end they gave up the struggle and what had been forest turned at last to a blasted heath. The long process of degradation ends in the garrigue. And even this blasted heath is not quite the end. Beyond the true garrigue, with its cistus, its broom, its prickly dwarf oak, there lie a series of false garrigues, vegetably speaking worse than the true. On purpose or by accident, somebody sets fire to the scrub. In the following spring the new shoots are eaten down to the ground. A coarse grass— baouco in Provençal—is all that manages to spring up. The shepherd is happy; his beasts can feed, as they could not do on the garrigue. But sheep and goats are ravenous. The new pasture is soon overgrazed. The baouco is torn up by the roots and disappears, giving place to ferocious blue thistles and the poisonous asphodel. With the asphodel the process is complete. Degradation can go no further. The asphodel is sheep-proof and even, thanks to its deeply planted tubers, fire-proof. And it allows very little else to grow in its neighborhood. If protected long enough from fire and animals, the garrigue will gradually build itself up again into a forest. But a desert of asphodels obstinately remains itself.

Efforts are now being made to reafforest the blasted heaths of Provence. In an age of cigarette-smoking tourists the task is difficult and the interruptions by fire frequent and disheartening. One can hardly doubt, however, of the ultimate success of the undertaking. The chemists may spare the olive trees; and yet the face of Provence may still be changed. For the proper background to the olive trees is the thinly fledged limestone of the hills—pinkish and white and pale blue in the distance, like Cézanne's Mont Sainte Victoire. Reafforested, these hills will be almost black with ilex and pine. Half the painter's paradise will have gone, if the desert is brought back to life. With the cutting of the olive trees the other half will follow.

(From *The Olive Tree*)

The Desert

Boundlessness and emptiness—these are the two most expressive symbols of that attributeless Godhead, of whom all that can be said is St. Bernard's *Nescio nescio* or the Vedantist's "not this, not this." The Godhead, says Meister Eckhart, must be loved "as not-God, not-Spirit, not-person, not-image, must be loved as He is, a sheer pure absolute One, sundered from all twoness, and in whom we must eternally sink from nothingness to nothingness." In the scriptures of Northern and Far Eastern Buddhism the spatial metaphors recur again and again. At the moment of death, writes the author of *Bardo Thodol,* "all things are like the cloudless sky; and the naked immaculate Intellect is like unto a translucent void without circumference or center." "The great Way," in Sosan's words, "is perfect, like unto vast space, with nothing wanting, nothing superfluous." "Mind," says Hui-neng (and he is speaking of that universal ground of consciousness, from which all beings, the unenlightened no less than the enlightened, take their source), "mind is like emptiness of space. . . . Space contains sun, moon, stars, the great earth, with its mountains and rivers. . . . Good men and bad men, good things and bad things, heaven and hell—they are all in empty space. The emptiness of Self-nature is in all people just like this." The theologians argue, the dogmatists declaim their credos; but their propositions "stand in no intrinsic relation to my inner light. This Inner Light" (I quote from Yoka Dashi's "Song of Enlightenment") "can be likened to space; it knows no boundaries; yet it is always here, is always with us, always retains its serenity and fullness. . . . You cannot take hold of it, and you cannot get rid of it; it goes on its own way. You speak and it is silent; you remain silent, and it speaks."

Silence is the cloudless heaven perceived by another sense. Like space and emptiness, it is a natural symbol of the divine. In the Mithraic mysteries, the candidate for initiation was told to lay a finger to his lips and whisper: "Silence! Silence!

Silence—symbol of the living imperishable God!" And long before the coming of Christianity to the Thebaid, there had been Egyptian mystery religions, for whose followers God was a well of life, "closed to him who speaks, but open to the silent." The Hebrew scriptures are eloquent almost to excess; but even here, among the splendid rumblings of prophetic praise and impetration and anathema, there are occasional references to the spiritual meaning and the therapeutic virtues of silence. "Be still, and know that I am God." "The Lord is in his holy temple; let all the world keep silence before him." "Keep thou silence at the presence of the Lord God." The desert, after all, began within a few miles of the gates of Jerusalem.

The facts of silence and emptiness are traditionally the symbols of divine immanence—but not, of course, for everyone, and not in all circumstances. "Until one has crossed a barren desert, without food or water, under a burning tropical sun, at three miles an hour, one can form no conception of what misery is." These are the words of a gold-seeker, who took the southern route to California in 1849. Even when one is crossing it at seventy miles an hour on a four-lane highway, the desert can seem formidable enough. To the forty-niners it was unmitigated hell. Men and women who are at her mercy find it hard to see in Nature and her works any symbols but those of brute power at the best and, at the worst, of an obscure and mindless malice. The desert's emptiness and the desert's silence reveal what we may call their spiritual meanings only to those who enjoy some measure of physiological security. The security may amount to no more than St. Anthony's hut and daily ration of bread and vegetables, no more than Milarepa's cave and barley meal and boiled nettles—less than what any sane economist would regard as the indispensable minimum, but still security, still a guarantee of organic life and, along with life, of the possibility of spiritual liberty and transcendental happiness.

But even for those who enjoy security against the assaults of the environment, the desert does not always or inevitably reveal its spiritual meanings. The early Christian hermits retired to the Thebaid because its air was purer, because there were fewer distractions, because God seemed nearer there than in the world of men. But, alas, dry places are notoriously the abode of unclean spirits, seeking rest and finding it not. If the immanence of God was sometimes more easily discoverable in the desert, so also, and all too frequently, was the immanence of the devil. St. Anthony's temptations have become a legend, and Cassian speaks of "the tempests of imagination" through which every newcomer to the eremitic life had to pass. Solitude, he writes, makes men feel "the many-winged folly of their souls ... ; they find the perpetual silence intolerable, and those whom no labor on the land could weary, are vanquished by doing nothing and worn out by the long duration of their peace." *Be still, and know that I am God;* be still, and know that *you* are the delinquent imbecile who snarls and gibbers in the basement of every human mind. The desert can drive men mad, but it can also help them to become supremely sane.

The enormous drafts of emptiness and silence prescribed by the eremites are safe medicine only for a few exceptional souls. By the majority the desert should be taken either dilute or, if at full strength, in small doses. Used in this way, it acts as a spiritual restorative, as an anti-hallucinant, as a de-tensioner and alterative.

In his book, *The Next Million Years,* Sir Charles Darwin looks forward to thirty thousand generations of ever more humans pressing ever more heavily on ever dwindling resources and being killed off in ever increasing numbers by famine, pestilence and war. He may be right. Alternatively, human ingenuity may somehow falsify his predictions. But even human ingenuity will find it hard to circumvent arithmetic. On a planet of limited area, the more people there are, the less vacant space there is bound to be. Over and above the material and sociological problems of increasing population, there is a serious psychological problem. In a completely home-made environment, such as is provided by any great metropolis, it is as hard to remain sane as it is in a completely natural environment such as the desert or the forest. O Solitude, where are thy charms? But, O Multitude, where are *thine*? The most wonderful thing about America is that, even in these middle years of the twentieth century, there are so few Americans. By taking a certain amount of trouble you might still be able to get yourself eaten by a bear in the state of New York. And without any trouble at all you can get bitten by a rattler in the Hollywood hills, or die of thirst, while wandering through an uninhabited desert, within a hundred and fifty miles of Los Angeles. A short generation ago you might have wandered and died within only a hundred miles of Los Angeles. Today the mounting tide of humanity has oozed through the intervening canyons and spilled out into the wide Mojave. Solitude is receding at the rate of four and a half kilometers per annum.

And yet, in spite of it all, the silence persists. For this silence of the desert is such that casual sounds, and even the systematic noise of civilization, cannot abolish it. They coexist with it—as small irrelevances at right angles to an enormous meaning, as veins of something analogous to darkness within an enduring transparency. From the irrigated land come the dark gross sounds of lowing cattle, and above them the plovers trail their vanishing threads of shrillness. Suddenly, startlingly, out of the sleeping sagebrush there bursts the shrieking of coyotes —Trio for Ghoul and Two Damned Souls. On the trunks of cottonwood trees, on the wooden walls of barns and houses, the woodpeckers rattle away like pneumatic drills. Picking one's way between the cactuses and the creosote bushes one hears, like some tiny whirring clockwork, the soliloquies of invisible wrens, the calling, at dusk, of the nightjars and even occasionally the voice of Homo sapiens—six of the species in a parked Chevrolet, listening to the broadcast of a prize fight, or else in pairs necking to the delicious accompaniment of Crosby. But the light forgives, the distances forget, and this great crystal of silence, whose base is as large as Europe and whose height, for all practical purposes, is infinite, can coexist with things of a far higher order of discrepancy than canned sentiment or vicarious sport. Jet planes, for example—the stillness is so massive that it can absorb even jet planes. The screaming crash mounts to its intolerable climax and fades again, mounts as another of the monsters rips through the air, and once more diminishes and is gone. But even at the height of the outrage the mind can still remain aware of that which surrounds it, that which preceded and will outlast it.

Progress, however, is on the march. Jet planes are already as characteristic of the desert as are Joshua trees or burrowing owls; they will soon be almost as numerous. The wilderness has entered the armament race, and will be in it to the end. In its multi-million-acred emptiness there is room enough to explode atomic bombs and experiment with guided missiles. The weather, so far as flying is concerned, is uniformly excellent, and in the plains lie the flat beds of many lakes, dry since the last Ice Age, and manifestly intended by Providence for hot-rod racing and jets. Huge airfields have already been constructed. Factories are going up. Oases are turning into industrial towns. In brand-new Reservations, surrounded by barbed wire and the FBI, not Indians but tribes of physicists, chemists, metallurgists, communication engineers and mechanics are working with the co-ordinated frenzy of termites. From their air-conditioned laboratories and machine shops there flows a steady stream of marvels, each one more expensive and each more fiendish than the last. The desert silence is still there; but so, ever more noisily, are the scientific irrelevancies. Give the boys in the reservations a few more years and another hundred billion dollars, and they will succeed (for with technology all things are possible) in abolishing the silence, in transforming what are now irrelevancies into the desert's fundamental meaning. Meanwhile, and luckily for us, it is noise which is exceptional; the rule is still this crystalline symbol of universal Mind.

The bulldozers roar, the concrete is mixed and poured, the jet planes go crashing through the air, the rockets soar aloft with their cargoes of white mice and electronic instruments. And yet for all this, "nature is never spent; there lives the dearest freshness deep down things."

And not merely the dearest, but the strangest, the most wonderfully unlikely. I remember, for example, a recent visit to one of the new Reservations. It was in the spring of 1952 and, after seven years of drought, the rains of the preceding winter had been copious. From end to end the Mojave was carpeted with flowers—sunflowers, and the dwarf phlox, chicory and coreopsis, wild hollyhock and all the tribe of garlics and lilies. And then, as we neared the Reservation, the flower carpet began to move. We stopped the car, we walked into the desert to take a closer look. On the bare ground, on every plant and bush innumerable caterpillars were crawling. They were of two kinds—one smooth, with green and white markings, and a horn, like that of a miniature rhinoceros, growing out of its hinder end. The caterpillar, evidently, of one of the hawk moths. Mingled with these, in millions no less uncountable, were the brown hairy offspring of (I think) the Painted Lady butterfly. They were everywhere —over hundreds of square miles of the desert. And yet, a year before, when the eggs from which these larvae had emerged were laid, California had been as dry as a bone. On what, then, had the parent insects lived? And what had been the food of their innumerable offspring? In the days when I collected butterflies and kept their young in glass jars on the window sill of my cubicle at school, no self-respecting caterpillar would feed on anything but the leaves to which its species had been predestined. Puss moths laid their eggs on poplars, spurge hawks on spurges; mulleins were frequented by the gaily piebald caterpillars of one rather rare and rigidly fastidious moth. Offered an alternative diet, my caterpillars would turn away in horror. They were like orthodox Jews confronted by pork or lobsters; they were like Brahmins at a feast of beef prepared by Untouchables. Eat? Never. They would rather die. And if the right food were not forthcoming, die they did. But these caterpillars of the desert were apparently different. Crawling into irrigated regions, they had devoured the young leaves of entire vineyards and vegetable gardens. They had broken with tradition, they had flouted the immemorial taboos. Here, near the Reservation, there was no

cultivated land. These hawk moth and Painted Lady caterpillars, which were all full grown, must have fed on indigenous
growths—but which, I could never discover; for when I saw
them the creatures were all crawling at random, in search
either of something juicier to eat or else of some place to spin
their cocoons. Entering the Reservation, we found them all
over the parking lot and even on the steps of the enormous
building which housed the laboratories and the administrative
offices. The men on guard only laughed or swore. But could
they be *absolutely* sure? Biology has always been the Russians' strongest point. These innumerable crawlers—perhaps
they were Soviet agents? Parachuted from the stratosphere,
impenetrably disguised, and so thoroughly indoctrinated, so
completely conditioned by means of post-hypnotic suggestions
that even under torture it would be impossible for them to
confess, even under DDT. . . .

Our party showed its pass and entered. The strangeness was
no longer Nature's; it was strictly human. Nine and a half
acres of floor space, nine and a half acres of the most extravagant improbability. Sagebrush and wild flowers beyond the
windows; but here, within, machine tools capable of turning
out anything from a tank to an electron microscope; million-
volt X-ray cameras; electric furnaces; wind tunnels; refrig-
erated vacuum tanks; and on either side of endless passages
closed doors bearing inscriptions which had obviously been
taken from last year's science fiction magazines. (This year's
space ships, of course, have harnessed gravitation and magnetism.) ROCKET DEPARTMENT, we read on door after door.
ROCKET AND EXPLOSIVES DEPARTMENT, ROCKET PERSONNEL
DEPARTMENT. And what lay behind the unmarked doors?
Rockets and Canned Tularemia? Rockets and Nuclear Fission?
Rockets and Space Cadets? Rockets and Elementary Courses
in Martian Language and Literature?

It was a relief to get back to the caterpillars. Ninety-nine
point nine recurring per cent of the poor things were going
to die—but not for an ideology, not while doing their best
to bring death to other caterpillars, not to the accompaniment of *Te Deums,* of *Dulce et decorums,* of "We shall not
sheathe the sword, which we have not lightly drawn, until . . ."
Until what? The only completely unconditional surrender will
come when everybody—but *everybody*—is a corpse.

For modern man, the really blessed thing about Nature is
its otherness. In their anxiety to find a cosmic basis for human
values, our ancestors invented an emblematic botany, a natural
history composed of allegories and fables, an astronomy that
told fortunes and illustrated the dogmas of revealed religion.
"In the Middle Ages," writes Émile Mâle, "the idea of a thing

which a man formed for himself, was always more real than the thing itself. . . . The study of things for their own sake held no meaning for the thoughtful man. . . . The task for the student of nature was to discover the eternal truth which God would have each thing express." These eternal truths expressed by things were not the laws of physical and organic being—laws discoverable only by patient observation and the sacrifice of preconceived ideas and autistic urges; they were the notions and fantasies engendered in the minds of logicians, whose major premises, for the most part, were other fantasies and notions bequeathed to them by earlier writers. Against the belief that such purely verbal constructions were eternal truths, only the mystics protested; and the mystics were concerned only with that "obscure knowledge," as it was called, which comes when a man "sees all in all." But between the real but obscure knowledge of the mystic and the clear but unreal knowledge of the verbalist, lies the clearish and realish knowledge of the naturalist and the man of science. It was knowledge of a kind which most of our ancestors found completely uninteresting.

Reading the older descriptions of God's creatures, the older speculations about the ways and workings of Nature, we start by being amused. But the amusement soon turns to the most intense boredom and a kind of mental suffocation. We find ourselves gasping for breath in a world where all the windows are shut and everything "wears man's smudge and shares man's smell." Words are the greatest, the most momentous of all our inventions, and the specifically human realm is the realm of language. In the stifling universe of medieval thought, the given facts of Nature were treated as the symbols of familiar notions. Words did not stand for things; things stood for pre-existent words. This is a pitfall which, in the natural sciences, we have learned to avoid. But in other contexts than the scientific—in the context, for example, of politics—we continue to take our verbal symbols with the same disastrous seriousness as was displayed by our crusading and persecuting ancestors. For both parties, the people on the other side of the Iron Curtain are not human beings, but merely the embodiments of the pejorative phrases coined by propagandists.

Nature is blessedly non-human; and insofar as we belong to the natural order, we too are blessedly non-human. The otherness of caterpillars, as of our own bodies, is an otherness underlain by a principal identity. The non-humanity of wild flowers, as of the deepest levels of our own minds, exists within a system which includes and transcends the human. In the given realm of the inner and outer not-self, we are all one. In the home-made realm of symbols we are separate and mutually hostile partisans. Thanks to words, we have been able to rise above the brutes; and thanks to words, we have often sunk to the level of the demons. Our statesmen have tried to come to an international agreement on the use of atomic power. They have not been successful. And even if they had, what then? No agreement on atomic power can do any lasting good, unless it be preceded by an agreement on language. If we make a wrong use of nuclear fission, it will be because we have made a wrong use of the symbols, in terms of which we think about ourselves and other people. Individually and collectively, men have always been the victims of their own words; but, except in the emotionally neutral field of science, they have never been willing to admit their linguistic ineptitude, and correct their mistakes. Taken too seriously, symbols have motivated and justified all the horrors of recorded history. On every level from the personal to the international, the letter kills. Theoretically we know this very well. In practice, nevertheless, we continue to commit the suicidal blunders to which we have become accustomed.

The caterpillars were still on the march when we left the Reservation, and it was half an hour or more, at a mile a minute, before we were clear of them. Among the phloxes and the sunflowers, millions in the midst of hundreds of millions, they proclaimed (along with the dangers of over-population) the strength, the fecundity, the endless resourcefulness of life. We were in the desert, and the desert was blossoming, the desert was crawling. I had not seen anything like it since that spring day, in 1948, when we had been walking at the other end of the Mojave, near the great earthquake fault, down which the highway descends to San Bernardino and the orange groves. The elevation here is around four thousand feet and the desert is dotted with dark clumps of juniper. Suddenly, as we moved through the enormous emptiness, we became aware of an entirely unfamiliar interruption to the silence. Before, behind, to right and to left, the sound seemed to come from all directions. It was a small sharp crackling, like the ubiquitous frying of bacon, like the first flames in the kindling of innumerable bonfires. There seemed to be no explanation. And then, as we looked more closely, the riddle gave up its answer. Anchored to a stem of sagebrush, we saw the horny pupa of cicada. It had begun to split and the full-grown insect was in process of pushing its way out. Each time it struggled, its case of amber-colored chitin opened a little more widely. The continuous crackling that we heard was caused by the simultaneous emergence of thousands upon thousands of individuals. How long they had spent underground I could never discover. Dr. Edmund Jaeger, who knows as much about the fauna and flora of the Western deserts as anyone now living, tells me that the habits of this particular cicada have never been closely studied. He himself had never witnessed the mass resurrection upon which we had had the good fortune to stumble. All one can be sure of is that these creatures had spent anything from two to seventeen years in the soil, and that they had all chosen this particular May morning to climb out of the grave, burst their coffins, dry their moist wings and embark upon their life of sex and song.

Three weeks later we heard and saw another detachment of the buried army coming out into the sun among the pines and the flowering fremontias of the San Gabriel Mountains. The chill of two thousand additional feet of elevation had postponed the resurrection; but when it came, it conformed exactly to the pattern set by the insects of the desert: the risen pupa, the crackle of splitting horn, the helpless imago waiting for the sun to bake it into perfection, and then the flight, the tireless singing, so unremitting that it becomes a part of the silence. The boys in the Reservations are doing their best; and perhaps, if they are given the necessary time and money, they may really succeed in making the planet uninhabitable. Applied Science is a conjuror, whose bottomless hat yields impartially the softest of Angora rabbits and the most petrifying of Medusas. But I am still optimist enough to credit life with invincibility, I am still ready to bet that the non-human otherness at the root of man's being will ultimately triumph over the all too human selves who frame the ideologies and engineer the collective suicides. For our survival, if we do survive, we shall be less beholden to our common sense (the name we give to what happens when we try to think of the world in terms of the unanalyzed symbols supplied by language and the local customs) than to our caterpillar- and cicada-sense, to intelligence, in other words, as it operates on the organic level. That intelligence is at once a will to persistence and an inherited knowledge of the physiological and psychological means by which, despite all the follies of the loquacious self, persistence can be achieved. And beyond survival is transfiguration; beyond and including animal grace is the grace of that other not-self, of which the desert silence and the desert emptiness are the most expressive symbols.

(From *Tomorrow and Tomorrow and Tomorrow*)

TRAVEL

The Palio at Siena

Our rooms were in a tower. From the windows one looked across the brown tiled roofs to where, on its hill, stood the cathedral. A hundred feet below was the street, a narrow canyon between high walls, perennially sunless; the voices of the passers-by came up, reverberating, as out of a chasm. Down there they walked always in shadow; but in our tower we were the last to lose the sunlight. On the hot days it was cooler, no doubt, down in the street; but we at least had the winds. The waves of the air broke against our tower and flowed past it on either side. And at evening, when only the belfries and the domes and the highest roofs were still flushed by the declining sun, our windows were level with the flight of the swifts and swallows. Sunset after sunset all through the long summer, they wheeled and darted round our tower. There was always a swarm of them intricately maneuvering just outside the window. They swerved this way and that, they dipped and rose, they checked their headlong flight with a flutter of their long pointed wings and turned about within their own length. Compact, smooth and tapering, they seemed the incarnation of airy speed. And their thin, sharp, arrowy cry was speed made audible. I have sat at my window watching them tracing their intricate arabesques until I grew dizzy; till their shrill crying sounded as though from within my ears and their flying seemed a motion, incessant, swift and bewilderingly multitudinous, behind my eyes. And all the while the sun declined, the shadows climbed higher up the houses and towers, and the light with which they were tipped became

29

more rosy. And at last the shadow had climbed to the very top and the city lay in a grey and violet twilight beneath the pale sky.

One evening, toward the end of June, as I was sitting at the window looking at the wheeling birds, I heard through the crying of the swifts the sound of a drum. I looked down into the shadowy street, but could see nothing. Rub-a-dub, dub, dub, dub—the sound grew louder and louder, and suddenly there appeared round the corner where our street bent out of sight, three personages out of a Pinturicchio fresco. They were dressed in liveries of green and yellow—yellow doublets slashed and tagged with green, parti-colored hose and shoes, with feathered caps of the same colors. Their leader played the drum. The two who followed carried green and yellow banners. Immediately below our tower the street opens out a little into a tiny piazza. In this clear space the three Pinturicchio figures came to a halt and the crowd of little boys and loafers who followed at their heels grouped themselves round to watch. The drummer quickened his beat and the two banner-bearers stepped forward into the middle of the little square. They stood there for a moment quite still, the right foot a little in advance of the other, the left fist on the hip and the lowered banners drooping from the right. Then, together, they lifted the banners and began to wave them round their heads. In the wind of their motion the flags opened out. They were the same size and both of them green and yellow, but the colors were arranged in a different pattern on each. And what patterns! Nothing more "modern" was ever seen. They might have been designed by Picasso for the Russian Ballet. Had they been by Picasso, the graver critics would have called them futuristic, the sprightlier (I must apologize for both these expressions) jazz. But the flags were not Picasso's; they were designed some four hundred years ago by the nameless genius who dressed the Sienese for their yearly pageant. This being the case, the critics can only take off their hats. The flags are classical, they are High Art; there is nothing more to be said.

The drum beat on. The bannermen waved their flags, so artfully that the whole expanse of patterned stuff was always unfurled and tremulously stretched along the air. They passed the flags from one hand to the other, behind their backs, under a lifted leg. Then, at last, drawing themselves together to make a supreme effort, they tossed their banners into the air. High they rose, turning slowly, over and over, hung for an instant at the height of their trajectory, then dropped back, the weighted stave foremost, toward their throwers, who caught them as they fell. A final wave, then the drum returned to its march rhythm, the bannermen shouldered their flags, and followed by the anachronistic children and idlers from the twentieth century, Pinturicchio's three young bravos swaggered off up the dark street out of sight and at length, the drum taps coming faintlier and ever faintlier, out of hearing.

Every evening after that, while the swallows were in full cry and flight about the tower, we heard the beating of the drum. Every evening, in the little piazza below us, a fragment of Pinturicchio came to life. Sometimes it was our friends in green and yellow who returned to wave their flags beneath our windows. Sometimes it was men from the other *contrade* or districts of the town, in blue and white, red and white, black, white and orange, white, green and red, yellow and scarlet. Their bright pied doublets and parti-colored hose shone out from among the drabs and funereal blacks of the twentieth-century crowd that surrounded them. Their spread flags waved in the street below, like the painted wings of enormous butterflies. The drummer quickened his beat, and to the accompaniment of a long-drawn rattle, the banners leapt up, furled and fluttering, into the air.

To the stranger who has never seen a Palio these little dress rehearsals are richly promising and exciting. Charmed by these present hints, he looks forward eagerly to what the day itself holds in store. Even the Sienese are excited. The pageant, however familiar, does not pall on them. And all the gambler in them, all the local patriot looks forward to the result of the race. Those last days of June before the first Palio, that middle week of August before the second, are days of growing excitement and tension in Siena. One enjoys the Palio the more for having lived through them.

Even the mayor and corporation are infected by the pervading excitement. They are so far carried away that, in the last days of June, they send a small army of men down in the great square before the Palazzo Comunale to eradicate every blade of grass or tuft of moss that can be found growing in the crannies between the flagstones. It amounts almost to a national characteristic, this hatred of growing things among the works of men. I have often, in old Italian towns, seen workmen laboriously weeding the less frequented streets and squares. The Colosseum, mantled till thirty or forty years ago with a romantic, Piranesian growth of shrubs, grasses and flowers, was officially weeded with such extraordinary energy that its ruinousness was sensibly increased. More stones were brought down in those few months of weeding than had fallen of their own accord in the previous thousand years. But the Italians were pleased; which is, after all, the chief thing that matters. Their hatred of weeds is fostered by their national pride; a great country, and one which specially piques itself on being modern, cannot allow weeds to grow even among its ruins. I entirely understand and sympathize with the Italian point of view. If Mr. Ruskin and his disciples had talked about my house and me as they talked about Italy and the Italians, I too should pique myself on being up-to-date; I should put in bathrooms, central heating and a lift, I should have all the moss scratched off the walls, I should lay cork lino on the marble floors. Indeed, I think that I should probably, in my irritation, pull down the whole house and build a new one. Considering the provocation they have received, it seems to me that the Italians have been remarkably moderate in the matter of weeding, destroying and rebuilding. Their moderation is due in part, no doubt, to their comparative poverty. Their ancestors built with such prodigious solidity that it would cost as much to pull down one of their old houses as to build a new one. Imagine, for example, demolishing the Palazzo Strozzi in Florence. It would be about as easy to demolish the Matterhorn. In Rome, which is predominantly a baroque, seventeenth-century city, the houses are made of flimsier stuff. Consequently, modernization progresses there much more rapidly than in most other Italian towns. In wealthier England very little antiquity has been permitted to stand. Thus, most of the great country houses of England were rebuilt during the eighteenth century. If Italy had preserved her independence and her prosperity during the seventeenth, eighteenth and nineteenth centuries, there would probably be very much less medieval or renaissance work now surviving than is actually the case. Money, then, is lacking to modernize completely. Weeding has the merit of being cheap and, at the same time, richly symbolic. When you say of a town that the grass grows in its streets, you mean that it is utterly dead. Conversely, if there is no grass in its streets, it must be alive. No doubt the mayor and corporation of Siena did not put the argument quite so explicitly. But that the argument was put, somehow, obscurely and below the surface of the mind, I do not doubt. The weeding was symbolic of modernity.

    With the weeders came other workmen who built up round the curving flanks of the great piazza a series of wooden stands, six tiers high, for the spectators. The piazza which is shaped, whether by accident or design I do not know, like an ancient theater, became for the time being indeed a theater. Between the seats and the central area of the place, a track was railed off and the slippery flags covered parsimoniously with sand. Expectation rose higher than ever.

    And at last the day came. The swallows and swifts wove their arabesques as usual in the bright golden light above the town. But their shrill crying was utterly inaudible, through the deep, continuous, formless murmur of the crowd that thronged the streets and the great piazza. Under its canopy of stone the great bell of the Mangia tower swung incessantly backwards and forwards; it too seemed dumb. The talking, the laughter, the shouting of forty thousand people rose up from the piazza in a column of solid sound, impenetrable to any ordinary noise.

It was after six. We took our places in one of the stands opposite the Palazzo Comunale. Our side of the piazza was already in the shade; but the sun still shone on the palace and its tall slender tower, making their rosy brickwork glow as though by inward fire. An immense concourse of people filled the square and all the tiers of seats round it. There were people in every window, even on the roofs. At the Derby, on boat-race days, at Wembley I have seen larger crowds; but never, I think, so many people confined within so small a space.

The sound of a gunshot broke through the noise of voices; and at the signal a company of mounted carabiniers rode into the piazza, driving the loungers who still thronged the track before them. They were in full dress uniform, black and red, with silver trimmings; cocked hats on their heads and swords in their hands. On their handsome little horses, they looked like a squadron of smart Napoleonic cavalry. The idlers re-treated before them, squeezing their way through every con-venient opening in the rails into the central area, which was soon densely packed. The track was cleared at a walk and, cleared, was rounded again at the trot, dashingly, in the best Carle Vernet style. The carabiniers got their applause and retired. The crowd waited expectantly. For a moment there was almost a silence. The bell on the tower ceased to be dumb. Some one in the crowd let loose a couple of balloons. They mounted perpendicularly into the still air, a red sphere and a purple. They passed out of the shadow into the sunlight; and the red became a ruby, the purple a glowing amethyst. When they had risen above the level of the roofs, a little breeze caught them and carried them away, still mounting all the time, over our heads, out of sight.

There was another gunshot and Vernet was exchanged for Pinturicchio. The noise of the crowd grew louder as they appeared, the bell swung, but gave no sound, and across the square the trumpets of the procession were all but inaudible. Slowly they marched round, the representatives of all the seventeen *contrade* of the city. Besides its drummer and its two bannermen, each *contrada* had a man-at-arms on horse-back, three or four halbardiers and young pages and, if it happened to be one of the ten competing in the race, a jockey, all of them wearing the Pinturicchian livery in its own particular colors. Their progress was slow; for at every fifty paces they stopped, to allow the bannermen to give an exhibition of their skill with the flags. They must have taken the best part of an hour to get round. But the time seemed only too short. The Palio is a spectacle of which one does not grow tired. I have seen it three times now and was as much delighted on the last occasion as on the first.

English tourists are often skeptical about the Palio. They remember those terrible "pageants" which were all the rage some fifteen years ago in their own country, and they imagine that the Palio will turn out to be something of the same sort. But let me reassure them; it is not. There is no poetry by Louis Napoleon Parker at Siena. There are no choruses of young ladies voicing high moral sentiments in low voices. There are no flabby actor-managers imperfectly disguised as Hengist and Horsa, no crowd of gesticulating supernumeraries dressed in the worst of taste and the cheapest of bunting. Nor finally does one often meet at Siena with that almost invariable accompaniment of the English pageant—rain. No, the Palio is just a show; having no "meaning" in particular, but by the mere fact of being traditional and still alive, signifying infinitely more than the dead-born English affairs for all their Parkerian blank verse and their dramatic re-evocations. For these pages and men-at-arms and bannermen come straight out of the Pinturicchian past. Their clothes are those designed for their ancestors, copied faithfully, once in a generation, in the same colors and the same rich materials. They walk, not in cotton or flannelette, but in silks and furs and velvets. And the colors were matched, the clothes originally cut by men whose taste was the faultless taste of the early renaissance. To be sure there are costumiers with as good a taste in these days. But it was not Paquin, not Lanvin or Poiret who dressed the actors of the English pageants; it was professional wig-makers and lady amateurs. I have already spoken of the beauty of the flags—the bold, fantastic, "modern" design of them. Everything else at the Palio is in keeping with the flags, daring, brilliant and yet always right, always irreproachably refined. The one false note is always the *Palio* itself—the painted banner which is given to the *contrada* whose horse wins the race. This banner is specially painted every year for the occasion. Look at it, where it comes along, proudly exposed on the great medieval war chariot which closes the procession —look at it, or preferably don't look at it. It is a typical property from the wardrobe of an English pageant committee. It is a lady amateur's masterpiece. Shuddering, one averts the eyes.

Preceded by a line of *quattrocento* pages carrying festoons and laurel leaves and escorted by a company of mounted knights, the war chariot rolled slowly and ponderously past, bearing aloft the unworthy trophy. And by now the trumpets at the head of the procession sounded, almost inaudibly for us, from the further side of the piazza. And at last the whole procession had made its round and was lined up in close order in front of the Palazzo Comunale. Over the heads of the spectators standing in the central area, we could see all the thirty-four banners waving and waving in a last concerted display and at last, together, all leaping high into the air, hesitating at the top of their leap, falling back, out of sight. There was a burst of applause. The pageant was over. Another gunshot. And in the midst of more applause, the racehorses were ridden to the starting place.

The course is three times round the piazza, whose shape, as I have said, is something like that of an ancient theater. Consequently, there are two sharp turns, where the ends of the semicircle meet the straight diameter. One of these, owing to the irregularity of the plan, is sharper than the other. The outside wall of the track is padded with mattresses at this point, to prevent impetuous jockeys who take the corner too fast from dashing themselves to pieces. The jockeys ride bareback; the horses run on a thin layer of sand spread over the flagstones of the piazza. The Palio is probably the most dangerous flat-race in the world. And it is made the more dangerous by the excessive patriotism of the rival *contrade*. For the winner of the race as he reins in his horse after passing the post, is set upon by the supporters of the other *contrade* (who all think that *their* horse should have won), with so real and earnest a fury that the carabiniers must always intervene to protect man and beast from lynching. Our places were at a point some two or three hundred yards beyond the post, so that we had an excellent view of the battle waged round the winning horse, as he slackened speed. Scarcely was the post passed when the crowd broke its ranks and rushed out into the course. Still cantering, the horse came up the track. A gang of young men ran in pursuit, waving sticks and shouting. And with them, their Napoleonic coat tails streaming in the wind of their own speed, their cocked hats bobbing, and brandishing swords in their white-gloved hands, ran the rescuing carabiniers. There was a brief struggle round the now stationary horse, the young men were repulsed, and surrounded by cocked hats, followed by a crowd of supporters from its native *contrada*, the beast was led off in triumph. We climbed down from our places. The piazza was now entirely shaded. It was only on the upper part of the tower and the battlements of the

great Palazzo that the sun still shone. Rosily against the pale
blue sky, they glowed. The swifts still turned and turned overhead in the light. It is said that at evening and at dawn these
light-loving birds mount on their strong wings into the sky to
bid a last farewell or earliest good-morrow to the sinking or
the rising sun. While we lie sleeping or have resigned ourselves
to darkness the swifts are looking down from their watch-
tower in the height of heaven over the edge of the turning
planet toward the light. Was it a fable, I wondered, looking
up at the wheeling birds? Or was it true? Meanwhile, some
one was swearing at me for not looking where I was going.
I postponed the speculation.

(From *Along the Road*)

Sabbioneta

"They call it the Palazzo del Te," said the maid at the little
inn in the back street where we had lunch, "because the Gonzaga used to go and take tea there." And that was all that she,
and probably most of the other inhabitants of Mantua, knew
about the Gonzaga or their palaces. It was surprising, perhaps,
that she should have known so much. Gonzaga—the name, at
least, still faintly reverberated. After two hundred years, how
many names are still remembered? Few indeed. The Gonzaga,
it seemed to me, enjoy a degree of immortality that might be
envied them. They have vanished, they are as wholly extinct
as the dinosaur; but in the cities they once ruled their name
still vaguely echoes, and for those who care to listen they have
left behind some of the most eloquent sermons on the vanity
of human wishes and the mutability of fortune that stones
have ever mutely preached.

I have seen many ruins and of every period. Stonehenge
and Ansedonia, Ostia and medieval Ninfa (which the duke
of Sermoneta is busily turning into the likeness of a neat
suburban park), Bolsover and the gruesome modern ruins in
Northern France. I have seen great cities dead or in decay:
Pisa, Bruges and the newly murdered Vienna. But over none,
it seemed to me, did there brood so profound a melancholy
as over Mantua; none seemed so dead or so utterly bereft of
glory; nowhere was desolation more pregnant with the memory
of splendor, the silence nowhere so richly musical with echoes.
There are a thousand rooms in the labyrinthine Reggia at
Mantua—Gothic rooms, rooms of the renaissance, baroque

rooms, rooms rich with the absurd pretentious decorations of
the first empire, huge presence chambers and closets and the
horribly exquisite apartments of the dwarfs—a thousand
rooms, and their walls enclose an emptiness that is the mournful ghost of departed plenitude. It is through Mallarmé's
creux néant musicien that one walks in Mantua.

And not in Mantua alone. For wherever the Gonzaga lived,
they left behind them the same pathetic emptiness, the same
pregnant desolation, the same echoes, the same ghosts of
splendor.

The Palazzo del Te is made sad and beautiful with the same
melancholy as broods in the Reggia. True, the stupid vulgarity
of Giulio Romano was permitted to sprawl over its wall in a
series of deplorable frescoes (it is curious, by the way, that
Giulio Romano should have been the only Italian artist of
whom Shakespeare had ever heard, or at least the only one
he ever mentioned); but the absurdities and grossnesses seem
actually to make the place more touching. The departed ten-
ants of the palace become in a manner more real to one, when
one discovers that their taste ran to *trompe l'œil* pictures of
fighting giants and mildly pornographic scenes out of pagan
mythology. And seeming more human, they seem also more
dead; and the void left by their disappearance is more than
ever musical with sadness.

Even the cadets of the Gonzaga house enjoyed a power of
leaving behind them a more than Pompeian desolation. Twenty
miles from Mantua, on the way to Cremona, is a village called
Sabbioneta. It lies near the Po, though not on its banks;
posseses, for a village, a tolerably large population, mostly
engaged in husbandry; is rather dirty and has an appearance
—probably quite deceptive—of poverty. In fact it is just like
all other villages of the Lombard plain, but with this difference: a Gonzaga once lived here. The squalor of Sabbioneta
is no common squalor; it is a squalor that was once magnificence. Its farmers and horse-copers live, dirtily and de-
structively, in treasures of late renaissance architecture. The
town hall is a ducal palace; in the municipal school, children
are taught under carved and painted ceilings, and when the
master is out of the room they write their names on the marble
bellies of the patient, battered caryatids who uphold the
scutcheoned mantel. The weekly cinema show is given in an
Olympic theater, built a few years after the famous theater at
Vicenza, by Palladio's pupil, Scamozzi. The people worship
in sumptuous churches, and if ever soldiers happen to pass
through the town, they are billeted in the deserted summer
palace.

The creator of all these splendors was Vespasiano, son of

that Luigi Gonzaga, the boon companion of kings, whom, for his valor and his fabulous strength, his contemporaries nicknamed Rodomonte. Luigi died young, killed in battle; and his son Vespasiano was brought up by his aunt, Giulia Gonzaga, one of the most perfectly courtly ladies of her age. She had him taught Latin, Greek, the mathematics, good manners and the art of war. This last he practiced with distinction, serving at one time or another under many princes, but chiefly under Philip II of Spain, who honored him with singular favors. Vespasiano seems to have been the typical Italian tyrant of his period—cultured, intelligent and only just so much of an ungovernably ferocious ruffian as one would expect a man to be who has been brought up in the possession of absolute power. It was in the intimacy of private life that he displayed his least amiable characteristics. He poisoned his first wife on a suspicion, probably unfounded, of her infidelity, murdered her supposed lover and exiled his relations. His second wife left him mysteriously after three years of married life and died of pure misery in a convent, carrying with her into the grave nobody knew what frightful secret. His third wife, it is true, lived to a ripe old age; but then Vespasiano himself died after only a few years of marriage. His only son, whom he loved with the anxious passion of the ambitious parvenu who desires to found a dynasty, one day annoyed him by not taking off his cap when he met him in the street. Vespasiano rebuked him for this lack of respect. The boy answered back impertinently. Whereupon Vespasiano gave him such a frightful kick in the groin that the boy died. Which shows that, even when chastising one's own children, it is advisable to observe the Queensberry rules.

It was in 1560 that Vespasiano decided to convert the miserable village from which he took his title into a capital worthy of its ruler. He set to work with energy. In a few years the village of squalid cottages clustering round a feudal castle had given place to a walled town, with broad streets, two fine squares, a couple of palaces and a noble Gallery of Antiques. These last Vespasiano had inherited from his father, Rodomonte, who had been at the sack of Rome in 1527 and had shown himself an industrious and discriminating looter. Sabbioneta was in its turn looted by the Austrians, who carried off Rodomonte's spoils to Mantua. The museum remains; but there is nothing in it but the *creux néant musicien* which the Gonzaga alone, of all the princes in Italy, had the special art of creating by their departure.

We had come to Sabbioneta from Parma. In the vast Farnese palace there is no musically echoing void—merely an ordinary, undisturbing emptiness. Only in the colossal

Estensian theater does one recapture anything like the Man-
tuan melancholy. We drove through Colorno, where the last
of the Este built a summer palace about as large as Hampton
Court. Over the Po, by a bridge of boats, through Casalmag-
giore and on, tortuously, by little by-roads across the plain. A
line of walls presented themselves, a handsome gate. We drove
in, and immediately faint ghostly oboes began to play around
us; we were in Sabbioneta among the Gonzaga ghosts.

The central piazza of the town is oblong; Vespasiano's
palace stands at one of the shorter ends, presenting to the
world a modest façade, five windows wide, once rich with
decorations, but now bare. It serves at present as town hall.
In the waiting-room on the first floor, stand four life-sized
equestrian figures, carved in wood and painted, representing
four of Vespasiano's ancestors. Once there was a squadron of
twelve; but the rest have been broken up and burned. This
crime, together with all the other ravages committed by time
or vandals in the course of three centuries, was attributed by
the mayor, who personally did us the honors of his munici-
pality, to the socialists who had preceded him in office. It is
unnecessary to add that he himself was a fascista.

We walked round in the emptiness under the superbly
carved and gilded ceilings. The porter sat among decayed
frescoes in the Cabinet of Diana. The town council held its
meetings in the Ducal Saloon. The Gallery of the Ancestors
housed a clerk and the municipal archives. The deputy mayor
had his office in the Hall of the Elephants. The Sala d'Oro
had been turned into an infants' class-room. We walked out
again into the sunlight fairly heart-broken.

The Olympic Theater is a few yards down the street. Accompanied by the obliging young porter from the Cabinet of
Diana, we entered. It is a tiny theater, but complete and
marvelously elegant. From the pit, five semicircular steps
rise to a pillared loggia, behind which—having the width of
the whole auditorium—is the ducal box. The loggia consists
of twelve Corinthian pillars, topped by a cornice. On the
cornice, above each pillar, stand a dozen stucco gods and
goddesses. Noses and fingers, paps and ears have gone the way
of all art; but the general form of them survives. Their white
silhouettes gesticulate elegantly against the twilight of the
hall.

The stage was once adorned with a fixed scene in perspective, like that which Palladio built at Vicenza. The mayor
wanted us to believe that it was his Bolshevik predecessors
who had destroyed it; but as a matter of fact it was taken
down about a century ago. Gone, too, are the frescoes with
which the walls were once covered. One year of epidemic the

theater was used as a fever hospital. When the plague had passed, it was thought that the frescoes needed disinfecting; they were thickly white-washed. There is no money to scrape the white-wash off again.

We followed the young porter out of the theater. Another two or three hundred yards and we were in the Piazza d'Armi. It is an oblong, grassy space. On the long axis of the rectangle, near one end there stands, handsomely pedestaled, a fluted marble column, topped by a statue of Athena, the tutelary goddess of Vespasiano's metropolis. The pedestal, the capital and the statue are of the late renaissance. But the column is antique, and formed a part of Rodomonte's Roman booty. Rodomonte was evidently no petty thief. If a thing is worth doing it is worth doing thoroughly; that, evidently, was his motto.

One of the long sides of the rectangle is occupied by the Gallery of Antiques. It is a superb building, architecturally by far the finest thing in the town. The lower story consists of an open arcade and the walls of the gallery above are ornamented with blind arches, having well-proportioned windows at the center of each and separated from one another by Tuscan pilasters. A very bold projecting cornice, topped by a low roof, finishes the design, which for sober and massive elegance is one of the most remarkable of its kind with which I am acquainted.

The opposite side of the piazza is open, a hedge separating it from the back gardens of the neighboring houses. It was here, I fancy, that the feudal castle originally stood. It was pulled down, however, during the eighteenth century (busy Bolsheviks!) and its bricks employed, more usefully but less aesthetically, to strengthen the dykes which defend the surrounding plain, none too impregnably, from the waters of the Po.

Its destruction has left Vespasiano's summer palace, or Palace of the Garden, isolated (save where it joins the Gallery of the Antiques), and rather forlorn at the end of the long piazza. It is a long, low building of only two stories, rather insignificant from outside. It is evident that Vespasiano built it as economically as he could. For him the place was only a week-end cottage, a holiday resort, whither he could escape from the metropolitan splendor and bustle of the palace in the market-place, a quarter of a mile away. Like all other rulers of small states, Vespasiano must have found it extremely difficult to take an effective holiday. He could not go ten miles in any direction without coming to a frontier. Within his dominions it was impossible to have a change of air. Wisely, therefore, he decided to concentrate his magnificences. He

built his Balmoral within five minutes' walk of his Buckingham
Palace.

We knocked at the door. The caretaker who opened to us
was an old woman who might have gone on to any stage and
acted Juliet's Nurse without a moment's rehearsal. Within
the first two minutes of our acquaintance with her she con-
fided to us that she had just got married—for the third time,
at the age of seventy. Her comments on the connubial state
were so very Juliet's Nurse, so positively Wife-of-Bath, that
we were made to feel quite early-Victorian in comparison
with this robustious old gammer from the *quattrocento*. After
having told us all that can be told (and much that cannot be
told, at any rate in polite society) about the married state, she
proceeded to do us the honors of the house. She led the way,
opening the shutters of each room in the long suite, as we entered it. And as the light came in through the unglazed windows, what Gonzagesque ravishments were revealed to us.
There was a Cabinet of Venus, with the remains of voluptuous
nudes, a Hall of the Winds with puffing cherubs and a mantel
in red marble; a Cabinet of the Caesars, floored with marble
and adorned with medallions of all the ruffians of antiquity;
a Hall of the Myths on whose ceiling, vaulted into the likeness
of a truncated pyramid seen from within, were five delightful
scenes from Lemprière—an Icarus, an Apollo and Marsyas,
a Phaeton, an Arachne and, in the midst, a to me somewhat
mysterious scene: a naked beauty sitting on the back, not of
a bull (that would have been simple enough), but of a reclin-
ing horse, which turns its head amorously toward her, while
she caresses its neck. Who was the lady and who the travestied
god I do not rightly know. Vague memories of an escapade
of Saturn's float through my mind. But perhaps I am slander-
ing a respectable deity.

But in any case, whatever its subject, the picture is charming. Vespasiano's principal artist was Bernardino Campi of
Cremona. He was not a good painter, of course; but at least
he was gracefully and charmingly, instead of vulgarly medi-
ocre, like Giulio Romano. About the Palazzo del Te there
hangs a certain faded frightfulness; but the Giardino is all
sweetness—mannered, no doubt, and rather feeble—but none
the less authentic in its ruinous decay.

The old caretaker expounded the pictures to us as we went
round—not out of any knowledge of what they represented,
but purely out of her imagination, which was a good deal
more interesting. In the Hall of the Graces, where the walls
are adorned with what remains of a series of very pretty little
grotteschi in the Pompeian manner, her fancy surpassed itself.
These, she said, were the records of the Duke's dreams. Each

time he dreamed a dream he sent for his painter and had it
drawn on the walls of this room. These—she pointed to a
pair of Chimeras—he saw in a nightmare; these dancing
satyrs visited his sleep after a merry evening; these four urns
were dreamt of after too much wine. As for the three naked
Graces, from whom the room takes its name, as for those—
over the Graces she once more became too Wife-of-Bath to
be recorded.

Her old cracked laughter went echoing down the empty
rooms; and it seemed to precipitate and crystallize all the
melancholy suspended, as it were, in solution within those
bleared and peeling walls. The sense of desolation, vaguely
felt before, became poignant. And when the old woman
ushered us into another room, dark and smelling of mold
like the rest, and threw open the shutters and called what the
light revealed the "Hall of the Mirrors," I could almost have
wept. For in the Hall of the Mirrors there are no more
mirrors, only the elaborate framing of them on walls and ceiling. Where the glasses of Murano once shone are spaces of
bare plaster that stare out like blind eyes, blankly and, it seems
after a little, reproachfully. "They used to dance in this room,"
said the old woman.

(From *Along the Road*)

Between Peshawar and Lahore

At Peshawar we were seized with one of our periodical financial panics. Money, in this country, slips rapidly between the
fingers, particularly between the fingers of the tourist. Great
wads of it have to be handed out every time one gets into the
train; for fares are high and distances enormous. No place
in India seems to be less than three hundred miles from any
other place; the longer journeys have to be measured in
thousands. Financial panics are justifiable. We decided to
travel second-class as far as Lahore.

For the first hour or so we were alone in our compartment.
We congratulated ourselves on having secured all the comfort
and privacy of first-class traveling at exactly half the price.
In future, we decided, we would always travel second. But
nature abhors a vacuum, and our compartment was evidently
the object of her special abhorrence. When the train stopped
at Campbellpur, we were invaded. In the twinkling of an eye
our luxurious emptiness was filled to overflowing with luggage

and humanity. And what queer specimens of humanity! The leader of the party which now entered the compartment was a middle-aged man wearing a yellow robe and, on his head, a kind of quilted bonnet with hanging ear-flaps. He was profusely garlanded with yellow chrysanthemums, and had been followed on to the platform by a large crowd of flower-bearing admirers and devotees. Our ignorance of the language did not permit us to discover who this exalted person might be. But he was evidently some kind of high priest, some Hindu pope of considerable holiness, to judge by the respect which was paid him by his numerous retinue and his admirers. His passage along the line must have been well advertised; for at every station our compartment was invaded by a swarm of devotees who came to kiss the great man's feet and to crave a blessing, which in most cases he seemed too lazy to give. Even the guards and ticket-collectors and stationmasters came in to pay their respects. The enthusiasm of one ticket-collector was so great that he traveled about thirty miles in our already packed compartment, simply in order to be near the holy man. He, meanwhile, passed the time by counting his money, which was contained in a large brass-bound box, by loudly eating and, later, dozing. Even at the stations he did not take the trouble to rouse himself, but reclined with closed eyes along his seat, and passively permitted the faithful to kiss his feet. When one is as holy as he evidently was, it is unnecessary to keep up appearances, behave decently, or do anything for one's followers. Office and hereditary honor claim the respect of a believing people quite as much as personal merit.

Judging by appearances, which are often deceptive, I should say that this particular holy man had no personal merit, but a very great office. His face, which had the elements of a fine and powerful face, seemed to have disintegrated and run to fat under the influence of a hoggish self-indulgence. To look at, he was certainly one of the most repulsive human specimens I have ever seen. But of course he may in reality have been a saint and an ascetic, a preacher and a practicer of the moral doctrines formulated in the Gita, or even one of those pure-souled oriental mystics who, we are told, are to leaven the materialism of our Western civilization. He may have been, but I doubt it. All that we could be certain of was that he looked unpleasant, and was undoubtedly dirty; also that he and his admirers exhaled the sour stink of garments long unwashed.

Tolstoy objected to too much cleanliness on the ground that to be too clean is a badge of class. It is only the rich who can afford the time and money to wash their bodies and shift their linen frequently. The laborer who sweats for his living, and whose house contains no bathroom, whose wardrobes no superfluous shirts, must stink. It is inevitable, and it is also right and proper, that he should. Work is prayer. Work is also stink. Therefore stink is prayer. So, more or less, argues Tolstoy, who goes on to condemn the rich for not stinking, and for bringing up their children to have a prejudice against all stinks however natural and even creditable. The non-stinker's prejudice against stink is largely a class prejudice, and therefore to be condemned.

Tolstoy is quite right, of course. We, who were brought up on open windows, clean shirts, hot baths, and sanitary plumbing, find it hard to tolerate twice-breathed air and all the odors which crowded humanity naturally exhales. Our physical education has been such that the majority of our fellow-beings, particularly those less fortunately circumstanced than ourselves, seem to us slightly or even extremely disgusting. A man may have strong humanitarian and democratic principles; but if he happens to have been brought up as a bath-taking, shirt-changing lover of fresh air, he will have to overcome certain physical repugnances before he can bring himself to put those principles into practice to the extent, at any rate, of associating freely with men and women whose habits are different from his own. It is a deplorable fact; but there it is. Tolstoy's remedy is that we should all stink together. Other reformers desire to make it economically possible for every man to have as many hot baths and to change his shirt as often as do the privileged non-stinkers at the present day. Personally, I prefer the second alternative.

Meanwhile, the crowd in our compartment increased. The day, as it advanced, grew hotter. And suddenly the holy man woke up and began to hawk and spit all over the compartment. By the time we reached Rawal Pindi we had decided that the twenty-two rupees we should economize by remaining seven hours longer among our second-class brothers were not enough. We had our luggage transferred into a first-class carriage and paid the difference. The only other occupant of the compartment was an English official of the Kashmir State, bound for his winter headquarters at Jammu. He was a dim little man; but at any rate his linen was clean, and he was not in the least holy. Nobody came in to kiss his feet.

For the rest of the journey I ruminated my anti-clericalism. Indian friends have assured me that the power of the priests is less than it was, and goes on rapidly waning. I hope they are right and that the process may be further accelerated. And not in India alone. There is still, for my taste, too much kissing of amethyst rings as well as of slippered feet. There are still too many black coats in the West, too many orange

ones in the East. *Écrasez l'infâme.* My traveling companion
had made me, for the moment, a thorough-going Voltairian.

It is a simple creed, Voltairianism. In its simplicity lies its
charm, lies the secret of its success—and also of its fallacious-
ness. For, in our muddled human universe, nothing so simple
can possibly be true, can conceivably "work."

If the *infâme* were squashed, if insecticide were scattered
on all the clerical beetles, whether black or yellow, if pure
rationalism became the universal faith, all would automatically
be well. So runs the simple creed of the anti-clericals. It is
too simple, and the assumptions on which it is based are too
sweeping. For, to begin with, is the *infâme* always infamous,
and are the beetles invariably harmful? Obviously not. Nor can
it be said that the behavior-value of pure rationalism (whatever the truth-value of its underlying assumptions) is necessarily superior to the behavior-value of irrational beliefs which
may be and, in general, almost certainly are untrue. And further, the vast majority of human beings are not interested in
reason or satisfied with what it teaches. Nor is reason itself
the most satisfactory instrument for the understanding of life.
Such are a few of the complications which render so simple a
formula as the anti-clerical's inapplicable to our real and
chaotic existence.

Man's progress has been contingent on his capacity to
organize societies. It is only when protected by surrounding
society from aggression, when freed by the organized labor of
society from the necessity of hunting or digging for his food,
it is only, that is to say, when society has tempered and to
a great extent abolished the struggle for personal existence,
that the man of talent can exercise his capacities to the full.
And it is only by a well-organized society that the results of
his labors can be preserved for the enrichment of succeeding
generations. Any force that tends to the strengthening of
society is, therefore, of the highest biological importance.
Religion is obviously such a force. All religions have been
unanimous in encouraging within limits that have tended to
grow wider and ever wider, the social, altruistic, humanitarian
proclivities of man and in condemning his anti-social, self-
assertive tendencies. Those who like to speak anthropomor-
phically would be justified in saying that religion is a device
employed by the Life Force for the promotion of its evolutionary designs. But they would be justified in adding that religion
is also a device employed by the Devil for the dissemination
of idiocy, intolerance, and servile abjection. My fellow passenger from Campbellpur did something, no doubt, to encourage brotherly love, forbearance, and mutual helpfulness
among his flock. But he also did his best to deepen their

congenital stupidity and prevent it from being tempered by the acquirement of correct and useful knowledge, he did his best to terrify them with imaginary fears into servility and to flatter them with groundless hopes into passive contentment with a life unworthy of human beings. What he did in the name of the evolutionary Life Force, he undid in the name of the Devil. I cherish a pious hope that he did just a trifle more than he undid, and that the Devil remained, as the result of his ministry, by ever so little the loser.

Jaipur

At Jaipur we were fortunate in having an introduction to one of the great *thakurs* of the State. He was a mighty land holder, the owner of twenty villages with populations ranging from five hundred to as many thousands, a feudal lord who paid for his fief (until, a year or two ago, a somewhat simpler and more modern system of tenure was introduced) by contributing to the State army one hundred and fifty armed and mounted men. This nobleman was kind enough to place his elephant at our disposal.

It was a superb and particularly lofty specimen, with gold-mounted tusks; ate two hundredweights of food a day and must have cost at least six hundred a year to keep. An expensive pet. But for a man in the *thakur*'s position, we gathered, indispensable, a necessity. Pachyderms in Rajputana are what glass coaches were in Europe a century and a half ago—essential luxuries.

The *thakur* was a charming and cultured man, hospitably kind as only Indians can be. But at the risk of seeming ungrateful, I must confess, that, of all the animals I have ever ridden, the elephant is the most uncomfortable mount. On the level, it is true, the motion is not too bad. One seems to be riding on a small chronic earthquake; that is all. The earthquake becomes more disquieting when the beast begins to climb. But when it goes downhill, it is like the end of the world. The animal descends very slowly and with an infinite caution, planting one huge foot deliberately before the other, and giving you time between each calculated step to anticipate the next convulsive spasm of movement—a spasm that seems to loosen from its place every organ in the rider's body, that twists the spine, that wrenches all the separate muscles of the loins and thorax. The hills round Jaipur are not very high. Fortunately; for by the end of the three or four hundred feet of our climbing and descending, we had almost reached the limits of our endurance. I returned full of admiration for Hannibal. He crossed the Alps on an elephant.

We made two expeditions with the pachyderm; one—over a rocky pass entailing, there and back, two climbs and two sickening descents—to the tanks and ruined temples of Galta, and one to the deserted palaces of Amber. Emerging from the palace precincts—I record the trivial and all too homely incident, because it set me mournfully reflecting about the cosmos—our monster halted and, with its usual deliberation, relieved nature, portentously. Hardly, the operation over, had it resumed its march when an old woman who had been standing at the door of a hovel among the ruins, expectantly waiting—we had wondered for what—darted forward and fairly threw herself on the mound of steaming excrement. There was fuel here, I suppose, for a week's cooking. "Salaam, Maharaj," she called up to us, bestowing in her gratitude the most opulent title she could lay her tongue to. Our passage had been to her like a sudden and unexpected fall of manna. She thanked us, she blessed the great and charitable Jumbo for his Gargantuan bounty.

Our earthquake lurched on. I thought of the scores of millions of human beings to whom the passage of an unconstipated elephant seems a godsend, a stroke of enormous good luck. The thought depressed me. Why are we here, men and women, eighteen hundred millions of us, on this remarkable and perhaps unique planet? To what end? Is it to go about looking for dung—cow dung, horse dung, the enormous and princely excrement of elephants? Evidently it is—for a good many of us at any rate. It seemed an inadequate reason, I thought, for our being here—immortal souls, first cousins of the angels, own brothers of Buddha and Mozart and Sir Isaac Newton.

But a little while later I saw that I was wrong to let the consideration depress me. If it depressed me, that was only because I looked at the whole matter from the wrong end, so to speak. In painting my mental picture of the dung-searchers I had filled my foreground with the figures of Sir Isaac Newton and the rest of them. These, I perceived, should have been relegated to the remote background and the foreground should have been filled with cows and elephants. The picture so arranged, I should have been able to form a more philosophical and proportionable estimate of the dung-searchers. For I should have seen at a glance how vastly superior were their activities to those of the animal producers of dung in the foreground. The philosophical Martian would admire the dung-searchers for having discovered a use for dung; no other animal, he would point out, has had the wit to do more than manufacture it.

We are not Martians and our training makes us reluctant to think of ourselves as animals. Nobody inquires why cows and elephants inhabit the world. There is as little *reason* why we should be here, eating, drinking, sleeping, and in the intervals reading metaphysics, saying prayers, or collecting dung. We *are* here, that is all; and like other animals we do what our native capacities and our environment permit of our doing. Our achievement, when we compare it with that of cows and elephants, is remarkable. They automatically make dung; we collect it and turn it into fuel. It is not something to be depressed about; it is something to be proud of. Still, in spite of the consolations of philosophy, I remained pensive.

(From *Jesting Pilate*)

Atitlan

The story of the Spanish conquest is true but incredible. That Tenochtitlan was taken, that Cortes marched from Mexico to Honduras, that Alvarado broke the power of the Quichés and Cakchiquels—these are facts, but facts so immoderately unlikely that I have never been able to believe them except on authority; reason and imagination withheld their assent. At Panajachel, I made an acquaintance who convinced me, for the first time, that everything in Prescott and Bernal Diaz had really happened. He was an old Spaniard who lived with an Indian wife and their family in a large rambling house by the lake, making his living as a taxidermist and dresser of skins. He was wonderfully expert at his job and had a first-hand knowledge of the birds, mammals and reptiles of the country. But it was not what he did or said that interested me most; it was what he was. As I watched him moving about the terrace of his house, a gaunt, bony figure, but active and powerful, his black beard aggressive in the wind, his nose like an eagle's, his eyes glittering, restless and fierce, I suddenly understood the how and the why of the Spanish conquest. The strength of the Indians is a strength of resistance, of passivity. Matched against these eager, violently active creatures from across the sea, they had no chance—no more chance than a rock against a sledge hammer. True, the Indian rock was a very large one, but the hammer, though small, was wielded with terrific force. Under its quick reiterated blows, the strangely sculptured monolith of American civilization broke into fragments. The bits are still there, indestructible, and perhaps some day they may be fused together again into a shapely whole; meanwhile they merely testify, in their scattered nullity, to the amazing force behind the Spanish hammer.

The old taxidermist went into the house and returned a moment later with a large bucket full of a glutinous and stinking liquid.

"Look here," he said; and he drew out of this disgusting soup yards and yards of an enormous snakeskin. *"Qué bonito!"* he kept repeating, as he smoothed it out. "Like silk. Nobody here knows how to tan a snakeskin as well as I."

I nodded and made the appropriate noises. But it was not at the skin that I was looking; it was at the old man's hands. They were big hands, with fingers long, but square-tipped; hands that moved with a deft power, that reached out and closed with a quick, unhesitating rapacity; the hands of a *conquistador.*

He asked too much for the skin he finally sold us; but I did not grudge the money; for, along with two yards of beautiful serpent's leather, I had bought the key to Spanish-American history, and to me that was worth several times the extra dollar I had paid for my python.

Sololà

The market at Sololà was a walking museum of fancy dress. Unlike the Indians of Mexico, who have mostly gone into white cotton pajamas, with a blanket slung over the shoulder in lieu of great-coat, the Guatemaltecos of the highlands have kept their old costumes. This conservatism has been to some extent affected by the slump and the persuasive salesmanship of shopkeepers and commercial travelers. Nobody starves in this self-supporting agricultural community; but money is a great deal scarcer than it was a few years ago, when the coffee *fincas* were in full production and called, during the picking season, for whole armies of workers from the hills. Those were the glorious times when a man could earn as much as twenty-five or thirty cents a day. The Quiché villages were rich: their *fiestas* were grand events and the more elaborate of their old dances were staged on a lavish scale; *aguardiente* flowed like water, and when a man needed a new suit of the traditional clothes he could afford to buy the hand-woven cloth, the richly patterned sashes and kerchiefs, the hat bands and tassels. Today he has to think twice and three times before he renews his wardrobe. A new outfit will cost him the equivalent of four or five pounds, and at the present moment this is, for a Quiché Indian, an enormous sum. At the local store the price of a suit of blue dungarees is only a few shillings, and when it is worn out, which it will be very soon, he will be able to afford to buy another. It looks, I am afraid, as though the traditional dress of the Indians were doomed. All the forces of industrialism are arrayed against it. Conservative prejudice cannot long resist the assaults of economics.

Meanwhile a majority of highlanders still wear the old costumes—a different one in every village. The most curious feature, for example, of the Sololà costume is the black varnished hat, which is a strangely flattened version of John Bull's topper. From another village (I never discovered which; but it cannot have been far from Sololà, for I saw several of its representatives at the market) came men in large mushroom-shaped hats, exactly like those worn by very distinguished old English ladies when they go gardening. I had a slight shock each time I saw one of them. It was as though Miss Jekyll had suddenly gone mad and taken to staining her face with walnut juice and wearing, with her old hat, a gray monkey-jacket and white cotton pants.

The most remarkable thing about these Indian costumes is that they are not Indian at all, but old European. Little scraps of seventeenth- and eighteenth-century Spain have been caught here and miraculously preserved, like flies in the hard amber of primitive conservatism. The Chichicastenango Indians, for example, wear a short-waisted embroidered jacket and knee-breeches of brown cloth, a gay woven sash and an embroidered kerchief tied round the head. It is, almost without modification, the costume of Sancho Panza. Elsewhere one finds a number of small variations on the Spanish theme. Thus, long kilts will sometimes be worn below a neatly tailored bull-fighter's jacket—a reminiscence, perhaps, of the loin-cloths of an earlier dispensation.

The women's dress has been much less profoundly affected by Spanish fashion than the men's. There is no sign here of the long trailing skirts and Lancashire-lassie shawls of the Mexicans. The Filipino lady's low-cut corsage and puffed sleeves, her white petticoat and coquettishly looped-up skirt are unheard of. True, the Quiché women's embroidered bodices may have borrowed something from European peasant costume; but their short skirts, reaching in many cases only to the knee—these are unquestionably Indian. Perhaps their color has changed since the conquest; for they are now dyed with indigo which was introduced by the Spaniards. But the cut is surely the same as it was when Alvarado passed this way.

Copan

We climbed into the plane and started off. The mist had all melted away and, in a little while, there below us, clear as a map, was the valley of Copan, narrow between hills, with its village, its fields of dust-colored stubble, its winding river, its tree-grown Maya acropolis rising sheer in a great wall from the water's edge. We came spiraling down. A small bald patch not far from the ruins was evidently the landing field. A herd of cows scattered in hysterical agitation as we descended. Avoiding these animals as best he could, and steering clear of the larger of the numerous rocks with which the airport was strewn, our pilot, who was fortunately a most skillful flyer, brought us safely to land. We stepped out and, accompanied by some small boys who offered to be our guides, walked off to see the ruins. Our pilot took the road to the village; the local authorities would be anxious, he knew, to prove their importance by lengthily examining his paper. If he did not indulge them, they might turn savage.

Time and its allies in destruction, vegetation and weather, play curious tricks on the works of man. A city left to their tender mercies is generally destroyed as an architectural and engineering whole, but spared in its decorative details. The great masses of masonry are buried and disrupted; tend, if the vegetation is strong, to vanish altogether, dissolved into their component parts; the statues, the reliefs, the fragile pots and jewels survive, very often, almost intact. At Copan, for example, a few mounds covered with trees, a wall here and there, some rubbish heaps of tumbled stones, are all that remain of the great complex of pyramids, of platforms, of walls and terraces, of sunken courtyards, which once occupied the site. Buried and, under the mold, disintegrated by the thrusting roots of the tropical vegetation, a sacred city of pure geometrical forms once stood here. Its sharp-edged planes of hewn stone, of white or painted stucco, shone smooth, like the surfaces of a crystal, in the perpendicular sunlight. But toiling up and down through the scrub, among the fallen stones, I found it all but impossible to reconstruct in my imagination the Mayas' huge embodiment of a mathematician's dream. I had read the writings of the archeologists and knew what sort of monument had been raised at Copan. But these almost shapeless barrows supplied my fancy with no visible foundations on which to rebuild the Mayas' prodigious works. Only the plastic decorations with which their mountains of solid geometry had been incidentally trimmed were still there, in unequivocal existence, before my eyes. The whole had gone; but a few of the ornamental parts remained. In a maize field at the foot of the wooded mounds—the mounds were the acropolis and principal pyramid, the maize field had been a great forum—stood a group of magnificent stelae, floridly carved in such deep relief that the stone was sometimes pierced from side to side. Using neolithic tools, the Maya sculptors had displayed an almost contemptuous mastery of their material; they had treated their twenty-foot monoliths as a Chinese craftsman might treat a piece of ivory. One is left bewildered by the spectacle of so much technical accomplishment displayed by people having such inadequate technical resources.

The stelae are not Copan's only monuments. Scrambling among the ruins, we found an astonishing wealth of carved stones. Here was a great cubic skull-symbol, its eye sockets glaring, its teeth deep in the grass and weeds; here, at the base of a broken wall, a dado of small death's heads in low relief; here the famous altar with its frieze of fantastically adorned astronomer-priests in scientific conference; here, carved in the round, a giant's head, grotesquely open-mouthed; here a pair of statues, broken, but still violently alive. The finest specimens of sculpture in the round are no longer at Copan. I saw nothing to compare in grace, in plastic subtlety, in emotional expressiveness, with the torso of the maize god at the British Museum, or with the lovely head of the same god now at Boston. These two pieces and certain others in American museums, are stylistically so close to one another that one is tempted to think of them as the works of a single sculptor of outstanding ability. Of the other carvings in the round still at Copan, none exhibited the kind of approach to reality exemplified in these extraordinary statues. The beauty of most Mayan sculpture is felt by us to be profoundly, incommensurably alien. But with this particular group of carvings from Copan one feels suddenly at home, on familiar emotional ground. The mind of the man, or men, who made them seems to have been gifted with the same kind of sensibilities as ours. Now that these works have been taken away, the European visitor at Copan enjoys no such comforting conviction. He looks at the astonishing works around him, but looks at them from across a gulf; they exist in a universe of sentiment and discourse that is not his universe. Those colossal skulls, for example—they have nothing to do with the macabre of our later middle ages, or the florid horrors of baroque sepulchral art.

> The flesh is bruckle, the fiend is slee
> *Timor mortis conturbat me.*

So wailed our ancestors. But I doubt if the Mayas were saying anything of the kind. In these great cubic monoliths, adorned (with what an unerring sense of the significantly decorative effect!) with eye sockets, nose hole, teeth, one finds no trace of our European lament for transience, our personal terror of extinction and decay. One finds—what? Confronted by the extraordinary objects themselves one can only ask the question, not hope to answer it. It is impossible to know by personal experience what the people who made such things felt and thought. Each life has its own private logic, and the logics of all the lives of people living at a given time, under a given cultural dispensation, have, at some point, a certain resemblance among themselves. The Mayas' life-logic was not the same as ours. The admiration with which we look at their works of art is tinged with a speculative incomprehension. What were they really up to? *Quien sabe?*

(From *Beyond the Mexique Bay*)

In a Tunisian Oasis

Waking at dawn, I looked out of the window. We were in the desert. On either side of the railway an immense plain, flat as Holland, but tawny instead of green, stretched out interminably. On the horizon, instead of windmills, a row of camels was silhouetted against the gray sky. Mile after mile, the train rolled slowly southward.

At Tozeur, when at last we arrived, it had just finished raining—for the first time in two and a half years—and now the wind had sprung up; there was a sandstorm. A thick brown fog, whirled into eddies by the wind, gritty to the skin, abolished the landscape from before our smarting eyes. We sneezed; there was sand in our ears, in our hair, between our teeth. It was horrible. I felt depressed, but not surprised. The weather is always horrible when I travel.

Once, in a French hotel, I was accused of having brought with me the flat black bugs, of whose presence among my bedclothes I complained to a self-righteous proprietress. I defended myself with energy against the impeachment. Bugs—no; I am innocent of bugs. But when it comes to bad weather, I have to plead guilty. Rain, frost, wind, snow, hail, fog—I bring them with me wherever I go. I bring them to places where they have never been heard of, at seasons when it is impossible that they should occur. What delightful skating there will be in the Spice Islands when I arrive! On this particular journey I had brought with me to every place on my itinerary the most appalling meteorological calamities. At Naples, for example, it was the snow. Coming out of the theater on the night of our arrival, we found it lying an inch deep under the palm trees in the public gardens. And Vesuvius, next morning, glittered white, like Fujiyama, against the pale spring sky. At Palermo there was a cloud-burst. "Between the Syrtes and soft Sicily" we passed through a tempest of hail, lightning and wind. At Tunis it very nearly froze. At Sousse the wind was so violent that the stiff board-like leaves of the cactuses swayed and trembled in the air like aspens. And now, on the day of our arrival at Tozeur, it had rained for the first time in thirty months, and there was a sandstorm. No, I was not in the least surprised; but I could not help feeling a little gloomy.

Toward evening the wind somewhat abated; the sand began to drop out of the air. At midday the brown curtain had been impenetrable at fifty yards. It thinned, grew gauzier; one could see objects at a hundred, two hundred yards. From the windows of the hotel bedroom in which we had sat all day, trying—but in vain, for it came through even invisible crannies—to escape from the wind-blown sand, we could see the fringes of a dense forest of palm trees, the dome of a little mosque, houses of sun-dried brick and thin brown men in flapping nightshirts walking, with muffled faces and bent heads, against the wind, or riding, sometimes astride, sometimes sideways, on the bony rumps of patient little asses. Two very professional tourists in sun helmets—there was no sun—emerged round the corner of a street. A malicious gust of wind caught them unawares; simultaneously the two helmets shot into the air, thudded, rolled in the dust. The too professional tourists scuttled in pursuit. The spectacle cheered us a little; we descended, we ventured out of doors.

A melancholy Arab offered to show us round the town. Knowing how hard it is to find one's way in these smelly labyrinths, we accepted his offer. His knowledge of French was limited; so too, in consequence, was the information he gave us. He employed what I may call the Berlitz method. Thus, when a column of whirling sand rose up and jumped at us round the corner of a street, our guide turned to us and said, pointing: *"Poussière."* We might have guessed it ourselves.

He led us interminably through narrow, many-cornered streets, between eyeless walls, half crumbled and tottering.

"Village," he explained. *"Très plaisant."* We did not altogether agree with him.

A walk through an Arab village is reminiscent of walks through Ostia or Pompeii. Roman remains are generally in a better state of preservation, and cleaner; that is all. One is astonished to see, among these dusty ruins, white-robed families crouching over their repasts.

Our guide patted a brown mud wall.

"Briques," he said, and repeated the word several times, so that we might be certain what he meant.

These bricks, which are of sun-dried mud, are sometimes, on the façades of the more considerable houses, arranged in a series of simple and pleasing patterns—diamonds, quincunxes, hexagons. A local art which nobody now takes the trouble to practice—nobody, that is, except the Europeans, who, with characteristic energy, have used and wildly abused the traditional ornamentation on the walls of the station and the principal hotel. It is a curious and characteristic fact that, whenever in Tunisia one sees a particularly Oriental piece of architecture, it is sure to have been built by the French, since 1881. The cathedral of Carthage, the law courts and schools of Tunis—these are more Moorish than the Alhambra, Moorish as only Oriental tea-rooms in Paris or London can be Moorish. In thirty years the French have produced buildings more typically and intensely Arabian than the Arabs themselves contrived to do in the course of thirteen centuries.

We passed into the market-place.

"Viande," said our guide, fingering as he passed a well-thumbed collop of mutton, lying among the dust and flies on a little booth.

We nodded.

"Très joli," commented our guide. *"Très plaisant."* Noisily he spat on the ground. The proprietor of the booth spat too. We hurried away; it needs time to grow inured to Tunisian habits. These frightful hoickings in the throat, these sibilant explosions and semi-liquid impacts are almost the national music of the country.

There are in the desert of southern Tunisia three great

oases. These are all of much the same size, each consisting
of some six or seven thousand acres of cultivated ground, and
are all three remarkable for their numerous and copious
springs. In the middle of the desert, suddenly, a hundred
fountains come welling out of the sand; rivers run, a network
of little canals is dug. An innumerable forest of date palms
springs up—a forest whose undergrowth is corn and roses,
vines and apricot trees, olives and pomegranates, pepper trees,
castor-oil trees, banana trees, every precious plant of the temperate and the sub-tropical zones. No rain falls on these little
Edens—except on the days of my arrival—but the springs,
fed from who knows what distant source, flow inexhaustibly
and have flowed at least since Roman times. Islanded among
the sands, their green luxuriance is a standing miracle. That
it should have been in a desert, with here and there such
islands of palm trees, that Judaism and Mohammedanism
took their rise is a thing which, since I have seen an oasis,
astonishes me. The religion which, in such a country, would
naturally suggest itself to me would be no abstract mono-
theism, but the adoration of life, of the forces of green and
growing nature. In an oasis, it seems to me, the worship of
Pan and of the Great Mother should be celebrated with an
almost desperate earnestness. The nymphs of water and of
trees ought surely, here, to receive a passionate gratitude. In
the desert, I should infallibly have invented the Greek mythology. The Jews and the Arabs discovered Jahweh and Allah.
I find it strange.

Of the three great Tunisian oases, my favorite is Nefta.
Gabes runs it close for beauty, while the proximity of the sea
gives it a charm which Nefta lacks. But, on the other hand,
Gabes is less fertile than Nefta and, socially, more sophisticated. There must be the best part of two hundred Europeans
living at Gabes. There is dancing once a week at the hotel.
Gabes is quite the little Paris. The same objection applies to
Tozeur, which has a railway station and positively teems with
French officials. Nefta, with fourteen thousand Arabs, has a
white population of a dozen or thereabouts. A hundred
Frenchmen can always make a Paris; twelve, I am happy
to say, cannot. The only non-Arabian feature of Nefta is its
hotel, which is clean, comfortable, French and efficient. At
Nefta one may live among barbarians, in the Middle Ages,
and at the same time, for thirty francs a day, enjoy the advantages of contemporary Western civilization. What could be
more delightful?

We set off next morning by car, across the desert. Every
now and then we passed a camel, a string of camels. Their
owners walked or rode on asses beside them. The womenfolk

were perched among the baggage on the hump—a testimony, most eloquent in this Mohammedan country, to the great discomfort of camel riding. Once we met a small Citroën lorry, crammed to overflowing with white-robed Arabs. In the Sahara, the automobile has begun to challenge the supremacy of the camel. Motor buses now ply across the desert. A line, we were told, was shortly to be inaugurated between Nefta and Touggourt, across two hundred kilometers of sand. In a few years, no doubt, we shall all have visited Lake Tchad and Timbuctoo. Should one be glad or sorry? I find it difficult to decide.

The hotel at Nefta is a long low building, occupying one whole side of the market-square. From your bedroom window you watch the Arabs living; they do it unhurriedly and with a dignified inefficiency. Endlessly haggling, they buy and sell. The vendor offers a mutton chop, slightly soiled; the buyer professes himself outraged by a price which would be exorbitant if the goods were spotlessly first-hand. It takes them half an hour to come to a compromise. On the ground white bundles doze in the sun; when the sun grows too hot, they roll a few yards and doze again in the shade. The notables of the town, the rich proprietors of palm trees, stroll past with the dignity of Roman senators. Their garments are of the finest wool; they carry walking sticks; they wear European shoes and socks, and on their bare brown calves—a little touch entirely characteristic of the real as opposed to the literary East—pale mauve or shell-pink sock suspenders. Wild men ride in from the desert. Some of them, trusting to common sense as well as Allah to preserve them from ophthalmia, wear smoked motor goggles. With much shouting, much reverberant thumping of dusty, moth-eaten hides, a string of camels is driven in. They kneel, they are unloaded. Supercilious and haughty, they turn this way and that, like the dowagers of very aristocratic families at a plebeian evening party. Then, all at once, one of them stretches out its long neck limply along the ground and shuts its eyes. The movement is one of hopeless weariness; the grotesque animal is suddenly pathetic. And what groanings, what gurglings in the throat, what enormous sighs when their masters begin to reload them! Every additional package evokes a bubbling protest, and when at last they have to rise from their knees, they moan as though their hearts were broken. Blind beggars sit patiently awaiting the alms they never receive. Their raw eyelids black with flies, small children play contentedly in the dust. If Allah wills it, they too will be blind one day: blessed be the name of Allah.

Sitting at our window, we watch the spectacle. And at night, after a pink and yellow sunset with silhouetted palm trees and domes against the sky (for my taste, I am afraid, altogether too like the colored plates in the illustrated Bible), at night huge stars come out in the indigo sky, the cafés are little caves of yellow light, draped figures move in the narrow streets with lanterns in their hands, and on the flat roofs of the houses one sees the prowling shadows of enormous watchdogs. There is silence, the silence of the desert: from time to time there comes to us, very distinctly, the distant sound of spitting.

Walking among the crowds of the market-place or along the narrow labyrinthine streets, I was always agreeably surprised by the apathetically courteous aloofness of Arab manners. There are beggars in plenty, of course, hawkers, guides, cab drivers; and when you pass, they faintly stir, it is true, from their impassive calm. They stretch out hands, they offer Arab antiquities of the most genuine German manufacture, they propose to take you the round of the sights, they invite you into their fly-blown vehicles. But they do all these things politely and quite uninsistently. A single refusal suffices to check their nascent importunity. You shake your head; they relapse once more into the apathy from which your appearance momentarily roused them—resignedly: nay, almost, you feel, with a sense of relief that it had not, after all, been necessary to disturb themselves. Coming from Naples, we had been particularly struck by this lethargic politeness. For in Naples the beggars claim an alms noisily and as though by right. If you refuse to ride, the cabmen of Pozzuoli follow you up the road, alternately cursing and whining, and at every hundred yards reducing their price by yet another ten per cent. The guides at Pompeii fairly insist on being taken; they cry aloud, they show their certificates, they enumerate their wives and starving children. As for the hawkers, they simply will not let you go. What, you don't want colored photographs of Vesuvius? Then look at these corals. No corals? But here is the last word in cigarette holders. You do not smoke? But in any case, you shave; these razor blades, now . . . You shake your head. Then toothpicks, magnifying glasses, celluloid combs. Stubbornly, you continue to refuse. The hawker plays his last card—an ace, it must be admitted, and of trumps. He comes very close to you, he blows garlic and alcohol confidentially into your face. From an inner pocket he produces an envelope; he opens it, he presses the contents into your hand. You may not want corals or razor blades, views of Vesuvius or celluloid combs; he admits it. But can you honestly say—honestly, with your hand on your heart—that you have no use for pornographic engravings?

And for nothing, sir, positively for nothing. Ten francs apiece; the set of twelve for a hundred. . . .

The touts, the pimps, the mendicants of Italy are the energetic members of a conquering, progressive race. The Neapolitan cabman is a disciple of Samuel Smiles; the vendors of pornographic post cards and the sturdy beggars live their lives with a strenuousness that would have earned the commendation of a Roosevelt. Self-help and the strenuous life do not flourish on the other shore of the Mediterranean. In Tunisia the tourist walks abroad unpestered. The Arabs have no future.

That they might still have a future if they changed their philosophy of life must be obvious to anyone who has watched the behavior of Arab children, who have not yet had time to be influenced by the prevailing fatalism of Islam. Arab children are as lively, as inquisitive, as tiresome and as charming as the children of the most progressively Western people. At Nefta the adult beggars and donkey drivers might leave us, resignedly, in peace; but the children were unescapable. We could never stir abroad without finding a little troop of them frisking around us. It was in vain that we tried to drive them away; they accompanied us, whether we liked it or no, on every walk, and, when the walk was over, claimed wages for their importunate fidelity.

To provide tourists with guidance they did not need—this, we found, was the staple profession of the little boys of Nefta. But they had other and more ingenious ways of making money. Close and acute observers of tourists, they had made an important psychological discovery about this curious race of beings. Foreigners, they found out, especially elderly female foreigners, have a preposterous tenderness for animals. The little boys of Nefta have systematically exploited this discovery. Their methods, which we had frequent opportunities of observing, are simple and effective. In front of the hotel a gang of little ruffians is perpetually on the watch. A tourist shows himself, or herself, on one of the balconies: immediately the general of the troop—or perhaps it would be better to call him the director of the company, for it is obvious that the whole affair is organized on a strictly business footing—runs forward to within easy coin-tossing distance. From somewhere about his person he produces a captive bird—generally some brightly colored little creature not unlike a goldfinch. Smiling up at the tourist, he shows his prize. "*Oiseau*," he explains in his pidgin French. When the tourist has been made to understand that the bird is alive, the little boy proceeds, with the elaborate gestures of a conjurer, to pretend to wring its neck, to pull off its legs and wings, to pluck out its feathers.

For a tender-hearted tourist the menacing pantomime is unbearable.

"Lâche la bête. Je te donne dix sous."

Released, the bird flaps ineffectually away, as well as its clipped wings will permit. In actual fact, we observed, they never did their victims any harm. A bird, it was obvious, was far too valuable to be lightly killed; goldfinches during the tourist season laid golden eggs. Besides, they were really very nice little boys and fond of their pets. When they saw that we had seen through their trick and could not be induced to pay ransom, they grinned up at us without malice and knowingly, as though we were their accomplices, and carefully put the birds away.

The importunity of the little boys was tiresome when one wanted to be alone. But if one happened to be in the mood for it, their company was exceedingly entertaining. The exploitation of the tourists was a monopoly which the most active of the children had arrogated, by force and cunning, to themselves. There was a little gang of them who shared the loot and kept competitors at a distance. By the time we left, we had got to know them very well. When we walked abroad, small strangers tried to join our party; but they were savagely driven away with shouts and blows. We were private property; no trespassing was tolerated. It was only by threatening to stop their wages that we could persuade the captains of the Nefta tourist industry to desist from persecuting their rivals. There was one particularly charming little boy—mythically beautiful, as only Arab children can be beautiful—who was the object of their special fury. The captains of the tourist industry were ugly: they dreaded the rivalry of this lovely child. And they were right; he was irresistible. We insisted on his being permitted to accompany us.

"But why do you send him away?" we asked.

"Lui méchant," the captains of industry replied in their rudimentary French. *"Lui casser un touriste."*

"He smashed a tourist?" we repeated in some astonishment.

They nodded. Blushing, even the child himself seemed reluctantly to admit the truth of their accusations. We could get no further explanations; none of them knew enough French to give them. *"Lui méchant. Lui casser un touriste."* That was all we could discover. The lovely child looked at us appealingly. We decided to run the risk of being smashed and let him come with us. I may add that we came back from all our walks quite intact.

Under the palm trees, through that labyrinth of paths and running streams, we wandered interminably with our rabble of little guides. Most often it was to that part of the oasis called the *Corbeille* that we went. At the bottom of a rounded valley, theater-shaped and with smooth steep sides of sand, a score of springs suddenly gush out. There are little lakes, jade green like those pools beneath the cypresses of the Villa d'Este at Tivoli. Round their borders the palm trees go jetting up, like fountains fixed in their upward aspiring gesture, their drooping crown of leaves a green spray arrested on the point of falling. Fountains of life—and five yards away the smooth unbroken slopes of sand glare in the sun. A little river flows out from the lakes, at first between high banks, then into an open sheet of water where the children paddle and bathe, the beasts come down to drink, the women do their washing. The river is the main road in this part of the oasis. The Arabs, when they want to get from place to place, tuck up their night-shirts and wade. Shoes and stockings, not to mention the necessity for keeping up their dignified prestige, do not permit Europeans to follow their example. It is only on mule-back that Europeans use the river road.

A fertile oasis possesses a characteristic color scheme of its own, which is entirely unlike that of any landscape in Italy or the north. The fundamental note is struck by the palms. Their foliage, except where the stiff shiny leaves metallically reflect the light, is a rich blue-green. Beneath them, one walks in a luminous aquarium shadow, broken by innumerable vivid shafts of sunlight that scatter gold over the ground or, touching the trunks of the palm trees, make them shine a pale ashy pink through the subaqueous shadow. There is pink, too, in the glaring whiteness of the sand beyond the fringes of the oasis. Under the palms, beside the brown or jade-colored water, glows the bright emerald green of corn or the deciduous trees of the north, with here and there the huge yellowish leaves of a banana tree, the smoky gray of olives, or the bare bone-white and writhing form of a fig tree.

As the sun gradually sinks, the aquarium shadow beneath the palm trees grows bluer, denser; you imagine yourself descending through layer after darkening layer of water. Only the pale skeletons of the fig trees stand out distinctly; the waters gleam like eyes in the dark ground; the ghost of a little marabout or chapel shows its domed silhouette, white and strangely definite in the growing darkness, through a gap in the trees. But looking up from the depths of this submarine twilight, one sees the bright pale sky of evening, and against it, still touched by the level, rosily-golden light, gleaming as though transmuted into sheets of precious metal, the highest leaves of the palm trees.

A little wind springs up; the palm leaves rattle together; it is suddenly cold. "*En avant*," we call. Our little guides quicken their pace. We follow them through the darkening mazes of the palm forest, out into the open. The village lies high on the desert plateau above the oasis, desert-colored, like an arid outcrop of the tawny rock. We mount to its nearest gate. Through passage-ways between blank walls, under long dark tunnels the children lead us—an obscure and tortuous way which we never succeeded in thoroughly mastering—back to the square market-place at the center of the town. The windows of the inn glimmer invitingly. At the door we pay off the captains of industry and the little tourist-smasher; we enter. Within the hotel it is provincial France.

(From "In a Tunisian Oasis," *The Olive Tree*)

Miracle in Lebanon

In one of the northern suburbs of Beirut there stands an ugly little Armenian church, to which, in the ordinary course of events, no tourist would ever dream of going. But in this month of May, 1954, the course of events had not been ordinary. The sight we had come to see was a miracle.

It had happened two or three days before. In the niche where, between services, the communion chalice was kept, a patch of light had appeared on the stone. There was no sunbeam to account for it, no indication, so we were assured, that the stone contained any phosphorescent or fluorescent substance. And yet the fact remained that, for the last few days, a soft glow had appeared every morning, persisted all day and faded out at night. For the Armenians, I suppose, the miracle clearly demonstrated how right their fathers had been to reject the competing orthodoxies of Rome and Byzantium in favor of the doctrine that, after his baptism (but not before), Christ's flesh consisted of ethereal fire and "was not subject to the ordinary phenomena of digestion, secretions and evacuations." For the rest of us, it was either a hoax, or an ordinary event in an unusual context, or else one of those delightful anomalies which distress the right-thinking scientist by actually turning up, every now and then, in all their mysterious pointlessness, and refusing to be explained away.

The church, when we arrived, was thronged, I was going to say, with pilgrims—but the word (at least in this present age of unfaith and, therefore, religious earnestness) calls up ideas of devotion; and of devotion, or even of decorum, there were no signs. But if these people were no pilgrims, in our non-Chaucerian sense of the term, neither were they mere sightseers. Curiosity was certainly one of their motives, but not, it was clear, the only or strongest one. What had brought most of them to the church was a form of self-interest. They had come there, as the forty-niners came to California, in search of sudden profit—a horde of spiritual prospectors looking for nuggets of *mana*, veins of twenty-two-carat good luck, something, in a word, for nothing.

Something for nothing—but, concretely, what? When crowds close in on a movie star, they can beg autographs, steal handkerchiefs and fountain pens, tear off pieces of his or her garments as relics. Similarly, in the Middle Ages persons dying in the odor of sanctity ran the risk, when their bodies lay in state, of being stripped naked or even dismembered by the faithful. Clothing would be cut to ribbons, ears cropped, hair pulled out, toes and fingers amputated, nipples snipped off and carried home as amulets. But here, unfortunately, there was no corpse; there was only light, and light is intangible. You cannot slice off an inch of the spectrum and put it in your pocket. The people who had come to exploit this Comstock Lode of the miraculous found themselves painfully frustrated; there was nothing here that they could take away with them. For all practical purposes, the glow in the niche was immaterial. Then, happily for all concerned, a young woman noticed that, for some reason or other, one of the chandeliers, suspended from the ceiling of the church, was wet. Drops of rather dirty water were slowly forming and, at lengthening intervals, falling. Nobody supposed that there was anything supernatural about the phenomenon; but at least it was taking place in a supernatural context. Moreover the water on the chandelier possessed one immense advantage over the light in the niche: it was tangible as well as merely visible. A boy was hoisted onto the shoulders of a tall man. Handkerchiefs were passed up to him, moistened in the oozings of the lamp and then returned to their owners, made happy now by the possession of a charged fetish, capable, no doubt, of curing minor ailments, restoring lost potency and mediating prayers for success in love or business.

But "the search for the miraculous" (to use Ouspensky's phrase) is not invariably motivated by self-interest. There are people who love truth for its own sake and are ready, like the founders of the Society for Psychical Research, to seek it at the bottom of even the muddiest, smelliest wells. Much more widespread than the love of truth is the appetite for marvels, the love of the Phony *an sich*, in itself and for its own sweet sake. There is also a curious psychological derangement, a kind of neurosis, sometimes mild, sometimes severe, which might be called "The Cryptogram-Secret Society Syndrome." What fun to be an initiate! How delicious to feel the paranoid glow which accompanies the consciousness of belonging to the innermost circle, of being one of the superior and privileged few who know, for example, that all history, past, present and future, is written into the stones of the Great Pyramid; that Jesus, like Madame Blavatsky, spent seven years in Tibet; that Bacon wrote all the works of Shakespeare and never died, merely vanished, to reappear a century later as the Comte de Saint-Germain, who is still living either (as Mrs. Annie Besant was convinced) in a Central European castle, or else, more probably, in a cave, with a large party of Lemurians, near the top of Mount Shasta; alternatively, that Bacon did die and was buried, not (needless to say) in what the vulgar regard as his tomb, but at Williamsburg, Virginia, or, better still, on an island off the coast of California, near Santa Barbara. To be privy to such secrets is a high, rare privilege, a distinction equivalent to that of being Mr. Rockefeller or a Knight of the Garter.

Esoteric phantasies about Fourth Dynasty monuments, sixteenth-century lawyers and eighteenth-century adventurers are harmless. But when practical politicians and power seekers go in for esotericism, the results are apt to be dangerous. Whether Fascist or revolutionary, every conspiratorial group has its quota of men and women afflicted by the Cryptogram-Secret Society Syndrome. Nor is this all. The intelligence services of every government are largely staffed by persons who (in happier circumstances or if their temperament were a little different), would be inoffensively engaged in hunting for Tibetan Masters, proving that the English are the Lost Ten Tribes, celebrating Black Masses or (the favorite occupation of Charles Williams's more eccentric characters) intoning the Tetragrammaton backwards. If these neurotics could be content to play the cloak-and-dagger game according to the rules of patriotism, all would be, relatively speaking, well. But the history of espionage demonstrates very clearly that many compulsive esotericists are not content to belong to only one Secret Society. To intensify their strange fun, they surreptitiously work for the enemy as well as their own gang, and end, in a delirium of duplicity, by doublecrossing everyone. The born secret agent, the man who positively enjoys spying, can never, because he is a neurotic, be relied upon. It may well be that a nation's actual security is in inverse ratio to the size of its security forces. The greater the number of its secret agents and hush-hush men, the more chances there are of betrayal.

But let us get back to our miracle. "What do you think of

it?" I asked our Lebanese companion. He stroked his black beard, he smiled, he shrugged his shoulders in expressive silence. Being himself a professional thaumaturge—trained by the dervishes to lie on beds of nails, to go into catalepsy, to perform feats of telepathy, to send people into hypnotic trance by simply touching a point on the neck or back—he knew how hard a man must work if he would acquire even the most trifling of paranormal powers. His skepticism in regard to amateur wonder-workers and spontaneous miracles was complete and unshakable.

A queue had formed at the foot of the altar steps. We got into line and shuffled slowly forward to get our peep, in due course, into the niche. That I personally saw nothing was the fault, not of the chalice, but of my own poor eyesight. To my companions and everyone else the glow was manifest. It was an Armenian miracle; but even Maronites, even Uniats, even Moslems and Druses had to admit that something had happened.

We made our way toward the door. Perched on the tall man's shoulders, the boy was still busy at his task of turning handkerchiefs into relics. In the sacristy picture postcards of the chalice and the illuminated niche were already on sale.

In Edward Conze's admirable account of Buddhism* there is a striking passage on the historical, and perhaps psychologically inevitable relationship between spirituality and superstition, between the highest form of religion and the lowest. "Historically," Conze notes, "the display of supernatural powers and the working of miracles were among the most potent causes of the conversion of tribes and individuals to Buddhism." Even the most "refined and intellectual" of Buddhists "would be inclined to think that a belief in miracles is indispensable to the survival of any spiritual life. In Europe, from the eighteenth century onwards, the conviction that spiritual forces can act on material events has given way to a belief in the inexorable rule of natural law. The result is that the experience of the spiritual has become more and more inaccessible to modern society. No known religion has become mature without embracing both the spiritual and the magical. If it rejects the spiritual, religion becomes a mere weapon to dominate the world. . . . Such was the case in Nazism and in modern Japan. If, however, religion rejects the magical side of life, it cuts itself off from the living forces of the world to such an extent that it cannot bring even the spiritual side of man to maturity." Buddhism (like Christianity in its heyday) has combined "lofty metaphysics with adherence to the most

* See pp. 84 ff. of *Buddhism, Its Essence and Development* by Edward Conze, Preface by Arthur Waley. New York, Philosophical Library, 1951.

commonly accepted superstitions of mankind. The Prajnapara-
mita text tells us that 'perfect wisdom can be attained only
by the complete and total extinction of self-interest.' And yet,
in the same texts, this supreme spiritual wisdom is 'recommended as a sort of magical talisman or lucky amulet.' . . .
Among all the paradoxes with which the history of Buddhism
presents us this combination of spiritual negation of self-interest with magical subservience to self-interest is perhaps one of
the most striking."

The same paradox is to be found in Christianity. The
mystical spirituality of the fourteenth century had as its background and context the system of ideas which called into
existence such men as Chaucer's Pardoner and the preacher
who, in the Decameron, tours the country exhibiting a tail
feather of the Holy Ghost. Or consider the flowering, three
centuries later, of French spirituality in Charles de Condren
and Olier, in Lallemant and Surin and Mme. de Chantal.
These worshipers in spirit of a God who is Spirit were contemporary with and, in Surin's case, deeply involved in the
most hideous manifestations of devil-centered superstition.
White sand is clean, but sterile. If you want a herbaceous
border, you must mulch your soil with dead leaves and, if
possible, dig in a load of dung. Shall we ever see, in religion,
the equivalent of hydroponics—spiritual flowers growing,
without benefit of excrement or decay, in a solution of pure
love and understanding? I devoutly hope so, but, alas, have
my doubts. Like dirtless farming, dirtless spirituality is likely
to remain, for a long time, an exception. The rule will be dirt
and plenty of it. Occult dirt, bringing forth, as usual, a few
mystical flowers and a whole crop of magicians, priests and
fanatics. Anti-occult dirt—the dirt of ideological and technological superstition—in which personal frustrations grow like
toadstools in the dark thickets of political tyranny. Or else
(and this will be the ultimate horror) a mixture of both kinds
of dirt, fertile in such monstrosities as mediumistic commis-
sars, clairvoyant engineers, NKVD's and FBI's equipped with
ESP as well as walky-talkies and concealed microphones.

(From "Miracle in Lebanon,"
Tomorrow and Tomorrow and Tomorrow)

LOVE, SEX,
AND PHYSICAL BEAUTY

Beauty in 1920

To those who know how to read the signs of the times it will
have become apparent, in the course of these last days and
weeks, that the Silly Season is close upon us. Already—and
this in July with the menace of three or four new wars
grumbling on the thunderous horizon—already a monster of
the deep has appeared at a popular seaside resort. Already
Mr. Louis McQuilland has launched in the *Daily Express* a
fierce onslaught on the younger poets of the Asylum. Already
the picture-papers are more than half-filled with photographs
of bathing nymphs—photographs that make one understand
the ease with which St. Anthony rebuffed his temptations.
The newspapermen, ramping up and down like wolves, seek
their prey wherever they may find it; and it was with a unanimous howl of delight that the whole Press went pelting after
the hare started by Mrs. Asquith in a recent installment of
her autobiography. Feebly and belatedly, let me follow the
pack.

Mrs. Asquith's denial of beauty to the daughters of the
twentieth century has proved a god-sent giant gooseberry. It
has necessitated the calling in of a whole host of skin-food
specialists, portrait-painters and photographers to deny this far
from soft impeachment. A great deal of space has been agreeably and inexpensively filled. Every one is satisfied, public,
editors, skin-food specialists and all. But by far the most
interesting contribution to the debate was a pictorial one,
which appeared, if I remember rightly, in the *Daily News.*
Side by side, on the same page, we were shown the photo-

graphs of three beauties of the eighteen-eighties and three of
the nineteen-twenties. The comparison was most instructive.
For a great gulf separates the two types of beauty represented
by these two sets of photographs.

I remember in *If*, one of those charming conspiracies of
E. V. Lucas and George Morrow, a series of parodied fashion-plates entitled "If Faces get any Flatter. Last year's standard, this year's Evening Standard." The faces of our living
specimens of beauty have grown flatter with those of their
fashion-plate sisters. Compare the types of 1880 and 1920.
The first is steep-faced, almost Roman in profile; in the contemporary beauties the face has broadened and shortened,
the profile is less noble, less imposing, more appealingly,
more alluringly pretty. Forty years ago it was the aristocratic
type that was appreciated; today the popular taste has shifted
from the countess to the soubrette. Photography confirms the
fact that the ladies of the 'eighties looked like Du Maurier
drawings. But among the present young generation one looks
in vain for the type; the Du Maurier damsel is as extinct as
the mesozoic reptile; the Fish girl and other kindred flat-faced
species have taken her place.

Between the 'thirties and 'fifties another type, the egg-faced
girl, reigned supreme in the affections of the world. From the
early portraits of Queen Victoria to the fashion-plates in the
Ladies' Keepsake this invariable type prevails—the egg-shaped
face, the sleek hair, the swan-like neck, the round, champagne-
bottle shoulders. Compared with the decorous impassivity of
the oviform girl our flat-faced fashion-plates are terribly abandoned and provocative. And because one expects so much in
the way of respectability from these egg-faces of an earlier
age, one is apt to be shocked when one sees them conducting
themselves in ways that seem unbefitting. One thinks of that
enchanting picture of Etty's, "Youth on the Prow and Pleasure at the Helm." The naiads are of the purest egg-faced type.
Their hair is sleek, their shoulders slope and their faces are
impassive as blanks. And yet they have no clothes on. It is
almost indecent; one imagined that the egg-faced type came
into the world complete with flowing draperies.

It is not only the face of beauty that alters with the changes
of popular taste. The champagne-bottle shoulders of the oviform girl have vanished from the modern fashion-plate and
from modern life. The contemporary hand, with its two middle fingers held together and the forefinger and little finger
splayed apart, is another recent product. Above all, the feet
have changed. In the days of the egg-faces no fashion-plate
had more than one foot. This rule will, I think, be found
invariable. That solitary foot projects, generally in a strangely

haphazard way as though it had nothing to do with a leg, from under the edge of the skirt. And what a foot! It has no relation to those provocative feet in Suckling's ballad:

> Her feet beneath her petticoat
> Like little mice stole in and out.

It is an austere foot. It is a small, black, oblong object like a tea-leaf. No living human being has ever seen a foot like it, for it is utterly unlike the feet of nineteen-twenty. Today the fashion-plate is always a biped. The tea-leaf has been replaced by two feet of rich baroque design, curved and florid, with insteps like the necks of Arab horses. Faces may have changed shape, but feet have altered far more radically. On the text, "the feet of the young women," it would be possible to write a profound philosophical sermon.

And while I am on the subject of feet I would like to mention another curious phenomenon of the same kind, but affecting, this time, the standards of male beauty. Examine the pictorial art of the eighteenth century, and you will find that the shape of the male leg is not what it was. In those days the calf of the leg was not a muscle that bulged to its greatest dimensions a little below the back of the knee, to subside, *decrescendo,* toward the ankle. No, in the eighteenth century the calf was an even crescent, with its greatest projection opposite the middle of the shin; the ankle, as we know it, hardly existed. This curious calf is forced upon one's attention by almost every minor picture-maker of the eighteenth century, and even by some of the great masters, as, for instance, Blake. How it came into existence I do not know. Presumably the crescent calf was considered, in the art schools, to approach more nearly to the Platonic Idea of the human leg than did the poor distorted Appearance of real life. Personally, I prefer my calves with the bulge at the top and a proper ankle at the bottom. But then I don't hold much with the *beau idéal.*

The process by which one type of beauty becomes popular, imposes its tyranny for a period and then is displaced by a dissimilar type is a mysterious one. It may be that patient historical scholars will end by discovering some law to explain the transformation of the Du Maurier type into the flat-face type, the tea-leaf foot into the baroque foot, the crescent calf into the normal calf. As far as one can see at present, these changes seem to be the result of mere hazard and arbitrary choice. But a time will doubtless come when it will be found that these changes of taste are as ineluctably predetermined as any chemical change. Given the South African War, the accession of Edward VII and the Liberal triumph of 1906, it was, no doubt, as inevitable that Du Maurier should have given place to Fish as that zinc subjected to sulphuric acid should break up into $ZnSO_4 + H_2$. But we leave it to others to formulate the precise workings of the law.

(From *On the Margin*)

Fashions in Love

Human nature does not change, or, at any rate, history is too short for any changes to be perceptible. The earliest known specimens of art and literature are still comprehensible. The fact that we can understand them all and can recognize in some of them an unsurpassed artistic excellence is proof enough that not only men's feelings and instincts, but also their intellectual and imaginative powers, were in the remotest times precisely what they are now. In the fine arts it is only the convention, the form, the incidentals that change: the fundamentals of passion, of intellect and imagination remain unaltered.

It is the same with the arts of life as with the fine arts. Conventions and traditions, prejudices and ideals and religious beliefs, moral systems and codes of good manners, varying according to the geographical and historical circumstances, mold into different forms the unchanging material of human instinct, passion, and desire. It is a stiff, intractable material— Egyptian granite, rather than Hindu bronze. The artists who carved the colossal statues of Rameses II may have wished to represent the Pharaoh standing on one leg and waving two or three pairs of arms over his head, as the Indians still represent the dancing Krishna. But with the best will in the world they could not have imposed such a form upon the granite. Similarly, those artists in social life whom we call statesmen, moralists, founders of religions, have often wished to mold human nature into forms of superhuman elegance; but the material has proved too stubborn for them, and they have had to be content with only a relatively small alteration in the form which their predecessors had given it. At any given historical moment human behavior is a compromise (enforced from without by law and custom, from within by belief in religious or philosophical myths) between the raw instinct on the one hand and the unattainable ideal on the other—a compromise, in our sculptural metaphor, between the unshaped block of stone and the many-armed dancing Krishna.

Like all the other great human activities, love is the product
of unchanging passions, instincts, and desires (unchanging,
that is to say, in the mass of humanity; for, of course, they
vary greatly in quantity and quality from individual to individual), and of laws and conventions, beliefs and ideals, which
the circumstances of time and place, or the arbitrary fiats of
great personalities, have imposed on a more or less willing
society. The history of love, if it were ever written (and
doubtless some learned German, unread, alas, by me, *has*
written it, and in several volumes), would be like the current
histories of art—a record of succeeding "styles" and "schools,"
of "influences," "revolutions," "technical discoveries." Love's
psychological and physiological material remains the same;
but every epoch treats it in a different manner, just as every
epoch cuts its unvarying cloth and silk and linen into garments of the most diverse fashion. By way of illustration, I
may mention that vogue of homosexuality which seems, from
all accounts, to have been universal in the Hellenic world.
Plutarch attributes the inception of this mode to the custom
(novel in the fifth century, according to Thucydides) of
exercising naked in the palestra.* But whatever may have
been its origin, there can be no doubt that this particular
fashion in love spread widely among people who were not
in the least congenitally disposed to homosexuality. Convention and public opinion molded the material of love into forms
which a later age has chosen to call "unnatural." A recrudescence of this amorous mode was very noticeable in Europe
during the years immediately following the War. Among the
determining causes of this recrudescence a future Plutarch will
undoubtedly number the writings of Proust and André Gide.

The present fashions in love are not so definite and universal as those in clothes. It is as though our age were dubiously
hesitating between crinolines and hobble skirts, trunk hose and
Oxford trousers. Two distinct and hostile conceptions of love
coexist in the minds of men and women, two sets of ideals,
of conventions, of public opinions, struggle for the right to
mold the psychological and physiological material of love.
One is the conception evolved by the nineteenth century out
of the ideals of Christianity on the one hand and romanticism on the other. The other is that still rather inchoate and
negative conception which contemporary youth is in process
of forming out of the materials provided by modern psychol-

* Plutarch, who wrote some five hundred years after the event, is by no
means an unquestionable authority. The habit of which he and Thucydides
speak may have facilitated the spread of the homosexual fashion. But that
the fashion existed before the fifth century is made sufficiently clear by Homer,
not to mention Sappho. Like many modern oriental peoples, the ancient
Greeks were evidently, in Sir Richard Burton's expressive phrase, "omnifu-
tuent."

ogy. The public opinion, the conventions, ideals, and prejudices which gave active force to the first convention and
enabled it, to some extent at least, to modify the actual practice of love, had already lost much of their strength when they
were rudely shattered, at any rate in the minds of the young,
by the shock of the War. As usually happens, practice preceded theory, and the new conception of love was called in
to justify existing post-War manners. Having gained a footing,
the new conception is now a cause of new behavior among
the youngest adolescent generation, instead of being, as it was
for the generation of the War, an explanation of war-time
behavior made after the fact.

Let us try to analyze these two coexisting and conflicting
conceptions of love. The older conception was, as I have said,
the product of Christianity and romanticism—a curious mixture of contradictions, of the ascetic dread of passion and the
romantic worship of passion. Its ideal was a strict monogamy,
such as St. Paul grudgingly conceded to amorous humanity,
sanctified and made eternal by one of those terrific exclusive
passions which are the favorite theme of poetry and drama.
It is an ideal which finds its most characteristic expression in
the poetry of that infinitely respectable rebel, that profoundly
anglican worshiper of passion, Robert Browning. It was
Rousseau who first started the cult of passion for passion's
sake. Before his time the great passions, such as that of Paris
for Helen, of Dido for Æneas, of Paolo and Francesca for one
another, had been regarded rather as disastrous maladies than
as enviable states of soul. Rousseau, followed by all the
romantic poets of France and England, transformed the
grand passion from what it had been in the Middle Ages—
a demoniac possession—into a divine ecstasy, and promoted
it from the rank of a disease to that of the only true and
natural form of love. The nineteenth-century conception of
love was thus doubly mystical, with the mysticism of Christian
asceticism and sacramentalism, and with the romantic mysticism of Nature. It claimed an absolute rightness on the
grounds of its divinity and of its naturalness.

Now, if there is one thing that the study of history and
psychology makes abundantly clear, it is that there are no
such things as either "divine" or "natural" forms of love.
Innumerable gods have sanctioned and forbidden innumerable
kinds of sexual behavior, and innumerable philosophers and
poets have advocated the return to the most diverse kinds of
"nature." Every form of amorous behavior, from chastity and
monogamy to promiscuity and the most fantastic "perver-
sions," is found both among animals and men. In any given
human society, at any given moment, love, as we have seen,

is the result of the interaction of the unchanging instinctive
and physiological material of sex with the local conventions
of morality and religion, the local laws, prejudices, and ideals.
The degree of permanence of these conventions, religious
myths, and ideals is proportional to their social utility in the
given circumstances of time and place.

The new twentieth-century conception of love is realistic.
It recognizes the diversity of love, not merely in the social
mass from age to age, but from individual to contemporary
individual, according to the dosage of the different instincts
with which each is born, and the upbringing he has received.
The new generation knows that there is no such thing as Love
with a large L, and that what the Christian romantics of the
last century regarded as the uniquely natural form of love is,
in fact, only one of the indefinite number of possible amorous
fashions, produced by specific circumstances at that particular
time. Psychoanalysis has taught it that all the forms of sexual
behavior previously regarded as wicked, perverse, unnatural,
are statistically normal (and normality is solely a question of
statistics), and that what is commonly called amorous normality is far from being a spontaneous, instinctive form of
behavior, but must be acquired by a process of education.
Having contracted the habit of talking freely and more or less
scientifically about sexual matters, the young no longer regard
love with that feeling of rather guilty excitement and thrilling
shame which was for an earlier generation the normal reaction
to the subject. Moreover, the practice of birth-control has
robbed amorous indulgence of most of the sinfulness traditionally supposed to be inherent in it by robbing it of its socially
disastrous effects. The tree shall be known by its fruits: where
there are no fruits, there is obviously no tree. Love has ceased
to be the rather fearful, mysterious thing it was, and become
a perfectly normal, almost commonplace, activity—an activity, for many young people, especially in America, of the same
nature as dancing or tennis, a sport, a recreation, a pastime.
For those who hold this conception of love, liberty and toleration are prime necessities. A strenuous offensive against the
old taboos and repressions is everywhere in progress.

Such, then, are the two conceptions of love which oppose
one another today. Which is the better? Without presuming to
pass judgment, I will content myself with pointing out the
defects of each. The older conception was bad, in so far as it
inflicted unnecessary and undeserved sufferings on the many
human beings whose congenital and acquired modes of love-
making did not conform to the fashionable Christian-romantic
pattern which was regarded as being uniquely entitled to call
itself Love. The new conception is bad, it seems to me, in so

far as it takes love too easily and lightly. On love regarded as
an amusement the last word is surely this of Robert Burns:

> I waive the quantum of the sin,
>   The hazard of concealing;
> But oh! it hardens all within
>   And petrifies the feeling.

Nothing is more dreadful than a cold, unimpassioned indulgence. And love infallibly becomes cold and unimpassioned
when it is too lightly made. It is not good, as Pascal remarked,
to have too much liberty. Love is the product of two opposed
forces—of an instinctive impulsion and a social resistance
acting on the individual by means of ethical imperatives justified by philosophical or religious myths. When, with the destruction of the myths, resistance is removed, the impulse
wastes itself on emptiness; and love, which is only the product
of conflicting forces, is not born. The twentieth century is re-
producing in a new form the error of the early nineteenth-
century romantics. Following Rousseau, the romantics imagined that exclusive passion was the "natural" mode of love,
just as virtue and reasonableness were the "natural" forms of
men's social behavior. Get rid of priests and kings, and men
will be for ever good and happy; poor Shelley's faith in this
palpable nonsense remained unshaken to the end. He believed
also in the complementary paralogism that you had only to
get rid of social restraints and erroneous mythology to make
the Grand Passion universally chronic. Like the Mussets and
Sands, he failed to see that the Grand Passion was produced
by the restraints that opposed themselves to the sexual impulse, just as the deep lake is produced by the dam that bars
the passage of the stream, and the flight of the aeroplane by
the air which resists the impulsion given to it by the motor.
There would be no air-resistance in a vacuum; but precisely
for that reason the machine would not leave the ground, or
even move at all. Where there are no psychological or external
restrains, the Grand Passion does not come into existence
and must be artificially cultivated, as George Sands and
Musset cultivated it—with what painful and grotesque results
the episode of Venice made only too ludicrously manifest.

"J'aime et je veux pâlir; j'aime et je veux souffrir," says
Musset, with his usual hysterically masochistic emphasis. Our
young contemporaries do not wish to suffer or grow pale; on
the contrary, they have a most determined desire to grow
pink and enjoy themselves. But too much enjoyment "blunts
the fine point of seldom pleasure." Unrestrained indulgence
kills not merely passion, but, in the end, even amusement.
Too much liberty is as life-destroying as too much restraint.

The present fashion in love-making is likely to be short, because love that is psychologically too easy is not interesting.
Such, at any rate, was evidently the opinion of the French,
who, bored by the sexual license produced by the Napoleonic
upheavals, reverted (so far, at any rate, as the upper and
middle classes were concerned) to an almost anglican strict-
ness under Louis-Philippe. We may anticipate an analogous
reaction in the not distant future. What new or what revived
mythology will serve to create those internal restraints without
which sexual impulse cannot be transformed into love? Christian morality and ascetic ideals will doubtless continue to play
their part, but there will no less certainly be other moralities
and ideals. For example, Mr. D. H. Lawrence's new mythology of nature (new in its expression, but reassuringly old in
substance) is a doctrine that seems to me fruitful in possibilities. The "natural love" which he sets up as a norm is a
passion less self-conscious and high-falutin, less obviously and
precariously artificial, than that "natural love" of the romantics, in which Platonic and Christian notions were essential ingredients. The restraints which Mr. Lawrence would
impose on sexual impulse, so as to transform it into love, are
not the restraints of religious spirituality. They are restraints
of a more fundamental, less artificial nature—emotional, not
intellectual. The impulse is to be restrained from promiscuous
manifestations because, if it were not, promiscuity would
"harden all within and petrify the feeling." The restraint is of
the same personal nature as the impulse. The conflict is between a part of the personality and the personality as an
organized whole. It does not pretend, as the romantic and
Christian conflict pretends, to be a battle between a diabolical
Lower Self and certain transcendental Absolutes, of which the
only thing that philosophy can tell us is that they are absolutely unknowable, and therefore, for our purposes, non-
existent. It only claims to be, what in fact it is, a psychological
conflict taking place in the more or less known and finite
world of human interests. This doctrine has several great advantages over previous systems of inward restraint. It does
not postulate the existence of any transcendental, non-human
entity. This is a merit which will be increasingly appreciated
as the significance of Kant's and Nietzsche's destructive criticism is more widely realized. People will cease to be interested
in unknowable absolutes; but they will never lose interest in
their own personalities. True, that "personality as a whole,"
in whose interests the sexual impulse is to be restrained and
turned into love, is, strictly speaking, a mythological figure.
Consisting, as we do, of a vast colony of souls—souls of
individual cells, of organs, of groups of organs, hunger-souls,

sex-souls, power-souls, herd-souls, of whose multifarious activities our consciousness (the Soul with a large S) is only very imperfectly and indirectly aware—we are not in a position to know the real nature of our personality as a whole. The only thing we can do is to hazard a hypothesis, to create a mythological figure, call it Human Personality, and hope that circumstances will not, by destroying us, prove our imaginative guesswork too hopelessly wrong. But myth for myth, Human Personality is preferable to God. We do at least know something of Human Personality, whereas of God we know nothing and, knowing nothing, are at liberty to invent as freely as we like. If men had always tried to deal with the problem of love in terms of known human rather than of grotesquely imagined divine interests, there would have been less "making of eunuchs for the kingdom of heaven's sake," less persecution of "sinners," less burning and imprisoning of the heretics of "unnatural" love, less Grundyism, less Comstockery, and, at the same time, less dirty Don-Juanism, less of that curiously malignant and vengeful love-making so characteristic of the debauchee under a Christian dispensation. Reacting against the absurdities of the old mythology, the young have run into absurdities no less inordinate at the other end of the scale. A sordid and ignoble realism offers no resistance to the sexual impulse, which now spends itself purposelessly, without producing love, or even, in the long-run, amusement, without enhancing vitality or quickening and deepening the rhythms of living. Only a new mythology of nature, such as, in modern times, Blake, Robert Burns, and Lawrence have defined it, an untranscendental and (relatively speaking) realistic mythology of Energy, Life, and Human Personality, will provide, it seems to me, the inward resistances necessary to turn sexual impulse into love, and provide them in a form which the critical intelligence of Post-Nietzschean youth can respect. By means of such a conception a new fashion in love may be created, a mode more beautiful and convenient, more healthful and elegant, than any seen among men since the days of remote and pagan antiquity.

(From *Do What You Will*)

Sermons in Cats

I met, not long ago, a young man who aspired to become a novelist. Knowing that I was in the profession, he asked me to tell him how he should set to work to realize his ambition. I did my best to explain. "The first thing," I said, "is to buy quite a lot of paper, a bottle of ink, and a pen. After that you merely have to write." But this was not enough for my young friend. He seemed to have a notion that there was some sort of esoteric cookery book, full of literary recipes, which you had only to follow attentively to become a Dickens, a Henry James, a Flaubert—"according to taste," as the authors of recipes say, when they come to the question of seasoning and sweetening. Wouldn't I let him have a glimpse of this cookery book? I said that I was sorry, but that (unhappily—for what an endless amount of time and trouble it would save!) I had never even seen such a work. He seemed sadly disappointed; so, to console the poor lad, I advised him to apply to the professors of dramaturgy and short-story writing at some reputable university; if any one possessed a trustworthy cookery book of literature, it should surely be they. But even this was not enough to satisfy the young man. Disappointed in his hope that I would give him the fictional equivalent of "One Hundred Ways of Cooking Eggs" or the "Carnet de la Ménagère," he began to cross-examine me about my methods of "collecting material." Did I keep a notebook or a daily journal? Did I jot down thoughts and phrases in a card-index? Did I systematically frequent the drawing-rooms of the rich and fashionable? Or did I, on the contrary, inhabit the Sussex downs? or spend my evenings looking for "copy" in East End gin-palaces? Did I think it was wise to frequent the company of intellectuals? Was it a good thing for a writer of novels to try to be well educated, or should he confine his reading exclusively to other novels? And so on. I did my best to reply to these questions—as non-committally, of course, as I could. And as the young man still looked rather disappointed, I volunteered a final piece of advice, gratuitously. "My young friend," I said, "if you want to be a psychological novelist and write about human beings, the best thing you can do is to keep a pair of cats." And with that I left him.

I hope, for his own sake, that he took my advice. For it was good advice—the fruit of much experience and many meditations. But I am afraid that, being a rather foolish young

man, he merely laughed at what he must have supposed was
only a silly joke: laughed, as I myself foolishly laughed when,
years ago, that charming and talented and extraordinary
man, Ronald Firbank, once told me that he wanted to write
a novel about life in Mayfair and so was just off to the West
Indies to look for copy among the Negroes. I laughed at the
time; but I see now that he was quite right. Primitive people,
like children and animals, are simply civilized people with the
lid off, so to speak—the heavy elaborate lid of manners,
conventions, traditions of thought and feeling beneath which
each one of us passes his or her existence. This lid can be
very conveniently studied in Mayfair, shall we say, or Passy,
or Park Avenue. But what goes on underneath the lid in these
polished and elegant districts? Direct observation (unless we
happen to be endowed with a very penetrating intuition) tells
us but little; and, if we cannot infer what is going on under
other lids from what we see, introspectively, by peeping under
our own, then the best thing we can do is to take the next
boat for the West Indies, or else, less expensively, pass a few
mornings in the nursery, or alternatively, as I suggested to
my literary young friend, buy a pair of cats.

Yes, a pair of cats. Siamese by preference; for they are
certainly the most "human" of all the race of cats. Also the
strangest, and, if not the most beautiful, certainly the most
striking and fantastic. For what disquieting pale blue eyes
stare out from the black velvet mask of their faces! Snow-
white at birth, their bodies gradually darken to a rich mulatto
color. Their forepaws are gloved almost to the shoulder like
the long black kid arms of Yvette Guilbert; over their hind
legs are tightly drawn the black silk stockings with which
Félicien Rops so perversely and indecently clothed his pearly
nudes. Their tails, when they have tails—and I would always
recommend the budding novelist to buy the tailed variety; for
the tail, in cats, is the principal organ of emotional expression
and a Manx cat is the equivalent of a dumb man—their tails
are tapering black serpents endowed, even when the body lies
in Sphinx-like repose, with a spasmodic and uneasy life of
their own. And what strange voices they have! Sometimes like
the complaining of small children; sometimes like the noise
of lambs; sometimes like the agonized and furious howling of
lost souls. Compared with these fantastic creatures, other cats,
however beautiful and engaging, are apt to seem a little insipid.

Well, having bought his cats, nothing remains for the would-
be novelist but to watch them living from day to day; to
mark, learn, and inwardly digest the lessons about human
nature which they teach; and finally—for, alas, this arduous

and unpleasant necessity always arises—finally write his book
about Mayfair, Passy, or Park Avenue, whichever the case
may be.

Let us consider some of these instructive sermons in cats,
from which the student of human psychology can learn so
much. We will begin—as every good novel should begin, instead of absurdly ending—with marriage. The marriage of
Siamese cats, at any rate as I have observed it, is an extraordinarily dramatic event. To begin with, the introduction of
the bridegroom to his bride (I am assuming that, as usually
happens in the world of cats, they have not met before their
wedding day) is the signal for a battle of unparalleled ferocity.
The young wife's first reaction to the advances of her would-
be husband is to fly at his throat. One is thankful, as one
watches the fur flying and listens to the piercing yells of rage
and hatred, that a kindly providence has not allowed these
devils to grow any larger. Waged between creatures as big
as men, such battles would bring death and destruction to
everything within a radius of hundreds of yards. As things
are, one is able, at the risk of a few scratches, to grab the
combatants by the scruffs of their necks and drag them, still
writhing and spitting, apart. What would happen if the newly-
wedded pair were allowed to go on fighting to the bitter end
I do not know, and have never had the scientific curiosity or
the strength of mind to try to find out. I suspect that, contrary to what happened in Hamlet's family, the wedding
baked meats would soon be serving for a funeral. I have
always prevented this tragical consummation by simply shutting up the bride in a room by herself and leaving the bridegroom for a few hours to languish outside the door. He does
not languish dumbly; but for a long time there is no answer,
save an occasional hiss or growl, to his melancholy cries of
love. When, finally, the bride begins replying in tones as soft
and yearning as his own, the door may be opened. The bridegroom darts in and is received, not with tooth and claw as on
the former occasion, but with every demonstration of affection.

At first sight there would seem, in this specimen of feline
behavior, no special "message" for humanity. But appearances
are deceptive; the lids under which civilized people live are
so thick and so profusely sculptured with mythological orna-
ments, that it is difficult to recognize the fact, so much insisted upon by D. H. Lawrence in his novels and stories, that
there is almost always a mingling of hate with the passion
of love and that young girls very often feel (in spite of their
sentiments and even their desires) a real abhorrence of the
fact of physical love. Unlidded, the cats make manifest this

ordinarily obscure mystery of human nature. After witnessing
a cats' wedding no young novelist can rest content with the
falsehood and banalities which pass, in current fiction, for
descriptions of love.

Time passes and, their honeymoon over, the cats begin to
tell us things about humanity which even the lid of civilization
cannot conceal in the world of men. They tell us—what, alas,
we already know—that husbands soon tire of their wives,
particularly when they are expecting or nursing families; that
the essence of maleness is the love of adventure and infidelity;
that guilty consciences and good resolutions are the psychological symptoms of that disease which spasmodically affects
practically every male between the ages of eighteen and sixty
—the disease called "the morning after"; and that with the
disappearance of the disease the psychological symptoms also
disappear, so that when temptation comes again, conscience
is dumb and good resolutions count for nothing. All these
unhappily too familiar truths are illustrated by the cats with
a most comical absence of disguise. No man has ever dared
to manifest his boredom so insolently as does a Siamese tom-
cat, when he yawns in the face of his amorously importunate
wife. No man has ever dared to proclaim his illicit amours so
frankly as this same tom caterwauling on the tiles. And how
slinkingly—no man was ever so abject—he returns next day
to the conjugal basket by the fire! You can measure the guilti-
ness of his conscience by the angle of his back-pressed ears,
the droop of his tail. And when, having sniffed him and so
discovered his infidelity, his wife, as she always does on these
occasions, begins to scratch his face (already scarred, like a
German student's, with the traces of a hundred duels), he
makes no attempt to resist; for, self-convicted of sin, he knows
that he deserves all he is getting.

It is impossible for me in the space at my disposal to
enumerate all the human truths which a pair of cats can
reveal or confirm. I will cite only one more of the innumerable
sermons in cats which my memory holds—an acted sermon
which, by its ludicrous pantomime, vividly brought home to
me the most saddening peculiarity of our human nature, its
irreducible solitariness. The circumstances were these. My she-
cat, by now a wife of long standing and several times a
mother, was passing through one of her occasional phases
of amorousness. Her husband, now in the prime of life and
parading that sleepy arrogance which is the characteristic of
the mature and conquering male (he was now the feline
equivalent of some herculean young Alcibiades of the
Guards), refused to have anything to do with her. It was in
vain that she uttered her love-sick mewing, in vain that she

walked up and down in front of him rubbing herself voluptu-
ously against doors and chairlegs as she passed, it was in vain
that she came and licked his face. He shut his eyes, he
yawned, he averted his head, or, if she became too importunate, got up and slowly, with an insulting air of dignity
and detachment, stalked away. When the opportunity presented itself, he escaped and spent the next twenty-four hours
upon the tiles. Left to herself, the wife went wandering dis-
consolately about the house, as though in search of a vanished
happiness, faintly and plaintively mewing to herself in a voice
and with a manner that reminded one irresistibly of Mélisande
in Debussy's opera. *"Je ne suis pas heureuse ici,"* she seemed
to be saying. And, poor little beast, she wasn't. But, like her
big sisters and brothers of the human world, she had to bear
her unhappiness in solitude, uncomprehended, unconsoled.
For in spite of language, in spite of intelligence and intuition
and sympathy, one can never really communicate anything
to anybody. The essential substance of every thought and feeling remains incommunicable, locked up in the impenetrable
strong-room of the individual soul and body. Our life is a
sentence of perpetual solitary confinement. This mournful
truth was overwhelmingly borne in on me as I watched the
abandoned and love-sick cat as she walked unhappily round
my room. *"Je ne suis pas heureuse ici,"* she kept mewing, *"je
ne suis pas heureuse ici."* And her expressive black tail would
lash the air in a tragical gesture of despair. But each time it
twitched, hop-la! from under the armchair, from behind the
book-case, wherever he happened to be hiding at the moment,
out jumped her only son (the only one, that is, we had not
given away), jumped like a ludicrous toy tiger, all claws out,
on to the moving tail. Sometimes he would miss, sometimes
he caught it, and getting the tip between his teeth would pretend to worry it, absurdly ferocious. His mother would have
to jerk it violently to get it out of his mouth. Then, he would
go back under his armchair again and, crouching down, his
hindquarters trembling, would prepare once more to spring.
The tail, the tragical, despairingly gesticulating tail, was for
him the most irresistible of playthings. The patience of the
mother was angelical. There was never a rebuke or a punitive
reprisal; when the child became too intolerable, she just moved
away; that was all. And meanwhile, all the time, she went on
mewing, plaintively, despairingly. *"Je ne suis pas heureuse ici,
je ne suis pas heureuse ici."* It was heartbreaking. The more
so as the antics of the kitten were so extraordinarily ludicrous.
It was as though a slap-stick comedian had broken in on the
lamentations of Mélisande—not mischievously, not wittingly,
for there was not the smallest intention to hurt in the little

cat's performance, but simply from lack of comprehension.
Each was alone serving his life-sentence of solitary confinement. There was no communication from cell to cell. Absolutely no communication. These sermons in cats can be
exceedingly depressing.

(From *Music at Night*)

Appendix

Every civilization is, among other things, an arrangement for
domesticating the passions and setting them to do useful work.
The domestication of sex presents a problem whose solution
must be attempted on two distinct levels of human experience,
the psycho-physiological and the social. On the social level
the relations of the sexes have everywhere been regulated by
law, by uncodified custom, by taboo and religious ritual. Hundreds of volumes have been filled with accounts of these
regulations, and it is unnecessary to do more than mention
them in passing. Our present concern is with the problem of
domesticating sex at the source, of civilizing its manifestations
in the individual lover. This is a subject to which, in our
Western tradition, we have paid much too little attention. Indeed, it is only in very recent years that, thanks to the declining influence of the Judaeo-Christian ethic, we have been able
to discuss it realistically. In the past the problem used to be
dealt with in one or other of three equally unsatisfactory ways.
Either it was not mentioned at all, with the result that adoles-
cents coming to maturity were left to work out their sexual
salvation, unassisted, within the framework of the prevailing,
and generally barbarous socio-legal system. Or else it was
mentioned—but mentioned on the one hand with obscene
delight or obscene disapproval (the tone of the pornographers
and the Puritan moralists), or with a vague and all too
"spiritual" sentimentality (the tone of the troubadours, Pe-
trarchians and romantic lyrists). Today we are condemned
neither to silence, nor obscenity, nor sentimentality; we are at
liberty, at last, to look at the facts and to ask ourselves what,
if anything, can be done about them. One of the best ways
of discovering what can be done is to look at what has been
done. What experiments have been made in this field, and
how successful have they been?

I shall begin not at the faraway beginning of everything,
among the Trobrianders, for example, or the Tahitians, but

rather at the beginning of our own current phase of civilization—in the middle years, that is to say, of the nineteenth
century.

Victoria had been on the throne for seven years when, in
1844, John Humphrey Noyes published his book, *Bible Communism.* (It is worth remarking that, for the American public
of a hundred years ago, Communism was essentially biblical.
It was preached and practiced by men and women who
wanted to emulate the earliest Christians. The appeal was not
to Marx's *Manifesto*—still unpublished when Noyes wrote
his book—but to the Acts of the Apostles.) In the fourth
chapter of *Bible Communism* and again, at greater length, in
his *Male Continence,* written more than twenty years later,
Noyes set forth his theories of sex and described the methods
employed by himself and his followers for transforming a
wild, God-eclipsing passion into a civilized act of worship, a
prime cause of crime and misery into a source of individual
happiness, social solidarity and good behavior.

"It is held in the world," Noyes writes in *Bible Communism,*
"that the sexual organs have two distinct functions—viz: the
urinary and the propagative. We affirm that they have three—
the urinary, the propagative and the amative., i.e. they are
conductors first of the urine, secondly of the semen and
thirdly of the social magnetism. . . ." After Mrs. Noyes had
come dangerously near to death as the result of repeated
miscarriages, Noyes and his wife decided that, henceforth,
their sexual relationships should be exclusively amative, not
propagative. But how were the specifically human aspects of
sex to be detached from the merely biological? Confronted
by this question, Robert Dale Owen had advocated *coitus
interruptus;* but Noyes had read his Bible and had no wish
to emulate Onan. Nor did he approve of contraceptives—
"those tricks," as he called them, "of the French voluptuaries."
Instead he advocated Male Continence and what Dr. Stock-
ham was later to call *Karezza.* With the most exemplary
scientific detachment he began by "analyzing the act of sexual
intercourse. It has a beginning, a middle and an end. Its beginning and most elementary form is the simple presence of
the male organ in the female." Presence is followed by motion, motion by crisis. But now "suppose the man chooses to
enjoy not only the simple presence, but also the reciprocal
motion, and yet to stop short of the crisis. . . . If you say
that this is impossible, I answer that I *know* it is possible—
nay, that it is easy." He knew because he himself had done
it. "Beginning in 1844, I experimented on the idea" (the idea
that the amative function of the sexual organs could be separated from the propagative) "and found that the self-control

it required is not difficult; also that my enjoyment was increased; also that my wife's experience was very satisfactory, which it had never been before; also that we had escaped the horrors and the fear of involuntary propagation." Noyes was a born prophet, a missionary in the bone. Having made a great discovery, he felt impelled to bring the good news to others—and to bring it, what was more, in the same package with what he believed to be true Christianity. He preached, he made disciples, he brought them together in a community, first in Vermont and later at Oneida, in upstate New York. "Religion," he declared, "is the first interest, and sexual morality the second in the great enterprise of establishing the Kingdom of God on earth." At Oneida the religion was Perfectionist Christianity and the sexual morality was based upon the psycho-physiological practices of Male Continence and the social law of Complex Marriage. Like all earlier founders of religious communities, Noyes disapproved of exclusive attachments between the members of his group. All were to love all, unpossessively, with a kind of impersonal charity which, at Oneida, included sexual relationships. Hence the establishment, within the community, of Complex Marriage. Noyes did not condemn monogamy; he merely believed that group love was better than exclusive love. "I would not," he wrote, "set up a distinction of right and wrong between general and special love, except that special love, when false, makes more mischief. I insist that all love, whether general or special, must have its authority in the sanction and the inspiration of the ascending fellowship. All love that is at work in a private corner, away from the general circulation, where there are no series of links connecting it with God, is false love; it rends and devours, instead of making unity, peace and harmony." At Oneida there was to be no love in a private corner, no idolatrous and God-eclipsing attachment of one for one, outside the general circulation. Each was married to all; and when any given pair decided (with the advice and permission of the Elders) to consummate their latent nuptials, Male Continence guaranteed that their union should be fruitful only of "social magnetism." Love was for love's sake and for God's, not for offspring.

The Oneida Community endured for thirty years and its members, from all accounts, were excellent citizens, singularly happy and measurably less neurotic than most of their Victorian contemporaries. The women of Oneida had been spared what one of Noyes's lady correspondents described as "the miseries of Married Life as it is in the World." The men found their self-denial rewarded by an experience, at once physical and spiritual, that was deeper and richer than that of unrestrained sexuality. Here is the comment of a young man who had lived in the community and learned the new Art of Love. "This Yankee nation," he wrote to Noyes, "claims to be a nation of inventors, but this discovery of Male Continence puts you, in my mind, at the head of all inventors." And here are Noyes's own reflections on the psychological, social and religious significance of his discovery. "The practice which we propose will advance civilization and refinement at railroad speed. The self-control, retention of life and advance out of sensualism, which must result from making freedom of love a bounty on the chastening of sensual indulgence, will at once raise the race to new vigor and beauty, moral and physical. And the refining effects of sexual love (which are recognized more or less in the world) will be increased a hundredfold when sexual intercourse becomes a method of ordinary conversation and each becomes married to all." Furthermore, "in a society trained in these principles, amative intercourse will have its place among the "fine arts." Indeed, it will take rank above music, painting, sculpture, etc.; for it combines the charms and benefits of them all. There is as much room for cultivation of taste and skill in this department as in any." And this is not all. Sexual love is a cognitive act. We speak—or at least we used to speak—of carnal knowledge. This knowledge is of a kind that can be deepened indefinitely. "To a true heart, one that appreciates God, the same woman is an endless mystery. And this necessarily flows from the first admission that God is unfathomable in depths of knowledge and wisdom." Male Continence transforms the sexual act into a prolonged exchange of "social magnetism"; and this prolonged exchange makes possible an ever deepening knowledge of the mystery of human nature—that mystery which merges ultimately, and becomes one with the mystery of Life itself.

Noyes's conception of the sexual act (when properly performed) as at once a religious sacrament, a mode of mystical knowledge and a civilizing social discipline has its counterpart in Tantra. In the twenty-seventh chapter of Sir John Woodroffe's *Shakti and Shakta* the interested reader will find a brief account of the Tantrik's sexual ritual, together with a discussion of the philosophy which underlies the practice. "Nothing in natural function is low or impure to the mind which recognizes it as Shakti and the working of Shakti. It is the ignorant and, in a true sense, vulgar mind which regards any natural function as low or coarse. The action in this case is seen in the light of the inner vulgarity of mind. . . . Once the reality of the world as grounded in the Absolute is established, the body seems to be less an obstacle to freedom;

for it is a form of that self-same Absolute." In Tantra the sexual sacrament borrows the method of Yoga, "not to frustrate, but to regulate enjoyment. Conversely enjoyment produces Yoga by the union of body and spirit. . . . Here are made one Yoga which liberates and Bhoga which enchains." In Hindu philosophy (which is not philosophy in the modern Western sense of the word, but rather the description and tentative explanation of a praxis aimed at the transformation of human consciousness), the relations between body, psyche, spirit and Divine Ground are described in terms of a kind of occult physiology, whose language comes nearer to expressing the unbroken continuity of experience, from the "lowest" to the "highest," than any hitherto devised in the West. "Coition," in terms of this occult physiology, "is the union of the Shakti Kundalini, the 'Inner Woman' in the lowest centre of the Sadhaka's body with the Supreme Shiva in the highest centre in the upper Brain. This, the Yogini Tantra says, is the best of all unions for those who are Yati, that is, who have controlled their passions."*

In the West the theory and practice of Tantra were never orthodox, except perhaps during the first centuries of Christianity. At this time it was common for ecclesiastics and pious laymen to have "spiritual wives," who were called Agapetae, Syneisaktoi or Virgines Subintroductae. Of the precise relationships between these spiritual wives and husbands we know very little; but it seems that, in some cases at least, a kind of Karezza, or bodily union without orgasm, was practiced as a religious exercise, leading to valuable spiritual experiences.

For the most part, Noyes's predecessors and the Christian equivalents of Tantra must be sought among the heretics— the Gnostics in the first centuries of our era, the Cathars in the early Middle Ages and the Adamites or Brethren and Sisters of the Free Spirit from the later thirteenth century onwards. In his monograph on *The Millennium of Hieronymus Bosch* Wilhelm Franger has brought together much interesting material on the Adamites. They practiced, we learn, a *modum specialem coeundi,* a special form of intercourse, which was identical with Noyes's Male Continence or the *coitus reservatus* permitted by Roman Catholic casuists. This kind of sexual intercourse, they declared, was known to Adam before the Fall and was one of the constituents of Paradise. It was a sacramental act of charity and, at the same time, of

* Male Continence, sex as a sacrament and coitus as a long-drawn cognitive exchange of "social magnetism" have been discussed in contemporary medical terms by Dr. Rudolf von Urban whose book *Sexual Perfection and Marital Happiness* is one of the most significant modern contributions to the solution of an age-old problem.

mystical cognition, and, as such, was called by the Brethren *acclivitas*—the upward path. According to Aegidius Cantor, the leader of the Flemish Adamites in the first years of the fifteenth century, "the natural sexual act can take place in such a manner that it is equal in value to a prayer in the sight of God." A Spanish follower of the Adamite heresy declared, at his trial that "after I had first had intercourse with her [the prophetess, Francisca Hernandez] for some twenty days, I could say that I had learned more wisdom in Valladolid than if I had studied for twenty years in Paris. For not Paris, but only Paradise could teach such wisdom." Like Noyes and his followers, the Adamites practiced a form of sexual communism, and practiced it not, as their enemies declared, out of a low taste for orgiastic promiscuity, but because Complex Marriage was a method by which every member of the group could love all the rest with an impartial and almost impersonal charity; could see and nuptially know in each beloved partner the embodiment of the original, un-fallen Adam—a godlike son or daughter of God.

Among literary testimonials to Male Continence, perhaps the most elegant is a little poem by Petronius. Long and inevitably disgusting experience had taught this arbiter of the elegancies that there must be something better than debauchery. He found it in physical tenderness and the peace of soul which such tenderness begets.

> Foeda est in coitu et brevis voluptas,
> et taedet Veneris statim peractae.
> Non ergo ut pecudes libidinosae
> caeci protinus irruamus illuc;
> nam languescit amor peritque flamma;
> sed sic sic sine fine feriati
> et tecum jaceamus osculantes.
> Hic nullus labor est ruborque nullus;
> hoc juvit, juvat et diu juvabit;
> hoc non deficit, incipitque semper.

Which was Englished by Ben Jonson, as follows:

> Doing, a filthy pleasure is, and short;
> And done, we straight repent us of the sport;
> Let us not then rush blindly on unto it,
> Like lustful beasts that only know to do it;
> For lust will languish, and that heat decay.
> But thus, thus, keeping endless holiday,
> Let us together closely lie and kiss;
> There is no labor, nor no shame in this;
> This hath pleased, doth please and long will please; never
> Can this decay, but is beginning ever.

And here, from a novelist and poet of a very different kind is a passage that hints at what is revealed by physical tenderness, when it is prolonged by Male Continence into a quasi-mystical experience. "She had sunk to a final rest," Lawrence writes, near the end of *The Plumed Serpent,** "within a great opened-out cosmos. The universe had opened out to her, new and vast, and she had sunk to the deep bed of pure rest. . . . She realized, almost with wonder, the death in her of the Aphrodite of the foam: the seething, frictional, ecstatic Aphrodite. By a swift dark instinct, Cipriano drew away from this in her. When, in their love, it came back on her, the seething electric female ecstasy, which knows such spasms of delirium, he recoiled from her. It was what she used to call her 'satisfaction.' She had loved Joachim for this, that again, and again, and again he could give her this orgiastic 'satisfaction,' in spasms that made her cry aloud.

"But Cipriano would not. By a dark and powerful instinct he drew away from her as soon as this desire rose again in her, for the white ecstasy of frictional satisfaction, the throes of Aphrodite of the foam. She could see that, to him, it was repulsive. He just removed himself, dark and unchangeable, away from her.

"And she, as she lay, would realize the worthlessness of this foam-effervescence, its strange externality to her. It seemed to come from without, not from within. And succeeding the first moment of disappointment, when this sort of 'satisfaction' was denied her, came the knowledge that she did not really want it, that it was really nauseous to her.

"And he in his dark, hot silence would bring her back to the new, soft, heavy, hot flow, when she was like a fountain gushing noiseless and with urgent softness from the deeps. There she was open to him soft and hot, yet gushing with a noiseless soft power. And there was no such thing as conscious 'satisfaction.' What happened was dark and untellable. So different from the beak-like friction of Aphrodite of the foam, the friction which flares out in circles of phosphorescent ecstasy, to the last wild spasm which utters the involuntary cry, like a death-cry, the final love-cry."

Male Continence is not merely a device for domesticating sexuality and heightening its psychological significance; it is also, as the history of the Oneida Community abundantly proves, a remarkably effective method of birth control. Indeed, under the name of *coitus reservatus,* it is one of the two methods of birth control approved by the authorities of the Roman Church—the other and more widely publicized method being the restriction of intercourse to the so-called

* By D. H. Lawrence. New York, Knopf, 1926.

safe periods. Unfortunately large-scale field experiments in India have shown that, in the kind of society which has the most urgent need of birth control, the safe period method is almost useless. And whereas Noyes, the practical Yankee, devoted much time and thought to the problem of training his followers in Male Continence, the Roman Church has done little or nothing to instruct its youth in the art of *coitus reservatus*. (How odd it is that while primitive peoples, like the Trobrianders, are careful to teach their children the best ways of domesticating sex, we, the Civilized, stupidly leave ours at the mercy of their wild and dangerous passions!)

Meanwhile, over most of the earth, population is rising faster than available resources. There are more people with less to eat. But when the standard of living goes down, social unrest goes up, and the revolutionary agitator, who has no scruples about making promises which he knows very well he cannot keep, finds golden opportunities. Confronted by the appalling dangers inherent in population increase at present rates, most governments have permitted and one or two have actually encouraged their subjects to make use of contraceptives. But they have done so in the teeth of protests from the Roman Church. By outlawing contraceptives and by advocating instead two methods of birth control, one of which doesn't work, while the other, effective method is never systematically taught, the prelates of that Church seem to be doing their best to ensure, first, a massive increase in the sum of human misery and, second, the triumph, within a generation or two, of World Communism.

(From *Tomorrow and Tomorrow and Tomorrow*)

LITERATURE

Subject-Matter of Poetry

It should theoretically be possible to make poetry out of anything whatsoever of which the spirit of man can take cognizance. We find, however, as a matter of historical fact, that most of the world's best poetry has been content with a curiously narrow range of subject-matter. The poets have claimed as their domain only a small province of our universe. One of them now and then, more daring or better equipped than the rest, sets out to extend the boundaries of the kingdom. But for the most part the poets do not concern themselves with fresh conquests; they prefer to consolidate their power at home, enjoying quietly their hereditary possessions. All the world is potentially theirs, but they do not take it. What is the reason for this, and why is it that poetical practice does not conform to critical theory? The problem has a peculiar relevance and importance in these days, when young poetry claims absolute liberty to speak how it likes of whatsoever it pleases.

Wordsworth, whose literary criticism, dry and forbidding though its aspects may be, is always illumined by a penetrating intelligence, Wordsworth touched upon this problem in his preface to *Lyrical Ballads*—touched on it and, as usual, had something of value to say about it. He is speaking here of the most important and the most interesting of the subjects which may, theoretically, be made into poetry, but which have, as a matter of fact, rarely or never undergone the transmutation: he is speaking of the relations between poetry and that vast world of abstractions and ideas—science and philosophy

—into which so few poets have ever penetrated. "The remotest discoveries of the chemist, the botanist, or mineralogist, will be as proper objects of the poet's art as any upon which he is now employed, if the time should ever come when these things shall be familiar to us, and the relations under which they are contemplated shall be manifestly and palpably material to us as enjoying and suffering beings." It is a formidable sentence; but read it well, read the rest of the passage from which it is taken, and you will find it to be full of critical truth.

The gist of Wordsworth's argument is this. All subjects— "the remotest discoveries of the chemist" are but one example of an unlikely poetic theme—can serve the poet with material for his art, on one condition: that he, and to a lesser degree his audience, shall be able to apprehend the subject with a certain emotion. The subject must somehow be involved in the poet's intimate being before he can turn it into poetry. It is not enough, for example, that he should apprehend it merely through his senses. (The poetry of pure sensation, of sounds and bright colors, is common enough nowadays; but amusing as we may find it for the moment, it cannot hold the interest for long.) It is not enough, at the other end of the scale, if he apprehends his subject in a purely intellectual manner. An abstract idea must be felt with a kind of passion, it must mean something emotionally significant, it must be as immediate and important to the poet as a personal relationship before he can make poetry of it. Poetry, in a word, must be written by "enjoying and suffering beings," not by beings exclusively dowered with sensations or, as exclusively, with intellect.

Wordsworth's criticism helps us to understand why so few subjects have ever been made into poetry when everything under the sun, and beyond it, is theoretically suitable for transmutation into a work of art. Death, love, religion, nature; the primary emotions and the ultimate personal mysteries— these form the subject-matter of most of the greatest poetry. And for obvious reasons. These things are "manifestly and palpably material to us as enjoying and suffering beings." But to most men, including the generality of poets, abstractions and ideas are not immediately and passionately moving. They are not enjoying or suffering when they apprehend these things —only thinking.

The men who do feel passionately about abstractions, the men to whom ideas are as persons—moving and disquietingly alive—are very seldom poets. They are men of science and philosophers, preoccupied with the search for truth and not, like the poet, with the expression and creation of beauty. It is very rarely that we find a poet who combines the power and the desire to express himself with that passionate apprehension of ideas and that passionate curiosity about strange remote facts which characterize the man of science and the philosopher. If he possessed the requisite sense of language and the impelling desire to express himself in terms of beauty, Einstein could write the most intoxicating lyrics about relativity and the pleasures of pure mathematics. And if, say, Mr. Yeats understood the Einstein theory—which, in company with most other living poets, he presumably does not, any more than the rest of us—if he apprehended it exultingly as something bold and profound, something vitally important and marvelously true, he too could give us, out of the Celtic twilight, his lyrics of relativity. It is those distressing little "ifs" that stand in the way of this happy consummation. The conditions upon which any but the most immediately and obviously moving subjects can be made into poetry are so rarely fulfilled, the combination of poet and man of science, poet and philosopher, is so uncommon, that the theoretical universality of the art has only very occasionally been realized in practice.

Contemporary poetry in the whole of the western world is insisting, loudly and emphatically through the mouths of its propagandists, on an absolute liberty to speak of what it likes how it likes. Nothing could be better; all that we can now ask is that the poets should put the theory into practice, and that they should make use of the liberty which they claim by enlarging the bounds of poetry.

The propagandists would have us believe that the subject-matter of contemporary poetry is new and startling, that modern poets are doing something which has not been done before. "Most of the poets represented in these pages," writes Mr. Louis Untermeyer in his *Anthology of Modern American Poetry,* "have found a fresh and vigorous material in a world of honest and often harsh reality. They respond to the spirit of their times; not only have their views changed, their vision has been widened to include things unknown to the poets of yesterday. They have learned to distinguish real beauty from mere prettiness, to wring loveliness out of squalor, to find wonder in neglected places, to search for hidden truths even in the dark caves of the unconscious." Translated into practice this means that contemporary poets can now write, in the words of Mr. Sandburg, of the "harr and boom of the blast fires," of "wops and bohunks." It means, in fact, that they are at liberty to do what Homer did—to write freely about the immediately moving facts of everyday life. Where Homer wrote of horses and the tamers of horses, our contemporaries write of trains, automobiles, and the various species of wops and bohunks who control the horsepower. That is all. Much too much stress has been laid on the newness of the new poetry; its newness is simply a return from the jeweled exquisiteness of the eighteen-nineties to the facts and feelings of ordinary life. There is nothing intrinsically novel or surprising in the introduction into poetry of machinery and industrialism, of labor unrest and modern psychology: these things belong to us, they affect us daily as enjoying and suffering beings; they are a part of our lives, just as the kings, the warriors, the horses and chariots, the picturesque mythology were part of Homer's life. The subject-matter of the new poetry remains the same as that of the old. The old boundaries have not been extended. There would be real novelty in the new poetry if it had, for example, taken to itself any of the new ideas and astonishing facts with which the new science has endowed the modern world. There would be real novelty in it if it had worked out a satisfactory artistic method for dealing with abstractions. It has not. Which simply means that that rare phenomenon, the poet in whose mind ideas are a passion and a personal moving force, does not happen to have appeared.

And how rarely in all the long past he has appeared! There was Lucretius, the greatest of all the philosophic and scientific poets. In him the passionate apprehension of ideas, and the desire and ability to give them expression, combined to produce that strange and beautiful epic of thought which is without parallel in the whole history of literature. There was Dante, in whose soul the medieval Christian philosophy was a force that shaped and directed every feeling, thought and action. There was Goethe, who focused into beautiful expression an enormous diffusion of knowledge and ideas. And there the list of the great poets of thought comes to an end. In their task of extending the boundaries of poetry into the remote and abstract world of ideas, they have had a few lesser assistants— Donne, for example, a poet only just less than the greatest; Fulke Greville, that strange, dark-spirited Elizabethan; John Davidson, who made a kind of poetry out of Darwinism; and, most interesting poetical interpreter of nineteenth-century science, Jules Laforgue.

Which of our contemporaries can claim to have extended the bounds of poetry to any material extent? It is not enough to have written about locomotives and telephones, "wops and bohunks," and all the rest of it. That is not extending the range of poetry; it is merely asserting its right to deal with the immediate facts of contemporary life, as Homer and as Chaucer did. The critics who would have us believe that there is something essentially unpoetical about a bohunk (whatever a bohunk may be), and something essentially poetical about Sir Lancelot of the Lake, are, of course, simply negligible; they may be dismissed as contemptuously as we have dismissed the pseudo-classical critics who opposed the freedoms of the Romantic Revival. And the critics who think it very new and splendid to bring bohunks into poetry are equally old-fashioned in their ideas.

It will not be unprofitable to compare the literary situation in this early twentieth century of ours with the literary situation of the early seventeenth century. In both epochs we see a reaction against a rich and somewhat formalized poetical tradition expressing itself in a determination to extend the range of subject-matter, to get back to real life, and to use more natural forms of expression. The difference between the two epochs lies in the fact that the twentieth-century revolution has been the product of a number of minor poets, none of them quite powerful enough to achieve what he theoretically meant to do, while the seventeenth-century revolution was the work of a single poet of genius, John Donne. Donne substituted for the rich formalism of non-dramatic Elizabethan poetry a completely realized new style, the style of the so-called metaphysical poetry of the seventeenth century. He was a poet-philosopher-man-of-action whose passionate curiosity about facts enabled him to make poetry out of the most unlikely aspects of material life, and whose passionate apprehension of ideas enabled him to extend the bounds of poetry beyond the frontiers of common life and its emotions into the void of intellectual abstraction. He put the whole life and the whole mind of his age into poetry.

We today are metaphysicals without our Donne. Theoretically we are free to make poetry of everything in the universe; in practice we are kept within the old limits, for the simple reason that no great man has appeared to show us how we can use our freedom. A certain amount of the life of the twentieth century is to be found in our poetry, but precious little of its mind. We have no poet today like that strange old Dean of St. Paul's three hundred years ago—no poet who can skip from the heights of scholastic philosophy to the heights of carnal passion, from the contemplation of divinity to the contemplation of a flea, from the rapt examination of self to an enumeration of the most remote external facts of science, and make all, by his strangely passionate apprehension, into an intensely lyrical poetry.

The few poets who do try to make of contemporary ideas the substance of their poetry, do it in a manner which brings little conviction or satisfaction to the reader. There is Mr. Noyes, who is writing four volumes of verse about the human side of science—in his case, alas, all too human. Then there is Mr. Conrad Aiken. He perhaps is the most successful exponent in poetry of contemporary ideas. In his case, it is clear, "the remotest discoveries of the chemist" are apprehended with a certain passion; all his emotions are tinged by his ideas. The trouble with Mr. Aiken is that his emotions are apt to degenerate into a kind of intellectual sentimentality, which expresses itself only too easily in his prodigiously fluent, highly colored verse.

One could lengthen the list of more or less interesting poets who have tried in recent times to extend the boundaries of their art. But one would not find among them a single poet of real importance, not one great or outstanding personality. The twentieth century still awaits its Lucretius, awaits its own philosophical Dante, its new Goethe, its Donne, even its up-to-date Laforgue. Will they appear? Or are we to go on producing a poetry in which there is no more than the dimmest reflection of that busy and incessant intellectual life which is the characteristic and distinguishing mark of this age?

(From *On the Margin*)

Tragedy and the Whole Truth

There were six of them, the best and bravest of the hero's companions. Turning back from his post in the bows, Odysseus was in time to see them lifted, struggling, into the air, to hear their screams, the desperate repetition of his own name. The survivors could only look on, helplessly, while Scylla "at the mouth of her cave devoured them, still screaming, still stretching out their hands to me in the frightful struggle." And Odysseus adds that it was the most dreadful and lamentable sight he ever saw in all his "explorings of the passes of the sea." We can believe it; Homer's brief description (the too poetical simile is a later interpolation) convinces us.

Later, the danger passed, Odysseus and his men went ashore for the night, and, on the Sicilian beach, prepared their supper —prepared it, says Homer, "expertly." The Twelfth Book of the *Odyssey* concludes with these words: "When they had satisfied their thirst and hunger, they thought of their dear companions and wept, and in the midst of their tears sleep came gently upon them."

The truth, the whole truth and nothing but the truth— how rarely the older literatures ever told it! Bits of the truth, yes; every good book gives us bits of the truth, would not be a good book if it did not. But the whole truth, no. Of the great writers of the past incredibly few have given us that. Homer —the Homer of the *Odyssey*—is one of those few.

"Truth?" you question. "For example, $2+2=4$? Or Queen Victoria came to the throne in 1837? Or light travels at the rate of 187,000 miles a second?" No, obviously, you won't find much of that sort of thing in literature. The "truth" of which I was speaking just now is in fact no more than an acceptable verisimilitude. When the experiences recorded in a piece of literature correspond fairly closely with our own actual experiences, or with what I may call our potential experiences—experiences, that is to say, which we feel (as the result of a more or less explicit process of inference from known facts) that we might have had—we say, inaccurately no doubt: "This piece of writing is true." But this, of course, is not the whole story. The record of a case in a text-book of psychology is scientifically true, in so far as it is an accurate account of particular events. But it might also strike the reader as being "true" with regard to himself—that is to say, acceptable, probable, having a correspondence with his own actual or potential experiences. But a text-book of psychology is not a work of art—or only secondarily and incidentally a work of art. Mere verisimilitude, mere correspondence of experience recorded by the writer with experience remembered or imaginable by the reader, is not enough to make a work of art seem "true." Good art possesses a kind of super-truth—is more probable, more acceptable, more convincing than fact itself. Naturally; for the artist is endowed with a sensibility and a power of communication, a capacity to "put things across," which events and the majority of people to whom events happen, do not possess. Experience teaches only the teachable, who are by no means as numerous as Mrs. Micawber's papa's favorite proverb would lead us to suppose. Artists are eminently teachable and also eminently teachers. They receive from events much more than most men receive and they can transmit what they have received with a peculiar penetrative force, which drives their communication deep into the reader's mind. One of our most ordinary reactions to a good piece of literary art is expressed in the formula: "This is what I have always felt and thought, but have never been able to put clearly into words, even for myself."

We are now in a position to explain what we mean, when we say that Homer is a writer who tells the Whole Truth. We mean that the experiences he records correspond fairly closely with our own actual or potential experiences—and correspond with our experiences not on a single limited sector,

but all along the line of our physical and spiritual being. And
we also mean that Homer records these experiences with a
penetrative artistic force that makes them seem peculiarly
acceptable and convincing.

So much, then, for truth in literature. Homer's, I repeat,
is the Whole Truth. Consider how almost any other of the
great poets would have concluded the story of Scylla's attack
on the passing ship. Six men, remember, have been taken and
devoured before the eyes of their friends. In any other poem
but the *Odyssey*, what would the survivors have done? They
would, of course, have wept, even as Homer made them
weep. But would they previously have cooked their supper,
and cooked it, what's more, in a masterly fashion? Would
they previously have drunken and eaten to satiety? And after
weeping, or actually while weeping, would they have dropped
quietly off to sleep? No, they most certainly would not have
done any of these things. They would simply have wept,
lamenting their own misfortune and the horrible fate of their
companions, and the Canto would have ended tragically on
their tears.

Homer, however, preferred to tell the Whole Truth. He
knew that even the most cruelly bereaved must eat; that
hunger is stronger than sorrow and that its satisfaction takes
precedence even of tears. He knew that experts continue to
act expertly and to find satisfaction in their accomplishment,
even when friends have just been eaten, even when the accomplishment is only cooking the supper. He knew that, when the
belly is full (and only when the belly is full), men can afford
to grieve, and that sorrow after supper is almost a luxury.
And finally he knew that, even as hunger takes precedence of
grief, so fatigue, supervening, cuts short its career and drowns
it in a sleep all the sweeter for bringing forgetfulness of
bereavement. In a word, Homer refused to treat the theme
tragically. He preferred to tell the Whole Truth.

Another author who preferred to tell the Whole Truth was
Fielding. *Tom Jones* is one of the very Odyssean books written
in Europe between the time of Aeschylus and the present age;
Odyssean, because never tragical; never—even when painful
and disastrous, even when pathetic and beautiful things are
happening. For they do happen; Fielding, like Homer, admits
all the facts, shirks nothing. Indeed, it is precisely because
these authors shirk nothing that their books are not tragical.
For among the things they don't shirk are the irrelevancies
which, in actual life, always temper the situations and characters that writers of tragedy insist on keeping chemically
pure. Consider, for example, the case of Sophy Western, that
most charming, most nearly perfect of young women. Fielding,

it is obvious, adored her (she is said to have been created in the image of his first, much-loved wife). But in spite of his adoration, he refused to turn her into one of those chemically pure and, as it were, focused beings who do not suffer in the world of tragedy. That innkeeper who lifted the weary Sophia from her horse—what need had he to fall? In no tragedy would he (nay, *could* he) have collapsed beneath her weight. For, to begin with, in the tragical context weight is an irrelevance; heroines should be above the law of gravitation. But that is not all; let the reader now remember what were the results of his fall. Tumbling flat on his back, he pulled Sophia down on top of him—his belly was a cushion, so that happily she came to no bodily harm—pulled her down head first. But head first is necessarily legs last; there was a momentary display of the most ravishing charms; the bumpkins at the inn door grinned and guffawed; poor Sophia, when they picked her up, was blushing in an agony of embarrassment and wounded modesty. There is nothing intrinsically improbable about this incident, which is stamped, indeed, with all the marks of literary truth. But however true, it is an incident which could never, never have happened to a heroine of tragedy. It would never have been allowed to happen. But Fielding refused to impose the tragedian's veto; he shirked nothing—neither the intrusion of irrelevant absurdities into the midst of romance or disaster, nor any of life's no less irrelevantly painful interruptions of the course of happiness. He did not want to be a tragedian. And, sure enough, that brief and pearly gleam of Sophia's charming posterior was sufficient to scare the Muse of Tragedy out of *Tom Jones* just as, more than five and twenty centuries before, the sight of stricken men first eating, then remembering to weep, then forgetting their tears in slumber had scared her out of the *Odyssey*.

In his *Principles of Literary Criticism* Mr. I. A. Richards affirms that good tragedy is proof against irony and irrelevance —that it can absorb anything into itself and still remain tragedy. Indeed, he seems to make of this capacity to absorb the untragical and the anti-tragical a touchstone of tragic merit. Thus tried, practically all Greek, all French and most Elizabethan tragedies are found wanting. Only the best of Shakespeare can stand the test. So, at least, says Mr. Richards. Is he right? I have often had my doubts. The tragedies of Shakespeare are veined, it is true, with irony and an often terrifying cynicism; but the cynicism is always heroic idealism turned neatly inside out, the irony is a kind of photographic negative of heroic romance. Turn Troilus's white into black and all his blacks into white and you have Thersites. Reversed, Othello and Desdemona become Iago. White Ophelia's negative is the irony of Hamlet, is the ingenuous bawdry of her own mad songs; just as the cynicism of mad King Lear is the black shadow-replica of Cordelia. Now, the shadow, the photographic negative of a thing is in no sense irrelevant to it. Shakespeare's ironies and cynicisms serve to deepen his tragic world, but not to widen it. If they had widened it, as the Homeric irrelevancies widened out the universe of the *Odyssey* —why, then, the world of Shakespearean tragedy would automatically have ceased to exist. For example, a scene showing the bereaved Macduff eating his supper, growing melancholy, over the whisky, with thoughts of his murdered wife and children, and then, with lashes still wet, dropping off to sleep, would be true enough to life; but it would not be true to tragic art. The introduction of such a scene would change the whole quality of the play; treated in this Odyssean style, *Macbeth* would cease to be a tragedy. Or take the case of Desdemona. Iago's bestially cynical remarks about her character are in no sense, as we have seen, irrelevant to the tragedy. They present us with negative images of her real nature and of the feelings she has for Othello. These negative images are always *hers*, are always recognizably the property of the heroine-victim of a tragedy. Whereas, if, springing ashore at Cyprus, she had tumbled, as the no less exquisite Sophia was to tumble, and revealed the inadequacies of sixteenth-century underclothing, the play would no longer be the *Othello* we know. Iago might breed a family of little cynics and the existing dose of bitterness and savage negation be doubled and trebled; *Othello* would still remain fundamentally *Othello*. But a few Fieldingesque irrelevancies would destroy it—destroy it, that is to say, as a tragedy; for there would be nothing to prevent it from becoming a magnificent drama of some other kind. For the fact is that tragedy and what I have called the Whole Truth are not compatible; where one is, the other is not. There are certain things which even the best, even Shakespearean tragedy, cannot absorb into itself.

To make a tragedy the artist must isolate a single element out of the totality of human experience and use that exclusively as his material. Tragedy is something that is separated from the Whole Truth, distilled from it, so to speak, as an essence is distilled from the living flower. Tragedy is chemically pure. Hence its power to act quickly and intensely on our feelings. All chemically pure art has this power to act upon us quickly and intensely. Thus, chemically pure pornography (on the rare occasions when it happens to be written convincingly, by some one who has the gift of "putting things across") is a quick-acting emotional drug of incomparably greater power than the Whole Truth about sensuality, or even (for many

people) than the tangible and carnal reality itself. It is because
of its chemical purity that tragedy so effectively performs its
function of catharsis. It refines and corrects and gives a style
to our emotional life, and does so swiftly, with power. Brought
into contact with tragedy, the elements of our being fall, for
the moment at any rate, into an ordered and beautiful pattern,
as the iron filings arrange themselves under the influence of
the magnet. Through all its individual variations, this pattern
is always fundamentally of the same kind. From the reading
or the hearing of a tragedy we rise with the feeling that

> *Our friends are exultations, agonies,*
> *And love, and man's unconquerable mind;*

with the heroic conviction that we too would be unconquerable
if subjected to the agonies, that in the midst of the agonies
we too should continue to love, might even learn to exult. It
is because it does these things to us that tragedy is felt to be
so valuable. What are the values of Wholly-Truthful art?
What does it do to us that seems worth doing? Let us try to
discover.

Wholly-Truthful art overflows the limits of tragedy and
shows us, if only by hints and implications, what happened
before the tragic story began, what will happen after it is
over, what is happening simultaneously elsewhere (and "elsewhere" includes all those parts of the minds and bodies of the
protagonists not immediately engaged in the tragic struggle).
Tragedy is an arbitrarily isolated eddy on the surface of a
vast river that flows on majestically, irresistibly, around, beneath, and to either side of it. Wholly-Truthful art contrives
to imply the existence of the entire river as well as of the eddy.
It is quite different from tragedy, even though it may contain,
among other constituents, all the elements from which tragedy
is made. (The "same thing" placed in different contexts, loses
its identity and becomes, for the perceiving mind, a succession
of different things.) In Wholly-Truthful art the agonies may
be just as real, love and the unconquerable mind just as
admirable, just as important, as in tragedy. Thus, Scylla's
victims suffer as painfully as the monster-devoured Hippolytus
in *Phèdre*; the mental anguish of Tom Jones when he thinks
he has lost his Sophia, and lost her by his own fault, is hardly
less than that of Othello after Desdemona's murder. (The fact
that Fielding's power of "putting things across" is by no means
equal to Shakespeare's, is, of course, merely an accident.)
But the agonies and indomitabilities are placed by the Wholly-
Truthful writer in another, wider context, with the result that
they cease to be the same as the intrinsically identical agonies
and indomitabilities of tragedy. Consequently, Wholly-Truth-

ful art produces in us an effect quite different from that produced by tragedy. Our mood, when we have read a Wholly-Truthful book, is never one of heroic exultation; it is one of resignation, of acceptance. (Acceptance can also be heroic.) Being chemically impure, Wholly-Truthful literature cannot move us as quickly and intensely as tragedy or any other kind of chemically pure art. But I believe that its effects are more lasting. The exultations that follow the reading or hearing of a tragedy are in the nature of temporary inebriations. Our being cannot long hold the pattern imposed by tragedy. Remove the magnet and the filings tend to fall back into confusion. But the pattern of acceptance and resignation imposed upon us by Wholly-Truthful literature, though perhaps less unexpectedly beautiful in design, is (for that very reason perhaps) more stable. The catharsis of tragedy is violent and apocalyptic; but the milder catharsis of Wholly-Truthful literature is lasting.

In recent times literature has become more and more acutely conscious of the Whole Truth—of the great oceans of irrelevant things, events and thoughts stretching endlessly away in every direction from whatever island point (a character, a story) the author may choose to contemplate. To impose the kind of arbitrary limitations, which must be imposed by any one who wants to write a tragedy, has become more and more difficult—is now indeed, for those who are at all sensitive to contemporaneity, almost impossible. This does not mean, of course, that the modern writer must confine himself to a merely naturalistic manner. One can imply the existence of the Whole Truth without laboriously cataloguing every object within sight. A book can be written in terms of pure phantasy and yet, by implication, tell the Whole Truth. Of all the important works of contemporary literature not one is a pure tragedy. There is no contemporary writer of significance who does not prefer to state or imply the Whole Truth. However different one from another in style, in ethical, philosophical and artistic intention, in the scales of values accepted, contemporary writers have this in common, that they are interested in the Whole Truth. Proust, D. H. Lawrence, André Gide, Kafka, Hemingway—here are five obviously significant and important contemporary writers. Five authors as remarkably unlike one another as they could well be. They are at one only in this: that none of them has written a pure tragedy, that all are concerned with the Whole Truth.

I have sometimes wondered whether tragedy, as a form of art, may not be doomed. But the fact that we are still profoundly moved by the tragic masterpieces of the past—that we can be moved, against our better judgment, even by the bad tragedies of the contemporary stage and film—makes me think that the day of chemically pure art is not over. Tragedy happens to be passing through a period of eclipse, because all the significant writers of our age are too busy exploring the newly discovered, or re-discovered, world of the Whole Truth to be able to pay any attention to it. But there is no good reason to believe that this state of things will last for ever. Tragedy is too valuable to be allowed to die. There is no reason, after all, why the two kinds of literature—the Chemically Impure and the Chemically Pure, the literature of the Whole Truth and the literature of Partial Truth—should not exist simultaneously, each in its separate sphere. The human spirit has need of both.

(From *Music at Night*)

Vulgarity in Literature

I

Vulgarity in literature must be distinguished from the vulgarity inherent in the profession of letters. Every man is born with his share of Original Sin, to which every writer adds a pinch of Original Vulgarity. Necessarily and quite inevitably. For exhibitionism is always vulgar, even if what you exhibit is the most exquisitely refined of souls.

Some writers are more squeamishly conscious than others of the essential vulgarity of their trade—so much so, that, like Flaubert, they have found it hard to commit that initial offense against good breeding: the putting of pen to paper.

It is just possible, of course, that the greatest writers have never written; that the world is full of Monsieur Testes and mute inglorious Miltons, too delicate to come before the public. I should like to believe it; but I find it hard. Your great writer is possessed by a devil, over which he has very little control. If the devil wants to come out (and, in practice, devils always do want to come out), it will do so, however loud the protests of the aristocratic consciousness, with which it uneasily cohabits. The profession of literature may be "fatally marred by a secret absurdity"; the devil simply doesn't care. *Scribo quia absurdum.*

II

To be pale, to have no appetite, to swoon at the slightest provocation—these, not so long ago, were the signs of maid-

enly good breeding. In other words, when a girl was marked
with the stigmata of anemia and chronic constipation, you
knew she was a lady. Virtues are generally fashioned (more
or less elegantly, according to the skill of the moral *couturier*)
out of necessities. Rich girls had no need to work; the aristocratic tradition discouraged them from voluntarily working;
and the Christian tradition discouraged them from compromis-
ing their maiden modesty by taking anything like violent
exercise. Good carriage-roads and, finally, railways spared
them the healthy fatigues of riding. The virtues of Fresh Air
had not yet been discovered and the Draft was still the
commonest, as it was almost the most dangerous, manifestation of the Diabolic Principle. More perverse than Chinese
foot-squeezers, the topiarists of European fashion had decreed
that the elegant should have all her viscera constricted and
displaced by tight lacing. In a word, the rich girl lived a life
scientifically calculated to make her unhealthy. A virtue was
made of humiliating necessity, and the pale ethereal swooner
of romantic literature remained for years the type and mirror
of refined young womanhood.

Something of the same kind happens from time to time in
the realm of literature. Moments come when too conspicuous
a show of vigor, too frank an interest in common things are
signs of literary vulgarity. To be really lady-like, the Muses,
like their mortal sisters, must be anemic and constipated. On
the more sensitive writers of certain epochs circumstances
impose an artistic wasting away, a literary consumption. This
distressing fatality is at once transformed into a virtue, which
it becomes a duty for all to cultivate.

"Vivre? Nos valets le feront pour nous." For, oh, the vulgarity of it! The vulgarity of this having to walk and talk;
to open and close the eyes; to think and drink and every day,
yes, every day, to eat, eat and excrete. And then this having
to pursue the female of one's species, or the male, whichever
the case may be; this having to cerebrate, to calculate, to
copulate, to propagate.... No, no—too gross, too stupidly
low. Such things, as Villiers de l'Isle-Adam says, are all very
well for footmen. But for a descendant of how many generations of Templars, of Knights of Rhodes and of Malta,
Knights of the Garter and the Holy Ghost and all the variously colored Eagles—obviously, it was out of the question;
it simply wasn't done. *Vivre? Nos valets le feront pour nous.*

At the same point, but on another plane, of the great spiral
of history, Prince Gotama, more than two thousand years
before, had also discovered the vulgarity of living. The sight
of a corpse rotting by the roadside had set him thinking. It
was his first introduction to death. Now, a corpse, poor thing,

is an untouchable and the process of decay is, of all pieces of
bad manners, the vulgarest imaginable. For a corpse is, by
definition, a person absolutely devoid of *savoir vivre*. Even
your sweeper knows better. But in every greatest king, in
every loveliest flowery princess, in every poet most refined,
every best dressed dandy, every holiest and most spiritual
teacher, there lurks, waiting, waiting for the moment to
emerge, an outcaste of the outcastes, a dung carrier, a dog,
lower than the lowest, bottomlessly vulgar.

What with making their way and enjoying what they have
won, heroes have no time to think. But the sons of heroes—
ah, they have all the necessary leisure. The future Buddha
belonged to the generation which has time. He saw the corpse,
he smelt it vulgarly stinking, he thought. The echoes of his
meditations still reverberate, rich with an accumulated wealth
of harmonics, like the memory of the organ's final chord
pulsing back and forth under the vaulting of a cathedral.

No less than that of war or statecraft, the history of economics has its heroic ages. Economically, the nineteenth century was the equivalent of those brave times about which we
read in Beowulf and the Iliad. Its heroes struggled, conquered
or were conquered, and had no time to think. Its bards, the
Romantics, sang rapturously, not of the heroes, but of higher
things (for they were Homers who detested Achilles), sang
with all the vehemence which one of the contemporary heroes
would have put into grinding the faces of the poor. It was
only in the second and third generation that men began to
have leisure and the necessary detachment to find the whole
business—economic heroism and romantic bardism—rather
vulgar. Villiers, like Gotama, was one who had time. That
he was the descendant of all those Templars and Knights of
this and that was, to a great extent, irrelevant. The significant
fact was this: he was, or at any rate chronologically might
have been, the son and grandson of economic heroes and
romantic bards—a man of the decadence. Sons have always
a rebellious wish to be disillusioned by that which charmed
their fathers; and, wish or no wish, it was difficult for a
sensitive man to see and smell the already putrefying corpse
of industrial civilization and not be shocked by it into distress-
ful thought. Villiers was duly shocked; and he expressed his
shockedness in terms of an aristocratic disdain that was almost
Brahminical in its intensity. But his feudal terminology was
hardly more than an accident. Born without any of Villiers'
perhaps legendary advantages of breeding, other sensitives of
the same post-heroic generation were just as profoundly
shocked. The scion of Templars had a more striking vocabulary than the others—that was all. For the most self-conscious

and intelligent artists of the last decades of the nineteenth
century, too frank an acceptance of the obvious actualities
of life, too hearty a manner and (to put it grossly) too many
"guts" were rather vulgar. *Vivre? Nos valets le feront pour
nous.* (Incidentally, the suicide rate took a sharp upward turn
during the 'sixties. In some countries it is nearly five times
what it was seventy years ago.) Zola was the master footman
of the age. That vulgar interest in actual life! And all those
guts of his—was the man preparing to set up as a tripe-
dresser?

A few aging ninetyites survive; a few young neo-ninetyites,
who judge of art and all other human activities in terms of
the Amusing and the Tiresome, play kittenishly around with
their wax flowers and stuffed owls and Early Victorian bead-
work. But, old and young, they are insignificant. Guts and an
acceptance of the actual are no longer vulgar. Why not? What
has happened? Three things: the usual reaction of sons against
fathers, another industrial revolution and a rediscovery of
mystery. We have entered (indeed, we have perhaps already
passed through) a second heroic age of economics. Its
Homers, it is true, are almost without exception skeptical,
ironic, denunciatory. But this skepticism, this irony, this de-
nunciation are as lively and vehement as that which is doubted
and denounced. Babbitt infects even his detractors with some
of his bouncing vitality. The Romantics, in the same way,
possessed an energy proportionate to that of their enemies,
the economic heroes who were creating modern industrialism.
Life begets life, even in opposition to itself.

Vivre? Nos valets le feront pour nous. But the physicists
and psychologists have revealed the universe as a place, in
spite of everything, so fantastically queer, that to hand it over
to be enjoyed by footmen would be a piece of gratuitous
humanitarianism. Servants must not be spoiled. The most
refined spirits need not be ashamed in taking a hearty interest
in the rediscovered mystery of the actual world. True, it is a
sinister as well as a fascinating and mysterious world. And
what a mess, with all our good intentions, we have made and
are busily making of our particular corner of it! The same old
industrial corpse—to some extent disinfected and galvanically
stimulated at the moment into a twitching semblance of
healthy life—still rots by the wayside, as it rotted in Villiers'
time. And as for Gotama's carrion—that of course is always
with us. There are, as ever, excellent reasons for personal
despair; while the reasons for despairing about society are
actually a good deal more cogent than at most times. A
Mallarméan shrinking away into pure poetry, a delicate
Henry-Jamesian avoidance of all the painful issues would

seem to be justified. But the spirit of the time—the industrially heroic time in which we live—is opposed to these re-
tirements, these handings over of life to footmen. It demands
that we should "press with strenuous tongue against our
palate" not only joy's grape, but every Dead Sea fruit. Even
dust and ashes must be relished with gusto. Thus, modern
American fiction, like the modern American fact which it so
accurately renders, is ample and lively. And yet, "Dust and
ashes, dust and ashes" is the fundamental theme and final
moral of practically every modern American novel of any
distinction. High spirits and a heroic vitality are put into the
expression of despair. The hopelessness is almost Rabelaisian.

III

It was vulgar at the beginning of the nineteenth century to
mention the word "handkerchief" on the French tragic stage.
An arbitrary convention had decreed that tragic personages
must inhabit a world, in which noses exist only to distinguish
the noble Romans from the Greeks and Hebrews, never to be
blown. Arbitrary conventions of one sort or another are essential to art. But as the sort of convention constantly varies, so
does the corresponding vulgarity. We are back among the
relativities.

In the case of the handkerchief we have a particular and
rather absurd application of a very widely accepted artistic
convention. This convention is justified by the ancient metaphysical doctrine, which distinguishes in the universe two
principles, mind and matter, and which attributes to mind an
immeasurable superiority. In the name of this principle many
religions have demanded the sacrifice of the body; their
devotees have responded by mortifying the flesh and, in
extreme cases, by committing self-castration and even suicide.
Literature has its Manichaeans as well as religion: men who
on principle would exile the body and its functions from the
world of their art, who condemn as vulgar all too particular
and detailed accounts of physical actuality, as vulgar any
attempt to relate mental or spiritual events to happenings in
the body. The inhabitants of their universe are not human
beings, but the tragical heroes and heroines who never blow
their noses.

Artistically, the abolition of handkerchiefs and all that
handkerchiefs directly or indirectly stand for has certain advantages. The handkerchiefless world of pure mind and spirit
is, for an adult, the nearest approach to that infinitely comfortable Freudian womb, toward which, as toward a lost
paradise, we are always nostalgically yearning. In the handker-

chiefless mental world we are at liberty to work things out
to their logical conclusions, we can guarantee the triumph of
justice, we can control the weather and (in the words of those
yearning popular songs which are the national anthems of
Wombland) make our Dreams come True by living under
Skies of Blue with You. Nature in the mental world is not that
collection of tiresomely opaque and recalcitrant objects, so
bewildering to the man of science, so malignantly hostile to
the man of action; it is the luminously rational substance of a
Hegelian nature-philosophy, a symbolic manifestation of the
principles of dialectic. Artistically, such a Nature is much
more satisfactory (because so much more easy to deal with)
than the queer, rather sinister and finally quite incomprehensible monster, by which, when we venture out of our
ivory towers, we are instantly swallowed. And man, than
whom, as Sophocles long since remarked, nothing is more
monstrous, more marvelous, more terrifyingly strange (it is hard
to find a single word to render his *deinoteron*)—man, too, is
a very unsatisfactory subject for literature. For this creature
of inconsistencies can live on too many planes of existence.
He is the inhabitant of a kind of psychological Woolworth
Building; you never know—he never knows himself—which
floor he'll step out at tomorrow, nor even whether, a minute
from now, he won't take it into his head to jump into the
elevator and shoot up a dozen or down perhaps twenty stories
into some totally different mode of being. The effect of the
Manichaean condemnation of the body is at once to reduce
this impossible skyscraper to less than half its original height.
Confined henceforward to the mental floors of his being, man
becomes an almost easily manageable subject for the writer.
In the French tragedies (the most completely Manichaean
works of art ever created) lust itself has ceased to be corporeal
and takes its place among the other abstract symbols, with
which the authors write their strange algebraical equations of
passion and conflict. The beauty of algebraical symbols lies in
their universality; they stand not for one particular case, but
for all cases. Manichaeans, the classical writers confined themselves exclusively to the study of man as a creature of pure
reason and discarnate passions. Now the body particularizes
and separates, the mind unites. By the very act of imposing
limitations the classicists were enabled to achieve a certain
universality of statement impossible to those who attempt to
reproduce the particularities and incompletenesses of actual
corporeal life. But what they gained in universality, they lost
in vivacity and immediate truth. You cannot get something
for nothing. Some people think that universality can be paid
for too highly.

To enforce their ascetic code the classicists had to devise a system of critical sanctions. Chief among these was the stigma of vulgarity attached to all those who insisted too minutely on the physical side of man's existence. Speak of handkerchiefs in a tragedy? The solecism was as monstrous as picking teeth with a fork.

At a dinner party in Paris not long ago I found myself sitting next to a French Professor of English, who assured me in the course of an otherwise very agreeable conversation that I was a leading member of the Neo-Classic school and that it was as a leading member of the Neo-Classic school that I was lectured about to the advanced students of contemporary English literature under his tutelage. The news depressed me. Classified, like a museum specimen, and lectured about, I felt most dismally posthumous. But that was not all. The thought that I was a Neo-Classic preyed upon my mind—a Neo-Classic without knowing it, a Neo-Classic against all my desires and intentions. For I have never had the smallest ambition to be a Classic of any kind, whether Neo, Palaeo, Proto or Eo. Not at any price. For, to begin with, I have a taste for the lively, the mixed and the incomplete in art, preferring it to the universal and the chemically pure. In the second place, I regard the classical discipline, with its insistence on elimination, concentration, simplification, as being, for all the formal difficulties it imposes on the writer, essentially an escape from, a getting out of, the greatest difficulty—which is to render adequately, in terms of literature, that infinitely complex and mysterious thing, actual reality. The world of mind is a comfortable Wombland, a place to which we flee from the bewildering queerness and multiplicity of the actual world. Matter is incomparably subtler and more intricate than mind. Or, to put it a little more philosophically, the consciousness of events which we have immediately, through our senses and intuitions and feelings, is incomparably subtler than any idea we can subsequently form of that immediate consciousness. Our most refined theories, our most elaborate descriptions are but crude and barbarous simplifications of a reality that is, in every smallest sample, infinitely complex. Now, simplifications must, of course, be made; if they were not, it would be quite impossible to deal artistically (or, for that matter, scientifically) with reality at all. What is the smallest amount of simplification compatible with comprehensibility, compatible with the expression of a humanly significant meaning? It is the business of the non-classical naturalistic writer to discover. His ambition is to render, in literary terms, the quality of immediate experience—in other words, to express the finally inexpressible. To come anywhere

near achieving this impossibility is much more difficult, it
seems to me, than, by eliminating and simplifying, to achieve
the perfectly realizable classical ideal. The cutting out of all
the complex particularities of a situation (which means, as we
have seen, the cutting out of all that is corporeal in it) strikes
me as mere artistic shirking. But I disapprove of the shirking
of artistic difficulties. Therefore I find myself disapproving of
classicism.

Literature is also philosophy, is also science. In terms of
beauty it enunciates truths. The beauty-truths of the best
classical works possess, as we have seen, a certain algebraic
universality of significance. Naturalistic works contain the
more detailed beauty-truths of particular observation. These
beauty-truths of art are truly scientific. All that modern psychologists, for example, have done is to systematize and de-
beautify the vast treasures of knowledge about the human soul
contained in novel, play, poem and essay. Writers like Blake
and Shakespeare, like Stendhal and Dostoevsky, still have
plenty to teach the modern scientific professional. There is a
rich scientific harvest to be reaped in the works even of minor
writers. By nature a natural historian, I am ambitious to add
my quota to the sum of particularized beauty-truths about
man and his relations with the world about him. (Incidentally,
this world of relationships, this borderland between "subjective" and "objective" is one which literature is peculiarly, perhaps uniquely, well fitted to explore.) I do not want to be a
Classical, or even a Neo-Classical, eliminator and generalizer.

This means, among other things, that I cannot accept the
Classicists' excommunication of the body. I think it not only
permissible, but necessary, that literature should take cognizance of physiology and should investigate the still obscure
relations between the mind and its body. True, many people
find the reports of such investigations, when not concealed in
scientific textbooks and couched in the decent obscurity of a
Graeco-Latin jargon, extremely and inexcusably vulgar; and
many more find them downright wicked. I myself have frequently been accused, by reviewers in public and by unpro-
fessional readers in private correspondence, both of vulgarity
and of wickedness—on the grounds, so far as I have ever been
able to discover, that I reported my investigations into certain
phenomena in plain English and in a novel. The fact that
many people should be shocked by what he writes practically
imposes it as a duty upon the writer to go on shocking them.
For those who are shocked by truth are not only stupid, but
morally reprehensible as well; the stupid should be educated,
the wicked punished and reformed. All these praiseworthy
ends can be attained by a course of shocking; retributive pain

will be inflicted on the truth-haters by the first shocking truths,
whose repetition will gradually build up in those who read
them an immunity to pain and will end by reforming and edu-
cating the stupid criminals out of their truth-hating. For a
familiar truth ceases to shock. To render it familiar is therefore a duty. It is also a pleasure. For, as Baudelaire says, *"ce
qu'il y a d'enivrant dans le mauvais goût, c'est le plaisir aristo-
cratique de déplaire."*

IV

The aristocratic pleasure of displeasing is not the only delight
that bad taste can yield. One can love a certain kind of vulgarity for its own sake. To overstep artistic restraints, to protest too much for the fun of baroquely protesting—such
offenses against good taste are intoxicatingly delightful to
commit, not because they displease other people (for to the
great majority they are rather pleasing than otherwise), but
because they are intrinsically vulgar, because the good taste
against which they offend is as nearly as possible an absolute
good taste; they are artistic offenses that have the exciting
quality of the sin against the Holy Ghost.

It was Flaubert, I think, who described how he was tempted,
as he wrote, by swarms of gaudy images and how, a new St.
Antony, he squashed them ruthlessly, like lice, against the bare
wall of his study. He was resolved that his work should be
adorned only with its own intrinsic beauty and with no ex-
traneous jewels, however lovely in themselves. The saintliness
of this ascetic of letters was duly rewarded; there is nothing
in all Flaubert's writings that remotely resembles a vulgarity.
Those who follow his religion must pray for the strength to
imitate their saint. The strength is seldom vouchsafed. The
temptations which Flaubert put aside are, by any man of
lively fancy and active intellect, incredibly difficult to be re-
sisted. An image presents itself, glittering, iridescent; capture
it, pin it down, however irrelevantly too brilliant for its context. A phrase, a situation suggests a whole train of striking or
amusing ideas that fly off at a tangent, so to speak, from the
round world on which the creator is at work; what an opportunity for saying something witty or profound! True, the ornament will be in the nature of a florid excrescence on the total
work; but never mind. In goes the tangent—or rather, out into
artistic irrelevancy. And in goes the effective phrase that is too
effective, too highly colored for what it is to express; in goes
the too emphatic irony, the too tragical scene, the too pathetic
tirade, the too poetical description. If we succumb to all these
delightful temptations, if we make welcome all these gaudy

lice instead of squashing them at their first appearance, our work will soon glitter like a South American parvenu, dazzling with parasitic ornament, and vulgar. For a self-conscious artist, there is a most extraordinary pleasure in knowing exactly what the results of showing off and protesting too much must be and then (in spite of this knowledge, or because of it) proceeding, deliberately and with all the skill at his command, to commit precisely those vulgarities, against which his conscience warns him and which he knows he will afterwards regret. To the aristocratic pleasure of displeasing other people, the conscious offender against good taste can add the still more aristocratic pleasure of displeasing himself. . . .

V

It is vulgar, in literature, to make a display of emotions which you do not naturally have, but think you ought to have, because all the best people do have them. It is also vulgar (and this is the more common case) to have emotions, but to express them so badly, with so many too many protestings, that you seem to have no natural feelings, but to be merely fabricating emotions by a process of literary forgery. Sincerity in art, as I have pointed out elsewhere, is mainly a matter of talent. Keats's love letters ring true, because he had great literary gifts. Most men and women are capable of feeling passion, but not of expressing it; their love letters (as we learn from the specimens read aloud at inquests and murder trials, in the divorce court, during breach of promise cases) are either tritely flat or tritely bombastic. In either case manifestly insincere, and in the second case also vulgar—for to protest too much is always vulgar, when the protestations are so incompetent as not to carry conviction. And perhaps such excessive protestations can never be convincing, however accomplished the protester. D'Annunzio, for example—nobody could do a job of writing better than D'Annunzio. But when, as is too often the case, he makes much ado about nothing, we find it hard to be convinced either of the importance of the nothing, or of the sincerity of the author's emotion about it—and this in spite of the incomparable splendor of D'Annunzio's much ado. True, excessive protestings may convince a certain public at a certain time. But when the circumstances, which rendered the public sensitive to the force and blind to the vulgarity of the too much protesting, have changed, the protests cease to convince. Mackenzie's *Man of Feeling,* for example, protests its author's sensibility with an extravagance that seems now, not merely vulgar, but positively ludicrous. At the time of its publication sentimentality was, for various reasons, extremely fashionable. Circumstances changed and *The Man of Feeling* revealed itself as vulgar to the point of ridiculousness; and vulgar and ridiculous it has remained ever since and doubtless will remain . . . .

The case of Dickens is a strange one. The really monstrous emotional vulgarity, of which he is guilty now and then in all his books and almost continuously in *The Old Curiosity Shop,* is not the emotional vulgarity of one who stimulates feelings which he does not have. It is evident, on the contrary, that Dickens felt most poignantly for and with his Little Nell; that he wept over her sufferings, piously revered her goodness and exulted in her joys. He had an overflowing heart; but the trouble was that it overflowed with such curious and even rather repellent secretions. The creator of the later Pickwick and the Cheeryble Brothers, of Tim Linkinwater the bachelor and Mr. Garland and so many other gruesome old Peter Pans was obviously a little abnormal in his emotional reactions. There was something rather wrong with a man who could take this lachrymose and tremulous pleasure in adult infantility. He would doubtless have justified his rather frightful emotional taste by a reference to the New Testament. But the child-like qualities of character commended by Jesus are certainly not the same as those which distinguish the old infants in Dickens's novels. There is all the difference in the world between infants and children. Infants are stupid and unaware and subhuman. Children are remarkable for their intelligence and ardor, for their curiosity, their intolerance of shams, the clarity and ruthlessness of their vision. From all accounts Jesus must have been child-like, not at all infantile. A child-like man is not a man whose development has been arrested; on the contrary, he is a man who has given himself a chance of continuing to develop long after most adults have muffled themselves in the cocoon of middle-aged habit and convention. An infantile man is one who has not developed at all, or who has regressed toward the womb, into a comfortable unawareness. So far from being attractive and commendable, an infantile man is really a most repulsive, because a truly monstrous and misshapen, being. A writer who can tearfully adore these stout or cadaverous old babies, snugly ensconced in their mental and economic womb-substitutes and sucking, between false teeth, their thumbs, must have something seriously amiss with his emotional constitution.

One of Dickens's most striking peculiarities is that, whenever in his writing he becomes emotional, he ceases instantly to use his intelligence. The overflowing of his heart drowns his head and even dims his eyes; for, whenever he is in the melting mood, Dickens ceases to be able and probably ceases even

to wish to see reality. His one and only desire on these occasions is just to overflow, nothing else. Which he does, with
a vengeance and in an atrocious blank verse that is meant to
be poetical prose and succeeds only in being the worst kind
of fustian. "When Death strikes down the innocent and young,
from every fragile form from which he lets the panting spirit
free, a hundred virtues rise, in shapes of mercy, charity and
love, to walk the world and bless it. Of every tear that sorrow-
ing mortals shed on such green graves, some good is born,
some gentler nature comes. In the Destroyer's steps there
spring up bright creations that defy his power, and his dark
path becomes a way of light to Heaven." And so on, a stanch-
less flux.

Mentally drowned and blinded by the sticky overflowings
of his heart, Dickens was incapable, when moved, of re-creating, in terms of art, the reality which had moved him, was
even, it would seem, unable to perceive that reality. Little
Nelly's sufferings and death distressed him as, in real life, they
would distress any normally constituted man; for the suffering
and death of children raise the problem of evil in its most unanswerable form. It was Dickens's business as a writer to re-
create in terms of his art this distressing reality. He failed.
The history of Little Nell is distressing indeed, but not as
Dickens presumably meant it to be distressing; it is distressing
in its ineptitude and vulgar sentimentality.

A child, Ilusha, suffers and dies in Dostoevsky's *Brothers
Karamazov*. Why is this history so agonizingly moving, when
the tale of Little Nell leaves us not merely cold, but derisive?
Comparing the two stories, we are instantly struck by the
incomparably greater richness in factual detail of Dostoevsky's
creation. Feeling did not prevent him from seeing and recording, or rather re-creating. All that happened round Ilusha's
deathbed he saw, unerringly. The emotion-blinded Dickens
noticed practically nothing of what went on in Little Nelly's
neighborhood during the child's last days. We are almost
forced, indeed, to believe that he didn't want to see anything.
He wanted to be unaware himself and he wanted his readers
to be unaware of everything except Little Nell's sufferings on
the one hand and her goodness and innocence on the other.
But goodness and innocence and the undeservedness of suffering and even, to some extent, suffering itself are only significant
in relation to the actual realities of human life. Isolated, they
cease to mean anything, perhaps to exist. Even the classical
writers surrounded their abstract and algebraical personages
with at least the abstract and algebraical implication of the
human realities, in relation to which virtues and vices are
significant. Thanks to Dickens's pathologically deliberate un-

awareness, Nell's virtues are marooned, as it were, in the midst
of a boundless waste of unreality; isolated, they fade and die.
Even her sufferings and death lack significance because of this
isolation. Dickens's unawareness was the death of death itself.
Unawareness, according to the ethics of Buddhism, is one of
the deadly sins. The stupid are wicked. (Incidentally, the
cleverest men can, sometimes and in certain circumstances,
reveal themselves as profoundly—criminally—stupid. You can
be an acute logician and at the same time an emotional cretin.)
Damned in the realm of conduct, the unaware are also damned
aesthetically. Their art is bad; instead of creating, they murder.

Art, as I have said, is also philosophy, is also science.
Other things being equal, the work of art which in its own
way "says" more about the universe will be better than the
work of art which says less. (The "other things" which have
to be equal are the forms of beauty, in terms of which the
artist must express his philosophic and scientific truths.) Why
is *The Rosary* a less admirable novel than *The Brothers Karamazov*? Because the amount of experience of all kinds
understood, "felt into," as the Germans would say, and artistically recreated by Mrs. Barclay is small in comparison
with that which Dostoevsky feelingly comprehended and knew
so consummately well how to re-create in terms of the novelist's art. Dostoevsky covers all Mrs. Barclay's ground and a
vast area beside. The pathetic parts of *The Old Curiosity Shop*
are as poor in understood and artistically re-created experience
as *The Rosary*—indeed, I think they are ever poorer. At the
same time they are vulgar (which *The Rosary,* that genuine
masterpiece of the servants' hall, is not). They are vulgar,
because their poverty is a pretentious poverty, because their
disease (for the quality of Dickens's sentimentality is truly
pathological) professes to be the most radiant health; because
they protest their unintelligence, their lack of understanding
with a vehemence of florid utterance that is not only shocking,
but ludicrous.

(From "Vulgarity in Literature," *Music at Night*)

D. H. Lawrence

It is impossible to write about Lawrence except as an artist.
He was an artist first of all, and the fact of his being an artist
explains a life which seems, if you forget it, inexplicably
strange. In *Son of Woman,* Mr. Middleton Murry has written

at great length about Lawrence—but about a Lawrence whom you would never suspect, from reading that curious essay in destructive hagiography, of being an artist. For Mr. Murry almost completely ignores the fact that his subject—his victim, I had almost said—was one whom "the fates had stigmatized 'writer.' " His book is *Hamlet* without the Prince of Denmark —for all its metaphysical subtleties and its Freudian inge- nuities, very largely irrelevant. The absurdity of his critical method becomes the more manifest when we reflect that no- body would ever have heard of a Lawrence who was not an artist.

An artist is the sort of artist he is, because he happens to possess certain gifts. And he leads the sort of life he does in fact lead, because he is an artist, and an artist with a particular kind of mental endowment. Now there are general abilities and there are special talents. A man who is born with a great share of some special talent is probably less deeply affected by nurture than one whose ability is generalized. His gift is his fate, and he follows a predestined course, from which no ordinary power can deflect him. In spite of Helvétius and Dr. Watson, it seems pretty obvious that no amount of education —including under that term everything from the Œdipus complex to the English Public School system—could have prevented Mozart from being a musician, or musicianship from being the central fact in Mozart's life. And how would a different education have modified the expression of, say, Blake's gift? It is, of course, impossible to answer. One can only express the unverifiable conviction that an art so pro- foundly individual and original, so manifestly "inspired," would have remained fundamentally the same whatever (with- in reasonable limits) had been the circumstances of Blake's upbringing. Lawrence, as Mr. F. R. Leavis insists, has many affinities with Blake. "He had the same gift of knowing what he was interested in, the same power of distinguishing his own feelings and emotions from conventional sentiment, the same 'terrifying honesty.' " Like Blake, like any man possessed of great special talents, he was predestined by his gifts. Explana- tions of him in terms of a Freudian hypothesis of nurture may be interesting, but they do not explain. That Lawrence was profoundly affected by his love for his mother and by her excessive love for him, is obvious to anyone who has read *Sons and Lovers*. None the less it is, to me at any rate, almost equally obvious that even if his mother had died when he was a child, Lawrence would still have been, essentially and funda- mentally, Lawrence. Lawrence's biography does not account for Lawrence's achievement. On the contrary, his achievement, or rather the gift that made the achievement possible, accounts for a great deal of his biography. He lived as he lived, because he was, intrinsically and from birth, what he was. If we would write intelligibly of Lawrence, we must answer, with all their implications, two questions: first, what sort of gifts did he have? and secondly, how did the possession of these gifts affect the way he responded to experience?

Lawrence's special and characteristic gift was an extraordinary sensitiveness to what Wordsworth called "unknown modes of being." He was always intensely aware of the mystery of the world, and the mystery was always for him a *numen,* divine. Lawrence could never forget, as most of us almost continuously forget, the dark presence of the otherness that lies beyond the boundaries of man's conscious mind. This special sensibility was accompanied by a prodigious power of rendering the immediately experienced otherness in terms of literary art.

Such was Lawrence's peculiar gift. His possession of it accounts for many things. It accounts, to begin with, for his attitude toward sex. His particular experiences as a son and as a lover may have intensified his preoccupation with the subject; but they certainly did not make it. Whatever his experiences, Lawrence *must* have been preoccupied with sex; his gift made it inevitable. For Lawrence, the significance of the sexual experience was this: that, in it, the immediate, non-mental knowledge of divine otherness is brought, so to speak, to a focus—a focus of darkness. Parodying Matthew Arnold's famous formula, we may say that sex is something not ourselves that makes for—not righteousness, for the essence of religion is not righteousness; there is a spiritual world, as Kierkegaard insists, beyond the ethical—rather, that makes for life, for divineness, for union with the mystery. Paradoxically, this something not ourselves is yet a something lodged within us; this quintessence of otherness is yet the quintessence of our proper being. "And God the Father, the Inscrutable, the Unknowable, we know in the flesh, in Woman. She is the door for our in-going and our out-coming. In her we go back to the Father; but like the witnesses of the transfiguration, blind and unconscious." Yes, blind and unconscious; otherwise it is a revelation, not of divine otherness, but of very human evil. "The embrace of love, which should bring darkness and oblivion, would with these lovers (the hero and heroine of one of Poe's tales) be a daytime thing, bringing more heightened consciousness, visions, spectrum-visions, prismatic. The evil thing that daytime love-making is, and all sex-palaver!" How Lawrence hated Eleonora and Ligeia and Roderick Usher and all such soulful Mrs. Shandies, male as well as female! What a horror, too, he had of all Don Juans, all knowing sensualists and conscious libertines! (About the time he was writing *Lady Chatterley's Lover* he read the memoirs of Casanova, and was profoundly shocked.) And how bitterly he loathed the Wilhelm-Meisterish view of love as an education, as a means to culture, a Sandow-exerciser for the soul! To *use* love in this way, consciously and deliberately, seemed to Lawrence wrong, almost a blasphemy. "It seems to me queer," he says to a fellow-writer, "that you prefer to present men chiefly—as if you cared for women not so much for what they were in themselves as for what the men saw in them. So that after all in your work women seem not to have an existence, save they are the projections of the men. . . . It's the *positivity* of women you seem to deny—make them sort of instrumental." The instrumentality of Wilhelm Meister's women shocked Lawrence profoundly . . . .

For someone with a gift for sensing the mystery of otherness, true love must necessarily be, in Lawrence's vocabulary, *nocturnal*. So must true knowledge. Nocturnal and tactual— a touching in the night. Man inhabits, for his own convenience, a home-made universe within the greater alien world of external matter and his own irrationality. Out of the illimitable blackness of that world the light of his customary thinking scoops, as it were, a little illuminated cave—a tunnel of brightness, in which, from the birth of consciousness to its death, he lives, moves and has his being. For most of us this bright tunnel is the whole world. We ignore the outer darkness; or if we cannot ignore it, if it presses too insistently upon us, we disapprove, being afraid. Not so Lawrence. He had eyes that could see, beyond the walls of light, far into the darkness, sensitive fingers that kept him continually aware of the environing mystery. He could not be content with the home-made, human tunnel, could not conceive that anyone else should be content with it. Moreover—and in this he was unlike those others, to whom the world's mystery is continuously present, the great philosophers and men of science—he did not want to increase the illuminated area; he approved of the outer darkness, he felt at home in it. Most men live in a little puddle of light thrown by the gig-lamps of habit and their immediate interest; but there is also the pure and powerful illumination of the disinterested scientific intellect. To Lawrence, both lights were suspect, both seemed to falsify what was, for him, the immediately apprehended reality—the darkness of mystery. "My great religion," he was already saying in 1912, "is a belief in the blood, the flesh, as being wiser than the intellect. We can go wrong in our minds. But what the blood feels, and believes, and says, is always true." Like Blake, who had prayed to be delivered from "single vision and

Newton's sleep": like Keats, who had drunk destruction to
Newton for having explained the rainbow, Lawrence disapproved of too much knowledge, on the score that it diminished men's sense of wonder and blunted their sensitiveness
to the great mystery. His dislike of science was passionate
and expressed itself in the most fantastically unreasonable
terms. "All scientists are liars," he would say, when I brought
up some experimentally established fact, which he happened
to dislike. "Liars, liars!" It was a most convenient theory. I
remember in particular one long and violent argument on
evolution, in the reality of which Lawrence always passionately disbelieved. "But look at the evidence, Lawrence," I
insisted, "look at all the evidence." His answer was characteristic. "But I don't care about evidence. Evidence doesn't mean
anything to me. I don't feel it *here*." And he pressed his two
hands on his solar plexus. I abandoned the argument and
thereafter never, if I could avoid it, mentioned the hated name
of science in his presence. Lawrence could give so much, and
what he gave was so valuable, that it was absurd and profitless
to spend one's time with him disputing about a matter in which
he absolutely refused to take a rational interest. Whatever the
intellectual consequences, he remained through thick and
thin unshakably loyal to his own genius. The *daimon* which
possessed him was, he felt, a divine thing, which he would
never deny or explain away, never even ask to accept a
compromise. This loyalty to his own self, or rather to his
gift, to the strange and powerful *numen* which, he felt, used
him as its tabernacle, is fundamental in Lawrence and accounts, as nothing else can do, for all that the world found
strange in his beliefs and his behavior. It was not an incapacity
to understand that made him reject those generalizations and
abstractions by means of which the philosophers and the men
of science try to open a path for the human spirit through
the chaos of phenomena. Not incapacity, I repeat; for Lawrence had, over and above his peculiar gift, an extremely
acute intelligence. He was a clever man as well as a man of
genius. (In his boyhood and adolescence he had been a great
passer of examinations.) He could have understood the aim
and methods of science perfectly well if he had wanted to.
Indeed, he did understand them perfectly well; and it was for
that very reason that he rejected them. For the methods of
science and critical philosophy were incompatible with the
exercise of his gift—the immediate perception and artistic
rendering of divine otherness. And their aim, which is to push
back the frontier of the unknown, was not to be reconciled
with his aim, which was to remain as intimately as possible
in contact with the surrounding darkness. And so, in spite of

their enormous prestige, he rejected science and critical philosophy; he remained loyal to his gift. Exclusively loyal. He would not attempt to qualify or explain his immediate knowledge of the mystery, would not even attempt to supplement it by other, abstract knowledge. "These terrible, conscious birds, like Poe and his Ligeia, deny the very life that is in them; they want to turn it all into talk, into *knowing*. And so life, which will not be known, leaves them." Lawrence refused to *know* abstractly. He preferred to live; and he wanted other people to live.

No man is by nature complete and universal; he cannot have first-hand knowledge of every kind of possible human experience. Universality, therefore, can only be achieved by those who mentally stimulate living experience—by the knowers, in a word, by people like Goethe (an artist for whom Lawrence always felt the most intense repugnance).

Again, no man is by nature perfect, and none can spontaneously achieve perfection. The greatest gift is a limited gift. Perfection, whether ethical or aesthetic, must be the result of knowing and of the laborious application of knowledge. Formal aesthetics are an affair of rules and the best classical models; formal morality, of the ten commandments and the imitation of Christ.

Lawrence would have nothing to do with proceedings so "unnatural," so disloyal to the gift, to the resident or visiting *numen*. Hence his aesthetic principle, that art must be wholly spontaneous, and, like the artist, imperfect, limited and transient. Hence, too, his ethical principle, that a man's first moral duty is not to attempt to live above his human station, or beyond his inherited psychological income.

The great work of art and the monument more perennial than brass are, in their very perfection and everlastingness, inhuman—too much of a good thing. Lawrence did not approve of them. Art, he thought, should flower from an immediate impulse toward self-expression or communication, and should wither with the passing of the impulse. Of all building materials Lawrence liked adobe the best; its extreme plasticity and extreme impermanence endeared it to him. There could be no everlasting pyramids in adobe, no mathematically accurate Parthenons. Nor, thank heaven, in wood. Lawrence loved the Etruscans, among other reasons, because they built wooden temples, which have not survived. Stone oppressed him with its indestructible solidity, its capacity to take and indefinitely keep the hard uncompromising forms of pure geometry. Great buildings made him feel uncomfortable, even when they were beautiful. He felt something of the same discomfort in the presence of any highly finished work of art.

In music, for example, he liked the folk-song, because it was a slight thing, born of immediate impulse. The symphony oppressed him; it was too big, too elaborate, too carefully and consciously worked out, too "would-be"—to use a character- istic Lawrencian expression. He was quite determined that none of his writings should be "would-be." He allowed them to flower as they liked from the depths of his being and would never use his conscious intellect to force them into a sem- blance of more than human perfection, or more than human universality. It was characteristic of him that he hardly ever corrected or patched what he had written. I have often heard him say, indeed, that he was incapable of correcting. If he was dissatisfied with what he had written, he did not, as most authors do, file, clip, insert, transpose; he rewrote. In other words, he gave the *daimon* another chance to say what it wanted to say. There are, I believe, three complete and totally distinct manuscripts of *Lady Chatterley's Lover*. Nor was this by any means the only novel that he wrote more than once. He was determined that all he produced should spring direct from the mysterious, irrational source of power within him. The conscious intellect should never be allowed to come and impose, after the event, its abstract pattern of perfection.

It was the same in the sphere of ethics as in that of art. "They want me to have form: that means, they want me to have *their* pernicious, ossiferous skin-and-grief form, and I won't." This was written about his novels; but it is just as applicable to his life. Every man, Lawrence insisted, must be an artist in life, must create his own moral form. The art of living is harder than the art of writing. "It is a much more delicate thing to make love, and win love, than to declare love." All the more reason, therefore, for practicing this art with the most refined and subtle sensibility; all the more rea- son for not accepting that "pernicious skin-and-grief form" of morality, which *they* are always trying to impose on one. It is the business of the sensitive artist in life to accept his own nature as it is, not to try to force it into another shape. He must take the material given him—the weaknesses and irra- tionalities, as well as the sense and the virtues; the mysterious darkness and otherness no less than the light of reason and the conscious ego—must take them all and weave them together into a satisfactory pattern; *his* pattern, not somebody else's pattern. "Once I said to myself: 'How can I blame—why be angry?' . . . Now I say: 'When anger comes with bright eyes, he may do his will. In me he will hardly shake off the hand of God. He is one of the archangels, with a fiery sword. God sent him—it is beyond my knowing.'" This was written in 1910. Even at the very beginning of his career Lawrence was envisaging man as simply the locus of a polytheism. Given his particular gifts of sensitiveness and of expression it was inevitable. Just as it was inevitable that a man of Blake's peculiar genius should formulate the very similar doctrine of the independence of states of being. All the generally accepted systems of philosophy and of ethics aim at policing man's polytheism in the name of some Jehovah of intellectual and moral consistency. For Lawrence this was an indefensible proceeding. One god had as much right to exist as another, and the dark ones were as genuinely divine as the bright. Perhaps (since Lawrence was so specially sensitive to the quality of dark godhead and so specially gifted to express it in art), perhaps even more divine. Anyhow, the polytheism was a democracy. This conception of human nature resulted in the formulation of two rather surprising doctrines, one ontological and the other ethical. The first is what I may call the Doctrine of Cosmic Pointlessness. "There is no point. Life and Love are life and love, a bunch of violets is a bunch of violets, and to drag in the idea of a point is to ruin everything. Live and let live, love and let love, flower and fade, and follow the natural curve, which flows on, pointless."

Ontological pointlessness has its ethical counterpart in the doctrine of insouciance. "They simply are eaten up with caring. They are so busy caring about Fascism or Leagues of Nations or whether France is right or whether Marriage is threatened, that they never know where they are. They certainly never live on the spot where they are. They inhabit abstract space, the desert void of politics, principles, right and wrong, and so forth. They are doomed to be abstract. Talking to them is like trying to have a human relationship with the letter x in algebra." As early as 1911 his advice to his sister was: "Don't meddle with religion. I would leave all that alone, if I were you, and try to occupy myself fully in the present.". . .

Lawrence's dislike of abstract knowledge and pure spirituality made him a kind of mystical materialist. Thus, the moon affects him strongly; therefore it cannot be a "stony cold world, like a world of our own gone cold. Nonsense. It is a globe of dynamic substance, like radium or phosphorus, coagulated upon a vivid pole of energy." Matter must be intrinsically as lively as the mind which perceives it and is moved by the perception. Vivid and violent spiritual effects must have correspondingly vivid and violent material causes. And, conversely, any violent feeling or desire in the mind must be capable of producing violent effects upon external matter. Lawrence could not bring himself to believe that the spirit can be moved, moved even to madness, without imparting the smallest corresponding movement to the external world. He was a subjectivist as well as a materialist; in other words, he believed in the possibility, in some form or another, of magic. Lawrence's mystical materialism found characteristic expression the curious cosmology and physiology of his speculative essays, and in his restatement of the strange Christian doctrine of the resurrection of the body. To his mind, the survival of the spirit was not enough; for the spirit is a man's conscious identity, and Lawrence did not want to be always identical to himself; he wanted to know otherness—to know it by being it, know it in the living flesh, which is always essentially *other*. Therefore there must be a resurrection of the body.

Loyalty to his genius left him no choice; Lawrence had to insist on those mysterious forces of otherness which are scattered without, and darkly concentrated within, the body and mind of man. He had to, even though, by doing so, he imposed upon himself, as a writer of novels, a very serious handicap. For according to his view of things most of men's activities were more or less criminal distractions from the proper business of human living. He refused to write of such distractions; that is to say, he refused to write of the main activities of the contemporary world. But as though this drastic limitation of his subject were not sufficient, he went still further and, in some of his novels, refused even to write of human personalities in the accepted sense of the term. *The Rainbow* and *Women in Love* (and indeed to a lesser extent all his novels) are the practical applications of a theory, which is set forth in a very interesting and important letter to Edward Garnett, dated June 5th, 1914. "Somehow, that which is physic—non-human in humanity, is more interesting to me than the old-fashioned human element, which causes one to conceive a character in a certain moral scheme and make him consistent. The certain moral scheme is what I object to. In Turgenev, and in Tolstoi, and in Dostoievsky, the moral scheme into which all the characters fit—and it is nearly the same scheme—is, whatever the extraordinariness of the characters themselves, dull, old, dead. When Marinetti writes: 'It is the solidity of a blade of steel that is interesting in itself, that is, the incomprehending and inhuman alliance of its molecules in resistance to, let us say, a bullet. The heat of a piece of wood or iron is in fact more passionate, for us, than the laughter or tears of a woman'—then I know what he means. He is stupid, as an artist, for contrasting the heat of the iron and the laugh of the woman. Because what is interesting in the laugh of the woman is the same as the binding of the molecules of steel or their action in heat: it is the

inhuman will, call it physiology, or like Marinetti, physiology
of matter, that fascinates me. I don't so much care about what
the woman *feels*—in the ordinary usage of the word. That
presumes an *ego* to feel with. I only care about what the
woman *is*—what she Is—inhumanly, physiologically, materially
—according to the use of the word. . . . You mustn't look in
my novel for the old stable *ego* of the character. There is
another *ego*, according to whose action the individual is
unrecognizable, and passes through, as it were, allotropic
states which it needs a deeper sense than any we've been used
to exercise, to discover are states of the same single radically
unchanged element. (Like as diamond and coal are the same
pure single element of carbon. The ordinary novel would trace
the history of the diamond—but I say, 'Diamond, what! This
is carbon.' And my diamond might be coal or soot, and my
theme is carbon.)". . .

Lawrence, then, possessed, or, if you care to put it the other
way round, was possessed by, a gift—a gift to which he was
unshakably loyal. I have tried to show how the possession and
the loyalty influenced his thinking and writing. How did they
affect his life? The answer shall be, as far as possible, in
Lawrence's own words. To Catherine Carswell Lawrence once
wrote: "I think you are the only woman I have met who is
so intrinsically detached, so essentially separate and isolated,
as to be a real writer or artist or recorder. Your relations with
other people are only excursions from yourself. And to want
children, and common human fulfillments, is rather a falsity
for you, I think. You were never made to 'meet and mingle,'
but to remain intact, *essentially*, whatever your experiences
may be."

Lawrence's knowledge of "the artist" was manifestly personal knowledge. He knew by actual experience that the "real
writer" is an essentially separate being, who must not desire
to meet and mingle and who betrays himself when he hankers
too yearningly after common human fulfillments. All artists
know these facts about their species, and many of them have
recorded their knowledge. Recorded it, very often, with distress; being intrinsically detached is no joke. Lawrence certainly suffered his whole life from the essential solitude to
which his gift condemned him. "What ails me," he wrote to
the psychologist, Dr. Trigant Burrow, "is the absolute frustration of my primeval societal instinct. . . . I think societal instinct much deeper than sex instinct—and societal repression
much more devastating. There is no repression of the sexual
individual comparable to the repression of the societal man
in me, by the individual ego, my own and everybody else's. . . .
Myself, I suffer badly from being so cut off. . . . At times one

is *forced* to be essentially a hermit. I don't want to be. But anything else is either a personal tussle, or a money tussle; sickening: except, of course, just for ordinary acquaintance, which remains acquaintance. One has no real human relations—that is so devastating." One has no real human relations: it is the complaint of every artist. The artist's first duty is to his genius, his *daimon*; he cannot serve two masters. Lawrence, as it happened, had an extraordinary gift for establishing an intimate relationship with almost anyone he met. "Here" (in the Bournemouth boarding-house where he was staying after his illness, in 1912), "I get mixed up in people's lives so—it's very interesting, sometimes a bit painful, often jolly. But I run to such close intimacy with folk, it is complicating. But I love to have myself in a bit of a tangle." His love for his art was greater, however, than his love for a tangle; and whenever the tangle threatened to compromise his activities as an artist, it was the tangle that was sacrificed: he retired. Lawrence's only deep and abiding human relationship was with his wife. ("It is hopeless for me," he wrote to a fellow-artist, "to try to do anything without I have a woman at the back of me. . . . Böcklin—or somebody like him—daren't sit in a café except with his back to the wall. I daren't sit in the world without a woman behind me. . . . A woman that I love sort of keeps me in direct communication with the unknown, in which otherwise I am a bit lost.") For the rest, he was condemned by his gift to an essential separateness. Often, it is true, he blamed the world for his exile. "And it comes to this, that the *oneness* of mankind is destroyed in me (by the war). I am I, and you are you, and all heaven and hell lie in the chasm between. Believe me, I am infinitely hurt by being thus torn off from the body of mankind, but so it is and it is right." It was right because, in reality, it was not the war that had torn him from the body of mankind; it was his own talent, the strange divinity to which he owed his primary allegiance. "I will not live any more in this time," he wrote on another occasion. "I know what it is. I reject it. As far as I possibly can, I will stand outside this time. I will live my life and, if possible, be happy. Though the whole world slides in horror down into the bottomless pit . . . I believe that the highest virtue is to be happy, living in the greatest truth, not submitting to the falsehood of these personal times." The adjective is profoundly significant. Of all the possible words of disparagement which might be applied to our uneasy age "personal" is surely about the last that would occur to most of us. To Lawrence it was the first. His gift was a gift of feeling and rendering the unknown, the mysteriously other. To one possessed by such a gift, almost any age would have seemed unduly and dangerously personal. He had to reject and escape. But when he had escaped, he could not help deploring the absence of "real human relationships." Spasmodically, he tried to establish contact with the body of mankind. There were the recurrent projects for colonies in remote corners of the earth; they all fell through . . . .

It was, I think, the sense of being cut off that sent Lawrence on his restless wanderings round the earth. His travels were at once a flight and a search: a search for some society with which he could establish contact, for a world where the times were not personal and conscious knowing had not yet perverted living; a search and at the same time a flight from the miseries and evils of the society into which he had been born, and for which, in spite of his artist's detachment, he could not help feeling profoundly responsible. He felt himself "English in the teeth of all the world, even in the teeth of England": that was why he had to go to Ceylon and Australia and Mexico. He could not have felt so intensely English in England without involving himself in corporative political action, without belonging and being attached; but to attach himself was something he could not bring himself to do, something that the artist in him felt as a violation. He was at once too English and too intensely an artist to stay at home. "Perhaps it is necessary for me to try these places, perhaps it is my destiny to know the world. It only excites the outside of me. The inside it leaves more isolated and stoic than ever. That's how it is. It is all a form of running away from oneself and the great problems, all this wild west and the strange Australia. But I try to keep quite clear. One forms not the faintest inward attachment, especially here in America."

His search was as fruitless as his flight was ineffective. He could not escape either from his homesickness or his sense of responsibility; and he never found a society to which he could belong. In a kind of despair, he plunged yet deeper into the surrounding mystery, into the dark night of that otherness whose essence and symbol is the sexual experience. In *Lady Chatterley's Lover* Lawrence wrote the epilogue to his travels and, from his long and fruitless experience of flight and search, drew what was, for him, the inevitable moral. It is a strange and beautiful book; but inexpressibly sad. But then so, at bottom, was its author's life.

Lawrence's psychological isolation resulted, as we have seen, in his seeking physical isolation from the body of mankind. This physical isolation reacted upon his thoughts. "Don't mind if I am impertinent," he wrote to one of his correspondents at the end of a rather dogmatic letter. "Living here alone one gets so different—sort of ex-cathedra." To live in isolation, above the medley, has its advantages; but it also imposes certain penalties. Those who take a bird's-eye view of the world often see clearly and comprehensively; but they tend to ignore all tiresome details, all the difficulties of social life and, ignoring, to judge too sweepingly and to condemn too lightly . . . .

Enough of explanation and interpretation. To those who knew Lawrence, not *why*, but *that* he was what he happened to be, is the important fact. I remember very clearly my first meeting with him. The place was London, the time 1915. But Lawrence's passionate talk was of the geographically remote and of the personally very near. Of the horrors in the middle distance—war, winter, the town—he would not speak. For he was on the point, so he imagined, of setting off to Florida— to Florida, where he was going to plant that colony of escape, of which up to the last he never ceased to dream. Sometimes the name and site of this seed of a happier and different world were purely fanciful. It was called Rananim, for example, and was an island like Prospero's. Sometimes it had its place on the map and its name was Florida, Cornwall, Sicily, Mexico and again, for a time, the English countryside. That wintry afternoon in 1915 it was Florida. Before tea was over he asked me if I would join the colony, and though I was an intellectually cautious young man, not at all inclined to enthusiasms, though Lawrence had startled and embarrassed me with sincerities of a kind to which my upbringing had not accustomed me, I answered yes.

Fortunately, no doubt, the Florida scheme fell through. Cities of God have always crumbled; and Lawrence's city— his village, rather, for he hated cities—his Village of the Dark God would doubtless have disintegrated like all the rest. It was better that it should have remained, as it was always to remain, a project and a hope. And I knew this even as I said I would join the colony. But there was something about Lawrence which made such knowledge, when one was in his presence, curiously irrelevant. He might propose impracticable schemes, he might say or write things that were demonstrably incorrect or even, on occasion (as when he talked about science), absurd. But to a very considerable extent it didn't matter. What mattered was always Lawrence himself, was the fire that burned within him, that glowed with so strange and marvelous a radiance in almost all he wrote.

My second meeting with Lawrence took place some years later, during one of his brief revisitings of that after-war England, which he had come so much to dread and to dislike. Then in 1925, while in India, I received a letter from Spotorno. He had read some essays I had written on Italian travel;

said he liked them; suggested a meeting. The next year we
were in Florence and so was he. From that time, till his death,
we were often together—at Florence, at Forte dei Marmi, for
a whole winter at Diablerets, at Bandol, in Paris, at Chexbres,
at Forte again, and finally at Vence where he died.

In a spasmodically kept diary I find this entry under the
date of December 27th, 1927: "Lunched and spent the p.m.
with the Lawrences. D. H. L. in admirable form, talking
wonderfully. He is one of the few people I feel real respect
and admiration for. Of most other eminent people I have met
I feel that at any rate I belong to the same species as they do.
But this man has something different and superior in kind, not
degree."

"Different and superior in kind." I think almost everyone
who knew him well must have felt that Lawrence was this.
A being, somehow, of another order, more sensitive, more
highly conscious, more capable of feeling than even the most
gifted of common men. He had, of course, his weaknesses and
defects; he had his intellectual limitations—limitations which
he seemed to have deliberately imposed upon himself. But
these weaknesses and defects and limitations did not affect
the fact of his superior otherness. They diminished him quan-
titively, so to speak; whereas the otherness was qualitative.
Spill half your glass of wine and what remains is still wine.
Water, however full the glass may be, is always tasteless and
without color.

To be with Lawrence was a kind of adventure, a voyage of
discovery into newness and otherness. For, being himself of a
different order, he inhabited a different universe from that of
common men—a brighter and intenser world, of which, while
he spoke, he would make you free. He looked at things with
the eyes, so it seemed, of a man who had been at the brink of
death and to whom, as he emerges from the darkness, the
world reveals itself as unfathomably beautiful and mysterious.
For Lawrence, existence was one continuous convalescence;
it was as though he were newly reborn from a mortal illness
every day of his life. What these convalescent eyes saw, his
most casual speech would reveal. A walk with him in the
country was a walk through that marvelously rich and significant landscape which is at once the background and the
principal personage of all his novels. He seemed to know, by
personal experience, what it was like to be a tree or a daisy
or a breaking wave or even the mysterious moon itself. He
could get inside the skin of an animal and tell you in the most
convincing detail how it felt and how, dimly, inhumanly, it
thought. Of Black-Eyed Susan, for example, the cow at his
New Mexican ranch, he was never tired of speaking, nor was

I ever tired of listening to his account of her character and her
bovine philosophy.

"He sees," Vernon Lee once said to me, "more than a
human being ought to see. Perhaps," she added, "that's why
he hates humanity so much." Why also he loved it so much.
And not only humanity: nature too, and even the supernatural. For wherever he looked, he saw more than a human
being ought to see; saw more and therefore loved and hated
more. To be with him was to find oneself transported to one
of the frontiers of human consciousness. For an inhabitant of
the safe metropolis of thought and feeling it was a most
exciting experience.

(From "D. H. Lawrence," *The Olive Tree*)

Famagusta or Paphos

Famagusta reminded me irresistibly of Metro-Goldwyn-
Mayer's back lot at Culver City. There, under the high fog
of the Pacific, one used to wander between the façades of
Romeo and Juliet's Verona into Tarzan's jungle, and out
again, through Bret Harte, into Harun al-Rashid and *Pride
and Prejudice*. Here, in Cyprus, the mingling of styles and
epochs is no less extravagant, and the sets are not merely
realistic—they are real. At Salamis, in the suburbs of Famagusta, one can shoot *Quo Vadis* against a background of solid
masonry and genuine marble. And downtown, overlooking the
harbor, stands the Tower of Othello (screen play by William
Shakespeare, additional dialogue by Louella Katz); and the
Tower of Othello is not the cardboard gazebo to which the
theater has accustomed us, but a huge High Renaissance gun
emplacement that forms part of a defense system as massive,
elaborate and scientific as the Maginot Line. Within the cir-
cuit of those prodigious Venetian walls lies the blank space
that was once a flourishing city—a blank space with a few
patches of modern Turkish squalor, a few Byzantine ruins and,
outdoing all the rest in intrinsic improbability, the Mosque.
Flanked by the domes and colonnades of a pair of pretty little
Ottoman buildings, the Mosque is a magnificent piece of thirteenth-century French Gothic, with a factory chimney, the
minaret, tacked onto the north end of its façade. Golden and
warm under the Mediterranean blue, this lesser Chartres rises
from the midst of palms and carob trees and Oriental coffee
shops. The muezzin (reinforced—for this is the twentieth cen-

tury—by loud-speakers) calls from his holy smoke stack, and in what was once the Cathedral of St. Nicholas, the Faithful— or, if you prefer, the Infidels—pray not to an image or an altar, but toward Mecca.

We climbed back into the car. "Paphos," I said to the chauffeur, as matter-of-factly as in more familiar surroundings one would say, "Selfridge's," or "the Waldorf-Astoria." But the birthplace of Venus, it turned out, was a long way off and the afternoon was already half spent. Besides, the driver assured us (and the books confirmed it) there was really nothing to see at Paphos. Better go home and read about the temple and its self-mutilated priests in Frazer. Better still, read nothing, but emulating Mallarmé, write a sonnet on the magical name. *Mes bouquins refermés sur le nom de Paphos.* "My folios closing on the name of Paphos, What fun, with nothing but genius, to elect A ruin blest by a thousand foams beneath The hyacinth of its triumphal days! Let the cold come, with silence like a scythe! I'll wail no dirge if, level with the ground, This white, bright frolic should deny to all Earth's sites the honor of the fancied scene. My hunger, feasting on no mortal fruits, finds in their studied lack an equal savor. Suppose one bright with flesh, human and fragrant! My foot upon some snake where our love stirs the fire, I dream much longer, passionately perhaps, Of the other fruit, the Amazon's burnt breast."

> Mes bouquins refermés sur le nom de Paphos,
> Il m'amuse d'élire avec le seul génie
> Une ruine, par mille écumes bénie
> Sous l'hyacinthe, au loin, de ses jours triomphaux.
>
> Coure le froid avec ses silences de faux,
> Je n'y hululerai pas de vide nénie
> Si ce très blanc ébat au ras du sol dénie
> À tout site l'honneur du paysage faux.
>
> Ma faim qui d'aucuns fruits ici ne se régale
> Trouve en leur docte manque une saveur égale:
> Qu'un éclate de chair humain et parfumant!
>
> Le pied sur quelque guivre où notre amour tisonne,
> Je pense plus longtemps, peut-être éperdument
> À l'autre, au sein brûlé d'une antique amazone.

How close this is to Keats's:

> Heard melodies are sweet, but those unheard
> Are sweeter; therefore, ye soft pipes, play on;
> Not to the sensual ear, but, more endeared,
> Pipe to the spirit ditties of no tone.

Parodying the Grecian Urn in terms of Mallarmé's Amazonian metaphor, we have: "Felt breasts are round, but those unfelt are rounder; therefore, absent paps, swell on." And the Keatsian formula can be applied just as well to Paphos. "Seen archeological remains are interesting; but those unseen are more impressively like what the ruins of Aphrodite's birthplace *ought* to be." All of which, in a judicial summing up, may be said to be, on the one hand, profoundly true and, on the other, completely false. Unvisited ruins, ditties of no tone, the solipsistic love of non-existent bosoms—these are all chemically pure, uncontaminated by those grotesque or horrible irrelevances which Mallarmé called "blasphemies" and which are the very stuff and substance of real life in a body. But this kind of chemical purity (the purity, in Mallarméan phraseology, of dream and Azure) is not the same as the saving purity of the Pure in Heart; this renunciation of irrelevant actuality is not the poverty in which the Poor in Spirit find the Kingdom of Heaven. Liberation is for those who react correctly to given reality, not to their own, or other people's notions and fancies. Enlightenment is not for the Quietists and Puritans who, in their different ways, deny the world, but for those who have learned to accept and transfigure it. Our own private silences are better, no doubt, than the heard melodies inflicted upon us by the juke box. But are they better than *Adieu m'Amour* or the slow movement of the second Razumovsky Quartet? Unless we happen to be greater musicians than Dufay or Beethoven, the answer is, emphatically, No. And what about a love so chemically pure that it finds in the studied lack of fruits a savor equal or superior to that of human flesh? Love is a cognitive process, and in this case nuptial knowledge will be only a knowledge of the lover's imagination in its relations to his physiology. And it is the same with the stay-at-home knowledge of distant ruins. In certain cases—and the case of Paphos, perhaps, is one of them —fancy may do a more obviously pleasing job than archeological research or a sightseer's visit. But, in general, imagination falls immeasurably short of the inventions of Nature and History. By no possibility could I, or even a great poet like Mallarmé, have fabricated Salamis-Famagusta. To which, of course, Mallarmé would have answered that he had no more wish to fabricate Salamis-Famagusta than to reproduce the real, historical Paphos. The picturesque detail, the unique and concrete datum—these held no interest for the poet whose advice to himself and others was: "Exclude the real, because vile; exclude the too precise meaning and *rature ta vague littérature*," correct your literature until it becomes (from the realist's point of view) completely vague. Mallarmé defined literature as the antithesis of journalism. Literature, for him, is never a piece of reporting, never an account of a *chose vue* —a thing seen in the external world or even a thing seen, with any degree of precision, by the inner eye. Both classes of seen things are too concretely real for poetry and must be avoided. Heredity and a visual environment conspired to make of Mallarmé a Manichean Platonist, for whom the world of appearances was nothing or worse than nothing, and the Ideal World everything. Writing in 1867 from Besançon where, a martyr to Secondary Education, he was teaching English to a pack of savage boys who found him boring and ridiculous, he described to his friend Henri Cazalis the consummation of a kind of philosophical conversion. "I have passed through an appalling year. Thought has come to think itself, and I have reached a Pure Conception. . . . I am now perfectly dead and the impurest region in which my spirit can venture is Eternity . . . I am now impersonal and no longer the Stéphane you have known—but the Spiritual Universe's capacity to see and develop itself through that which once was I." In another historical context Mallarmé could have devoted himself to Quietism, to the attainment of a Nirvana apart from and antithetical to the world of appearances. But he lived under the Second Empire and the Third Republic; such a course was out of the question. Besides, he was a poet and, as such, dedicated to the task of "giving a purer meaning to the words of the tribe"—*un sens plus pur aux mots de la tribu.*

"Words," he wrote, "are already sufficiently themselves not to receive any further impression from outside." This "outside," this world of appearances, was to be reduced to nothing, and a world of autonomous and, in some sort, absolute words substituted for it. In other, Mallarméan words, "the pure cup of no liquor but inexhaustible widowhood announces a rose in the darkness"—a mystic rose of purged, immaculate language that is, in some sort, independent of the given realities for which it is supposed to stand, that exists in its own right, according to the laws of its own being. These laws are simultaneously syntactical, musical, etymological and philosophical. To create a poem capable of living autonomously according to these laws is an undertaking to which only the literary equivalent of a great contemplative saint is equal. Such a saint-surrogate was Mallarmé—the most devout and dedicated man of letters who ever lived. But "patriotism is not enough." Nor are letters. The poet's cup can be filled with something more substantial than words and inexhaustible widowhood, and still remain undefiled. It would be possible, if one were sufficiently gifted, to write a sonnet about Salamis-Famagusta as it really is, in all the wild incongruous confusion left by three thousand years of history—a sonnet that should be as perfect a work of art, as immaculate and, though referring to the world of appearances, as self-sufficient and absolute as that which Mallarmé wrote on the name of Paphos and the fact of absence. All *I* can do, alas, is to describe and reflect upon this most improbable reality in words a little less impure, perhaps, than those of the tribe, and in passing to pay my homage to that dedicated denier of reality, that self-mortified saint of letters, whose art enchants me as much today as it did forty years ago when, as an undergraduate, I first discovered it. Dream, azure, blasphemy, studied lack, inexhaustible widowhood—fiddlesticks! But how incredibly beautiful are the verbal objects created in order to express this absurd philosophy!

> Tel qu'en Lui-même enfin l'éternité le change . . .

> Cet unanime blanc conflit
> D'une guirlande avec la même . . .

> Le pur vase d'aucun breuvage
> Que l'inexhaustible veuvage . . .

> O si chère de loin et proche et blanche, si
> Délicieusement toi, Mary, que je songe
> À quelque baume rare émané par mensonge
> Sur aucun bouquetier de cristal obscurci . . .

Treasures of sound and syntax, such lines are endowed with some of the intense *thereness* of natural objects seen by the transfiguring eye of the lover or the mystic. Utterly dissimilar from the given marvels of the world, they are yet, in some obscure way, the equivalents of the first leaves in springtime, of a spray of plum blossom seen against the sky, of moss growing thick and velvety on the sunless side of oaks, of a seagull riding the wind. The very lines in which Mallarmé exhorts the poet to shut his eyes to given reality partake, in some measure at least, of that reality's divine and apocalyptic nature.

> Ainsi le choeur des romances
> À la levre vole-t-il
> Exclus-en si tu commences
> Le réel parce que vil
> Le sens trop précis rature
> Ta vague littérature.

Reading, one smiles with pleasure—smiles with the same smile as is evoked by the sudden sight of a woodpecker on a tree trunk, of a hummingbird poised on the vibration of its wings before a hibiscus flower.

(From *Tomorrow and Tomorrow and Tomorrow*)

PAINTING

Breughel

Most of our mistakes are fundamentally grammatical. We create our own difficulties by employing an inadequate language to describe facts. Thus, to take one example, we are constantly giving the same name to more than one thing, and more than one name to the same thing. The results, when we come to argue, are deplorable. For we are using a language which does not adequately describe the things about which we are arguing.

The word "painter" is one of those names whose indiscriminate application has led to the worst results. All those who, for whatever reason and with whatever intentions, put brushes to canvas and make pictures, are called without distinction, painters. Deceived by the uniqueness of the name, aestheticians have tried to make us believe that there is a single painter-psychology, a single function of painting, a single standard of criticism. Fashion changes and the views of art critics with it. At the present time it is fashionable to believe in form to the exclusion of subject. Young people almost swoon away with excess of aesthetic emotion before a Matisse. Two generations ago they would have been wiping their eyes before the latest Landseer. (Ah, those more than human, those positively Christ-like dogs—how they moved, what lessons they taught! There had been no religious painting like Landseer's since Carlo Dolci died.)

These historical considerations should make us chary of believing too exclusively in any single theory of art. One kind of painting, one set of ideas are fashionable at any given moment. They are made the basis of a theory which condemns all other kinds of painting and all preceding critical theories. The process constantly repeats itself.

At the present moment, it is true, we have achieved an unprecedentedly tolerant eclecticism. We are able, if we are up-to-date, to enjoy everything, from Negro sculpture to Locca della Robbia and from Magnasco to Byzantine mosaics. But it is an eclecticism achieved at the expense of almost the whole content of the various works of art considered. What we have learned to see in all these works is their formal qualities, which we abstract and arbitrarily call essential. The subject of the work, with all that the painter desired to express in it beyond his feelings about formal relations, contemporary criticism rejects as unimportant. The young painter scrupulously avoids introducing into his pictures anything that might be mistaken for a story, or the expression of a view of life, while the young *Kunstforscher* turns, as though at an act of exhibitionism, from any manifestation by a contemporary of any such forbidden interest in drama or philosophy. True, the old masters are indulgently permitted to illustrate stories and express their thoughts about the world. Poor devils, they knew no better! Your modern observer makes allowance for their ignorance and passes over in silence all that is not a matter of formal relations. The admirers of Giotto (as numerous today as were the admirers of Guido Reni a hundred years ago) contrive to look at the master's frescoes without considering what they represent, or what the painter desired to express. Every germ of drama or meaning is disinfected out of them; only the composition is admired. The process is analogous to reading Latin verses without understanding them —simply for the sake of the rhythmical rumbling of the hexameters.

It would be absurd, of course, to deny the importance of formal relations. No picture can hold together without composition and no good painter is without some specific passion for form as such—just as no good writer is without a passion for words and the arrangement of words. It is obvious that no man can adequately express himself, unless he takes an interest in the terms which he proposes to use as his medium of expression. Not all painters are interested in the same sort of forms. Some, for example, have a passion for masses and the surfaces of solids. Others delight in lines. Some compose in three dimensions. Others like to make silhouettes on the flat. Some like to make the surface of the paint smooth and, as it were, translucent, so that the objects represented in the picture can be seen distinct and separate, as through a sheet of glass. Others (as for example Rembrandt) love to make a rich thick surface which shall absorb and draw together into one whole all the objects represented, and that in spite of the depth of the composition and the distance of the objects from the plane of the picture. All these purely aesthetic considerations are, as I have said, important. All artists are interested in them; but almost none are interested in them to the exclusion of everything else. It is very seldom indeed that we find a painter who can be inspired merely by his interest in form and texture to paint a picture. Good painters of "abstract" subjects or even of still lives are rare. Apples and solid geometry do not stimulate a man to express his feelings about form and make a composition. All thoughts and emotions are interdependent. In the words of the dear old song,

> The roses round the door
> Make me love mother more.

One feeling is excited by another. Our faculties work best in a congenial emotional atmosphere. For example, Mantegna's faculty for making noble arrangements of forms was stimulated by his feelings about heroic and god-like humanity. Expressing those feelings, which he found exciting, he also expressed—and in the most perfect manner of which he was capable—his feelings about masses, surfaces, solids, and voids. "The roses round the door"—his hero worship—"made him love mother more"—made him, by stimulating his faculty for composition, paint better. If Isabella d'Este had made him paint apples, table napkins and bottles, he would have produced, being uninterested in these objects, a poor composition. And yet, from a purely formal point of view, apples, bottles and napkins are quite as interesting as human bodies and faces. But Mantegna—and with him the majority of painters—did not happen to be very passionately interested in these inanimate objects. When one is bored one becomes boring.

> The apples round the door
> Make me a frightful bore.

Inevitably; unless I happen to be so exclusively interested in form that I can paint anything that has a shape; or unless I happen to possess some measure of that queer pantheism, that animistic superstition which made Van Gogh regard the humblest of common objects as being divinely or devilishly alive. *"Crains dans le mur aveugle un regard qui t'épie."* If a painter can do that, he will be able, like Van Gogh, to make pictures of cabbage fields and the bedrooms of cheap hotels that shall be as wildly dramatic as a Rape of the Sabines.

The contemporary fashion is to admire beyond all others

the painter who can concentrate on the formal side of his art and produce pictures which are entirely devoid of literature. Old Renoir's apophthegm, *"Un peintre, voyez-vous, qui a le sentiment du téton et des fesses, est un homme sauvé,"* is considered by the purists suspiciously latitudinarian. A painter who has the sentiment of the pap and the buttocks is a painter who portrays real models with gusto. Your pure aesthete should only have a feeling for hemispheres, curved lines and surfaces. But this "sentiment of the buttocks" is common to all good painters. It is the lowest common measure of the whole profession. It is possible, like Mantegna, to have a passionate feeling for all that is solid, and at the same time to be a stoic philosopher and a hero-worshiper; possible, with Michelangelo, to have a complete realization of breasts and also an interest in the soul or, like Rubens, to have a sentiment for human greatness as well as for human rumps. The greater includes the less; great dramatic or reflective painters know everything that the aestheticians who paint geometrical pictures, apples or buttocks know, and a great deal more besides. What they have to say about formal relations, though important, is only a part of what they have to express. The contemporary insistence on form to the exclusion of everything else is an absurdity. So was the older insistence on exact imitation and sentiment to the exclusion of form. There need be no exclusions. In spite of the single name, there are many different kinds of painters and all of them, with the exception of those who cannot paint, and those whose minds are trivial, vulgar and tedious, have a right to exist.

All classifications and theories are made after the event; the facts must first occur before they can be tabulated and methodized. Reversing the historical process, we attack the facts forearmed with theoretical prejudice. Instead of considering each fact on its own merits, we ask how it fits into the theoretical scheme. At any given moment a number of meritorious facts fail to fit into the fashionable theory and have to be ignored. Thus El Greco's art failed to conform with the ideal of good painting held by Philip the Second and his contemporaries. The Sienese primitives seemed to the seventeenth and eighteenth centuries incompetent barbarians. Under the influence of Ruskin, the later nineteenth century contrived to dislike almost all architecture that was not Gothic. And the early twentieth century, under the influence of the French, deplores and ignores, in painting, all that is literary, reflective or dramatic.

In every age theory has caused men to like much that was bad and reject much that was good. The only prejudice that the ideal art critic should have is against the incompetent, the mentally dishonest and the futile. The number of ways in which good pictures can be painted is quite incalculable, depending only on the variability of the human mind. Every good painter invents a new way of painting. Is this man a competent painter? Has he something to say, is he genuine? These are the questions a critic must ask himself. Not, Does he conform with my theory of imitation, or distortion, or moral purity, or significant form?

There is one painter against whom, it seems to me, theoretical prejudice has always most unfairly told. I mean the elder Breughel. Looking at his best paintings I find that I can honestly answer in the affirmative all the questions which a critic may legitimately put himself. He is highly competent aesthetically; he has plenty to say; his mind is curious, interesting and powerful; and he has no false pretensions, is entirely honest. And yet he has never enjoyed the high reputation to which his merits entitle him. This is due, I think, to the fact that his work has never quite squared with any of the various critical theories which since his days have had a vogue in the aesthetic world.

A subtle colorist, a sure and powerful draftsman, and possessing powers of composition that enable him to marshal the innumerable figures with which his pictures are filled into pleasingly decorative groups (built up, as we see, when we try to analyze his methods of formal arrangement, out of individually flat, silhouette-like shapes standing in a succession of receding planes), Breughel can boast of purely aesthetic merits that ought to endear him even to the strictest sect of the Pharisees. Coated with this pure aesthetic jam, the bitter pill of his literature might easily, one would suppose, be swallowed. If Giotto's dalliance with sacred history be forgiven him, why may not Breughel be excused for being an anthropologist and a social philosopher? To which I tentatively answer: Giotto is forgiven, because we have so utterly ceased to believe in Catholic Christianity that we can easily ignore the subject matter of his pictures and concentrate only on their formal qualities; Breughel, on the other hand, is unforgivable because he made comments on humanity that are still interesting to us. From his subject matter we cannot escape; it touches us too closely to be ignored. That is why Breughel is despised by all up-to-date *Kunstforschers*.

And even in the past, when there was no theoretical objection to the mingling of literature and painting, Breughel failed, for another reason, to get his due. He was considered low, gross, a mere comedian, and as such unworthy of serious consideration. Thus, the *Encyclopedia Britannica*, which in these matters may be safely relied on to give the current opinion of a couple of generations ago, informs us, in the eleven lines which it parsimoniously devotes to Peter Breughel that "the subjects of his pictures are chiefly humorous figures, like those of D. Teniers; and if he wants the delicate touch and silvery clearness of that master, he has abundant spirit and comic power."

Whoever wrote these words—and they might have been written by any one desirous, fifty years ago, of playing for safety and saying the right thing—can never have taken the trouble to look at any of the pictures painted by Breughel when he was a grown and accomplished artist.

In his youth, it is true, he did a great deal of hack work for a dealer who specialized in caricatures and devils in the manner of Hieronymus Bosch. But his later pictures, painted when he had really mastered the secrets of his art, are not comic at all. They are studies of peasant life, they are allegories, they are religious pictures of the most strangely reflective cast, they are exquisitely poetical landscapes. Breughel died at the height of his powers. But there is enough of his mature work in existence—at Antwerp, at Brussels, at Naples and above all at Vienna—to expose the fatuity of the classical verdict and exhibit him for what he was: the first landscape painter of his century, the acutest student of manners, and the wonderfully skillful pictorial expounder or suggester of a view of life. It is at Vienna, indeed, that Breughel's art can best be studied in all its aspects. For Vienna possesses practically all his best pictures of whatever kind. The scattered pictures at Antwerp, Brussels, Paris, Naples and elsewhere give one but the faintest notion of Breughel's powers. In the Vienna galleries are collected more than a dozen of his pictures, all belonging to his last and best period. The Tower of Babel, the great Calvary, the Numbering of the People at Bethlehem, the two Winter Landscapes and the Autumn Landscape, the Conversion of Saint Paul, the Battle between the Israelites and the Philistines, the Marriage Feast and the Peasants' Dance—all these admirable works are here. It is on these that he must be judged.

There are four landscapes at Vienna: the Dark Day (January) and Huntsmen in the Snow (February), a November landscape (the Return of the Cattle), and the Numbering of the People at Bethlehem which in spite of its name is little more than a landscape with figures. This last, like the February Landscape and the Massacre of the Innocents at Brussels, is a study of snow. Snow scenes lent themselves particularly well to Breughel's style of painting. For a snowy background has the effect of making all dark or colored objects seen against it appear in the form of very distinct, sharp-edged silhouettes. Breughel does in all his compositions what the snow does in nature. All the objects in his pictures (which are composed in a manner that reminds one very much of the Japanese) are paper-thin silhouettes arranged, plane after plane, like the theatrical scenery in the depth of the stage. Consequently in the painting of snow scenes, where nature starts by imitating his habitual method, he achieves an almost disquieting degree of fundamental realism. Those hunters stepping down over the brow of the hill toward the snowy valley with its frozen ponds are Jack Frost himself and his crew. The crowds who move about the white streets of Bethlehem have their being in an absolute winter, and those ferocious troopers looting and innocent-hunting in the midst of a Christmas card landscape are a part of the very army of winter, and the innocents they kill are the young green shoots of the earth.

Breughel's method is less fundamentally compatible with the snowless landscapes of January and November. The different planes stand apart a little too flatly and distinctly. It needs a softer, bloomier kind of painting to recapture the intimate quality of such scenes as those he portrays in these two pictures. A born painter of Autumn, for example, would have fused the beasts, the men, the trees and the distant mountains into a hazier unity, melting all together, the near and the far, in the rich surface of his paint. Breughel painted too transparently and too flatly to be the perfect interpreter of such landscapes. Still, even in terms of his not entirely suitable convention he has done marvels. The Autumn Day is a thing of the most exquisite beauty. Here, as in the more somberly dramatic January Landscape, he makes a subtle use of golds and yellows and browns, creating a sober yet luminous harmony of colors. The November Landscape is entirely placid and serene; but in the Dark Day he has staged one of those natural dramas of the sky and earth—a conflict between light and darkness. Light breaks from under clouds along the horizon, shines up from the river in the valley that lies in the middle distance, glitters on the peaks of the mountains. The foreground, which represents the crest of a wooded hill, is dark; and the leafless trees growing on the slopes are black against the sky. These two pictures are the most beautiful sixteenth-century landscapes of which I have any knowledge. They are intensely poetical, yet sober and not excessively picturesque or romantic. Those fearful crags and beetling precipices of which the older painters were so fond do not appear in these examples of Breughel's maturest work.

Breughel's anthropology is as delightful as his nature poetry. He knew his Flemings, knew them intimately, both in their

prosperity and during the miserable years of strife, of rebellion, of persecution, of war and consequent poverty which
followed the advent of the Reformation in Flanders.

A Fleming himself, and so profoundly and ineradicably a
Fleming that he was able to go to Italy, and, like his great
countryman in the previous century, Roger van der Weyden,
return without the faintest tincture of Italianism—he was perfectly qualified to be the natural historian of the Flemish folk.
He exhibits them mostly in those moments of orgiastic gaiety
with which they temper the laborious monotony of their
daily lives: eating enormously, drinking, uncouthly dancing,
indulging in that peculiarly Flemish scatological waggery. The
Wedding Feast and the Peasants' Dance, both at Vienna, are
superb examples of this anthropological type of painting. Nor
must we forget those two curious pictures, the Battle between
Carnival and Lent and the Children's Games. They too show
us certain aspects of the joyous side of Flemish life. But the
view is not of an individual scene, casually seized at its height
and reproduced. These two pictures are systematic and ency-
clopedic. In one he illustrates all children's games; in the
other all the amusements of carnival, with all the forces arrayed on the side of asceticism. In the same way he represents,
in his extraordinary Tower of Babel, all the processes of
building. These pictures are handbooks of their respective
subjects.

Breughel's fondness for generalizing and systematizing is
further illustrated in his allegorical pieces. The Triumph of
Death, at the Prado, is appalling in its elaboration and com-
pleteness. The fantastic "Dulle Griet" at Antwerp is an almost
equally elaborate triumph of evil. His illustrations to proverbs
and parables belong to the same class. They show him to have
been a man profoundly convinced of the reality of evil and of
the horrors which this mortal life, not to mention eternity,
hold in store for suffering humanity. The world is a horrible
place; but in spite of this, or precisely because of this, men
and women eat, drink and dance, Carnival tilts against Lent
and triumphs, if only for a moment; children play in the
streets, people get married in the midst of gross rejoicings.

But of all Breughel's pictures the one most richly suggestive
of reflection is not specifically allegorical or systematic. Christ
carrying the Cross is one of his largest canvases, thronged with
small figures rhythmically grouped against a wide and romantic background. The composition is simple, pleasing in itself,
and seems to spring out of the subject instead of being imposed
on it. So much for pure aesthetics.

Of the Crucifixion and the Carrying of the Cross there are
hundreds of representations by the most admirable and diverse

masters. But of all that I have ever seen this Calvary of Breughel's is the most suggestive and, dramatically, the most appalling. For all other masters have painted these dreadful scenes from within, so to speak, outwards. For them Christ is the center, the divine hero of the tragedy; this is the fact from which they start; it affects and transforms all the other facts, justifying, in a sense, the horror of the drama and ranging all that surrounds the central figure in an ordered hierarchy of good and evil. Breughel, on the other hand, starts from the outside and works inwards. He represents the scene as it would have appeared to any casual spectator on the road to Golgotha on a certain spring morning in the year 33 A.D. Other artists have pretended to be angels, painting the scene with a knowledge of its significance. But Breughel resolutely remains a human onlooker. What he shows is a crowd of people walking briskly in holiday joyfulness up the slopes of a hill. On the top of the hill, which is seen in the middle distance on the right, are two crosses with thieves fastened to them, and between them a little hole in the ground in which another cross is soon to be planted. Round the crosses, on the bare hill top stands a ring of people, who have come out with their picnic baskets to look on at the free entertainment offered by the ministers of justice. Those who have already taken their stand round the crosses are the prudent ones; in these days we should see them with camp stools and thermos flasks, six hours ahead of time, in the vanguard of the queue for a Melba night at Covent Garden. The less provident or more adventurous people are in the crowd coming up the hill with the third and greatest of the criminals whose cross is to take the place of honor between the other two. In their anxiety not to miss any of the fun on the way up, they forget that they will have to take back seats at the actual place of execution. But it may be, of course, that they have reserved their places, up there. At Tyburn one could get an excellent seat in a private box for half a crown; with the ticket in one's pocket, one could follow the cart all the way from the prison, arrive with the criminal and yet have a perfect view of the performance. In these later days, when cranky humanitarianism has so far triumphed that hangings take place in private and Mrs. Thompson's screams are not even allowed to be recorded on the radio, we have to be content with reading about executions, not with seeing them. The impresarios who sold seats at Tyburn have been replaced by titled newspaper proprietors who sell juicy descriptions of Tyburn to a prodigiously much larger public. If people were still hanged at Marble Arch, Lord Riddell would be much less rich.

That eager, tremulous, lascivious interest in blood and

beastliness which in these more civilized days we can only satisfy at one remove from reality in the pages of our newspapers, was franklier indulged in Breughel's day; the naïve ingenuous brute in man was less sophisticated, was given longer rope, and joyously barks and wags its tail round the appointed victim. Seen thus, impassively, from the outside, the tragedy does not purge or uplift; it appalls and makes desperate; or it may even inspire a kind of gruesome mirth. The same situation may often be either tragic or comic, according as it is seen through the eyes of those who suffer or those who look on. (Shift the point of vision a little and Macbeth could be paraphrased as a roaring farce.) Breughel makes a concession to the high tragic convention by placing in the foreground of his picture a little group made up of the holy women weeping and wringing their hands. They stand quite apart from the other figures in the picture and are fundamentally out of harmony with them, being painted in the style of Roger van der Weyden. A little oasis of passionate spirituality, an island of consciousness and comprehension in the midst of the pervading stupidity and brutishness. Why Breughel put them into his picture is difficult to guess; perhaps for the benefit of the conventionally religious, perhaps out of respect for tradition; or perhaps he found his own creation too depressing and added this noble irrelevance to reassure himself.

(From *Along the Road*)

Meditation on El Greco

The pleasures of ignorance are as great, in their way, as the pleasures of knowledge. For though the light is good, though it is satisfying to be able to place the things that surround one in the categories of an ordered and comprehensible system, it is also good to find oneself sometimes in the dark, it is pleasant now and then to have to speculate with vague bewilderment about a world, which ignorance has reduced to a quantity of mutually irrelevant happenings dotted, like so many unexplored and fantastic islands, on the face of a vast ocean of incomprehension. For me, one of the greatest charms of travel consists in the fact that it offers unique opportunities for indulging in the luxury of ignorance. I am not one of those conscientious travelers who, before they visit a new country, spend weeks mugging up its geology, its economics,

its art history, its literature. I prefer, at any rate during my
first few visits, to be a thoroughly unintelligent tourist. It is
only later, when my ignorance has lost its virgin freshness,
that I begin to read what the intelligent tourist would have
known by heart before he bought his tickets. I read—and
forthwith, in a series of apocalypses, my isolated and mysteriously odd impressions begin to assume significance, my
jumbled memories fall harmoniously into patterns. The pleasures of ignorance have given place to the pleasures of
knowledge.

I have only twice visited Spain—not often enough, that is
to say, to have grown tired of ignorance. I still enjoy bewilderedly knowing as little as possible about all I see between
the Pyrenees and Cape Trafalgar. Another two or three visits,
and the time will be ripe for me to go to the London Library
and look up "Spain" in the subject index. In one of the numerous, the all too numerous, books there catalogued I shall find,
no doubt, the explanation of a little mystery that has mildly
and intermittently puzzled me for quite a number of years—
ever since, at one of those admirable Loan Exhibitions in
Burlington House, I saw for the first time a version of El
Greco's *Dream of Philip II*.

This curious composition, familiar to every visitor to the
Escorial, represents the king, dressed and gloved like an
undertaker in inky black, kneeling on a well-stuffed cushion
in the center foreground; beyond him, on the left, a crowd
of pious kneelers, some lay, some clerical, but all manifestly
saintly, are looking upwards into a heaven full of waltzing
angels, cardinal virtues and biblical personages, grouped in a
circle round the Cross and the luminous monogram of the
Saviour. On the right a very large whale gigantically yawns,
and a vast concourse, presumably of the damned, is hurrying
(in spite of all that we learned in childhood about the
anatomy of whales) down its crimson throat. A curious
picture, I repeat, and, as a work of art, not remarkably good;
there are many much better Grecos belonging even to the same
youthful period. Nevertheless, in spite of its mediocrity, it is
a picture for which I have a special weakness. I like it for the
now sadly unorthodox reason that the subject interests me.
And the subject interests me, because I do not know what the
subject is. For this dream of King Philip—what was it? Was
it a visionary anticipation of the Last Judgment? A mystical
peep into Heaven? An encouraging glimpse of the Almighty's
short way with heretics? I do not know—do not at present
even desire to know. In the face of so extravagant a phantasy
as this of Greco's, the pleasures of ignorance are peculiarly
intense. Confronted by the mysterious whale, the undertaker

king, the swarming aërial saints and scurrying sinners, I give my fancy license and fairly wallow in the pleasure of bewilderedly not knowing.

The fancy I like best of all that have occurred to me is the one which affirms that this queer picture was painted as a prophetic and symbolic autobiography, that it was meant to summarize hieroglyphically the whole of Greco's future development. For that whale in the right foreground—that great-grandfather of Moby Dick, with his huge yawn, his crimson gullet and the crowd of the damned descending, like bank clerks at six o'clock into the Underground—that whale, I say, is the most significantly autobiographical object in all El Greco's early pictures. For whither are they bound, those hastening damned? "Down the red lane," as our nurses used to say when they were encouraging us to swallow the uneatable viands of childhood. Down the red lane into a dim inferno of tripes. Down, in a word, into that strange and rather frightful universe which Greco's spirit seems to have come more and more exclusively, as he grew older, to inhabit. For in the Cretan's later painting every personage is a Jonah. Yes, *every* personage. Which is where *The Dream of Philip II* reveals itself as being imperfectly prophetic, a mutilated symbol. It is for the damned alone that the whale opens his mouth. If El Greco had wanted to tell the whole truth about his future development, he would have sent the blessed to join them, or at least have provided his saints and angels with another monster of their own, a supernal whale floating head downwards among the clouds, with a second red lane ascending, straight and narrow, toward a swallowed Heaven. Paradise and Purgatory, Hell, and even the common Earth—for El Greco in his artistic maturity, every department of the universe was situated in the belly of a whale. His Annunciations and Assumptions, his Agonies and Transfigurations and Crucifixions, his Martyrdoms and Stigmatizations are all, without exception, visceral events. Heaven is no larger than the Black Hole of Calcutta, and God Himself is whale-engulfed.

Critics have tried to explain El Greco's pictorial agorophobia in terms of his early, Cretan education. There is no space in his pictures, they assure us, because the typical art of that Byzantium, which was El Greco's spiritual home, was the mosaic, and the mosaic is innocent of depth. A specious explanation, whose only defect is that it happens to be almost entirely beside the point. To begin with, the Byzantine mosaic was not invariably without depth. Those extraordinary eighth-century mosaics in the Omeyyid mosque at Damascus, for example, are as spacious and airy as impressionist landscapes. They are, it is true, somewhat exceptional specimens of the

art. But even the commoner shut-in mosaics have really
nothing to do with El Greco's painting, for the Byzantine
saints and kings are enclosed, or, to be more accurate, are
flatly inlaid in a kind of two-dimensional abstraction—in a
pure Euclidean, plane-geometrical Heaven of gold or blue.
Their universe never bears the smallest resemblance to that
whale's belly in which every one of El Greco's personages
has his or her mysterious and appalling being. El Greco's
world is no Flatland; there is depth in it—just a little depth.
It is precisely this that makes it seem such a disquieting
world. In their two-dimensional abstraction the personages of
the Byzantine mosaists are perfectly at home; they are adapted
to their environment. But, solid and three-dimensional, made
to be the inhabitants of a spacious universe, El Greco's people are shut up in a world where there is perhaps just room
enough to swing a cat, but no more. They are in prison and,
which makes it worse, in a visceral prison. For all that surrounds them is organic, animal. Clouds, rock, drapery have
all been mysteriously transformed into mucus and skinned
muscle and peritoneum. The Heaven into which Count Orgaz
ascends is like some cosmic operation for appendicitis. The
Madrid *Resurrection* is a resurrection in a digestive tube. And
from the later pictures we receive the gruesome impression
that all the personages, both human and divine, have begun to
suffer a process of digestion, are being gradually assimilated
to their visceral surroundings. Even in the Madrid *Resurrection* the forms and texture of the naked flesh have assumed a
strangely tripe-like aspect. In the case of the nudes in *Laocoon*
and *The Opening of the Seventh Seal* (both of them works of
El Greco's last years) this process of assimilation has been
carried a good deal further. After seeing their draperies and
the surrounding landscape gradually peptonized and transformed, the unhappy Jonahs of Toledo discover, to their
horror, that they themselves are being digested. Their bodies,
their arms and legs, their faces, fingers, toes are ceasing to be
humanly their own; they are becoming—the process is slow
but inexorably sure—part of the universal Whale's internal
workings. It is lucky for them that El Greco died when he
did. Twenty years more, and the Trinity, the Communion of
Saints and all the human race would have found themselves
reduced to hardly distinguishable excrescences on the surface
of a cosmic gut. The most favored might perhaps have aspired
to be taenias and trematodes.

For myself, I am very sorry that El Greco did not live to
be as old as Titian. At eighty or ninety he would have been
producing an almost abstract art—a cubism without cubes,
organic, purely visceral. What pictures he would then have

painted! Beautiful, thrilling, profoundly appalling. For appalling are even the pictures he painted in middle age, dreadful in spite of their extraordinary power and beauty. This swallowed universe into which he introduces us is one of the most disquieting creations of the human mind. One of the most puzzling too. For what were El Greco's reasons for driving mankind down the red lane? What induced him to take God out of His boundless Heaven and shut Him up in a fish's gut? One can only obscurely speculate. All that I am quite certain of is that there were profounder and more important reasons for the whale than the memory of the mosaics—the wholly unvisceral mosaics—which he may have seen in the course of a Cretan childhood, a Venetian and Roman youth. Nor will a disease of the eye account, as some have claimed, for his strange artistic development. Diseases must be very grave indeed before they become completely coextensive with their victims. That men are affected by their illnesses is obvious; but it is no less obvious that, except when they are almost *in extremis,* they are something more than the sum of their morbid symptoms. Dostoevsky was not merely personified epilepsy, Keats was other things besides a simple lump of pulmonary tuberculosis. Men make use of their illnesses at least as much as they are made use of by them. It is likely enough that El Greco had something wrong with his eyes. But other people have had the same disease without for that reason painting pictures like the *Laocoon* and *The Opening of the Seventh Seal.* To say that El Greco was just a defective eyesight is absurd; he was a man who used a defective eyesight.

Used it for what purpose? to express what strange feeling about the world, what mysterious philosophy? It is hard indeed to answer. For El Greco belongs as a metaphysician (every significant artist is a metaphysician, a propounder of beauty-truths and form-theories) to no known school. The most one can say, by way of classification, is that, like most of the great artists of the Baroque, he believed in the validity of ecstasy, of the non-rational, "numinous" experiences out of which, as a raw material, the reason fashions the gods or the various attributes of God. But the kind of ecstatic experience artistically rendered and meditated on by El Greco was quite different from the kind of experience which is described and symbolically "rationalized" in the painting, sculpture and architecture of the great Baroque artists of the *seicento.* Those mass-producers of spirituality, the Jesuits, had perfected a simple technique for the fabrication of orthodox ecstasies. They had cheapened an experience, hitherto accessible only to the spiritually wealthy, and so placed it within the reach of all. What the Italian *seicento* artists so brilliantly and copiously rendered was this cheapened experience and the metaphysic in terms of which it could be rationalized. "St. Teresa for All." "A John of the Cross in every Home." Such were, or might have been, their slogans. Was it to be wondered at if their sublimities were a trifle theatrical, their tenderness treacly, their spiritual intuitions rather commonplace and vulgar? Even the greatest of the Baroque artists were not remarkable for subtlety and spiritual refinement.

With these rather facile ecstasies and the orthodox Counter-Reformation theology in terms of which they could be interpreted, El Greco has nothing to do. The bright reassuring Heaven, the smiling or lachrymose, but always all too human divinities, the stage immensities and stage mysteries, all the stock-in-trade of the *seicentisti*, are absent from his pictures. There is ecstasy and flamy aspiration; but always ecstasy and aspiration, as we have seen, within the belly of a whale. El Greco seems to be talking all the time about the physiological root of ecstasy, not the spiritual flower; about the primary corporeal facts of numinous experience, not the mental derivatives from them. However vulgarly, the artists of the Baroque were concerned with the flower, not the root, with the derivatives and theological interpretations, not the brute facts of immediate physical experience. Not that they were ignorant of the physiological nature of these primary facts. Bernini's astonishing *St. Teresa* proclaims it in the most unequivocal fashion; and it is interesting to note that in this statue (as well as in the very similar and equally astonishing *Ludovica Albertoni* in San Franceso a Ripa) he gives to the draperies a kind of organic and, I might say, intestinal lusciousness of form. A little softened, smoothed and simplified, the robe of the great mystic would be indistinguishable from the rest of the swallowed landscape inside El Greco's whale. Bernini saves the situation (from the Counter-Reformer's point of view) by introducing into his composition the figure of the dart-brandishing angel. This aerial young creature is the inhabitant of an unswallowed Heaven. He carries with him the implication of infinite spaces. Charmingly and a little preposterously (the hand which holds the fiery dart has a delicately crook'd little finger, like the hand of some too refined young person in the act of raising her tea-cup), the angel symbolizes the spiritual flower of ecstasy, whose physiological root is the swooning Teresa in her peritoneal robe. Bernini is, spiritually speaking, a *plein-airiste*.

Not so El Greco. So far as he is concerned, there is nothing outside the whale. The primary physiological fact of religious experience is also, for him, the final fact. He remains consistently on the plane of that visceral consciousness which we so largely ignore, but with which our ancestors (as their language proves) did so much of their feeling and thinking. "Where is thy zeal and thy strength, the sounding of the bowels and of thy mercies toward me?" "My heart is turned within me, my repentings are kindled together." "I will bless the Lord who hath given me counsel; my reins also instruct me in the night season." "For God is my record, how greatly I long after you all in the bowels of Jesus Christ." "For Thou hast possessed my reins." "Is Ephraim my dear son? . . . Therefore my bowels are troubled for him." The Bible abounds in such phrases—phrases which strike the modern reader as queer, a bit indelicate, even repellent. We are accustomed to thinking of ourselves as thinking entirely with our heads. Wrongly, as the physiologists have shown. For what we think and feel and are is to a great extent determined by the state of our ductless glands and our viscera. The Psalmist drawing instruction from his reins, the Apostle with his yearning bowels, are thoroughly in the modern physiological movement.

El Greco lived at a time when the reality of the primary visceral consciousness was still recognized—when the heart and the liver, the spleen and reins did all a man's feeling for him, and the four humors of blood, phlegm, choler and melancholy determined his character and imposed his passing moods. Even the loftiest experiences were admitted to be primarily physiological. Teresa knew God in terms of an exquisite pain in her heart, her side, her bowels. But while Teresa, and along with her the generality of human beings, found it natural to pass from the realm of physiology into that of the spirit—from the belly of the whale out into the wide open sky—El Greco obstinately insisted on remaining swallowed. His meditations were all of religious experience and ecstasy—but always of religious experience in its raw physiological state, always of primary, immediate, visceral ecstasy. He expressed these meditations in terms of Christian symbols—of symbols, that is to say, habitually employed to describe experiences quite different from the primary physiological states on which he was accustomed to dwell. It is the contrast between these symbols, with their currently accepted significance, and the special private use to which El Greco puts them—it is this strange contrast which gives to El Greco's pictures their peculiarly disquieting quality. For the Christian symbols remind us of all the spiritual open spaces—the open spaces of altruistic feeling, the open spaces of abstract thought, the open spaces of free-floating spiritual ecstasy. El Greco imprisons them, claps them up in a fish's gut. The symbols of the spiritual open spaces are compelled by him to serve as a

language in terms of which he talks about the close imme-
diacies of visceral awareness, about the ecstasy that anni-
hilates the personal soul, not by dissolving it out into universal
infinity, but by drawing it down and drowning it in the warm,
pulsating, tremulous darkness of the body.

Well, I have wandered far and fancifully from the undertaker king and his enigmatic nightmare of whales and Jonahs.
But imaginative wandering is the privilege of the ignorant.
When one doesn't know one is free to invent. I have seized
the opportunity while it presented itself. One of these days I
may discover what the picture is about, and when that has
happened I shall no longer be at liberty to impose my own
interpretations. Imaginative criticism is essentially an art of
ignorance. It is only because we don't know what a writer
or artist meant to say that we are free to concoct meanings of
our own. If El Greco had somewhere specifically told us what
he meant to convey by painting in terms of Black Holes and
mucus, I should not now be in a position to speculate. But
luckily he never told us; I am justified in letting my fancy
loose to wander.

(From Music at Night)

Form and Spirit in Art

A painter or a sculptor can be simultaneously representational and nonrepresentational. In their architectural backgrounds and, above all, in their draperies, many works even
of the Renaissance and the Baroque incorporate passages of
almost unadulterated abstraction. These are often expressive
in the highest degree. Indeed, the whole tone of a representational work may be established, and its inner meaning expressed, by those parts of it which are most nearly abstract.
Thus, the pictures of Piero della Francesca leave upon us
an impression of calm, of power, of intellectual objectivity
and stoical detachment. From those of Cosimo Tura there
emanates a sense of disquiet, even of anguish. When we
analyze the purely pictorial reasons for our perception of
a profound difference in the temperaments of the two artists,
we find that a very important part is played by the least representational elements in their pictures—the draperies. In
Piero's draperies there are large unbroken surfaces, and the
folds are designed to emphasize the elementary solid-geo-
metrical structure of the figures. In Tura's draperies the sur-

faces are broken up, and there is a profusion of sharp angles, of jagged and flame-like forms. Something analogous may be found in the work of two great painters of a later period, Poussin and Watteau. Watteau's draperies are broken into innumerable tiny folds and wrinkles, so that the color of a mantle or a doublet is never the same for half an inch together. The impression left upon the spectator is one of extreme sensibility and the most delicate refinement. Poussin's much broader treatment of these almost non-representational accessories seems to express a more masculine temperament and a philosophy of like akin to Piero's noble stoicism.

In some works the non-representational passages are actually more important than the representational. Thus, in many of Bernini's statues, only the hands, feet and face are fully representational; all the rest is drapery—that is to say, a writhing and undulant abstraction. It is the same with El Greco's paintings. In some of them a third, a half, even as much as two thirds of the entire surface is occupied by low-level organic abstractions, to which, because of their representational context, we give the name of draperies, or clouds, or rocks. These abstractions are powerfully expressive, and it is through them that, to a considerable extent, El Greco tells the private story that underlies the official subject matter of his paintings.

At this point the pure abstractionist will come forward with a question. Seeing that the non-representational passages in representational works are so expressive, why should anyone bother with representation? Why trouble to tell a high-level story about recognizable objects when the more important low-level story about the artist's temperament and reactions to life can be told in terms of pure abstractions? I myself have no objection to pure abstractions which, in the hands of a gifted artist, can achieve their own kind of aesthetic perfection. But this perfection, it seems to me, is a perfection without rather narrow limits. The Greeks called the circle "a perfect figure." And so it is—one cannot improve on it. And yet a composition consisting of a red circle inscribed within a black square would strike us, for all its perfection, as being a little dull. Even aesthetically the perfect figure of a circle is less interesting than the perfect figure of a young woman. This does not mean, of course, that the representation of the young woman by a bad artist will be more valuable, as a picture, than a composition of circles, squares and triangles devised by a good one. But it does mean, I think, that Nature is a richer source of forms than any textbook of plane or solid geometry. Nature has evolved innumerable forms and, as we ourselves move from point to point, we see large numbers of these forms, grouped in an endless variety of ways and thus creating an endless variety of new forms, all of which may be used as the raw materials of works of art. What is given is incomparably richer than what we can invent. But the richness of Nature is, from our point of view, a chaos upon which we, as philosophers, men of science, technicians and artists, must impose various kinds of unity. Now, I would say that, other things being equal, a work of art which imposes aesthetic unity upon a large number of formal and psychological elements is a greater and more interesting work than one in which unity is imposed upon only a few elements. In other words, there is a hierarchy of perfections. Bach's Two-Part Inventions are perfect, in their way. But his *Chromatic Fantasia* is also perfect; and since its perfection involves the imposition of aesthetic unity upon a larger number of elements it is (as we all in fact recognize) a greater work. The old distinction between the Fine Arts and the crafts is based to some extent upon snobbery and other non-aesthetic considerations. But not entirely. In the hierarchy of perfections a perfect vase or a perfect carpet occupies a lower rank than that, say, of Giotto's frescoes at Padua, or Rembrandt's *Polish Rider,* or the *Grande Jatte* of Georges Seurat. In these and a hundred other masterpieces of painting the pictorial whole embraces and unifies a repertory of forms much more numerous, varied, strange and interesting than those which come together in the wholes organized by even the most gifted craftsmen. And, over and above this richer and subtler formal perfection, we are presented with the non-pictorial bonus of a story and, explicit or implicit, a criticism of life. At their best, non-representational compositions achieve perfection; but it is a perfection nearer to that of the jug or rug than to that of the enormously complex and yet completed unified masterpieces of representational art—most of which, as we have seen, contain expressive passages of almost pure abstraction. At the present time it would seem that the most sensible and rewarding thing for a painter to do is (like Braque, for example) to make the best and the most of both worlds, representational as well as non-representational.

Within his own Byzantine-Venetian tradition El Greco did precisely this, combining representation with abstraction in a manner which we are accustomed to regard as characteristically modern. His intention was to use this powerful artistic instrument to express, in visual terms, man's capacity for union with the divine. But the artistic means he employed were such that it was not possible for him to carry out that intention. The existence of a spiritual reality transcendent and yet immanent, absolutely other and yet the sustaining spiritual essence of every being, has frequently been rendered in visual symbols—but not symbols of the kind employed by El Greco. The agitation of quasi-visceral forms in an overcrowded and almost spaceless world, from which non-human Nature has been banished, cannot, in the very nature of things, express man's union with the Spirit who must be worshiped in spirit.

Landscape and the human figure in repose—these are the symbols through which, in the past, the spiritual life has been most clearly and powerfully expressed. "Be still and know that I am God." Recollectedness is the indispensable means to the unitive knowledge of spiritual reality; and though recollectedness should, and by some actually can, be practiced in the midst of the most violent physical activity, it is most effectively symbolized by a body in repose and a face that expresses an inner serenity. The carved or painted Buddhas and Bodhisattvas of India and the Far East are perhaps the most perfect examples of such visual symbols of the spiritual life. Hardly less adequate are the majestic Byzantine figures of Christ, the Virgin and the saints. It seems strange that El Greco, who received his first training from Byzantine masters, should not have recognized the symbolical value of repose, but should have preferred to represent or, through his accessory abstractions, to imply, an agitation wholly incompatible with the spiritual life of which he had read in the pages of Dionysius.

No less strange is the fact that a disciple of Titian should have ignored landscape and that a Neo-Platonist should have failed to perceive that, in the aged master's religious pictures, the only hint of spirituality was to be found, not in the all too human figures, but in the backgrounds of Alpine foothills, peaks and skies. Civilized man spends most of his life in a cozy little universe of material artifacts, of social conventions and of verbalized ideas. Only rarely, if he is the inhabitant of a well-ordered city, does he come into direct contact with the mystery of the non-human world, does he become aware of modes of being incommensurable with his own, of vast, indefinite extensions, of durations all but everlasting. From time immemorial deity has been associated with the boundlessness of earth and sky, with the longevity of trees, rivers and mountains, with Leviathan and the whirlwind, with sunshine and the lilies of the field. Space and time on the cosmic scale are symbols of the infinity and eternity of Spirit. Non-human Nature is the outward and visible expression of the mystery which confronts us when we look into the depths of our own being. The first artists to concern themselves with the spiritual significance of Nature were the Taoist landscape painters of China. "Cherishing the Way, a virtuous man responds to objects. Clarifying his mind, a wise man appreciates forms. As to landscapes, they exist in material substance and soar into the realm of spirit. . . . The virtuous man follows the Way by spiritual insight; the wise man takes the same approach. But the lovers of landscape are led into the Way by a sense of form. . . . The significance which is too subtle to be communicated by means of words of mouth may be grasped by the mind through books and writings. Then how much more so in my case, when I have wandered among the rocks and hills and carefully observed them with my own eyes! I render form by form and appearance by appearance. . . . The truth comprises the expression received through the eyes and recognized by the mind. If, in painting, therefore, the likeness of an object is skillfully portrayed, both the eye and the mind will approve. When the eyes respond and the mind agrees with the objects, the divine spirit may be felt and truth may be attained in the painting." So wrote Tsung Ping who was a contemporary of St. Augustine, in an *Introduction to Landscape Painting,* which has become a Chinese classic. When, twelve hundred years later, European artists discovered landscape, they developed no philosophy to explain and justify what they were doing. That was left to the poets—to Wordsworth, to Shelley, to Whitman. The Presence which they found in Nature, "the Spirit of each spot," is identical with Hsuan P'in, the mysterious Valley Spirit of the Tao Te Ching, who reveals herself to the landscape painter and, by him, is revealed to others in his pictures. But the lack of an explanatory philosophy did not prevent the best of the European landscape painters from making manifest that

> something far more deeply interfused,
> Whose dwelling is the light of setting suns,
> And the round ocean, and the living air,
> And the blue sky, and in the mind of man.

"This is not drawing," Blake exclaimed, when he was shown one of Constable's sketches, "this is inspiration." And though Constable himself protested that it was only drawing, the fact remains that the best of his landscapes are powerful and convincing renderings of the spiritual reality in which all things have their being. Indeed, they are much more adequate as symbols of spiritual life than the majority of the works in which Blake consciously tried to express his spiritualist philosophy. Much less gifted as painter than as poet, and brought up in a deplorable artistic tradition, Blake rarely produced a picture that "comes off" to the extent of expressing what he says so perfectly in his lyrics and in isolated passages of the *Prophetic Books.* Constable, on the other hand, is a great

Nature mystic without knowing or intending it. In this he reminds us of Seurat. "They see poetry in what I do," complained that consummate master of landscape. "No; I apply my method and that is all there is to it." But the method was applied by a painter who combined the most exquisite sensibility with intellectual powers of the first order. Consequently what Seurat supposed to be merely *pointillisme* was in fact inspiration—a vision of the world in which material reality is the symbol and, one might say, the incarnation of an all-embracing spiritual reality. The famous method was the means whereby he told this Taoistic and Wordsworthian story; *pointillisme,* as he used it, permitted him to render empty space as no other painter has ever done, and to impose, through color, an unprecedented degree of unity upon his composition. In Seurat's paintings the near and the far are separate and yet are one. The emptiness which is the symbol of infinity is of the same substance as the finite forms it contains. The transient participates in the eternal, *samsara* and *nirvana* are one and the same. Such is the poetry with which, in spite of himself, Seurat filled those wonderful landscapes of Honfleur and Gravelines and the Seine. And such is the poetry which El Greco, in spite of what seems to have been a conscious desire to imply it, was forced by the nature of his artistic instrument to exclude from every picture he painted. His peculiar treatment of space and form tells a story of obscure happenings in the subconscious mind—of some haunting fear of wide vistas and the open air, some dream of security in the imagined equivalent of a womb. The conscious aspiration toward union with, and perfect freedom in, the divine Spirit is overridden by a subconscious longing for the consolations of some ineffable uterine state.

When we think of it in relation to the great world of human experience, El Greco's universe of swallowed spirit and visceral rapture seems curiously oppressive and disquieting. But considered as an isolated artistic system, how strong and coherent it seems, how perfectly unified, how fascinatingly beautiful. And because of this inner harmony and coherence, it asserts in one way all that it had denied in another. El Greco's conscious purpose was to affirm man's capacity for union with the divine. Unconsciously, by his choice of forms and his peculiar treatment of space, he proclaimed the triumph of the organic and the incapacity of spirit, so far as he personally was concerned, to transfigure the matter with which it is associated. But at the same time he was a painter of genius. Out of the visceral forms and cramped spaces, imposed upon him by a part of his being beyond his voluntary control, he was able to create a new kind of order and perfection and, through this order and perfection, to reaffirm the possibility of man's union with the Spirit—a possibility which the raw materials of his pictures had seemed to rule out.

There is no question here of a dialectical process of thesis, antithesis and synthesis. A work of art is not a becoming, but a multiple being. It exists and has significance on several levels at once. In most cases these significances are of the same kind and harmoniously reinforce one another. Not always, however. Occasionally it happens that each of the meanings is logically exclusive of all the rest. There is then a happy marriage of incompatibles, a perfect fusion of contradictions. It is one of those states which, though inconceivable, actually occur. Such things cannot be; and yet, when you enter the Prado, when you visit Toledo, there they actually are.

(From "Variations on El Greco," *Themes and Variations*)

Variations on Goya

There are anthologies of almost everything—from the best to the worst, from the historically significant to the eccentric, from the childish to the sublime. But there is one anthology, potentially the most interesting of them all, which, to the best of my knowledge, has never yet been compiled; I mean, the Anthology of Later Works.

To qualify for inclusion in such an anthology, the artist would have to pass several tests. First of all, he must have avoided a premature extinction and lived on into artistic and chronological maturity. Thus the last poems of Shelley, the last compositions of Schubert and even of Mozart would find no place in our collection. Consummate artists as they were, these men were still psychologically youthful when they died. For their full development they needed more time than their earthly destiny allowed them. Of a different order are those strange beings whose chronological age is out of all proportion to their maturity, not only as artists, but as human spirits. Thus, some of the letters written by Keats in his early twenties and many of the paintings which Seurat executed before his death at thirty-two might certainly qualify as Later Works. But, as a general rule, a certain minimum of time is needed for the ripening of such fruits. For the most part, our hypothetical anthologist will make his selections from the art of elderly and middle-aged men and women.

But by no means all middle-aged and elderly artists are

capable of producing significant Later Works. For the last half century of a long life, Wordsworth preserved an almost unbroken record of dullness. And in this respect he does not stand alone. There are many, many others whose Later Works are their worst. All these must be excluded from our anthology, and I would pass a similar judgment on that other large class of Later Works which, though up to the standard of the earlier, are not significantly different from them. Haydn lived to a ripe old age and his right hand never forgot its cunning; but it also failed to learn a new cunning. Peter Pan-like, he continued, as an old man, to write the same sort of thing he had written twenty, thirty and forty years before. Where there is nothing to distinguish the creations of a man's maturity from those of his youth it is superfluous to include any of them in a selection of characteristically Later Works.

This leaves us, then, with the Later Works of those artists who have lived without ever ceasing to learn of life. The field is relatively narrow; but within it, what astonishing and sometimes what disquieting treasures! One thinks of the ineffable serenity of the slow movement of Beethoven's *A-Minor Quartet,* the peace passing all understanding of the orchestral prelude to the *Benedictus* of his *Missa Solemnis.* But this is not the old man's only mood; when he turns from the contemplation of eternal reality to a consideration of the human world, we are treated to the positively terrifying merriment of the last movement of his *B-Flat-Major Quartet*—merriment quite inhuman, peals of violent and yet somehow abstract laughter echoing down from somewhere beyond the limits of the world. Of the same nature, but if possible even more disquieting, is the mirth which reverberates through the last act of Verdi's *Falstaff,* culminating in that extraordinary final chorus in which the aged genius makes his maturest comment on the world—not with bitterness or sarcasm or satire, but in a huge, contrapuntal paroxysm of detached and already posthumous laughter.

Turning to the other arts, we find something of the same non-human, posthumous quality in the Later Works of Yeats and, coupled with a prodigious majesty, in those of Piero della Francesca. And then, of course there is *The Tempest*— a work charged with something of the unearthly serenity of Beethoven's *Benedictus* but concluding in the most disappointing anti-climax, with Prospero giving up his magic for the sake (heaven help us!) of becoming once again a duke. And the same sort of all too human anti-climax saddens us at the end of the second part of *Faust,* with its implication that draining fens is Man's Final End, and that the achievement of this end automatically qualifies the drainer for the beatific vision.

And what about the last El Grecos—for example, that unimaginable *Immaculate Conception* at Toledo with its fantastic harmony of brilliant, ice-cold colors, its ecstatic gesticulations in a heaven with a third dimension no greater than that of a mine-shaft, its deliquescence of flesh and flowers and drapery into a set of ectoplasmic abstractions? What about them, indeed? All we know is that, beautiful and supremely enigmatic, they will certainly take their place in our hypothetical anthology.

And finally, among these and all other extraordinary Later Works, we should have to number the paintings, drawings and etchings of Goya's final twenty-five or thirty years.

The difference between the young Goya and the old may be best studied and appreciated by starting in the basement of the Prado, where his cartoons for the tapestries are hung; climbing thence to the main floor, where there is a room full of his portraits of royal imbeciles, grandees, enchanting duchesses, *majas,* clothed and unclothed; walking thence to the smaller room containing the two great paintings of the Second of May—Napoleon's Mamelukes cutting down the crowd and, at night, when the revolt has been quelled, the firing squads at work upon their victims by the light of lanterns; and finally mounting to the top floor where hang the etchings and drawings, together with those unutterably mysterious and disturbing "black paintings," with which the deaf and aging Goya elected to adorn the dining room of his house, the Quinta del Sordo. It is a progress from lighthearted eighteenth-century art, hardly at all unconventional in subject matter or in handling, through fashionable brilliancy and increasing virtuosity, to something quite timeless both in technique and spirit —the most powerful of commentaries on human crime and madness, made in terms of an artistic convention uniquely fitted to express precisely that extraordinary mingling af hatred and compassion, despair and sardonic humor, realism and fantasy.

"I show you sorrow," said the Buddha, "and the ending of sorrow"—the sorrow of the phenomenal world in which man, "like an angry ape, plays such fantastic tricks before high heaven as make the angels weep," and the ending of sorrow in the beatific vision, the unitive contemplation of transcendental reality. Apart from the fact that he is a great and, one might say, uniquely original artist, Goya is significant as being, in his Later Works, the almost perfect type of the man who knows only sorrow and not the ending of sorrow.

In spite of his virulent anti-clericalism, Goya contrived to remain on sufficiently good terms with the Church to receive periodical commissions to paint religious pictures. Some of

these, like the frescoes in the cupola of La Florida, are
frankly and avowedly secular. But others are serious essays
in religious painting. It is worth looking rather closely at what
is probably the best of these religious pieces—the fine *Agony
in the Garden*. With outstretched arms, Christ raises toward
the comforting angel a face whose expression is identical with
that of the poor creatures whom we see, in a number of un-
forgettably painful etchings and paintings, kneeling or standing in an excruciating anticipation before the gun barrels of
a French firing squad. There is no trace here of that loving
confidence which, even in the darkest hours, fills the hearts
of men and women who live continually in the presence of
God; not so much as a hint of what François de Sales calls
"holy indifference" to suffering and good fortune, of the
fundamental equanimity, the peace passing all understanding,
which belongs to those whose attention is firmly fixed upon
a transcendental reality.

For Goya the transcendental reality did not exist. There
is no evidence in his biography or his works that he ever
had even the most distant personal experience of it. The
only reality he knew was that of the world around him; and
the longer he lived the more frightful did that world seem—
the more frightful, that is to say, in the eyes of his rational
self; for his animal high spirits went on bubbling up irrepres-
sibly, whenever his body was free from pain or sickness, to
the very end. As a young man in good health, with money
and reputation, a fine position and as many women as he
wanted, he had found the world a very agreeable place—
absurd, of course, and with enough of folly and roguery to
furnish subject matter for innumerable satirical drawings, but
eminently worth living in. Then all of a sudden came deaf-
ness, and, after the joyful dawn of the Revolution, Napoleon
and French imperialism and the atrocities of war; and, when
Napoleon's hordes were gone, the unspeakable Ferdinand VII
and clerical reaction and the spectacle of Spaniards fighting
among themselves; and all the time, like the drone of a bag-
pipe accompanying the louder noises of what is officially
called history, the enormous stupidity of average men and
women, the chronic squalor of their superstitions, the bestiality
of their occasional violences and orgies.

Realistically or in fantastic allegories, with a technical
mastery that only increased as he grew older, Goya recorded
it all—not only the agonies endured by his people at the
hands of the invaders, but also the follies and crimes committed by these same people in their dealings with one another. The great canvases of the Madrid massacres and executions, the incomparable etchings of *War's Disasters*, fill us

with an indignant compassion. But then we turn to the *Disparates* and the *Pinturas Negras*. In these, with a sublimely impartial savagery, Goya sets down exactly what he thinks of the martyrs of the Dos de Mayo when they are not being martyred. Here, for example, are two men—two Spaniards—sinking slowly toward death in an engulfing quicksand, but busily engaged in knocking one another over the head with bludgeons. And here is a rabble coming home from a pilgrimage—scores of low faces, distorted as though by reflection in the back of a spoon, all open-mouthed and yelling. And all the blank black eyes stare vacantly and idiotically in different directions.

These creatures who haunt Goya's Later Works are inexpressibly horrible, with the horror of mindlessness and animality and spiritual darkness. And above the lower depths where they obscenely pullulate is a world of bad priests and lustful friars, of fascinating women whose love is a "dream of lies and inconstancy," of fatuous nobles and, at the top of the social pyramid, a royal family of half-wits, sadists, Messalinas and perjurers. The moral of it all is summed up in the central plate of the *Caprichos*, in which we see Goya himself, his head on his arms, sprawled across his desk and fitfully sleeping, while the air above is peopled with the bats and owls of necromancy and just behind his chair lies an enormous witch's cat, malevolent as only Goya's cats can be, staring at the sleeper with baleful eyes. On the side of the desk are traced the words, "The dream of reason produces monsters." It is a caption that admits of more than one interpretation. When reason sleeps, the absurd and loathsome creatures of superstition wake and are active, goading their victim to an ignoble frenzy. But this is not all. Reason may also dream without sleeping, may intoxicate itself, as it did during the French Revolution, with the daydreams of inevitable progress, of liberty, equality and fraternity imposed by violence, of human self-sufficiency and the ending of sorrow, not by the all too arduous method which alone offers any prospect of success, but by political rearrangements and a better technology. The *Caprichos* were published in the last year of the eighteenth century; in 1808 Goya and all Spain were given the opportunity of discovering the consequences of such daydreaming. Murat marched his troops into Madrid; the *Desastres de la Guerra* were about to begin.

Goya produced four main sets of etchings—the *Caprichos,* the *Desastres de la Guerra,* the *Tauromaquia* and the *Disparates* or *Proverbios.* All of them are Later Works. The *Caprichos* were not published until he was fifty-three; the plates of the *Desastres* were etched between the ages of sixty-five and seventy-five; the *Tauromaquia* series first saw the light when he was sixty-nine (and at the age of almost eighty he learnt the brand-new technique of lithography in order to be able to do justice to his beloved bulls in yet another medium); the *Disparates* were finished when he was seventy-three.

For the non-Spaniard the plates of the *Tauromaquia* series will probably seem the least interesting of Goya's etchings. They are brilliant records of the exploits of the bull ring; but unfortunately, or fortunately, most of us know very little about bullfighting. Consequently, we miss the finer shades of the significance of these little masterpices of documentary art. Moreover, being documentary, the etchings of the *Tauromaquia* do not lend themselves to being executed with that splendid audacity, that dramatic breadth of treatment, which delights us in the later paintings and the etchings of the other three series. True, we find in this collection a few plates that are as fine as anything Goya ever produced—for example, that wonderful etching of the bull which has broken out of the arena and stands triumphant, a corpse hanging limp across its horns, among the spectators' benches. But by and large it is not to the *Tauromaquia* that we turn for the very best specimens of Goya's work in black and white, or for the most characteristic expressions of his mature personality. The nature of the subject matter makes it impossible for him, in these plates to reveal himself fully either as a man or as an artist.

Of the three other sets of etchings two, the *Caprichos* and *Disparates,* are fantastic and allegorical in subject matter, while the third, the *Desastres,* though for the most part it represents real happenings under the Napoleonic terror, represents them in a way which, being generalized and symbolical rather than directly documentary, permits of, and indeed demands, a treatment no less broad and dramatic than is given to the fantasies of the other collections.

War always weakens and often completely shatters the crust of customary decency which constitutes a civilization. It is a thin crust at the best of times, and beneath it lies—what? Look through Goya's *Desastres* and find out. The abyss of bestiality and diabolism and suffering seems almost bottomless. There is practically nothing of which human beings are not capable when war or revolution or anarchy gives them the necessary opportunity and excuse; and to their pain death alone imposes a limit.

Goya's record of disaster has a number of recurrent themes. There are those shadowy archways, for example, more sinister than those even of Piranesi's *Prisons,* where women are violated, captives squat in a hopeless stupor, corpses lie rotting, emaciated children starve to death. Then there are the vague street corners at which the famine-stricken hold out their hands; but the whiskered French hussars and carabiniers look on without pity, and even the rich Spaniards pass by indifferently, as though they were "of another lineage." Of still more frequent occurrence in the series are the crests of those naked hillocks on which lie the dead, like so much garbage. Or else, in dramatic silhouette against the sky above those same hilltops, we see the hideous butchery of Spanish men and women, and the no less hideous vengeance meted out by infuriated Spaniards upon their tormentors. Often the hillock sprouts a single tree, always low, sometimes maimed by gunfire. Upon its branches are impaled, like the beetles and caterpillars in a butcher bird's larder, whole naked torsos, sometimes decapitated, sometimes without arms, or else a pair of amputated legs, or a severed head—warnings, set there by the conquerors, of the fate awaiting those who dare oppose the Emperor. At other times the tree is used as a gallows—a less efficient gallows, indeed, than that majestic oak which, in Callot's *Misères de la Guerre,* is fruited with more than a score of swinging corpses, but good enough for a couple of executions *en passant,* except, of course, in the case recorded in one of Goya's most hair-raising plates, in which the tree is too stumpy to permit of a man's hanging clear of the ground. But the rope is fixed, none the less, and to tighten the noose around their victim's neck, two French soldiers tug at the legs, while with his foot a third man thrusts with all his strength against the shoulders.

And so the record proceeds, horror after horror, unalleviated by any of the splendors which other painters have been able to discover in war; for, significantly, Goya never illustrates an engagement, never shows us impressive masses of troops marching in column or deployed in the order of battle. His concern is exclusively with war as it affects the civilian population, with armies disintegrated into individual thieves and ravishers, tormentors and executioners—and occasionally, when the *guerilleros* have won a skirmish, into individual victims tortured in their turn and savagely done to death by the avengers of their own earlier atrocities. All he shows us is war's disasters and squalors, without any of the glory or even picturesqueness.

In the two remaining series of etchings we pass from tragedy to satire and from historical fact to allegory and pictorial metaphor and pure fantasy. Twenty years separate the *Caprichos* from the *Disparates,* and the later collection is at once more somber and more enigmatic than the earlier. Much of the satire of the *Caprichos* is merely Goya's sharper version of what may be called standard eighteenth-century humor. A plate such as Hasta la Muerte, showing the old hag before her mirror, coquettishly trying on a new headdress, is just Rowlandson-with-a-difference. But in certain other etchings a stranger and more disquieting note is struck. Goya's handling of his material is such that standard eighteenth-century humor often undergoes a sea-change into something darker and queerer, something that goes below the anecdotal surface of life into what lies beneath—the unplumbed depths of original sin and original stupidity. And in the second half of the series the subject matter reinforces the effect of the powerful and dramatically sinister treatment; for here the theme of almost all the plates is basely supernatural. We are in a world of demons, witches and familiars, half horrible, half comic, but wholly disquieting inasmuch as it reveals the sort of thing that goes on in the squalid catacombs of the human mind.

In the *Disparates* the satire is on the whole less direct than in the *Caprichos,* the allegories are more general and more mysterious. Consider, for example, the technically astonishing plate, which shows a large family of three generations perched like huddling birds along a huge dead branch that projects into the utter vacancy of a dark sky. Obviously, much more is meant than meets the eye. But what? The question is one upon which the commentators have spent a great deal of ingenuity—spent it, one may suspect, in vain. For the satire, it would seem, is not directed against this particular social evil or that political mistake, but rather against unregenerate human nature as such. It is a statement, in the form of an image, about life in general. Literature and the scriptures of all the great religions abound in such brief metaphorical verdicts on human destiny. Man turns the wheel of sorrow, burns in the fire of craving, travels through a vale of tears, leads a life that is no better than a tale told by an idiot signifying nothing.

> Poor man, what art? A tennis ball of error,
> A ship of glass tossed in a sea of terror:
> Issuing in blood and sorrow from the womb,
> Crawling in tears and mourning to the tomb.
> How slippery are thy paths, how sure thy fall!
> How art thou nothing, when thou art most of all!

And so on. Good, bad and indifferent, the quotations could be multiplied almost indefinitely. In the language of the plastic arts, Goya has added a score of memorable contributions to the stock of humanity's gnomic wisdom.

The *Disparates* of the dead branch is relatively easy to

understand. So is the comment on Fear contained in the plate
which shows soldiers running in terror from a gigantic cowled
figure, spectral against a jet black sky. So is the etching of
the ecstatically smiling woman riding a stallion that turns its
head and, seizing her skirts between its teeth, tries to drag
her from her seat. The allegorical use of the horse, as a symbol of the senses and the passions, and of the rational rider
or charioteer who is at liberty to direct or be run away with, is
at least as old as Plato.

But there are other plates in which the symbolism is less
clear, the allegorical significance far from obvious. That horse
on a tightrope, for example, with a woman dancing on its
back; the men who fly with artificial wings against a sky of
inky menace; the priests and the elephant; the old man wandering among phantoms: what is the meaning of these things?
And perhaps the answer to that question is that they have no
meaning in any ordinary sense of the word; that they refer
to strictly private events taking place on the obscurer levels
of their creator's mind. For us who look at them, it may be
that their real point and significance consist precisely in the
fact that they image forth so vividly, and yet, of necessity,
so darkly and incomprehensibly, some at least of the unknown
quantities that exist at the heart of every personality.

Goya once drew a picture of an ancient man tottering along
under the burden of years, but with the accompanying caption,
"I'm still learning." That old man was himself. To the end
of a long life, he went on learning. As a very young man he
paints like the feeble eclectics who were his masters. The first
signs of power and freshness and originality appear in the
cartoons for the tapestries, of which the earliest were executed
when he was thirty. As a portraitist, however, he achieves
nothing of outstanding interest until he is almost forty. But
by that time he really knows what he's after, and during the
second forty years of his life he moves steadily forward toward the consummate technical achievements, in oils, of the
Pinturas Negras, and, in etching, of the *Desastres* and the
Disparates. Goya's is a stylistic growth away from restraint
and into freedom, away from timidity and into expressive
boldness.

From the technical point of view the most striking fact
about almost all Goya's successful paintings and etchings is
that they are composed in terms of one or more clearly delimited masses standing out from the background—often
indeed, silhouetted against the sky. When he attempts what
may be called an "all-over" composition, the essay is rarely
successful. For he lacks almost completely the power which

Rubens so conspicuously possessed—the power of filling the entire canvas with figures or details of landscape, and upon that *plenum* imposing a clear and yet exquisitely subtle three-dimensional order. The lack of this power is already conspicuous in the tapestry cartoons, of which the best are invariably those in which Goya does his composing in terms of silhouetted masses and the worst those in which he attempts to organize a collection of figures distributed all over the canvas. And compare, from this point of view, the two paintings of the Dos de Mayo—the Mamelukes cutting down the crowd in the Puerta del Sol, and the firing squads at work in the suburbs, after dark. The first is an attempt to do what Rubens would have done with an almost excessive facility—to impose a formally beautiful and dramatically significant order upon a crowd of human and animal figures covering the greater part of the canvas. The attempt is not successful, and in spite of its power and the beauty of its component parts, the picture as a whole is less satisfying as a composition, and for that reason less moving as a story, than is the companion piece, in which Goya arranges his figures in a series of sharply delimited balancing groups, dramatically contrasted with one another and the background. In this picture the artist is speaking his native language, and he is therefore able to express what he wants to say with the maximum force and clarity. This is not the case with the picture of the Mamelukes. Here, the formal language is not truly his own, and consequently his eloquence lacks the moving power it possesses when he lets himself go in the genuine Goyescan idiom.

Fortunately, in the etchings, Goya is very seldom tempted to talk in anything else. Here he composes almost exclusively in terms of bold separate masses, silhouetted in luminous grays and whites against a darkness that ranges from stippled pepper-and-salt to intense black, or in blacks and heavily shaded grays against the whiteness of virgin paper. Sometimes there is only one mass, sometimes several, balanced and contrasted. Hardly ever does he make the, for him, almost fatal mistake of trying to organize his material in an all-over composition.

With the *Desastres* and the *Disparates* his mastery of this, his predestined method of composition, becomes, one might say, absolute. It is not, of course, the only method of composition. Indeed, the nature of this particular artistic idiom is such that there are probably certain things that can never be expressed in it—things which Rembrandt, for example, was able to say in his supremely beautiful and subtle illustrations to the Bible. But within the field that he chose to cultivate—

that the idiosyncrasies of his temperament and the quality of his artistic sensibilities compelled him to choose—Goya remains incomparable.

(From *Themes and Variations*; originally published in COMPLETE ETCHINGS OF GOYA. Used by permission of Crown Publishers, Inc.)

Landscape Painting as a Vision-Inducing Art

Let us begin by asking a question. What landscapes—or, more generally, what representations of natural objects—are most transporting, most intrinsically vision inducing? In the light of my own experience and of what I have heard other people say about their reactions to works of art, I will risk an answer. Other things being equal (for nothing can make up for lack of talent), the most transporting landscapes are, first, those which represent natural objects a very long way off, and, second, those which represent them at close range.

Distance lends enchantment to the view; but so does propinquity. A Sung painting of faraway mountains, clouds and torrents is transporting; but so are the closeups of tropical leaves in the Douanier Rousseau's jungles. When I look at the Sung landscape, I am reminded of the crags, the boundless expanses of plain, the luminous skies and seas of that Other World which lies at the self-conscious mind's antipodes. And those disappearances into mist and cloud, those sudden emergences of some strange, intensely definite form, a weathered rock, for example, an ancient pine tree twisted by years of struggle with the wind—these too, are transporting. For they remind me, consciously or unconsciously, of the Other World's essential alienness and unaccountability.

It is the same with the close-up. I look at those leaves with their architecture of veins, their stripes and mottlings, I peer into the depths of interlacing greenery, and something in me is reminded of those living patterns, so characteristic of the visionary world, of those endless births and proliferations of geometrical forms that turn into objects, of things that are forever being transmuted into other things.

This painted close-up of a jungle is what, in one of its aspects, the Other World is like, and so it transports me, it makes me see with eyes that transfigure a work of art into something else, something beyond art.

I remember—very vividly, though it took place many years ago—a conversation with Roger Fry. We were talking about Monet's "Water Lilies." They had no right, Roger kept insisting, to be so shockingly unorganized, so totally without a proper compositional skeleton. They were all wrong, artistically speaking. And yet, he had to admit, and yet. . . . And yet, as I should now say, they were transporting. An artist of astounding virtuosity had chosen to paint a close-up of natural objects seen in their own context and without reference to merely human notions of what's what, or what ought to be what. Man, we like to say, is the measure of all things. For Monet, on this occasion, water lilies were the measure of water lilies; and so he painted them.

The same non-human point of view must be adopted by any artist who tries to render the distant scene. How tiny, in the Chinese painting, are the travelers who make their way along the valley! How frail the bamboo hut on the slope above them! And all the rest of the vast landscape is emptiness and silence. This revelation of the wilderness, living its own life according to the laws of its own being, transports the mind toward its antipodes; for primeval Nature bears a strange resemblance to that inner world where no account is taken of our personal wishes or even of the enduring concerns of man in general.

Only the middle distance and what may be called the remoter foreground are strictly human. When we look very near or very far, man either vanishes altogether or loses his primacy. The astronomer looks even further afield than the Sung painter and sees even less of human life. At the other end of the scale the physicist, the chemist, the physiologist pursue the close-up—the cellular close-up, the molecular, the atomic and sub-atomic. Of that which, at twenty feet, even at arm's length, looked and sounded like a human being no trace remains.

Something analogous happens to the myopic artist and the happy lover. In the nuptial embrace personality is melted down; the individual (it is the recurrent theme of Lawrence's poems and novels) ceases to be himself and becomes a part of the vast impersonal universe.

And so it is with the artist who chooses to use his eyes at the near point. In his work humanity loses its importance, even disappears completely. Instead of men and women playing their fantastic tricks before high heaven, we are asked to consider the lilies, to meditate on the unearthly beauty of "mere things," when isolated from their utilitarian context and rendered as they are, in and for themselves. Alternatively, (or, at an earlier stage of artistic development, exclusively) the non-human world of the near point is rendered in patterns. These patterns are abstracted for the most part from leaves and flowers—the rose, the lotus, the acanthus, palm, papyrus—and are elaborated, with recurrences and variations, into something transportingly reminiscent of the living geometries of the Other World.

Freer and more realistic treatments of Nature at the near point make their appearance at a relatively recent date—but far earlier than those treatments of the distant scene, to which alone (and mistakenly) we give the name of landscape painting. Rome, for example, had its close-up landscapes. The fresco of a garden, which once adorned a room in Livia's villa, is a magnificent example of this form of art.

For theological reasons, Islam had to be content, for the most part, with "arabesques"—luxuriant and (as in visions) continually varying patterns, based upon natural objects seen at the near point. But even in Islam the genuine close-up landscape was not unknown. Nothing can exceed in beauty and in vision-inducing power the mosaics of gardens and buildings in the great Omayyad mosque at Damascus.

In medieval Europe, despite the prevailing mania for turning every datum into a concept, every immediate experience into a mere symbol of something in a book, realistic close-ups of foliage and flowers were fairly common. We find them carved on the capitals of Gothic pillars, as in the Chapter House of Southwell Cathedral. We find them in paintings of the chase—paintings whose subject was that ever-present fact of medieval life, the forest, seen as the hunter or the strayed traveler sees it, in all its bewildering intricacy of leafy detail.

The frescoes in the papal palace at Avignon are almost the sole survivors of what, even in the time of Chaucer, was a widely practiced form of secular art. A century later this art of the forest close-up came to its self-conscious perfection in such magnificent and magical works as Pisanello's "St. Hubert" and Paolo Uccello's "Hunt in a Wood," now in the Ashmolean Museum at Oxford. Closely related to the wall paintings of forest close-ups were the tapestries, with which the rich men of northern Europe adorned their houses. The best of these are vision-inducing works of the highest order. In their own way they are as heavenly, as powerfully reminiscent of what goes on at the mind's antipodes, as are the great masterpieces of landscape painting at the farthest point —Sung mountains in their enormous solitude, Ming rivers interminably lovely, the blue sub-Alpine world of Titian's distances, the England of Constable; the Italies of Turner and Corot; the Provences of Cézanne and Van Gogh; the Île de France of Sisley and the Île de France of Vuillard.

Vuillard, incidentally, was a supreme master both of the transporting close-up and of the transporting distant view. His bourgeois interiors are masterpieces of vision-inducing art, compared with which the works of such conscious and so to say professional visionaries as Blake and Odilon Redon seem feeble in the extreme. . . .

At the near point Vuillard painted interiors for the most part, but sometimes also gardens. In a few compositions he managed to combine the magic of propinquity with the magic of remoteness by representing a corner of a room in which there stands or hangs one of his own, or someone else's, representations of a distant view of trees, hills and sky. It is an invitation to make the best of both worlds, the telescopic and the microscopic, at a single glance.

For the rest, I can think of only a very few close-up landscapes by modern European artists. There is a strange "Thicket" by Van Gogh at the Metropolitan. There is Constable's wonderful "Dell in Helmington Park" at the Tate. There is a bad picture, Millais's "Ophelia," made magical, in spite of everything, by its intricacies of summer greenery seen from the point of view, very nearly, of a water rat. And I remember a Delacroix, glimpsed long ago at some loan exhibition, of bark and leaves and blossom at the closest range. There must, of course, be others; but either I have forgotten, or have never seen them. In any case there is nothing in the West comparable to the Chinese and Japanese renderings of nature at the near point. A spray of blossoming plum, eighteen inches of a bamboo stem with its leaves, tits or finches seen at hardly more than arm's length among the bushes, all kinds of flowers and foliage, of birds and fish and small mammals. Each tiny life is represented as the center of its own universe, the purpose, in its own estimation, for which this world and all that is in it were created; each issues its own specific and individual declaration of independence from human imperialism; each, by ironic implication, derides our absurd pretensions to lay down merely human rules for the conduct of the cosmic game; each mutely repeats the divine tautology: I am that I am.

Nature at the middle distance is familiar—so familiar that we are deluded into believing that we really know what it is all about. Seen very close at hand, or at a great distance, or from an odd angle, it seems disquietingly strange, wonderful beyond all comprehension. The closeup landscapes of China and Japan are so many illustrations of the theme that samsara and nirvana are one, that the Absolute is manifest in every appearance. These great metaphysical, and yet pragmatic, truths were rendered by the Zen-inspired artists of the

Far East in yet another way. All the objects of their near-point scrutiny were represented in a state of unrelatedness against a blank of virgin silk or paper. Thus isolated, these transient appearances take on a kind of absolute Thing-in-Itselfhood. Western artists have used this device when painting sacred figures, portraits and, sometimes, natural objects at a distance. Rembrandt's "Mill" and Van Gogh's "Cypresses" are examples of long-range landscapes in which a single feature has been absolutized by isolation. The magical power of many of Goya's etchings, drawings and paintings can be accounted for by the fact that his compositions almost always take the form of a few silhouettes, or even a single silhouette, seen against a blank. These silhouetted shapes possess the visionary quality of intrinsic significance, heightened by isolation and unrelatedness to preternatural intensity. In nature, as in a work of art, the isolation of an object tends to invest it with absoluteness, to endow it with that more-than-symbolic meaning which is identical with being.

> —But there's a Tree—of many, *one*,
> A *single* Field which I have looked upon,
> Both of them speak of something that is gone.

The something which Wordsworth could no longer see was the "visionary gleam." That gleam, I remember, and that intrinsic significance were the properties of a solitary oak that could be seen from the train, between Reading and Oxford, growing from the summit of a little knoll in a wide expanse of plowland, and silhouetted against the pale northern sky.

The effects of isolation combined with proximity may be studied, in all their magical strangeness, in an extraordinary painting by a seventeenth-century Japanese artist, who was also a famous swordsman and a student of Zen. It represents a butcherbird, perched on the very tip of a naked branch, "waiting without purpose, but in the state of highest tension." Beneath, above and all around is nothing. The bird emerges from the Void, from that eternal namelessness and formlessness, which is yet the very substance of the manifold, concrete and transient universe. That shrike on its bare branch is first cousin to Hardy's wintry thrush. But whereas the thrush insists on teaching us some kind of a lesson, the Far Eastern butcherbird is content simply to exist, to be intensely and absolutely there.

(From *Heaven and Hell*)

MUSIC

Popular Music

There is a certain jovial, bouncing, hoppety little tune with which any one who has spent even a few weeks in Germany, or has been tended in childhood by a German nurse, must be very familiar. Its name is "Ach, du lieber Augustin." It is a merry little affair in three-four time; in rhythm and melody so simple, that the village idiot could sing it after a first hearing; in sentiment so innocent that the heart of the most susceptible maiden would not quicken by a beat a minute at the sound of it. Rum ti-tiddle, Um tum tum, Um tum tum, Um tum tum: Rum ti-tiddle, Um tum tum, Um tum tum, TUM. By the very frankness of its cheerful imbecility the thing disarms all criticism.

Now for a piece of history. "Ach, du lieber Augustin" was composed in 1770, and it was the first waltz. The first waltz! I must ask the reader to hum the tune to himself, then to think of any modern waltz with which he may be familiar. He will find in the difference between the tunes a subject richly suggestive of interesting meditations.

The difference between "Ach, du lieber Augustin" and any waltz tune composed at any date from the middle of the nineteenth century onwards, is the difference between one piece of music almost completely empty of emotional content and another, densely saturated with amorous sentiment, languor and voluptuousness. The susceptible maiden who, when she hears "Ach, du lieber Augustin," feels no emotions beyond a general sense of high spirits and cheerfulness, is fairly made to palpitate by the luscious strains of the modern waltz. Her

173

soul is carried swooning along, over waves of syrup; she seems
to breathe an atmosphere heavy with ambergris and musk.
From the jolly little thing it was at its birth, the waltz has
grown into the voluptuous, heart-stirring affair with which we
are now familiar.

And what has happened to the waltz has happened to all
popular music. It was once innocent but is now provocative;
once pellucid, now richly clotted; once elegant, now deliberately barbarous. Compare the music of *The Beggar's Opera*
with the music of a contemporary revue. They differ as life
in the garden of Eden differed from life in the artistic quarter
of Gomorrah. The one is prelapsarian in its airy sweetness,
the other is rich, luscious and loud with conscious savagery.

The evolution of popular music has run parallel on a lower
plane, with the evolution of serious music. The writers of
popular tunes are not musicians enough to be able to invent
new forms of expression. All they do is to adapt the discoveries
of original geniuses to the vulgar taste. Ultimately and indirectly, Beethoven is responsible for all the languishing waltz
tunes, all the savage jazzings, for all that is maudlin and violent in our popular music. He is responsible because it was
he who first devised really effective musical methods for the
direct expression of emotion. Beethoven's emotions happened
to be noble; moreover, he was too intellectual a musician to
neglect the formal, architectural side of music. But unhappily
he made it possible for composers of inferior mind and
character to express in music their less exalted passions and
vulgarer emotions. He made possible the weakest sentimen-
talities of Schumann, the baroque grandiosities of Wagner,
the hysterics of Scriabine; he made possible the waltzes of all
the Strausses, from the *Blue Danube* to the waltz from *Salome*.
And he made possible, at a still further remove, such masterpieces of popular art as "You made me love you" and "That
coal black mammy of mine."

For the introduction of a certain vibrant sexual quality into
music, Beethoven is perhaps less directly responsible than the
nineteenth-century Italians. I used often to wonder why it was
that Mozart's operas were less popular than those of Verdi,
Leoncavallo and Puccini. You couldn't ask for more, or more
infectiously "catchy" tunes than are to be found in *Figaro* or
Don Giovanni. The music though "classical," is not obscure,
nor forbiddingly complex. On the contrary it is clear, simple
with that seemingly easy simplicity which only consummate
genius can achieve and thoroughly engaging. And yet for every
time *Don Giovanni* is played, *La Bohème* is played a hundred.
Tosca is at least fifty times as popular as *Figaro*. And if you
look through a catalogue of gramophone records you will

find that, while you can buy *Rigoletto* complete in thirty discs, there are not more than three records of *The Magic Flute*. This seems as first sight extremely puzzling. But the reason is not really far to seek. Since Mozart's day composers have learned the art of making music throatily and palpitatingly sexual. The arias of Mozart have a beautiful clear purity which renders them utterly insipid compared with the sobbing, catch-in-the-throaty melodies of the nineteenth-century Italians. The public, having accustomed itself to this stronger and more turbid brewage, finds no flavor in the crystal songs of Mozart.

No essay on modern popular music would be complete without some grateful reference to Rossini, who was, as far as I know, the first composer to show what charms there are in vulgar melody. Melodies before Rossini's day were often exceedingly commonplace and cheap; but almost never do they possess that almost indefinable quality of low vulgarity which adorns some of the most successful of Rossini's airs, and which we recognize as being somehow a modern, contemporary quality. The methods which Rossini employed for the achievement of his melodic vulgarity are not easy to analyze. His great secret, I fancy, was the very short and easily memorable phrase frequently repeated in different parts of the scale. But it is easiest to define by example. Think of Moses' first aria in *Moses in Egypt*. That is an essentially vulgar melody; and it is quite unlike the popular melodies of an earlier date. Its affinities are with the modern popular tune. It is to his invention of vulgar tunes that Rossini owed his enormous contemporary success. Vulgar people before his day had to be content with Mozart's delicate airs. Rossini came and revealed to them a more congenial music. That the world fell down and gratefully worshiped him is not surprising. If he has long ceased to be popular, that is because his successors, profiting by his lessons, have achieved in his own vulgar line triumphs of which he could not have dreamed.

Barbarism has entered popular music from two sources—from the music of barbarous people, like the Negroes, and from serious music which has drawn upon barbarism for its inspiration. The technique of being barbarous effectively has come, of course, from serious music. In the elaboration of this technique no musicians have done more than the Russians. If Rimsky-Korsakoff had never lived, modern dance music would not be the thing it is.

Whether, having grown inured to such violent and purely physiological stimuli as the clashing and drumming, the rhythmic throbbing and wailing glissandos of modern jazz music can supply, the world will ever revert to something less crudely direct, is a matter about which one cannot prophesy.

Even serious musicians seem to find it hard to dispense with barbarism. In spite of the monotony and the appalling lack of subtlety which characterize the process, they persist in banging away in the old Russian manner, as though there were nothing more interesting or exciting to be thought of. When, as a boy, I first heard Russian music, I was carried off my feet by its wild melodies, its persistent, its relentlessly throbbing rhythms. But my excitement grew less and less with every hearing. Today no music seems to me more tedious. The only music a civilized man can take unfailing pleasure in is civilized music. If you were compelled to listen every day of your life to a single piece of music, would you choose Stravinsky's "Oiseau de Feu" or "Beethoven's "Grosse Fugue"? Obviously, you would choose the fugue, if only for its intricacy and because there is more in it to occupy the mind than in the Russian's too simple rhythms. Composers seem to forget that we are, in spite of everything and though appearances may be against us, tolerably civilized. They overwhelm us not merely with Russian and negroid noises, but with Celtic caterwaulings on the black notes, with dismal Spanish wailings, punctuated by the rattle of the castanets and the clashing harmonies of the guitar. When serious composers have gone back to civilized music—and already some of them are turning from barbarism—we shall probably hear a corresponding change for the more refined in popular music. But until serious musicians lead the way, it will be absurd to expect the vulgarizers to change their style.

(From *Along the Road*)

Music at Night

Moonless, this June night is all the more alive with stars. Its darkness is perfumed with faint gusts from the blossoming lime trees, with the smell of wetted earth and the invisible greenness of the vines. There is silence; but a silence that breathes with the soft breathing of the sea and, in the thin shrill noise of a cricket, insistently, incessantly harps on the fact of its own deep perfection. Far away, the passage of a train is like a long caress, moving gently, with an inexorable gentleness, across the warm living body of the night.

Music, you say; it would be a good night for music. But I have music here in a box, shut up, like one of those bottled djinns in the *Arabian Nights*, and ready at a touch to break out of its prison. I make the necessary mechanical magic, and

suddenly, by some miraculously appropriate coincidence (for
I had selected the record in the dark, without knowing what
music the machine would play), suddenly the introduction to
the *Benedictus* in Beethoven's *Missa Solemnis* begins to trace
its patterns on the moonless sky.

The *Benedictus*. Blessed and blessing, this music is in some
sort the equivalent of the night, of the deep and living darkness, into which, now in a single jet, now in a fine interweav-
ing of melodies, now in pulsing and almost solid clots of
harmonious sound, it pours itself, stanchlessly pours itself, like
time, like the rising and falling, falling trajectories of a life.
It is the equivalent of the night in another mode of being,
as an essence is the equivalent of the flowers, from which it
is distilled.

There is, at least there sometimes seems to be, a certain
blessedness lying at the heart of things, a mysterious blessedness, of whose existence occasional accidents or providences
(for me, this night is one of them) make us obscurely, or it
may be intensely, but always fleetingly, alas, always only for
a few brief moments aware. In the *Benedictus* Beethoven gives
expression to this awareness of blessedness. His music is the
equivalent of this Mediterranean night, or rather of the
blessedness as it would be if it could be sifted clear of
irrelevance and accident, refined and separated out into its
quintessential purity.

"*Benedictus, benedictus . . .*" One after another the voices
take up the theme propounded by the orchestra and lovingly
mediated through a long and exquisite solo (for the blessedness reveals itself most often to the solitary spirit) by a single
violin. "*Benedictus, benedictus . . .*" And then, suddenly,
the music dies; the flying djinn has been rebottled. With a
stupid insect-like insistence, a steel point rasps and rasps the
silence.

At school, when they taught us what was technically
known as English, they used to tell us to "express in our own
words" some passage from whatever play of Shakespeare was
at the moment being rammed, with all its annotations—particularly the annotations—down our reluctant throats. So
there we would sit, a row of inky urchins, laboriously translat-
ing "now silken dalliance in the wardrobe lies" into "now
smart silk clothes lie in the wardrobe," or "To be or not to
be" into "I wonder whether I ought to commit suicide or
not." When we had finished, we would hand in our papers,
and the presiding pedagogue would give us marks, more or
less, according to the accuracy with which "our own words"
had "expressed" the meaning of the Bard.

He ought, of course, to have given us naught all round with a hundred lines to himself for ever having set us the silly exercise. Nobody's "own words," except those of Shakespeare himself, can possibly "express" what Shakespeare meant. The substance of a work of art is inseparable from its form; its truth and its beauty are two and yet, mysteriously, one. The verbal expression of even a metaphysic or a system of ethics is very nearly as much of a work of art as a love poem. The philosophy of Plato expressed in the "own words" of Jowett is not the philosophy of Plato; nor in the "own words" of, say, Billy Sunday, is the teaching of St. Paul St. Paul's teaching.

"Our own words" are inadequate even to express the meaning of other words; how much more inadequate, when it is a matter of rendering meanings which have their original expression in terms of music or one of the visual arts! What, for example, does music "say"? You can buy at almost any concert an analytical program that will tell you exactly. Much too exactly; that is the trouble. Every analyst has his own version. Imagine Pharaoh's dream interpreted successively by Joseph, by the Egyptian soothsayers, by Freud, by Rivers, by Adler, by Jung, by Wohlgemuth: it would "say" a great many different things. Not nearly so many, however, as the Fifth Symphony has been made to say in the verbiage of its analysts. Not nearly so many as the Virgin of the Rocks and the Sistine Madonna have no less lyrically said.

Annoyed by the verbiage and this absurd multiplicity of attributed "meanings," some critics have protested that music and painting signify nothing but themselves; that the only things they "say" are things, for example, about modulations and fugues, about color values and three-dimensional forms. That they say anything about human destiny or the universe at large is a notion which these purists dismiss as merely nonsensical.

If the purists were right, then we should have to regard painters and musicians as monsters. For it is strictly impossible to be a human being and not to have views of some kind about the universe at large, very difficult to be a human being and not to express those views, at any rate by implication. Now, it is a matter of observation that painters and musicians are *not* monsters. Therefore . . . The conclusion follows, unescapably.

It is not only in program music and problem pictures that composers and painters express their views about the universe. The purest and most abstract artistic creations can be, in their own peculiar language, as eloquent in this respect as the most deliberately tendencious.

Compare, for example, a Virgin by Piero della Francesca

with a Virgin by Tura. Two Madonnas—and the current
symbolical conventions are observed by both artists. The
difference, the enormous difference between the two pictures
is a purely pictorial difference, a difference in the forms and
their arrangement, in the disposition of the lines and planes
and masses. To any one in the least sensitive to the eloquence
of pure form, the two Madonnas say utterly different things
about the world.

Piero's composition is a welding together of smooth and
beautifully balanced solidities. Everything in his universe is
endowed with a kind of supernatural substantiality, is much
more "there" than any object of the actual world could possibly be. And how sublimely rational, in the noblest, the most
humane acceptation of the word, how orderedly philosophical
is the landscape, are all the inhabitants of this world! It is the
creation of a god who "ever plays the geometer."

What does she say, this Madonna from San Sepolcro? If I
have not wholly mistranslated the eloquence of Piero's forms,
she is telling us of the greatness of the human spirit, of its
power to rise above circumstance and dominate fate. If you
were to ask her, "How shall I be saved?" "By Reason," she
would probably answer. And, anticipating Milton, "Not only,
not mainly upon the Cross," she would say, "is Paradise
regained, but in those deserts of utter solitude where man puts
forth the strength of his reason to resist the Fiend." This
particular mother of Christ is probably not a Christian.

Turn now to Tura's picture. It is fashioned out of a substance that is like the living embodiment of flame—flame-
flesh, alive and sensitive and suffering. His surfaces writhe
away from the eye, as though shrinking, as though in pain.
The lines flow intricately with something of that disquieting
and, you feel, magical calligraphy, which characterizes certain
Tibetan paintings. Look closely; feel your way into the picture, into the painter's thoughts and intuitions and emotions.
This man was naked and at the mercy of destiny. To be able
to proclaim the spirit's stoical independence, you must be able
to raise your head above the flux of things; this man was sunk
in it, overwhelmed. He could introduce no order into his
world; it remained for him a mysterious chaos, fantastically
marbled with patches, now of purest heaven, now of the most
excruciating hell. A beautiful and terrifying world, is this
Madonna's verdict; a world like the incarnation, the material
projection, of Ophelia's madness. There are no certainties in
it but suffering and occasional happiness. And as for salvation,
who knows the way of salvation? There may perhaps be
miracles, and there is always hope.

The limits of criticism are very quickly reached. When he

has said "in his own words" as much, or rather as little, as "own words" can say, the critic can only refer his readers to the original work of art: let them go and see for themselves. Those who overstep the limit are either rather stupid, vain people, who love their "own words" and imagine that they can say in them more than "own words" are able in the nature of things to express. Or else they are intelligent people who happen to be philosophers or literary artists and who find it convenient to make the criticism of other men's work a jumping-off place for their own creativity.

What is true of painting is equally true of music. Music "says" things about the world, but in specifically musical terms. Any attempt to reproduce these musical statements "in our own words" is necessarily doomed to failure. We cannot isolate the truth contained in a piece of music; for it is a beauty-truth and inseparable from its partner. The best we can do is to indicate in the most general terms the nature of the musical beauty-truth under consideration and to refer curious truth-seekers to the original. Thus, the introduction to the *Benedictus* in the *Missa Solemnis* is a statement about the blessedness that is at the heart of things. But this is about as far as "own words" will take us. If we were to start describing in our "own words" exactly what Beethoven felt about this blessedness, how he conceived it, what he thought its nature to be, we should very soon find ourselves writing lyrical nonsense in the style of the analytical program makers. Only music, and only Beethoven's music, and only this particular music of Beethoven, can tell us with any precision what Beethoven's conception of the blessedness at the heart of things actually was. If we want to know, we must listen—on a still June night, by preference, with the breathing of the invisible sea for background to the music and the scent of lime trees drifting through the darkness, like some exquisite soft harmony apprehended by another sense.

(From *Music at Night*)

Gesualdo:
Variations on a Musical Theme

Space has been explored, systematically and scientifically, for more than five centuries; time, for less than five generations. Modern geography began in the fourteen-hundreds with the voyages of Prince Henry the Navigator. Modern history and modern archeology came in with Queen Victoria. Except in the Antarctic there is today no such thing as a *terra incognita*; all the corners of all the other continents have now been visited. In contrast, how vast are the reaches of history which still remain obscure! And how recently acquired is most of our knowledge of the past! Almost everything we know about paleolithic and neolithic man, about the Sumerian, Hittite and Minoan civilizations, about pre-Buddhist India and pre-Columbian America, about the origins of such fundamental human arts as agriculture, metallurgy and writing, was discovered within the last sixty or seventy years. And there are still new worlds of history to conquer. Even in such well-dug regions as the Near and Middle East literally thousands of sites await the burrowing archeologist, and thousands more are scattered far and wide over Asia, Africa and the Americas. Moreover, there is work for the explorer in times and cultures much nearer home. For, strange as it may seem, it is only within the last generation that certain aspects of quite recent European history have come to be critically investigated. A very striking example of this failure to explore our own back yard is supplied by the history of music. Practically everybody likes music; but practically nobody has heard any music composed before 1680. Renaissance poetry, painting and sculpture have been studied in minutest detail, and the labors of five generations of scholars have been made available to the public in hundreds of monographs, general histories, critical appreciations and guidebooks. But Renaissance music —an art which was fully the equal of Renaissance poetry, painting and sculpture—has received relatively little attention from scholars and is almost unknown to the concert-going public. Donatello and Piero della Francesca, Titian and Michelangelo—their names are household words and, in the original or in reproduction, their works are familiar to everyone. But how few people have heard, or even heard of, the music of Dufay and Josquin, of Okeghem and Obrecht, of Ysaac and Wert and Marenzio, of Dunstable, Byrd and Victoria! All that can be said is that, twenty years ago, the number was still smaller than it is today. And a couple of generations earlier the ignorance was almost total. Even so great a historian as Burckhardt—the man who wrote with such insight, such a wealth of erudition, about every other aspect of the Renaissance in Italy—knew next to nothing about the music of his chosen period. It was not his fault; there were no modern editions of the music and nobody ever played or sang it. Consider, by way of example, the *Vespers*, composed in 1610 by one of the most famous, one of the most historically important of Italian musicians, Claudio Monteverdi. After the middle of the seventeenth century this extraordinary masterpiece was never again performed until the year 1935. One can say without any exaggeration that, until very recent times, more was known about the Fourth Dynasty Egyptians, who built the pyramids, than about the Flemish and Italian contemporaries of Shakespeare who wrote the madrigals.

This sort of thing, let us remember, has happened before. From the time of the composer's death in 1750 to the performance under Mendelssohn, in 1829, of the *Passion According to St. Matthew,* no European audience had ever heard a choral work by John Sebastian Bach. What Mendelssohn and the nineteenth-century musicologists, critics and virtuosi did for Bach another generation of scholars and performers has begun to do for Bach's predecessors, whose works have been rediscovered, published in critical editions, performed here and there and even occasionally recorded. It is gradually dawning upon us that the three centuries before Bach are just as interesting musically speaking, as the two centuries after Bach.

There exists in Los Angeles a laudable institution called the Southern California Chamber Music Society. This society sponsors a series of Monday evening concerts, at which, besides much fine and seldom-heard classical and contemporary music, many pre-Bach compositions are performed. Among these earlier compositions one group stands out in my memory as uniquely interesting—a group of madrigals and motets by an almost exact contemporary of Shakespeare, Carlo Gesualdo. Another English poet, John Milton, was an admirer of Gesualdo and, while in Italy, bought a volume of his madrigals which, with a number of other books, he sent home by ship from Venice. Milton's admiration is understandable; for Gesualdo's music is so strange and, in its strangeness, so beautiful that it haunts the memory and fires the imagination. Listening to it, one is filled with questioning wonder. What sort of a man was it who wrote such music? Where does it fit into the general musical scheme, and what is its relevance for us? In the paragraphs that follow I shall try, in the light of my sadly limited knowledge of Gesualdo's time and of Gesualdo's art, to answer, or at least to speculate about, these questions.

Let us begin, then, with the biographical facts. Carlo Gesualdo was born in or about 1560, either at Naples or in one of his father's numerous castles in the neighborhood of Naples. The Gesualdi were of ancient and noble lineage, had been barons for fifteen generations, counts for eight, dukes for four or five, and, for the past three generations, hereditary Princes of Venosa. Carlo's mother hailed from northern Italy and was a sister of the great Cardinal Carlo Borromeo, who died in 1584 and was canonized in 1610. In his later years Gesualdo could speak not only of my father, the Prince, but even (going one better) of my uncle, the Saint. Of the boy's education we know nothing and can only infer, from his later achievements, that he must have had a very thorough grounding in music.

Every age has its own characteristic horrors. In ours there are the Communists and nuclear weapons, there are nationalism and the threat of overpopulation. The violence in which we indulge is truly monstrous; but it is, so to say, official violence, ordered by the proper authorities, sanctioned by law, ideologically justified and confined to periodical world wars, between which we enjoy the blessings of law, order and internal peace. In the Naples of Gesualdo's day, violence was ruggedly individualistic, unorganized and chronic. There was little nationalism and world wars were unknown; but dynastic squabbles were frequent and the Barbary Corsairs were incessantly active, raiding the coasts of Italy in search of slaves and booty. But the citizen's worst enemies were not the pirates and the foreign princes; they were his own neighbors. Between the wars and the forays of the infidels there were no lucid intervals, such as we enjoy between our wholesale massacres, of civic decency, but an almost lawless and policeless freefor-all in a society composed of a class of nobles, utterly corrupted by Spanish ideas of honor (Naples was then a Spanish colony), a small and insignificant middle class and a vast mob of plebeians living in bestial squalor and savagery, and sunk, head over ears, in the most degrading superstition. It was in this monstrous environment that Carlo grew up, an immensely talented and profoundly neurotic member of the overprivileged minority.

In 1586 he married Maria d'Avalos, a girl of twenty, but already a widow. (Her previous husband, it was whispered, had died of too much connubial bliss.) Gesualdo had two children by this lady, one of his own begetting, the other almost certainly not; for after two years of marriage, the lovely and lively Donna Maria had taken a lover, Don Fabrizio Carafa, Duke of Andria. On the night of October 16, 1590, accompanied by three of his retainers, armed with swords, halberds and arquebuses, Gesualdo broke into his wife's room, found the lovers in bed and had them killed. After which he took horse and galloped off to one of his castles where, after liquidating his second child (the one of doubtful paternity), he remained for several months—not to escape the law (for he was never prosecuted and, if he had been, would certainly have been acquitted as having done only what any injured husband had the right and even the duty to do), but to avoid the private vengeance of the Avalos and Carafa families. These last were outraged, not so much by the murder (which was entirely in order) as by the fact that the killing had been done by lackeys and not by Gesualdo himself. According to the code of honor, blue blood might be spilled only by the possessor of blue blood, never by a member of the lower classes.

Time passed and the storm, as all storms finally do, blew over. From his feudal keep in the hills Gesualdo was able to return to Naples and the cultivated society of madrigal-singing amateurs and professional musicians. He began composing, he even published. Second and third editions of his madrigals were called for. He was almost a best seller.

The Prince of Venosa, the *Serenissimo* as he was called by his respectful contemporaries, was now an eligible widower, and sometime in 1592 or 1593 his paternal uncle, the Archbishop of Naples, entered into negotiations with Alfonso II, Duke of Ferrara, with a view to securing for his nephew a princess of the great house of Este. Suitable financial arrangements were made, and in February, 1594, the nuptials of Carlo Gesualdo and Donna Leonora d'Este were celebrated at Ferrara with all the usual pomp. After a short stay in the south, Gesualdo returned to Ferrara with his bride, now pregnant, rented a palace and settled down for a long stay.

Ferrara in 1594 was a setting sun, still dazzling, but on the brink of darkness. Three years later, on the death of Duke Alfonso without a male heir, the city, which was a papal fief, reverted to its overlord, the Pope, and was incorporated into the States of the Church. The glory that was Ferrara vanished overnight, forever.

That Ferrara should ever have become a glory is one of the unlikeliest facts in that long succession of actualized improbabilities which make up human history. The ducal territory was small and, in those malarious days, unhealthy. Its material resources were scanty, and the most important local industry was the smoking of eels, caught in the winding channels of the delta of the Po. Militarily, the state was feeble in the extreme. Powerful and not always friendly neighbors surrounded it and, to make matters worse, it lay on the invasion route from Germany and Austria. In spite of which Ferrara became and for a hundred and fifty years—from the middle of the fifteenth to the end of the sixteenth century—remained not only a sovereign state of considerable political importance, but also one of the most brilliant intellectual centers of Western Europe. This position the city owed entirely to the extraordinary ability and good taste of its rulers, the dukes of the house of Este. In the game of international and inter-dynastic politics, the Estensi were consummately skillful players. At home they were not too tyrannical, and had a happy knack, when discontent ran high, of blaming their ministers for everything and so maintaining their own popularity.

Their domestic life was relatively harmonious. Unlike many of the ruling families of Italy, the Estensi seldom murdered one another. True, a few years before Carlo's marriage to Leonora, the Duke had had his sister's lover strangled. But this was an exceptional act—and anyhow he refrained from strangling the lady; the integrity of the clan was preserved. But from our present point of view the most remarkable thing about the Dukes of Ferrara was their steady patronage of talent, especially in the fields of literature and music. The greatest Italian poets of the sixteenth century—from Ariosto at the beginning to Guarini and Tasso at the end—were summoned to Ferrara, where the dukes either gave them jobs in the administration of the state, or else paid them a pension, so that they might devote the whole of their time to literature. Musicians were no less welcome than poets. From 1450 to 1600 most of the greatest composers of the time visited Ferrara, and many of them stayed at the court for long periods. They came from Burgundy and Flanders, the most productive centers of early Renaissance music; they came from France, they came even from faraway England. And later, when the Italians had learned their lesson from the North and had become, in their turn, the undisputed leaders in the field, they came from all over the peninsula. The huge square *castello* at the heart of the city, the ducal hunting lodges, the summer palaces by the sea, the mansions of the nobles and the foreign ambassadors—all of them resounded with music: Learned polyphonic music and popular songs and dances. Music for lutes (there was a functionary at the ducal court whose sole duty it was to keep the lutes perpetually in tune) and music for the organ, for viols, for wind instruments, for the earliest forms of harpsichord and clavichord. Music performed by amateurs sitting around the fire or at a table, and music rendered by professional virtuosi. Music in church, music at home and (this was a novelty) music in the concert hall. For there were daily concerts in the various ducal palaces, concerts in which as many as sixty players and singers would take part. On grand occasions—and at Ferrara there seems to have been a grand occasion at least twice a week— there were masques with choral interludes, there were plays with overtures and incidental music, there were performances, in those sunset years of decline, of the first rudimentary operas. And what wonderful voices could be heard at Alfonso's court!

Ferrara's Three Singing Ladies were world famous. There was Lucrezia Bendidio, there was Laura Peperara and, most remarkable of the trio, there was the beautiful, learned and many-talented Tarquinia Molza. But every Eden, alas, has its serpent, and, in Tarquinia's musical paradise, there was not merely a reptile to rear its ugly head; there were several Adams as well.

Tarquinia married and was widowed; then, in her middle thirties she fell under the spell of that most charming and romantic of men, Torquato Tasso. The poet, who wrote a great deal about love, but very seldom made it, was alarmed, and, putting up a barrage of platonic verse, beat a hasty retreat. Tarquinia had to be content, for several years, with lovers of less exalted intellectual rank. Then, in her forties, she found another man of genius, the great Flemish composer, Giaches Wert, who was in the employ of the Duke of Mantua. Their passion was reciprocal and so violent that it created a scandal. The unhappy Tarquinia was exiled to Modena and Wert returned, alone, to the court of the Gonzagas.

For a man of Gesualdo's gifts and sensibilities, Ferrara combined the advantages of a seat of higher education with those of a heaven on earth. It was a place where he could simultaneously enjoy himself and learn. And learn he certainly did. The madrigals he composed before 1594 are admirable in their workmanship; but their style, though his own, is still within the bounds of sixteenth-century music. The madrigals and motets written after his stay at Ferrara are beyond those bounds—far out in a kind of no-man's land.

Gesualdo left no memoirs and, in spite of his high contemporary reputation and his exalted position in the world, very little is known of his later life, except that he was unhappy and dogged by misfortune. His son by his second wife died in childhood. His son by the murdered Donna Maria, the heir to all the family titles and estates, grew up to loathe his father and long for his death; but it was he who died first. One of Gesualdo's daughters went to the bad and presented him with several illegitimate grandchildren. Meanwhile he was constantly tormented, says a contemporary gossip writer, by a host of demons. His lifelong neurosis had deepened, evidently into something like insanity. Apart from music, which he went on composing with undiminished powers, his only pleasure seems to have been physical pain. He would, we are told, submit ecstatically to frequent whippings. These at last became a physiological necessity. According to that much persecuted philosopher, Tommaso Campanella, the Prince of Venosa could never go to the bathroom (*cacare non poterat*) unless he had first been flogged by a servant specially trained to perform this duty. Remorse for the crimes of his youth weighed heavily on Gesualdo's conscience. The law might excuse, public opinion might even approve; but Holy Writ was explicit: *Thou shalt not kill.* A few years before his death in 1613 he endowed a Capuchin friary in his native town of Gesualdo and built a handsome church. Over the altar hung a huge penitential picture, painted to the prince's order and under his personal direction. This picture, which still survives, represents Christ the Judge seated on high and flanked by the Blessed Virgin and the Archangel Michael. Below Him, arranged symmetrically, in descending tiers, to right and left, are Saint Francis and Saint Mary Magdalen, Saint Dominic and Saint Catherine of Siena, all of them, to judge by their gestures, emphatically interceding with the Savior on behalf of Carlo Gesualdo, who kneels in the lower left-hand corner, dressed in black velvet and an enormous ruff, while, splendid in the scarlet robes of a Prince of the Church, his uncle, the Saint, stands beside him, with one hand resting protectively on the sinner's shoulder. Opposite them kneels Carlo's aunt, Isabella Borromeo, in the costume of a nun, and at the center of this family group is the murdered child, as a heavenly cherub. Below, at the very bottom of the composition, Donna Maria and the Duke of Andria are seen roasting everlastingly in those flames from which the man who had them butchered still hopes against hope to be delivered.

So much for the facts of our composer's life—facts which confirm an old and slightly disquieting truth: namely, that between an artist's work and his personal behavior there is no very obvious correspondence. The work may be sublime,the behavior anything from silly to insane and criminal. Conversely the behavior may be blameless and the work uninteresting or downright bad. Artistic merit has nothing to do with any other kind of merit. In the language of theology, talent is a gratuitous grace, completely unconnected with saving grace or even with ordinary virtue or sanity.

From the man we now pass to his strange music. Like most of the great composers of his day, Gesualdo wrote exclusively for the human voice—to be more precise, for groups of five or six soloists singing contrapuntally. All his five- or six-part compositions belong to one or other of two closely related musical forms, the madrigal and the motet. The motet is the older of the two forms and consists of a setting, for any number of voices from three to twelve, of a short passage, in Latin, from the Bible or some other sacred text. Madrigals may be defined as nonreligious motets. They are settings, not of sacred Latin texts, but of short poems in the vernacular. In most cases, these settings were for five voices; but the composer was free to write for any number of parts from three to eight or more.

The madrigal came into existence in the thirties of the sixteenth century and, for seventy or eighty years, remained the favorite art form of all composers of secular music. Contrapuntal writing in five parts is never likely to be popular, and the madrigal made its appeal, not to the general public, but to a select audience of professional musicians and highly educated amateurs, largely aristocratic and connected for the most part with one or other of the princely or ecclesiastical courts of the day. (One is amazed, when one reads the history of renaissance music, by the good taste of Europe's earlier rulers. Popes and emperors, kings, princes and cardinals— they never make a mistake. Invariably, one might almost say infallibly, they choose for their chapel masters and court composers the men whose reputation has stood the test of time and whom we now recognize as the most gifted musicians of their day. Left to themselves, what sort of musicians would our twentieth-century monarchs and presidents choose to patronize? One shudders to think.)

Gesualdo wrote madrigals, and a madrigal, as we have seen, is a non-religious motet. But what else is it? Let us begin by saying what it is not. First and foremost, the madrigal, though sung, is not a song. It does not, that is to say, consist of a tune, repeated stanza after stanza. Nor has it anything to do with the art form known to later musicians as the aria. An aria is a piece of music for a solo voice, accompanied by instruments or by other voices. It begins, in most cases, with an introduction, states a melodic theme in one key, states a second theme in another key, goes into a series of modulations and ends with a recapitulation of one or both themes in the original key. Nothing of all this is to be found in the madrigal. In the madrigal there is no solo singing. All the five or more voices are of equal importance, and they move, so to speak, straight ahead, whereas the aria and the song move in the equivalent of circles or spirals. In other words, there are, in the madrigal, no returns to a starting point, no systematic recapitulations. Its form bears no resemblance to the sonata form or even to the suite form. It might be described as a choral tone poem, written in counterpoint. When counterpoint is written within a structural pattern, such as the fugue or canon, the listener can follow the intricacies of the music almost indefinitely. But where the counterpoint has no structural pattern imposed upon it, where it moves forward freely, without any returns to a starting point, the ear finds it very hard to follow it, attentively and understandingly, for more than a few minutes at a stretch. Hence the brevity of the typical madrigal, the extraordinary succinctness of its style.

During the three quarters of a century of its existence, the madrigal underwent a steady development in the direction of completer, ever intenser expressiveness. At the beginning of the period it is a piece of emotionally neutral polyphony, whose whole beauty consists in the richness and complexity of its many-voiced texture. At the end, in the work of such masters as Marenzio, Monteverdi and, above all, Gesualdo, it has become a kind of musical miracle, in which seemingly incompatible elements are reconciled in a higher synthesis. The intricacies of polyphony are made to yield the most powerfully expressive effects, and this polyphony has become so flexible that it can, at any moment, transmute itself into blocks of chords or a passage of dramatic declamation.

During his stay at Ferrara, Gesualdo was in contact with the most "advanced" musicians of his day. A few miles away, at Mantua, the great Giaches Wert, sick and prematurely old, was still composing; and at the same court lived a much younger musician, Claudio Monteverdi, who was to carry to completion the revolution in music begun by Wert. That revolution was the supersession of polyphony by monody, the substitution of the solo voice, with instrumental or vocal accompaniment, for the madrigalist's five or six voices of equal importance. Gesualdo did not follow the Mantuans into monody; but he was certainly influenced by Wert's essays in musical expressionism. Those strange cries of grief, pain and despair, which occur so frequently in his later madrigals, were echoes of the cries introduced by Wert into his dramatic cantatas.

At Ferrara itself Gesualdo's closest musical friends were Count Fontanelli and a professional composer and virtuoso, Luzzasco Luzzaschi. Like Gesualdo, Fontanelli was an aristocrat and had murdered an unfaithful wife; unlike Gesualdo, he was not a man of genius, merely a good musician passionately interested in the latest developments of the art. Luzzaschi was a writer of madrigals, and had invented a number of expressive devices, which Gesualdo employed in his own later productions. More important, he was the only man who knew how to play on, and even compose for, an extraordinary machine, which was the greatest curiosity in Duke Alfonso's collection of musical instruments. This was the archicembalo, a large keyboard instrument belonging to the harpsichord family, but so designed that a player could distinguish, for example, between B flat and A sharp, could descend chromatically from E, through E flat, D sharp, D, D flat, C sharp to a final C major chord. The archicembalo required thirty-one keys to cover each octave and must have been fantastically difficult to play and still harder, one would imagine, to compose for. The followers of Schoenberg are far behind Luzzaschi; *their* scale has only twelve tones, *his*, thirty-one. Luzzaschi's thirty-one-tone compositions (none of which, unfortunately, survive) and his own experiments on the archicembalo profoundly influenced the style of Gesualdo's later madrigals. Forty years ago, the Oxford musicologist, Ernest Walker, remarked that Gesualdo's most famous madrigal, *Moro lasso*, sounded like "Wagner gone wrong." Hardly an adequate criticism of Gesualdo, but not without significance.

The mention of Wagner is fully justified; for the incessant chromaticisms of Gesualdo's later writing found no parallel in music until the time of *Tristan*. As for the "gone-wrongness" —this is due to Gesualdo's unprecedented and, until recent times, almost unimitated treatment of harmonic progression. In his madrigals successive chords are related in ways which conform neither to the rules of sixteenth-century polyphony, nor to the rules of harmony which hold good from the middle of the seventeenth century to the beginning of the twentieth. An infallible ear is all that, in most cases, preserves these strange and beautiful progressions from seeming altogether arbitrary and chaotic. Thanks to that infallible ear of his, Gesualdo's harmonies move, always astonishingly, but always with a logic of their own, from one impossible, but perfectly satisfying, beauty to another. And the harmonic strangeness is never allowed to continue for too long at a stretch. With consummate art, Gesualdo alternates these extraordinary passages of Wagner-gone-wrong with passages of pure traditional polyphony. To be fully effective, every elaboration must be shown in a setting of simplicity, every revolutionary novelty should emerge from a background of the familiar. For the composers of arias, the simple and familiar background for their floridly expressive melodies was a steady, rhythmically constant accompaniment. For Gesualdo, simplicity and familiarity meant the rich, many-voiced texture of contrapuntal writing. The setting for Wagner-gone-wrong is Palestrina.

Every madrigal is the setting of a short poem in the vernacular, just as every motet is the setting of a short passage from the Vulgate or some other piece of sacred Latin literature. The texts of the motets were generally in prose, and the early polyphonists saw no obvious reason for imposing upon this essentially rectilinear material a circular musical form. After the invention of the aria, the composers of music for prose texts habitually distorted the sense and rhythm of their words in order to force them into the circular, verselike patterns of their new art form. From Alessandro Scarlatti, through Bach and Handel, Mozart, Haydn and Mendelssohn —all the great composers from 1650 to 1850 provide examples, in their musical settings, of what may be called the versification of prose. To do this, they were compelled to repeat phrases and individual words again and again, to prolong single syllables to inordinate length, to recapitulate, note for note, or with variations, entire paragraphs. How different was the procedure of the madrigalists! Instead of versifying prose, they found it necessary, because of the nature of their art form, to prosify verse. The regular recurrences of lines and stanzas—these have no place in the madrigal, just as they have no place in the motet. Like good prose, the madrigal is rectilinear, not circular. Its movement is straight ahead, irreversible, asymmetrical. When they set a piece of poetry to music, the madrigalists set it phrase by phrase, giving to each phrase, even each word, its suitable expression and linking the successive moods by a constant adaptation of the polyphonic writing, not by the imposition from outside of a structural pattern. Every madrigal, as I have said, is a choral tone poem. But instead of lasting for a whole hour, like the huge, spectacular machines of Liszt and Richard Strauss, it concentrates its changing moods into three or four minutes of elaborate and yet intensely expressive counterpoint.

The Italian madrigalists chose their texts, for the most part, from the best poets. Dante was considered too harsh and old-fashioned; but his great fourteenth-century successor, Petrarch, remained a perennial favorite. Among more recent poets, Ariosto, though set fairly frequently, was much less popular than Guarini and Tasso, whose emotional tone was more emphatic and who took pleasure in just those violent contrasts of feeling which lent themselves most perfectly to the purposes of the madrigalist. In their shorter pieces (pieces written expressly to be set to music) Tasso and his contemporaries made use of a kind of epigrammatic style, in which antithesis, paradox and oxymoron played a major part and were turned into a literary convention, so that every versifier now talked of dolorous joy, sweet agony, loathing love and living death— to the immense delight of the musicians, for whom these emotional ambiguities, these abrupt changes of feeling offered golden opportunities.

Gesualdo was a personal friend of Torquato Tasso and, during the last, mad, wandering years of the poet's life, helped him with money and letters of introduction. As we should expect, he set a number of Tasso's poems to music. For the rest he made use of anything that came to hand. Many of his finest madrigals are based on snatches of verse having no literary merit whatsoever. That they served his purpose was due to the fact that they were written in the current idiom and contained plenty of emphatically contrasting words, which he could set to appropriately expressive music. Gesualdo's indifference to the poetical quality of his texts, and his methods of setting words to music, are very clearly illustrated in one of the most astonishing of his madrigals, *Ardita zanzaretta*—a work, incidentally, whose performance at Los Angeles in the Autumn of 1955 was probably the first in more than three hundred years. This extraordinary little masterpiece compresses into less than three minutes every mood from the cheerfully indifferent to the perversely voluptuous, from the gay to the tragic, and in the process employs every musical resource, from traditional polyphony to Wagner-gone-wrong chromaticism and the strangest harmonic progressions, from galloping rhythms to passages of long, suspended notes. Then we look at the text and discover that this amazing music is the setting of half-a-dozen lines of doggerel. The theme of *Ardita zanzaretta* is the same as the theme of a tiny poem by Tasso, tasteless enough in all conscience, but written with a certain elegance of style. A little mosquito (*zanzaretta*) settles on the bosom of the beloved, bites and gets swatted by the exasperated lady. What a delicious fate, muses Tasso, to die in a place where it is such bliss to swoon away!

> *Felice te felice*
> *più che nel rogo oriental Fenice!*

(Oh happy, happy bug—more happy than the Phoenix on its oriental pyre!)

Gesualdo's nameless librettist takes the same subject, robs it of whatever charm Tasso was able to lend it, and emphasizes the bloodiness of the mosquito's fate by introducing—twice over in the space of only six lines—the word *stringere*, meaning to squeeze, squash, squelch. Another improvement on Tasso is the addition of a playful sally by the lover. Since he longs to share the mosquito's fate, he too will take a bite in the hope of being squashed to death on the lady's bosom. What follows is a literal translation of this nonsense, accompanied by a description of the music accompanying each phrase. "A bold little mosquito bites the fair breast of her who consumes my heart." This is set to a piece of pure neutral polyphony, very rapid and, despite its textural richness, very light. But the lady is not content with consuming the lover's heart; she also "keeps in cruel pain." Here the dancing polyphony of the first bars gives place to a series of chords moving slowly from dissonance to unprepared dissonance. The pain, however unreal in the text, becomes in the music genuinely excruciating. Now the mosquito "makes its escape, but rashly flies back to that fair breast which steals my heart away. Whereupon she catches it." All this is rendered in the same kind of rapid, emotionally neutral polyphony as was heard in the opening bars. But now comes another change. The lady not only catches the insect, "she squeezes it and gives it death." The word *morte*, death, occurs in almost all Gesualdo's madrigals. Sometimes it carries its literal meaning; more often, however, it is used figuratively, to signify sensual ecstasy, the swoon of love. But this makes no difference to Gesualdo. Whatever its real significance, and whoever it is that may be dying (the lover metaphorically or, in a literal sense, a friend, a mosquito, the crucified Savior), he gives the word, *morte*, a musical expression of the most tragic and excruciating kind. For the remorseful assassin, death was evidently the most terrifying of prospects.

From the insect's long-drawn musical martyrdom, we return to cheerfulness and pure polyphony. "To share its happy fate, I too will bite you." Gesualdo was a pain-loving masochist and this playful suggestion of sadism left him unmoved. The counterpoint glides along in a state of emotional neutrality. Then comes a passage of chromatic yearning on the words "my beloved, my precious one." Then polyphony again. "And if you catch and squeeze me...." After this, the music becomes unadulterated Gesualdo. There is a cry of pain—*ahi!*—and then "I will swoon away and, upon that fair breast, taste delicious poison." The musical setting of these final words is a concentrated version of the love-potion scene in *Tristan*—the chief difference being that Gesualdo's harmonic progressions are far bolder than any attempted, two and a half centuries later, by Richard Wagner.

Should pictures tell stories? Should music have a connection with literature? In the past the answer would have been, unanimously, yes. Every great painter was a raconteur of Biblical or mythological anecdotes; every great composer was a setter-to-music of sacred or profane texts. Today the intrusion of literature into the plastic arts is regarded almost as a crime. In the field of music, this anti-literary reign of terror has been less savage. Program music is deplored (not without reason, considering the horrors bequeathed to us by the Victorian era); but in spite of much talk about "pure music," good composers still write songs, masses, operas and cantatas. Good painters would do well to follow their example and permit themselves to be inspired to still better painting by the promptings of a literary theme. In the hands of a bad painter, pictorial storytelling, however sublime the subject matter, is merely comicstrip art on a large scale. But when a good painter tells the same story, the case is entirely different. The exigencies of illustration—the fact that he has to show such-and-such personages, in such-and-such an environment, performing such-and-such actions—stimulates his imagination on every level, including the purely pictorial level, with the result that he produces a work which, though literary, is of the highest quality as a formal composition. Take any famous painting of the past—Botticelli's "Calumny of Apelles," for example, or Titian's "Bacchus and Ariadne." Both of these are admirable illustrations; but both are much more than illustrations—they are very complex and yet perfectly harmonious and unified arrangements of forms and colors. Moreover the richness of their formal material is a direct consequence of their literary subject matter. Left to itself, the pictorial imagination even of a painter of genius could never conjure up such a subtle and complicated pattern of shapes and hues as we find in these illustrations of texts by Lucian and Ovid. To achieve their purely plastic triumphs, Botticelli and Titian required to be stimulated by a literary theme. It is a highly significant fact that, in no abstract or non-representational painting of today, do we find a purely formal composition having anything like the richness, the harmonious complexity, created in the process of telling a story, by the masters of earlier periods. The traditional distinction between the crafts and the fine arts is based, among other things, on degrees of complexity. A good picture is a greater work of art than a good bowl or a good vase. Why? Because it unifies in one harmonious whole more, and more diverse, elements of human experience than are or can be unified and harmonized in the pot. Some of the non-representational pictures painted in the course of the last fifty years are very beautiful; but even the best of them are minor works, inasmuch as the number of elements of human experience which they combine and harmonize is pitifully small. In them we look in vain for that ordered profusion, that lavish and yet perfectly controlled display of intellectual wealth, which we discover in the best works of the "literary" painters of the past.

In this respect the composer is more fortunate than the painter. It is psychologically possible to write "pure music" that shall be just as harmoniously complex, just as rich in unified diversities, as music inspired by a literary text. But even in music the intrusion of literature has often been beneficent. But for the challenge presented by a rather absurd anecdote couched in very feeble language, Beethoven would never have produced the astonishing "pure music" of the second act of *Fidelio*. And it was Da Ponte, with his rhymed versions of the stories of Figaro and Don Giovanni, who stimulated Mozart to reveal himself in the fullness of his genius. Where music is a matter of monody and harmony, with a structural pattern (the sonata form or the suite form) imposed, so to speak, from the outside, it is easy to write "pure music," in which the successive moods shall be expressed, at some length, in successive movements. But where there is no structural pattern, where the style is polyphonic and the movement of the music is not circular, but straight ahead, irreversible and rectilinear, the case is different. Such a style demands extreme brevity and the utmost succinctness of expression. To meet these demands for brevity and succinctness, the musical imagination requires a text—and a text, moreover, of the kind favored by the madrigalists, paradoxical, antithetical, full of

> All things counter, original, spare, strange
> Whatever is fickle, freckled (who know how?)
> With swift, slow; sweet, sour; adazzle, dim.

Contemporary musicians, who aspire to write "pure music" in forms as rich, subtle and compact as those devised by Gesualdo and his contemporaries, would do well to turn once more to the poets.

(From *Tomorrow and Tomorrow and Tomorrow*)

MATTERS OF
TASTE AND STYLE

Variations on a Baroque Tomb

"The skeleton," as we all know, "was invisible in the happy days of pagan art." And invisible it remained, in spite of Christianity, for most of the centuries that followed. Throughout the Middle Ages, the knights, the mitered bishops, the ladies who warm their feet on the backs of little dogs—all are reassuringly in the flesh. No skulls adorn their tombs, no bones, no grisly reapers. Artists in words may cry, "Alas, my heart will break in three; *Terribilis mors conturbat me.*" Artists in stone are content to carve the likeness of a sleeper upon a bed. The Renaissance comes and still the sleep persists, tranquil amid the sculptured dreams of a paradise half earthly, half celestial.

> Those Pans and Nymphs ye wot of, and perchance
> Some tripod, thyrsus, with a vase or so,
> The Savior at his sermon on the mount,
> St. Praxed in a glory, and one Pan
> Ready to twitch the Nymph's last garment off,
> And Moses with the tables.

But by the middle of the sixteenth century a change has taken place. The effigy no longer sleeps, but opens its eyes and sits up—ideally noble, as on the Medicean tombs, or soberly a portrait, like any one of those admirable busts in their round niches between the pilasters of a classical design. And at the base, below the Latin inscription, it not infrequently happens (at any rate in Rome and after 1550) that a little skull, in bone-white marble, reminds the onlooker of what he himself

197

will soon be, of what the original of the portrait has already become.

Why should the death's head have become fashionable at this particular moment of history? The religiously minded might surmise that it had something to do with the Counter Reformation; the medically minded, that it was connected with that sixteenth-century pandemic of syphilis, whose noseless victims were a constant reminder of man's latter end; the artistically minded, that some mortuary sculptor of the time had a taste for, and a happy knack with, bones. I do not venture to decide between the possible alternatives, but am content to record the fact, observable by anyone who has been in Rome, that there, after the middle of the century, the skulls indubitably are.

As the years pass these reminders of mortality assume an even greater importance. From being miniatures they grow in a short time into full-blown, death-sized replicas of the thing behind the face. And suddenly, imitating those bodiless seraphs of medieval and Renaissance painting, they sprout a pair of wings and learn to fly. Meanwhile the art of the late Renaissance has become the Baroque. By an aesthetic necessity, because it is impossible for self-conscious artists to go on doing what has been supremely well done by their predecessors, the symmetrical gives place to the disbalanced, the static to the dynamic, the formalized to the realistic. Statues are caught in the act of changing their positions; pictorial compositions try to break out of their frames. Where there was understatement, there is now emphasis; where there was measure and humanity, there is now the enormous, the astounding, the demigod and the epileptic sub-man.

Consider, for example, those skulls on the monuments. They have grown in size; their truth to death is overpowering and, to heighten the effect of verisimilitude, the sculptor has shifted them from their old place on the central axis and now shows them, casual and unposed, in profile or three-quarters face, looking up to heaven or down into the grave. And their wings! Vast, wildly beating, windblown—the wings of vultures in a hurricane. The appetite for the inordinate grows with what it feeds upon, and along with it grow the virtuosity of the artists and the willingness of their patrons to pay for ever more astounding monuments. By 1630 the skull is no longer adequate as a memento mori; it has become necessary to represent the entire skeleton.

The most grandiose of these reminders of our mortality are the mighty skeletons which Bernini made for the tombs of Urban VIII and Alexander VII in St. Peter's. Majestic in his vestments and intensely alive, each of the two Popes sits there aloft, blessing his people. Some feet below him, on either side, are his special Virtues—Faith, Temperance, Fortitude, who knows? In the middle, below the Pontiff, is the gigantic emblem of death. On Urban's tomb the skeleton is holding (slightly cock-eyed, for it would be intolerably old-fashioned and unrealistic if the thing were perfectly level) a black marble scroll inscribed with the Pope's name and title; on Alexander's the monster has been "stopped," as the photographers say, in the act of shooting up from the doorway leading into the vault. Up it comes, like a rocket, at an angle of sixty or seventy degrees, and as it rises it effortlessly lifts six or seven tons of the red marble drapery, which mitigates the rigidities of architecture and transforms the statically geometrical into something mobile and indeterminate.

The emphasis, in these two extraordinary works, is not on heaven, hell, and purgatory, but on physical dissolution and the grave. The terror which inspired such works as the *Dies Irae* was of the second death, the death inflicted by an angry judge upon the sinner's soul. Here, on the contrary, the theme is the first death, the abrupt passage from animation to insensibility and from worldly glory to supper with the convocation of politic worms.

> *Chi un tempo, carco d'amorose prede,*
> *ebbe l'ostro alle guance e l'oro al crine,*
> *deforme, arido teschio, ecco, si vede.*

Bernini's tombs are by no means unique. The Roman churches are full of cautionary skeletons. In Santa Maria sopra Minerva, for example, there is a small monument attached to one of the columns on the north side of the church. It commemorates a certain Vizzani, if I remember rightly, a jurisconsult who died some time before the middle of the seventeenth century. Here, as in the wall monuments of the High Renaissance, a bust looks out of a rounded niche placed above the long Latin catalogue of the dead man's claims upon the attention of posterity. It is the bust, so intensely life-like as to be almost a caricature, of a florid individual in his middle forties, no fool evidently, but wearing an expression of serene and unquestioning complacency. Socially, professionally, financially, what a huge success his life has been! And how strongly, like Milton, he feels that "nothing profits more than self-esteem founded on just and right"! But suddenly we become aware that the bust in its round frame is being held in an almost amorous embrace by a great skeleton in high relief, whizzing diagonally, from left to right, across the monument. The lawyer and all his achievements, all his self-satisfaction, are being wafted away into darkness and oblivion.

Of the same kind, but still more astounding, are the tombs of the Pallavicino family in San Francesco a Ripa. Executed by Mazzuoli at the beginning of the eighteenth century, these monuments are among the last and at the same time the most extravagant outflowerings of the Baroque spirit. Admirably carved, the usual Virtues keep guard at the base of each of the vast pyramidal structures. Above them, flapping huge wings, a ten-foot skeleton in bronze holds up for our inspection a pair of oval frames, containing busts of the departed Pallavicini. On one side of the family chapel we see the likenesses of two princely ecclesiastics. Death holds them with a studied carelessness, tilting their frames a little, one to the left, the other to the right, so that the grave ascetic faces look out, as though through the ports of a rolling ship. Opposite them, in the hands of another and, if possible, even more frightful skeleton, are two more members of the family—an elderly princess, this time, and her spouse. And what a spouse! Under the majestic wig the face is gross, many-chinned, complacently imbecile. High blood pressure inflates the whole squat person almost to bursting point; pride keeps the pig-snout chronically pointing to the skies. And it is Death who now holds him aloft; it is Corruption who, with triumphant derision, exhibits him, forever pilloried in marble, a grotesque and pitiable example of human bumptiousness.

Looking at the little fat man up there in the skeleton's clutches, one reflects, with a certain astonishment, that some Pallavicino must have ordered and presumably paid for this strange monument to a departed relative. With what intentions? To display the absurdity of the old gentleman's pretensions to grandeur? To make a mock of everything he had lived for? The answer to these questions is, at least in part, affirmative. All these Baroque tombs were doctrinally sound. The heirs of popes and princes laid out huge sums to celebrate the glories of their distinguished forebears—but laid them out on monuments whose emphatically Christian theme is the transience of earthly greatness and the vanity of human wishes. After which they addressed themselves with redoubled energy to the task of satisfying their own cravings for money, position and power. A belief in hell and the knowledge that every ambition is doomed to frustration at the hands of a skeleton have never prevented the majority of human beings from behaving as though death were no more than an unfounded rumor and survival, a thing beyond the bounds of possibility. The men of the Baroque differed from those of other epochs not in what they actually did, not even in what they thought about those doings, but in what they were ready to express of their thoughts. They liked an art that harps on

death and corruption, and were neither better nor worse than
we who are reticent about such things.

The fantastic dance of death in San Francesco a Ripa is
almost the last of its kind. Thirty years after it was carved,
Robert Blair could achieve a modest popularity by writing
such lines as these:

> Methinks I see thee with thy head low laid,
> While surfeited upon thy damask cheek
> The high-fed worm, in lazy volumes rolled,
> Riots unscared.

But eighteenth-century sculptors made no attempt to realize
these gruesome images. On graves and monuments Death no
longer comments upon the mad pretensions of his victims.
Broken columns, extinguished torches, weeping angels and
muses—these are now the emblems in vogue. The artist and
his patron are concerned to evoke sentiments less painful than
the horror of corruption. With the nineteenth century we
enter an age of stylistic revivals; but there is never a return
to the mortuary fashions of the Baroque. From the time of
Mazzuoli until the present day no monument to any important European has been adorned with death's heads or
skeletons.

We live habitually on at least three levels—the level of
strictly individual existence, the level of intellectual abstraction
and the level of historical necessity and social convention.
On the first of these levels our life is completely private; on
the others it is, at least partially, a shared and public life.
Thus, writing about death, I am on the level of intellectual
abstraction. Participating in the life of a generation to which
the mortuary art of the Baroque seems odd and alien, I am
on the level of history. But when I actually come to die, I
shall be on the first level, the level of exclusively individual
experience. That which, in human life, is shared and public
has always been regarded as more respectable than that which
is private. Kings have their Astronomers Royal, emperors their
official Historiographers; but there are no Royal Gastron-
omers, no Papal or Imperial Pornographers. Among crimes,
the social and the historical are condoned as last infirmities
of noble minds, and their perpetrators are very generally
admired. The lustful and intemperate, on the contrary, are
condemned by all—even by themselves (which was why Jesus
so much preferred them to the respectable Pharisees). We
have no God of Brothels, but the God of Battles, alas, is still
going strong.

Baroque mortuary sculpture has as its basic subject matter
the conflict, on one important front, between the public and

the private, between the social and the individual, between the historical and the existential. The prince in his curly wig, the Pope in his vestments, the lawyer with his Latin eulogy and his smirk of self-satisfaction—all these are pillars of society, representatives of great historical forces and even makers of history. But under smirk and wig and tiara is the body with its unsharable physiological processes, is the psyche with its insights and sudden graces, its abysmal imbecilities and its unavowable desires. Every public figure—and to some extent we are all public figures—is also an island universe of private experiences; and the most private of all these experiences is that of falling out of history, of being separated from society— in a word, the experience of death.

Based as they always are upon ignorance—invincible in some cases, voluntary and selective in others—historical generalizations can never be more than partially true. In spite of which and at the risk of distorting the facts to fit a theory, I would suggest that, at any given period, preoccupation with death is in inverse ratio to the prevalence of a belief in man's perfectibility through and in a properly organized society. In the art and literature of the age of Condorcet, of the age of Herbert Spencer and Karl Marx, of the age of Lenin and the Webbs there are few skeletons. Why? Because it was during the eighteenth and nineteenth centuries that men came to believe in progress, in the march of history toward an ever bigger and better future, in salvation, not for the individual, but for society. The emphasis is on history and environment, which are regarded as the primary determinants of individual destiny. Indeed, among orthodox Marxians they are now (since the canonization of Lysenko and the anathema pronounced on "reactionary Morganism") regarded as the sole determinants. Predestination, whether Augustinian or Mendelian, whether *karmic* or genetic, has been ruled out, and we are back with Helvétius and his shepherd boys who can all be transformed into Newtons, back with Dr. Watson and his infinitely conditionable infants. But meanwhile the fact remains that, in this still unregenerate world, each of us inherits a physique and a temperament. Moreover the career of every individual man or woman is essentially non-progressive. We reach maturity only to decline into decrepitude and the body's death. Could anything be more painfully obvious? And yet how rarely in the course of the past two hundred and fifty years has death been made the theme of any considerable work of art! Among the great painters only Goya has chosen to treat of death, and then only of death by violence, death in war. The mortuary sculptors, as we have seen, harp only on the sentiments surrounding death—sentiments ranging from the noble to the tender and even the voluptuous. (The most delicious buttocks in the whole repertory of art are to be found on Canova's monument to the last of the Stuarts.)

In the literature of this same period death has been handled more frequently than in painting or sculpture, but only once (to my knowledge, at least) with complete adequacy. Tolstoy's *The Death of Ivan Ilyitch* is one of the artistically most perfect and at the same time one of the most terrible books ever written. It is the story of an utterly commonplace man who is compelled to discover, step by agonizing step, that the public personage with whom, all his life, he has identified himself is hardly more than a figment of the collective imagination, and that his essential self is the solitary, insulated being who falls sick and suffers, rejects and is rejected by the world and finally (for the story has a happy ending) gives in to his destiny and in the act of surrender, at the very moment of death, finds himself alone and naked in the presence of the Light. The Baroque sculptors are concerned with the same theme but they protest too much and their conscious striving for sublimity is apt to defeat its own object. Tolstoy is never emphatic, indulges in no rhetorical flourishes, speaks simply of the most difficult matters and flatly, matter-of-factly of the most terrible. That is why his book has such power and is so profoundly disturbing to our habitual complacency. We are shocked by it in much the same way as we are shocked by pornography—and for the same reason. Sex is almost as completely private a matter as death, and a work of art which powerfully expresses the truth about either of them is very painful to the respectable public figure we imagine ourselves to be. Nobody can have the consolations of religion or philosophy unless he has first experienced their desolations. And nothing is more desolating than a thorough knowledge of the private self. Hence the utility of such books as *Ivan Ilyitch* and, I would venture to add, such books as Henry Miller's *Tropic of Cancer*.

And here let me add a parenthetical note on the pornography of the age which witnessed the rise of the ideas of progress and social salvation. Most of it is merely pretty, an affair of wish-fulfillments—Boucher carried to his logical conclusion. The most celebrated pornographer of the time, the Marquis de Sade, is a mixture of escapist maniac and *philosophe*. He lives in a world where insane phantasy alternates with post-Voltairean ratiocination; where impossible orgies are interrupted in order that the participants may talk, sometimes shrewdly, but more often in the shallowest eighteenth-century way, about morals, politics and metaphysics. Here, for example, is a typical specimen of Sadian

sociology. "Is incest dangerous? Certainly not. It extends
family ties and consequently renders more active the citizen's
love of his fatherland." In this passage, as throughout the
work of this oddest product of the Enlightenment, we see the
public figure doing his silly best to rationalize the essentially
unrationalizable facts of private existence. But what we need,
if we are to know ourselves, is the truthful and penetrating
expression in art of precisely these unrationalizable facts—
the facts of death, as in *Ivan Ilyitch,* the facts of sex, as in
Tropic of Cancer, the facts of pain and cruelty, as in Goya's
Disasters, the facts of fear and disgust and fatigue, as in that
most horrifyingly truthful of war books, *The Naked and the
Dead.* Ignorance is a bliss we can never afford; but to know
only ourselves is not enough. If it is to be a fruitful desolation,
self-knowledge must be made the road to a knowledge of the
Other. Unmitigated, it is but another form of ignorance and
can lead only to despair or complacent cynicism. Floundering
between time and eternity, we are amphibians and must accept
the fact. *Noverim me, noverim Te,* the prayer expresses an
essentially realistic attitude toward the universe in which,
willy-nilly, we have to live and to die.

Death is not the only private experience with which Baroque art concerns itself. A few yards from the Pallavicino
tombs reclines Bernini's statue of Blessed Ludovica Albertoni
in ecstasy. Here, as in the case of the same artist's more celebrated St. Teresa, the experience recorded is of a privacy so
special that, at a first glance, the spectator feels a shock of
embarrassment. Entering those rich chapels in San Francesco
and Santa Maria della Vittoria, one has the impression of
having opened a bedroom door at the most inopportune of
moments, almost of having opened *The Tropic of Cancer* at
one of its most startling pages. The posture of the ecstatics,
their expression and the exuberance of the tripe-like drapery
which surrounds them and, in the Albertoni's case, overflows
in a kind of peritoneal cataract onto the altar below—all con-
spire to emphasize the fact that, though saints may be important historical figures, their physiology is as disquietingly
private as anyone else's.

By the inner logic of the tradition within which they
worked, Baroque artists were committed to a systematic exploitation of the inordinate. Hence the epileptic behavior of
their gesticulating or swooning personages, and hence, also,
their failure to find an adequate artistic expression for the
mystical experience. This failure seems all the more surprising
when one remembers that their period witnessed a great
efflorescence of mystical religion. It was the age of St. John
of the Cross and Benet of Canfield, of Mme. Acarie and

Father Lallemant and Charles de Condren, of Augustine Baker and Surin and Olier.

All these had taught that the end of the spiritual life is the unitive knowledge of God, an immediate intuition of Him beyond discursive reason, beyond imagination, beyond emotion. And all had insisted that visions, raptures and miracles were not the "real thing," but mere by-products which, if taken too seriously, could become fatal impediments to spiritual progress. But visions, raptures and miracles are astounding and picturesque occurrences; and astounding and picturesque occurrences were the predestined subject matter of artists whose concern was with the inordinate. In Baroque art the mystic is represented either as a psychic with supernormal powers, or as an ecstatic, who passes out of history in order to be alone, not with God, but with his or her physiology in a state hardly distinguishable from that of sexual enjoyment. And this in spite of what all the contemporary masters of the spiritual life were saying about the dangers of precisely this sort of thing.

Such a misinterpretation of mysticism was made inevitable by the very nature of Baroque art. Given the style in which they worked, the artists of the seventeenth century could not have treated the theme in any other way. And, oddly enough, even at times when the current style permitted a treatment of the less epileptic aspects of religion, no fully adequate rendering of the contemplative life was ever achieved in the plastic arts of Christendom. The peace that passes all understanding was often sung and spoken; it was hardly ever painted or carved. Thus, in the writings of St. Bernard, of Albertus Magnus, of Eckhart and Tauler and Ruysbroeck one may find passages that express very clearly the nature and significance of mystical contemplation. But the saints who figure in medieval painting and sculpture tell us next to nothing about this anticipation of the beatific vision. There are no equivalents of those Far Eastern Buddhas and Bodhisattvas who incarnate, in stone and paint, the experience of ultimate reality. Moreover the Christian saints have their being in a world from which non-human Nature (that mine of supernatural beauties and transcendent significances) has been almost completely excluded. In his handbook on painting Cennini gives a recipe for mountains. Take some large jagged stones, arrange them on a table, draw them and, lo and behold, you will have a range of Alps or Apennines good enough for all the practical purposes of art. In China and Japan mountains were taken more seriously. The aspiring artist was advised to go and live among them, to make himself alertly passive in their presence, to contemplate them lovingly until he could understand the mode of their being and feel within them the workings of the immanent and transcendent Tao. As one might have expected, the medieval artists of Christendom painted mere backgrounds, whereas those of the Far East painted landscapes that are the equivalent of mystical poetry—formally perfect renderings of man's experience of being related to the Order of Things.

This experience is, of course, perfectly private, non-historical and unsocial. That is why, to the organizers of churches and the exponents of salvation through the State, it has always seemed to be suspect, shady and even indecent. And yet, like sex and pain and death, there it remains, one of the brute facts with which, whether we like them or not, we have to come to terms. Maddeningly, unbearably, an occasional artist rubs our noses in his rendering of these facts. Confronted by the pornographies of suffering, of sensuality, of dissolution, by *The Disasters of War* and *The Naked and the Dead,* by *Tropic of Cancer,* by *Ivan Ilyitch* and even (despite their ludicrous sublimity) by the Baroque tombs, we shrink and are appalled. And in another way there is something hardly less appalling in the pornographies (as many good rationalists regard them) of mysticism. Even the consolations of religion and philosophy are pretty desolating for the average sensual man, who clings to his ignorance as the sole guarantee of happiness. *Terribilis mors conturbat me*; but so does *terribilis Vita.*

(From *Themes and Variations*)

Faith, Taste, and History

Among tall stories, surely one of the tallest is the history of Mormonism. A founder whose obviously homemade revelations were accepted as more-than-gospel truth by thousands of followers; a lieutenant and successor who was "for daring a Cromwell, for intrigue a Machiavelli, for executive force a Moses, and for utter lack of conscience a Bonaparte"; a body of doctrine combining the most penetrating psychological insights with preposterous history and absurd metaphysics; a society of puritanical but theater-going and music-loving polygamists; a chuch once condemned by the Supreme Court as an organized rebellion, but now a monolith of respectability; a passionately loyal membership distinguished, even in these middle years of the twentieth century, by the old-fashioned Protestant and pioneering virtues of self-reliance

and mutual aid—together, these make up a tale which no
self-respecting reader even of Spillane, even of science fiction,
should be asked to swallow. And yet, in spite of its total lack
of plausibility, the tale happens to be true.

My book knowledge of its truth had been acquired long
since and intermittently kept up to date. It was not, however,
until the spring of 1953 that I had occasion actually to see
and touch the concrete evidences of that strange history.

We had driven all day in torrential rain, sometimes even in
untimely snow, across Nevada. Hour after hour in the vast
blankness of desert plains, past black bald mountains that
suddenly closed in through the driving rain, to recede again,
after a score of wintry miles, into the gray distance.

At the state line the weather had cleared for a little, and
there below us, unearthly in a momentary gleam of sunshine,
lay the Great Salt Desert of Utah, snow-white between the
nearer crags, with the line of blue or inky peaks rising, far
off, from the opposite shore of that dry ghost of an inland sea.

There was another storm as we entered Salt Lake City, and
it was through sheets of falling water that we caught our first
glimpse, above the chestnut trees, of a flood-lit object quite
as difficult to believe in, despite the evidence of our senses, as
the strange history it commemorates.

The improbability of this greatest of the Mormon Temples
does not consist in its astounding ugliness. Most Victorian
churches are astoundingly ugly. It consists in a certain combination of oddity, dullness and monumentality unique, so far
as I know, in the annals of architecture.

For the most part Victorian buildings are more or less
learned pastiches of something else—something Gothic, something Greek or nobly Roman, something Elizabethan or Flam-
boyant Flemish or even vaguely Oriental. But this Temple
looks like nothing on earth—looks like nothing on earth and
yet contrives to be completely unoriginal, utterly and uniformly prosaic.

But whereas most of the churches built during the past
century are gimcrack affairs of brick veneered with imitation
stone, of lattice work plastered to look like masonry, this
vast essay in eccentric dreariness was realized, from crypt to
capstone, in the solidest of granite. Its foundations are cyclopean, its walls are three yards thick. Like the Escorial, like
the Great Pyramid, it was built to last indefinitely. Long after
the rest of Victorian and twentieth-century architecture shall
have crumbled back to dust, this thing will be standing in the
Western desert, an object, to the neo-neolithic savages of
post-atomic times, of uncomprehending reverence and superstitious alarm.

To what extent are the arts conditioned by, or indebted to, religion? And is there, at any given moment of history, a common socio-psychological source that gives to the various arts—music and painting, architecture and sculpture—some kind of common tendency? What I saw that night in Temple Square and what I heard next day during an organ recital in the Tabernacle, brought up the old problem in a new and, in many ways, enlightening context.

Here, in the floodlights, was the most grandiose by far of all Western cathedrals. This Chartres of the desert was begun and largely built under economic and social conditions hardly distinguishable from those prevailing in France or England in the tenth century. In 1853, when the Temple's foundation stone was laid, London could boast its Crystal Palace, could look back complacently on its Exhibition of the marvels of Early Victorian technology. But here in Utah men were still living in the Dark Ages—without roads, without towns, with no means of communication faster than the ox wagon or mule train, without industry, without machines, without tools more elaborate than saws and scythes and hammers—and with precious few even of those. The granite blocks of which the Temple is built were quarried by man power, dressed by man power, hauled over twenty miles of trackless desert by man power and ox power, hoisted into position by man power. Like the cathedrals of medieval Europe the Temple is a monument, among other things, to the strength and heroic endurance of striped muscle.

In the Spanish colonies, as in the American South, striped muscle was activated by the whip. But here in the West there were no African slaves and no local supply of domesticable aborigines. Whatever the settlers wanted to do had to be done by their own hands. The ordinary run of settlers wanted only houses and mills and mines and (if the nuggets were large enough) Paris fashions imported at immense expense around the Horn. But these Mormons wanted something more—a granite Temple of indestructible solidity. Within a few years of their arrival in Utah they set to work. There were no whips to stimulate their muscles, only faith—but in what abundance! It was the kind of mountain-moving faith that gives men power to achieve the impossible and bear the intolerable, the kind of faith for which men die and kill and work themselves beyond the limits of human capacity, the kind of faith that had launched the Crusades and raised the towers of Angkor-Vat. Once again it performed its historic miracle. Against enormous odds, a great cathedral was built in the wilderness. Alas, instead of Bourges or Canterbury, it was *This.*

Faith, it is evident, may be relied on to produce sustained action and, more rarely, sustained contemplation. There is, however, no guarantee that it will produce good art. Religion is always a patron of the arts, but its taste is by no means impeccable. Religious art is sometimes excellent, sometimes atrocious; and the excellence is not necessarily associated with fervor nor the atrocity with lukewarmness. Thus, at the turn of our era, Buddhism flourished in Northwestern India. Piety, to judge by the large number of surviving monuments, ran high; but artistic merit ran pretty low. Or consider Hindu art. For the last three centuries it has been astonishingly feeble. Have the many varieties of Hinduism been taken less seriously than in the times when Indian art was in its glory? There is not the slightest reason to believe it. Similarly there is not the slightest reason to believe that Catholic fervor was less intense in the age of the Mannerists than it had been three generations earlier. On the contrary, there is good reason to believe that, during the Counter-Reformation, Catholicism was taken more seriously by more people than at any time since the fourteenth century. But the bad Catholicism of the High Renaissance produced superb religious art; the good Catholicism of the later sixteenth and seventeenth centuries produced a great deal of rather bad religious art. Turning now to the individual artist—and after all, there is no such thing as "Art," there are only men at work—we find that the creators of religious masterpieces are sometimes, like Fra Angelico, extremely devout, sometimes no more than conventionally orthodox, sometimes (like Perugino, the supreme exponent of pietism in art) active and open disbelievers.

For the artist in his professional capacity, religion is important because it offers him a wealth of interesting subject matter and many opportunities to exercise his skill. Upon the quality of his production it has little or no influence. The excellence of a work of religious art depends on two factors, neither of which has anything to do with religion. It depends primarily on the presence in the artist of certain tendencies, sensibilities and talents; and, secondarily, it depends on the earlier history of his chosen art, and on what may be called the logic of its formal relations. At any given moment that internal logic points toward conclusions beyond those which have been reached by the majority of contemporary artists. A recognition of this fact may impel certain artists—especially young artists—to try to realize those possible conclusions in concrete actuality. Sometimes these attempts are fully successful; sometimes, in spite of their author's talents, they fail. In either case, the outcome does not depend on the nature of the artist's metaphysical beliefs, nor on the warmth with which he entertains them.

The Mormons had faith, and their faith enabled them to realize a prodigious ideal—the building of a Temple in the wilderness. But though faith can move mountains, it cannot of itself shape those mountains into cathedrals. It will activate muscle, but has no power to create architectural talent where none exists. Still less can it alter the facts of artistic history and the internal logic of forms.

For a great variety of reasons, some sociological and some intrinsically aesthetic, some easily discernible and others obscure, the traditions of the European arts and crafts had disintegrated, by the middle years of the nineteenth century, into a chaos of fertile bad taste and ubiquitous vulgarity. In their fervor, in the intensity of their concern with metaphysical problems, in their readiness to embrace the most eccentric beliefs and practices, the Mormons, like their contemporaries in a hundred Christian, Socialist or Spiritualist communities, belonged to the Age of the Gnostics. In everything else they were typical products of rustic nineteenth-century America. And in the field of the plastic arts nineteenth-century America, especially rustic America, was worse off even than nineteenth-century Europe. Barry's Houses of Parliament were as much beyond these Temple-builders as Bourges or Canterbury.

Next morning, in the enormous wooden tabernacle, we listened to the daily organ recital. There was some Bach and a piece by César Franck and finally some improvised variations on a hymn tune. These last reminded one irresistibly of the good old days of the silent screen—the days when, in a solemn hush and under spotlights, the tail-coated organist at the console of his Wurlitzer would rise majestically from the cellarage, would turn and bend his swanlike loins in acknowledgment of the applause, would resume his seat and slowly extend his white hands. Silence, and then boom! the picture palace was filled with the enormous snoring of thirty-two-foot contratrombones and bombardes. And after the snoring would come the "Londonderry Air" on the *vox humana,* "A Little Grey Home in the West" on the *vox angelica,* and perhaps (what bliss!) "The End of a Perfect Day" on the *vox treacliana,* the *vox bedroomica,* the *vox unementionabilis.*

How strange, I found myself reflecting, as the glutinous tide washed over me, how strange that people should listen with apparently equal enjoyment to this kind of thing and the Prelude and Fugue in E-flat Major. Or had I got hold of the wrong end of the stick? Perhaps mine was the strange, the essentially abnormal attitude. Perhaps there was something wrong with a listener who found it difficult to adore both these warblings around a hymn tune *and* the Prelude and Fugue.

From these unanswerable questions my mind wandered to others, hardly less puzzling, in the domain of history. Here was this huge instrument. In its original and already monumental state, it was a product of pioneering faith. An Australian musician and early Mormon convert, Joseph Ridges, had furnished the design and supervised the work. The timber used for making the pipes was hauled by oxen from forests three hundred miles to the south. The intricate machinery of a great organ was home-made by local craftsmen. When the work was finished, what kind of music, one wonders, was played to the Latter-day Saints assembled in the tabernacle? Hymns, of course, in profusion. But also Handel, also Haydn and Mozart, also Mendelssohn and perhaps even a few pieces by that queer old fellow whom Mendelssohn had resurrected, John Sebastian Bach.

It is one of the paradoxes of history that the people who built the monstrosities of the Victorian epoch should have been the same as the people who applauded, in their hideous halls and churches, such masterpieces of orderliness and unaffected grandeur as *The Messiah,* and who preferred to all his contemporaries that most elegantly classical of the moderns, Felix Mendelssohn. Popular taste in one field may be more or less completely at variance with popular taste outside that field. Still more surprisingly, the fundamental tendencies of professionals in one of the arts may be at variance with the fundamental tendencies of professionals in other arts.

Until very recently the music of the fifteenth, sixteenth and early seventeenth centuries was, to all but learned specialists, almost completely unknown. Now, thanks to long-playing phonograph records, more and more of this buried treasure is coming to the surface. The interested amateur is at last in a position to hear for himself what, before, he could only read about. He knows, for example, what people were singing when Botticelli was painting "Venus and Mars"; what Van Eyck might have heard in the way of love songs and polyphonic masses; what kind of music was being sung or played in St. Mark's while Tintoretto and Veronese were at work, next door, in the Doge's Palace; what developments were taking place in the sister art during the more than sixty years of Bernini's career as sculptor and architect.

Dunstable and Dufay, Ockeghem and Josquin, Lassus, Palestrina, Victoria—their overlapping lives cover the whole of the fifteenth and sixteenth centuries. Music, in those two centuries, underwent momentous changes. The dissonances of the earlier, Gothic polyphony were reduced to universal consonance; the various artifices—imitation, diminution, augmentation and the rest—were perfected and, by the greater masters, used to create rhythmical patterns of incredible subtlety and richness. But through the whole period virtually all serious music retained those open-ended, free-floating forms which it had inherited from the Gregorian Chant and, more remotely, from some Oriental ancestor. European folk music was symmetrical, four-square, with regular returns to the same starting point and balanced phrases, as in metrical poetry, of pre-established and foreseeable length. Based upon plain chant and written, for the part, as a setting to the liturgical texts, learned music was analogous, not to scanned verse, but to prose. It was a music without bars—that is to say, with no regularity of emphasis. Its component elements were of different lengths, there were no returns to recognizable starting points, and its geometrical analogue was not some closed figure like the square or circle, but an open curve undulating away to infinity. That such a music ever reached a close was due, not to the internal logic of its forms, but solely to the fact that even the longest liturgical texts come at last to their Amen. Some attempt to supply a purely musical reason for not going on forever was made by those composers who wrote their masses around a *cantus firmus*—a melody borrowed, almost invariably, from the closed, symmetrical music of popular songs. Sung or played in very slow time, and hidden in the tenor, sometimes even in the bass, the *cantus firmus* was, for all practical purposes, inaudible. It existed for the benefit, not of listeners, but of the composer; not to remind bored church-goers of what they had heard last night in the tavern, but to serve a strictly artistic purpose. Even when the *cantus firmus* was present, the general effect of unconditioned, free-floating continuousness persisted. But, for the composer, the task of organization had been made easier; for, buried within the fluid heart of the music, was the unbending armature of a fully metrical song.

While Dufay was still a choir boy at Cambrai, Ghiberti was at work on the bronze doors of Santa Maria del Fiore, the young Donatello had been given his first commissions. And when Victoria, the last and greatest of the Roman masters, died in 1613, Lorenzo Bernini was already a full-blown infant prodigy. From Early Renaissance to Baroque, the fundamental tendency of the plastic arts was through symmetry and beyond it, away from closed forms toward unbalanced openness and the implication of infinity. In music, during this same period, the fundamental tendency was through openness and beyond it, away from floating continuousness toward meter, toward four-square symmetry, to-

ward regular and foreseeable recurrence. It was in Venice
that the two opposite tendencies, of painting and of music,
first became conspicuous. While Tintoretto and Veronese
moved toward openness and the asymmetrical, the two Ga-
brielis moved, in their motets and their instrumental music,
toward harmony, toward regular scansion and the closed
form. In Rome, Palestrina and Victoria continued to work
in the old free-floating style. At St. Mark's, the music of the
future—the music which in due course was to develop into
the music of Purcell and Couperin, of Bach and Handel—
was in process of being born. By the sixteen-thirties, when
even sculpture had taken wing for the infinite, Bernini's older
contemporary, Heinrich Schuetz, the pupil of Giovanni Gabrieli, was writing (not always, but every now and then)
symmetrical music that sounds almost like Bach.

For some odd reason this kind of music has recently been
labeled "baroque." The choice of this nickname is surely unfortunate. If Bernini and his Italian, German and Austrian
followers are baroque artists (and they have been so desig-
nated for many years), then there is no justification, except
in the fact that they happened to be living at the same time,
for applying the same epithet to composers, whose fundamental tendencies in regard to form were radically different
from theirs.

About the only seventeenth-century composer to whom the
term "baroque" can be applied in the same sense as we apply
it to Bernini, is Claudio Monteverdi. In his operas and his
religious music, there are passages in which Monteverdi combines the openness and boundlessness of the older polyphony
with a new expressiveness. The feat is achieved by setting an
unconditionally soaring melody to an accompaniment, not of
other voices, but of variously colored chords. The so-called
baroque composers are baroque (in the established sense of
the word) only in their desire for a more direct and dramatic
expression of feeling. To realize this desire, they developed
modulation within a fully tonal system, they exchanged polyphony for harmony, they varied the tempo of their music
and the volume of its sound, and they invented modern
orchestration. In this concern with expressiveness they were
akin to their contemporaries in the fields of painting and
sculpture. But in their desire for squareness, closedness and
symmetry they were poles apart from men whose first wish
was to overthrow the tyranny of centrality, to break out of
the cramping frame or niche, to transcend the merely finite
and the all too human.

Between 1598 and 1680—the years of Bernini's birth and
death—baroque painting and sculpture moved in one direc-

tion, baroque music, as it is miscalled, moved in another, almost opposite direction. The only conclusion we can draw is that the internal logic and the recent history of the art in which a man is working exercise a more powerful influence upon him than do the social, religious and political events of the time in which he lives. Fifteenth-century sculptors and painters inherited a tradition of symmetry and closedness. Fifteenth-century composers inherited a tradition of openness and asymmetry. On either side the intrinsic logic of the forms was worked out to its ultimate conclusion. By the end of the sixteenth century neither the musical nor the plastic artists could go any further along the roads they had been following. Going beyond themselves, the painters and sculptors pursued the path of open-ended asymmetry, the free-floating musicians turned to the exploration of regular recurrence and the closed form. Meanwhile the usual wars and persecutions and sectarian throat-cuttings were in full swing; there were economic revolutions, political and social revolutions, revolutions in science and technology. But these merely historical events seem to have affected artists only materially—by ruining them or making their fortunes, by giving or withholding the opportunity to display their skill, by changing the social or religious status of potential patrons. Their thought and feeling, their fundamental artistic tendencies were reactions to events of a totally different order—events not in the social world, but in the special universe of each man's chosen art.

Take Schuetz, for example. Most of his adult life was spent in running away from the recurrent horrors of the Thirty Years' War. But the changes and chances of a discontinuous existence left no corresponding traces upon his work. Whether at Dresden or in Italy, in Denmark or at Dresden again, he went on drawing the artistically logical conclusions from the premises formulated under Gabrieli at Venice and gradually modified, through the years, by his own successive achievements and the achievements of his contemporaries and juniors.

Man is a whole, but a whole with an astounding capacity for living, simultaneously or successively, in water-tight compartments. What happens here has little or no effect on what happens there. The seventeenth-century taste for closed forms in music was inconsistent with the seventeenth-century taste for asymmetry and openness in the plastic arts. The Victorian taste for Mendelssohn and Handel was inconsistent with the Victorian taste for Mormon Temples, Albert Halls and St. Pancras Railway Stations. But in fact these mutually exclusive tastes coexisted and had no perceptible effect on one another. Consistency is a verbal criterion, which cannot be applied to the phenomena of life. Taken together, the various activities of a single individual may "make no sense," and yet be perfectly compatible with biological survival, social success and personal happiness.

Objective time is the same for every member of a human group and, within each individual, for each inhabitant of a watertight compartment. But the self in one compartment does not necessarily have the same *Zeitgeist* as the selves in other compartments or as the selves in whom other individuals do their equally inconsistent living. When the stresses of history are at a maximum, men and women tend to react to them in the same way. For example, if their country is involved in war, most individuals become heroic and self-sacrificing. And if the war produces famine and pestilence, most of them die. But where the historical pressures are more moderate, individuals are at liberty, within rather wide limits, to react to them in different ways. We are always synchronous with ourselves and others; but it often happens that we are not contemporary with either.

At Logan, for example, in the shadow of another Temple, whose battlemented turrets gave it the air of an Early Victorian "folly," of a backdrop to Edmund Kean in *Richard III*, we got into conversation with a charming contemporary, not of Harry Emerson Fosdick or Bishop Barnes, but of Brother Juniper—a Mormon whose faith had all the fervor, all the unqualified literalness, of peasant faith in the thirteenth century. He talked to us at length about the weekly baptisms of the dead. Fifteen hundred of them baptized by proxy every Saturday evening and thus, at long last, admitted to that heaven where all the family ties persist throughout the aeons. To a member of a generation brought up on Freud, these posthumous prospects seemed a bit forbidding. Not so to Brother Juniper. He spoke of them with a kind of quiet rapture. And how celestially beautiful, in his eyes, was this cyclopean gazebo! How inestimable the privilege, which he had earned, of being allowed to pass through its doors! Doors forever closed to all Gentiles and even to a moiety of the Latter-day Saints. Around that heavenly Temple the lilac trees were in full scent and the mountains that ringed the fertile valley were white with the snowy symbol of divine purity. But time pressed. We left Brother Juniper to his paradise and drove on.

That evening, in the tiny Natural History Museum at Idaho Falls, we found ourselves talking to two people from a far remoter past—a fascinating couple straight out of a cave. Not one of your fancy Magdalenian caves with all that modernistic art work on the walls. No, no—a good old-fashioned, down-to-earth cave belonging to nice ordinary people three thousand generations before the invention of painting. These were Australopiths, whose reaction to the stuffed grizzly was a remark about sizzling steaks of bear meat; these were early Neanderthalers who could not see a fish or bird or four-footed beast without immediately dreaming of slaughter and a guzzle.

"Boy!" said the cave lady, as we stood with them before the solemn, clergyman-like head of an enormous moose. "Would *he* be good with onions!"

It was fortunate, I reflected, that we were so very thin, they so remarkably well fed and therefore, for the moment, so amiable.

(From *Tomorrow and Tomorrow and Tomorrow*)

HISTORY

Maine de Biran: The Philosopher in History

Systematic knowledge of historical trends and "waves of the future" is sought only by the intellectual few. But every individual lives here and now, and is more or less profoundly affected by the fact that now is not then, nor here somewhere else. What are, and what should be, the relations between the personal and the historical, the existential and the social? Our philosopher, Maine de Biran never posed this question in so many words; consequently we have to infer his answers from what he says in other contexts. What he seems to suggest, throughout the *Journal Intime,* is that the individual's relation to history and society is normally that of victim to monster. This being so, every reasonable person should try, so far as he can, to escape from history—but into what? Into abstract thought and the inner life, or else (and this was the conclusion reached by our philosopher toward the end of his career) into the loving contemplation of the divine Spirit.

The problem is so important that it deserves a more thorough examination than Biran chose to give it. Let us begin with an analogy drawn from inanimate matter. The laws of gases are concerned with the interdependence of volume, pressure and temperature. But the individual molecules of which the gas is composed have neither temperature nor pressure, but only kinetic energy and a tendency to random movement. In a word, the laws of single molecules are entirely different from the laws of the gases they constitute. Something of the same kind is true of individuals and societies. In groups consisting of large numbers of human individuals,

217

certain regularities can be detected and certain sociological laws can be formulated. Because of the relatively small size of even the most considerable human groups, and because of the enormous differences, congenital and acquired, between individual and individual, these regularities have numerous exceptions and these sociological laws are rather inexact. But this is no reason for dismissing them. For, in the words of Edgar Zilser, from whose essay on "The Problems of Empiricism" I have borrowed this simile of molecules and gases, "no physicist or astronomer would disregard a regularity on the ground that it did not always hold."

For our purposes the important thing about the sociological laws is not their inexactness but the fact that they are quite different from the psychological and physiological laws which govern the individual person. "If," says Zilser, "we look for social regularities by means of empathy"—feeling ourselves into a situation by imagining what would be our own behavior in regard to it—"we may never find them, since ideas, wishes and actions might not appear in them at all." In a word, changes in quantity, if sufficiently great, result in changes in kind. Between the individual and the social, the personal and the historical, there is a difference amounting to incommensurability. Nobody now reads Herbert Spencer's *Man Versus the State*. And yet the conflict between what is good for a psycho-physical person and what is good for an organization wholly innocent of feelings, wishes and ideas is real and seems destined to remain forever unresolved. One of the many reasons for the bewildering and tragic character of human existence is the fact that social organization is at once necessary and fatal. Men are forever creating such organizations for their own convenience and forever finding themselves the victims of their homemade monsters. History reveals the Church and the State as a pair of indispensable Molochs. They protect their worshiping subjects, only to enslave and destroy them. The relations between social organizations and the individuals who live under them is symbolically expressed by the word "shepherd," as applied to the priests and rulers, who like to think of themselves as God's earthly representatives, and even to God Himself. The metaphor is of high, but not the highest, antiquity; for it was first used by the herd-owning, land-destroying, meat-eating and war-waging peoples who replaced the horticulturists of the first civilization and put an end to that Golden Age of Peace, which not long since was regarded as a mere myth but is now revealed by the light of archaeology as a proto- and pre-historical reality. By force of unreflecting habit we go on talking sentimentally about the Shepherd of his people, about

Pastors and their flocks, about stray lambs and a Good Shepherd. We never pause to reflect that a shepherd is "not in business for his health," still less for the health of his sheep. If he takes good care of the animals, it is in order that he may rob them of their wool and milk, castrate their male offspring and finally cut their throats and convert them into mutton. Applied to most of the States and Churches of the last two or three thousand years, this pastoral metaphor is seen to be exceedingly apt—so apt, indeed, that one wonders why the civil and ecclesiastical herders of men should ever have allowed it to gain currency. From the point of view of the individual lambs, rams and ewes there is, of course, no such thing as a *good* shepherd; their problem is to find means whereby they may enjoy the benefits of a well-ordered social life without being exposed to the shearings, milkings, geldings and butcheries which have always been associated with the pastoral office. To discuss those means would lead us too far afield. Let it suffice to say that, given, first, the manifest unfitness of almost all human beings to exercise much power for very long, and, second, the tendency for social institutions to become pseudo-divine ends, to which individual men and women are merely means, it follows that every grant of authority should be hedged about with effective reservations; that political, economic and religious organizations should be small and co-operative, never large, and therefore inhuman and hierarchical; that the centralization of economic and political power should be avoided at all costs; and that nations and groups of nations should be organized as federations of local and professional bodies, having wide powers of self-government. At the present time, unfortunately, all signs point, not to decentralization and the abolition of man-herders, but rather to a steady increase in the power of the Big Shepherd and his oligarchy of bureaucratic dogs, to a growth in the size, the complexity, the machine-like efficiency and rigidity of social organizations, and to a completer deification of the State, accompanied by a completer reification, or reduction to thing-hood, of individual persons.

Maine de Biran's temperament was such that, even when he found himself on the winning side, even when—as Quaestor of the Chamber under Louis XVIII—he was an official personage of some importance, he continued to regard the social and the historical with the same apprehensive dislike as he had felt toward them in the days of Bonaparte and the Jacobins. In his diary the longing to escape from his pigeonhole in the social hierarchy, to break out of contemporary history and return to a purely private life, is expressed almost as frequently as the longing to be delivered from the body of this death. And yet he remained to the end embedded in politics and chained to his legislative functions. Why? To begin with, our philosopher was far from rich and found it very hard, without his official salary, to make both ends meet. Next there was his sense of duty. He felt morally obliged to do all he could for the royal house and for his rustic neighbors in Périgord. And finally there was his very unphilosophical desire to seem important, to be a personage among the pompous personages of the great world. Groaning and reluctant, yet perennially hopeful of the miracle that should transform him from a tongue-tied introvert into the brilliant and commanding herder of men, he went on clinging to his barbed perch among the great. It was death, and not his own will, that finally relaxed that agonizing clutch.

Fortunately for Biran, his martyrdom was not continuous. Even at moments when history pressed upon him most alarmingly, he found it possible to take a complete holiday in abstract thought. Sometimes he did not even have to *take* his holiday; it came to him, spontaneously, gratuitously, in the form of an illumination or a kind of ecstasy. Thus, to our philosopher, the spring of 1794 was memorable not for the executions of Hébert and Danton, not because Robespierre had now dedicated the Terror to the greater glory of the Supreme Being, but on account of an event that had nothing whatever to do with history or the social environment. "Today, the 27th of May, I had an experience too beautiful, too remarkable by its rarity ever to be forgotten. I was walking by myself a few minutes before sundown. The weather was perfect; spring was at its freshest and most brilliant; the whole world was clothed in that charm which can be felt by the soul, but not described in words. All that struck my senses filled my heart with a mysterious, sad sweetness. The tears stood in my eyes. Ravishment succeeded ravishment. If I could perpetuate this state, what would be lacking to my felicity? I should have found upon this earth the joys of heaven."

During the Hundred Days Biran was a good deal closer to history, than he had been at his ancestral estate of Grateloup in 1794. Every event that occurred between the return from Elba and Waterloo filled him with a bitter indignation. "I am no longer kind, for men exasperate me. I can now see only criminals and cowards. Pity for misfortune, the need to be useful and to serve my fellows, the desire to relieve distress, all the expansive and generous sentiments which were, up till now, my principles of action, are suffering a daily diminution in my heart."

Such are the ordinary psychological consequences of violent

events on the historical level. Individuals react to these events
with a chronic uncharitableness punctuated by paroxysms of
hate, rage and fear. Happily, in the long run, malice is always
self-destructive. If it were not, this earth would be, not a
Middle World of inextricably mingled good and evil, but plain,
unmitigated Hell. In the short run, however, the war-born
uncharitableness of many individuals constitutes a public
opinion in favor of yet more collective violence.

In Biran's case the bitterness with which he reacted to
contemporary history filled only his heart. "My mind, meanwhile, is occupied with abstract speculations, foreign to all
the interests of this world. The speculations keep me from
thinking about my fellow men—and this is fortunate; for I
cannot think of them except to hate and despise."

The life of every individual occupies a certain position in
time, is contemporary with certain political events and runs
parallel, so to speak, with certain social and cultural movements. In a word, the individual lives surrounded by history.
But to what extent does he actually live *in* history? And what
precisely is this history by which individuals are surrounded
and within which each of them does at least some of his
living?

Let us begin by considering the second of these two questions: What *is* history? Is history something which exists, in
its intelligible perfection, only in the minds of historians? Or
is it something actually experienced by the men and women
who are born into time, live out their lives, die and are succeeded by their sons and daughters?

Mr. Toynbee puts the question somewhat differently:
"What," he asks, "will be singled out as the salient event of
our time by future historians? Not, I fancy, any of those
sensational or tragic or catastrophic political and economic
events which occupy the headlines of our newspapers and the
foregrounds of our minds," but rather, "the impact of Western Civilization upon all the other societies of the world,"
followed by the reaction (already perceptible) of those other
civilizations upon Western Civilization and the ultimate
emergence of a religion affirming "the unity of mankind." This
is an answer to our question as well as to Mr. Toynbee's. For,
obviously, the processes he describes are not a part of anybody's immediate experience. Nobody now living is intimately
aware of them; nobody feels that they are happening to himself or sees them happening to his children or his friends. But
the (to a philosophical historian) unimportant tragedies and
catastrophes, which fill the headlines, actually happen to some
people, and their repercussions are part of the experience of
almost everybody. If the philosophical historians are right,

everything of real importance in history is a matter of very long durations and very large numbers. Between these and any given person, living at any given moment of time, lie the events predominantly "tragic or catastrophic" which are the subject matter of unphilosophical history. Some of these events can become part of the immediate experience of persons, and, conversely, some persons can to some extent modify the tragedies and control the catastrophes. Inasmuch as they involve fairly large numbers and fairly long durations, such events are a part of history. But from the philosophical historian's point of view they are important only in so far as they are at once the symptoms of a process involving much greater numbers and longer durations, and the means to the realization of that process. Individuals can never actually experience the long-range process which, according to the philosophical historians, gives meaning to history. All that they can experience (and this experience is largely subconscious) is the circumambient culture. And should they be intellectually curious, they can discover, through appropriate reading, that the culture by which they are surrounded is different in certain respects from the culture which surrounded their ancestors. Between one state of a culture and another later state there is not, and there cannot be, a continuity of experience. Every individual simply finds himself where in fact he is—here, not there; now, not then. Necessarily ignorant of the meaningful processes of long-range history, he has to make the best of that particular tract of short-range tragedy and catastrophe, that particular section of a cultural curve, against which his own personal life traces its organic pattern of youth, maturity and decay. Once again, it is a case of the gas and its constituent molecules. Gas laws are not the same as the laws governing the particles within the gas. Though he himself must act, suffer and enjoy as a molecule, the philosophical historian does his best to think as a gas—or rather (since a society is incapable of thought) as the detached observer of a gas. It is, of course, easy enough to take the gaseous view of a period other than one's own. It is much more difficult to take it in regard to the time during which one is oneself a molecule within the social gas. That is why a modern historian feels himself justified in revising the estimates of their own time made by the authors of his documents—in correcting, for example, the too unfavorable view of the age of Aquinas and the cathedral-builders taken by all thirteenth-century moralists, or the too favorable view of industrial civilization taken by many Victorian moralists.

History as something experienced can never be fully recorded. For, obviously, there are as many such histories as there have been experiencing human beings. The nearest approach to a general history-as-something-experienced would be an anthology of a great variety of personal documents. Professor Coulton has compiled a number of excellent anthologies of this kind covering the medieval period. They should be read by anyone who wants to know, not what modern historians think about the Middle Ages, but what it actually felt like to be a contemporary of St. Francis, or Dante, or Chaucer.

History-as-something-experienced being unwritable, we must perforce be content with history-as-something-in-the-minds-of-historians. This last is of two kinds: the short-range history of tragedies and catastrophes, political ups and downs, social and economic revolutions; and the long-range, philosophical history of those very long durations and very large numbers in which it is possible to observe meaningful regularities, recurrent and developing patterns. No two philosophical historians discover precisely the same regularities or meanings; and even among the writers of the other kind of history there is disagreement in regard to the importance of the part played by individuals in the short-range political and economic movements which are their chosen subject matter. These divergences of opinion are unfortunate but, in view of our present ignorance, inevitable.

We may now return to the first of our two questions: To what extent does the individual, who lives surrounded by history, actually live in history? How much is his existence conditioned by the sociologists' trinity of Place, Work and Folk? How is he related to the circumambient culture? In what ways is his molecular personality affected by the general state of the social gas and his own position within it? The answer, it is evident, will be different in each particular case; but it is possible, nonetheless, to cast up a reckoning sufficiently true to average experience to have at least some significance for every one of us.

Let us begin with the obvious but nonetheless very strange fact that all human beings pass nearly a third of their lives in a state that is completely non-historical, non-social, non-cultural—and even non-spatial and non-temporal. In other words, for eight hours out of every twenty-four they are asleep. Sleep is the indispensable condition of physical health and mental sanity. It is in sleep that our body repairs the damage caused by the day's work and the day's amusements; in sleep that the *vis medicatrix naturae* overcomes our disease; in sleep that our conscious mind finds some respite from the cravings and aversions, the fears, anxieties and hatreds, the planning and calculating which drive it during waking hours to the brink of nervous exhaustion and sometimes beyond. Many of us are chronically sick and more or less far gone in neurosis. That we are not much sicker and much madder than we are is due exclusively to that most blessed and blessing of all natural graces, sleep. Even a Himmler, even a Marquis de Sade, even a Jay Gould and a Zaharoff must resign themselves to being, during thirty per cent of their existence, innocent, sane and obscurely at one with the divine ground of all being. One of the most dreadfully significant facts about political, social and ecclesiastical institutions is that they never sleep. In so far as individual human beings create and direct them, they embody the ideals and the calculating cleverness, inextricably combined with the conscious or unconscious cravings, aversions and fears, of a group of waking selves. Every large organization exists in a state of chronic insomnia and so can never receive directly those accessions of new life and wisdom which, in dreams and dreamless unconsciousness, come sometimes trickling, sometimes pouring in from the depths of the sleeper's being or even from some source beyond those depths. An institution can be revivified only by individuals who, because they are capable of sleep and inspiration, are capable of becoming more than themselves.

The enlightened person, as the word "Buddha" implies, is fully and forever awake—but with a wakefulness radically different from that of the social organization; for he is awake even during the day to that which the unregenerate can approach only in sleep, that which social organizations never approach at all. When such organizations are left to their insomnia, when they are permitted to function according to the laws of their own being, subordinating individual insights to collective tradition, they become mad—not like an individual lunatic, but with a solemn, traditional and systematic madness that is at once majestic and ludicrous, grotesque and terrifying. There is a hymn which exhorts us to thank God that the Church unsleeping her watch is keeping. Instead of rejoicing in the fact we should lament and deplore. Unsleeping, the Church kept watch, century after century, over its bank accounts, its lands, its prestige, its political influence, its idolatrously worshiped dogmas, rites and traditions. All the enormous evils and imbecilities recorded in ecclesiastical history are the products of this fatal incapacity of a social organization to go to sleep.

Conversely all the illuminations and charities of personal religion have their source in the Spirit, which transcends and yet is the most inward ground of our own being, and with which, gratuitously in sleep, and in moments of insight and illumination prepared for by a deliberate "dying to self," the individual spirit is able to establish contact.

One culture gives us the pyramids, another the Escorial, a third, Forest Lawn. But the act of dying remains always and everywhere identical. Like sleep, death is outside the pale of history—a molecular experience unaffected by the state of the social gas. Every individual has to die alone, to die by himself to himself. The experience cannot be shared; it can only be privately undergone. "How painful it is," writes Shestov, "to read Plato's account of the last days of Socrates! His hours are numbered, and he talks, talks, talks. . . . That is what comes of having disciples. They won't allow you even to die in peace. The best death is the death we consider the worst, when one is alone, far from home, when one dies in the hospital like a dog in a ditch. Then at least one cannot spend one's last moments pretending, talking, teaching. One is allowed to keep silence and prepare oneself for the terrible and perhaps specially important event. Pascal's sister reports that he too talked a great deal before he died. Musset, on the contrary, wept like a child. May it not be that Socrates and Pascal talked as much as they did because they were afraid of crying?"

Hardly less unhistorical than death is old age. Modern medicine has done something to make the last years of a long life a little more comfortable, and pension plans have relieved the aged of a dependence upon charity or their children. Nevertheless, in spite of vitamins and social security, old age is still essentially what it was for our ancestors—a period of experienced decline and regression, to which the facts of contemporary history, the social and economic movements of the day are more or less completely irrelevant. The aging man of the middle twentieth century lives, not in the public world of atomic physics and conflicting ideologies, of welfare states and supersonic speed, but in his strictly private universe of physical weakness and mental decay.

It was the same with our philosopher. Laplace was his older contemporary; Cuvier and Ampère were his friends. But his last years were lived, not in the age of scientific progress which history records, but in the intimate experience of dying ever more completely to love, to pleasure, to enthusiasm, to sensibility, even to his intellect. "The most painful manner of dying to oneself," he writes, "is to be left with only so much of a reflective personality as suffices to recognize the successive degradation of those faculties, on account of which one could feel some self-esteem." Compared with these facts of his immediate experience, the social and the historical seemed unimportant.

Progress is something that exists on the level of the species (as increasing freedom from and control over natural environment) and perhaps also on the level of the society or the civilization (as an increase in prosperity, knowledge and skill, an improvement in laws and manners). For the individual it does not exist, except as an item of abstract knowledge. Like the other trends and movements recorded in books of history-as-something-in-the-mind-of-the-historian, it is never an object of individual experience. And this for two reasons. The first of these must be sought in the fact that man's organic life is intrinsically non-progressive. It does not keep on going up and up, in the manner of the graphs representing literacy, or national income, or industrial production. On the contrary, it is a curve like a flattened cocked hat. We are born, rise through youth to maturity, continue for a time on one level, then drop down through old age and decrepitude into death. An aging member of even the most progressive society experiences only molecular decay, never gaseous expansion.

The second reason for the individual's incapacity to experience progress is purely psychological and has nothing to do with the facts of physiology. Most human beings have an almost infinite capacity for taking things for granted. By the mere fact of having come into existence, the most amazing novelty becomes in a few months, even a few days, a familiar and, as it were, self-evident part of the environment. Every aspiration is for a golden ceiling overhead; but the moment that ceiling has been reached, it becomes a commonplace and disregarded floor, on which we dance or trudge in a manner indistinguishable, so far as our feeling-tone is concerned, from that in which we danced and trudged on the floor below. Moreover, every individual is born into a world having a social and technological floor of a particular kind, and is completely unaware, except through reading and by hearsay, that there was ever any other kind of floor. Between the members of one generation and the members of the preceding and subsequent generations there is no continuity of immediate experience. This means that one can read or write books about progress, but that one cannot feel it or live it in the same way as one feels a pain or lives one's old age.

Sleep and old age account for about thirty years of our allotted three score and ten. In other words, nearly half of every life is passed either completely outside of the social and the historical or in a world of enforced privacy, to which the social and the historical are only slightly relevant. Like the experience of old age, the experience of sickness takes the individual out of history and society. This does not mean, of course, that history is without effect on the bodily and mental health of individuals. What it does mean, however, is that, though certain diseases are less common and less dangerous than in the past, though hospitals are better and medical treatment more rational, sickness still causes an alienation from the world of history, and that, while it lasts, this alienation is as complete as ever it was in the past. Moreover, in spite of the progress in hygiene and medicine, in spite of the elimination from many parts of the earth of the contagious diseases which used to plague our forefathers, sickness is still appallingly common. Chronic, degenerative ailments are on the increase, and so are mental disorders, ranging from mild neuroses, with their accompanying physical disabilities, to severe and often incurable psychoses. Our fever hospitals are empty, but our asylums are full to bursting. Thanks to events which can be recorded in social history, a person living in the twentieth century is much less likely to catch the plague than was a person living in the fourteenth, but rather more likely to develop cancer, diabetes, coronary disease, hypertension, neurosis, psychosis and all the varieties of psychosomatic disorders.

Like death, sickness has had a great variety of cultural concomitants; but these changing concomitants have not changed the essential fact that sick persons experience an alienation from their culture and society, that they temporarily fall out of history into their private world of pain and fever.

Thus, because Biran was a child of the century which had perfected the chronometer and the clockwork flute player, he always, though a strenuous anti-mechanist, referred to his body as "the machine." And because St. Francis had been brought up in thirteenth-century Umbria, among peasants and their beasts, he always referred to *his* body as "Brother Ass." Differences in place, work and folk account for these differences in terminology. But when "the machine" suffered, it suffered in just the same way as "Brother Ass" had suffered nearly six hundred years before, in just the same way as St. Paul's "body of this death" had suffered in the first century.

Sickness, then, and old age take us out of history. Does this mean that the young and the healthy are permanently in history? Not at all. In the normal person, all the physiological processes are in their nature unhistorical and incommunicably non-social. The arts of breathing and assimilation, for example, of regulating body temperature and the chemistry of the blood, were acquired before our ancestors were even human. Digestion and excretion have no history; they are always there, as given facts of experience, as permanent elements in the destiny of every individual man and woman who has ever lived. The pleasures of good and the discomforts of bad digestion are the same at all times, in all places, under whatever political regime or cultural dispensation.

Maine de Biran, as we learn from his Journal, had a very delicate and capricious digestion. When it worked well, he found life worth living and experienced a sense of well-being which made even a dinner party at his mother-in-law's seem delightful. But when it worked badly, he felt miserable, found it impossible to think his own thoughts or even to understand what he read. "Van Helmont," he thinks, "was quite right when he situated in the stomach the center of all our affections and the active cause of our intellectual dispositions and even our ideas." This is not a piece of cheap cynicism, for never was any man less cynical than our philosopher. It is simply the statement of a fact in the life of incarnated spirits —a fact which has to be accepted, whether we like it or not, and made the best of. A great Catholic mystic has recorded his inability to place his mind in the presence of God during the half hour which followed his principal repast. It was the same with Biran. After dinner he was generally incapable of any but the most physiologically private life. The psychologist and the metaphysician disappeared, and for an hour or two their place was taken by the mere dim consciousness of a stomach. Biran felt these humiliations profoundly and never ceased to bemoan them. His friend Ampère, on the contrary, preferred to treat his body with a slightly theatrical defiance. "You ask of my health," he writes in reply to an inquiry from Maine de Biran. "As if that were the question! Between us there can be no question but of what is eternal." Noble words! And yet all knowledge is in the knower according to the mode of the knower. Can the man who has an unsound body acquire an undistorted knowledge of the eternal? Perhaps health is not without its importance even for philosophers.

Though themselves non-historical, physiological processes can, of course, be influenced by the kind of events that are recorded in short-range, non-philosophical history books. By way of obvious example, wars and revolutions ordinarily result in famine, and famine strikes at the very roots of organic life in countless individuals. On a smaller scale, the same effects may be produced by a slump or, for certain classes of a population, by a faulty distribution of purchasing power.

As an organic experience, sex is as private and unhistorical a matter as death or sleep, digestion or sickness. As a psychological experience it may be shared to some extent by two people—not indeed completely, for no experience can be shared completely, but as much as any experience of one person can be participated in by another. *Je crois bien,* says Mallarmé.

> *Je crois bien que deux bouches n'ont*
> *Bu, ni son amant, ni ma mère,*
> *Jamais à la même Chimère.*

In the final analysis the poet is right. But fortunately analysis is rarely pushed to the limit. For the practical purposes of life, the Chimeras which two lovers drink at one another's lips are sufficiently alike to be regarded as identical.

Social control of sex behavior is through laws, religious precepts, ethical ideals and codes of manners. At every period of history great organizations and a host of individuals have dedicated themselves to the task of compelling or persuading people to conform, in sexual matters, to the locally accepted norm. To what extent has this drive for conformity been successful? The evidence on which an accurate answer to this question might be based is simply not available. But such evidence as we have tends rather emphatically to suggest that collective efforts to make the sexual life of individuals conform to a socially acceptable pattern are seldom successful. In a minority of cases they are evidently successful enough to produce more or less severe mental conflicts and even neuroses. But the majority go their private way without paying more than lip-service to religion and respectability.

Thus, fifty years ago, the rules of sexual decorum were much more rigid than they are today, and yet, if the Kinsey Report may be believed, the actual behavior of men who were young at the beginning of our century was very similar to the behavior of those who were young in its middle forties. Among the writers of memoirs, diaries and autobiographies few indeed have left us an honest and unvarnished account of their sexual behavior. But if we read such all but unique documents as Jean-Jacques Bouchard's account of a seventeenth-century adolescence and youth, or as Samuel Pepys's day-by-day record of how the average sensual man comported himself a generation later, we shall be forced to the conclusion that laws and precepts, ideals and conventions have a good deal less influence on private life than most educators would care to admit. Pepys grew to manhood under the Commonwealth; Bouchard, during the revival of French Catholicism after the close of the religious wars. Both were piously brought up; both had to listen to innumerable sermons and exhortations; both were assured that sexual irregularity would lead them infallibly to Hell. And each behaved like a typical case from the pages of Ellis or Ebbing or Professor Kinsey. The same enormous gulf between theory and actual behavior is revealed by the casuists of the Counter Reformation and, in the Middle Ages, by the denunciatory moralists and the secular tellers of tales. Modern authors sometimes write as though the literary conventions of chivalrous or Platonic love, which have appeared at various times in European history, were the reflections of an unusually refined behavior on the part of writers and the members of their public. Again, such evidence as we have points to quite different conclusions. The fact that he was the author of all those sonnets did not prevent Petrarch from acting, in another poet's words, "as doves and sparrows do." And the man who transformed Beatrice into a heavenly principle was not only a husband and father, but also, if we may believe his first biographer—and there seems to be absolutely no reason why we should question Boccaccio's good faith or the truthfulness of his informants—a frequenter of prostitutes. Culture's relation to private life is at once more superficial, more spotty and more Pickwickian than most historians are ready to admit.

In the individual's intellectual, artistic and religious activities history plays, as we might expect, a much more considerable part than in the strictly private life of physiological processes and personal emotions. But even here we find enclaves, as it were, and Indian Reservations of the purest non-historicity. The insights and inspirations of genius are gratuitous graces, which seem to be perfectly independent of the kind of events that are described in the works of philosophical or non-philosophical historians. Certain favored persons were as richly gifted a thousand or five thousand years ago as similarly favored persons are today. Talent exists within a particular cultural and social framework, but itself belongs to realms outside the pales of culture and society.

At any given moment the state of the gas sets certain limits to what the creative molecules can think and do. But within those limits the performance of the exceptionally gifted is as remarkable, aesthetically speaking, in one age as another. In this context I remember a conversation between the directors of two of the world's largest and best museums. They agreed that, from the resources at their disposal, they could put on an exhibition of Art in the Dark Ages which should be as fine (within the limits imposed by the social conditions of the time) and as aesthetically significant as an exhibition of the art of any other period. Historians have tried to find social and cultural explanations for the fact that some epochs are very rich in men of talent, others abnormally poor. And, in effect, it may be that certain environments are favorable to the development of creative gifts, while others are unfavorable. But meanwhile we must remember that every individual

has his or her genes, that mating combines and recombines
these genes in an indefinite number of ways, and that the
chances against the kind of combination that results in a
Shakespeare or a Newton are a good many millions to one.
Moreover, in any game of hazard we observe that, though in
the long run everything conforms to the laws of probability,
in the short run there may be the most wildly improbable runs
of good or bad luck. Periclean Athens, Renaissance Italy,
Elizabethan England—these may be the equivalents, on the
genetic plane, of those extraordinary freaks of chance which
sometimes permit roulette players to break the bank. To those
politically minded people who believe that man can be perfected from outside and that environment can do everything,
this is, of course, an intolerable conclusion. Hence Lysenko
and the current Soviet attack upon reactionary, idealist Men-
delo-Morganism. The issue between Soviet geneticists and the
geneticists of the West is similar in essence to that which
divided the Pelagians from the Augustinians. Like Helvétius
and the Behaviorists, Pelagius affirmed that we are born *non
pleni* (without an inherited character) and that we are affected
by the sin of Adam *non propagine sed exemplo*—in our modern jargon, through social heredity rather than physical, individual heredity.

Augustine and his followers retorted than man in his nature
is totally depraved, that he can do nothing by his own efforts
and that salvation is only through grace. According to Soviet
theory, Western geneticists are pure Augustinians. In reality
they occupy a position halfway between Augustine and Pelagius. Like Augustine, they affirm that we are born with
"original sin," not to mention "original virtue"; but they hold,
with Pelagius, that we are not wholly predestined, but can do
quite a lot to help ourselves. For example, we can make it
easier for gifted individuals to develop their creative talents,
but we cannot, by modifying the environment, increase the
number of such individuals.

Where religion is concerned, the experiences of individuals
may be classified under two main heads: experiences related
to homemade deities and all too human notions, feelings and
imaginings about the universe; and experiences related to the
primordial fact of an immanent and transcendent Spirit.
Experiences of the first class have their source in history; those
of the second class are non-historical. In so far as they are
non-historical and immediately given, the religious experiences
of all times and places resemble one another and convey a
knowledge of the divine nature. In so far as they are concerned with the all too human, the homemade and the historically conditioned, the various religions of the world are

dissimilar and tell us little or nothing about the primordial fact. The direct apprehension of the immanence of a transcendent Spirit is an experience of which we have records going far back in time, an experience which, it would seem, can be had by persons belonging to very primitive cultures. At what point in their development human beings became capable of this apprehension we do not know; but for practical purposes we are probably justified in saying that, at least for some persons, this apprehension is as much an immediate datum, as little conditioned by history, as the experience of a world of objects. Only the verbal descriptions of the mystical experience are historically conditioned; the experiences themselves are not. Compare, for example, the literary styles of William Law and Jacob Boehme, the first exquisitely pure, lucid and elegant, the second barbarous, obscure, crabbed in the extreme. And yet Law chose Boehme as his spiritual master—chose him because, through the verbal disguises, he could recognize a spiritual experience essentially similar to his own. Or consider our philosopher and his English contemporary, William Wordsworth. Both were "Nature mystics," to whom were vouchsafed ecstatic insights into the divine ground of all being. Their immediate experiences were essentially similar. We may add, I think, that they were both essentially non-historical.

In Europe, it is true, the capacity to see in the more savage aspects of Nature, not only terrifying power, but also beauty, love and wisdom is of fairly recent growth and may be regarded as being, in some measure, historically conditioned. In the Far East, on the contrary, this capacity is of very high antiquity. Moreover Nature is not invariably savage, and at all times and in all places many persons have had no difficulty in perceiving that her more smiling aspects were manifestations of the divine. The ubiquitous cult of trees, the myths of Eden and Avalon, of Ava-iki and the Garden of the Hesperides, are sufficient proof that "Nature mysticism" is primordial and permanent, as unconditionally "built-in" and non-historical as any other unchanging datum of our psycho-physical experience. Biran and Wordsworth were among those moderns who had not chosen or been compelled to close the doors of their perception. They actually saw—as all might see if they were not self-blinded or the victims of unfavorable circumstances—the divine mystery that manifests itself in Nature.

But while Wordsworth (in his youth) was a great poet, capable of creating, within the splendid tradition of English poetry, a new medium of expression as nearly adequate to ineffable experience as any expression can be, Biran at his

most lyrical was merely an imitator, and an imitator merely
of Jean-Jacques Rousseau. Both historically and non-histori-
cally, as inheritor of a stylistic tradition and as literary genius,
he was far less well equipped than Wordsworth to tell of what
he had actually perceived and understood. And yet there is
no reason to suppose that his experiences at Grateloup and in
the Pyrenees were intrinsically inferior to the experiences
which Wordsworth had in the Lake Country or at Tintern.

We see, then, that while every person's life is lived within
a given culture and a given period of history, by no means
all the experiences in that life are historically conditioned.
And those which are not historically conditioned—sleep, for
example, all the processes of our organic life in health or
sickness, all our unmediated apprehensions of God as Spirit
and of God as manifest in Nature and persons—are more
fundamental, more important for us in our amphibious existence between time and eternity, than those which are so
conditioned.

Gas laws are entirely different from the laws governing
molecules. Individuals think, feel and variously apprehend;
societies do not. Men achieve their Final End in a timeless
moment of conscious experience. Societies are incapable of
conscious experience, and therefore can never, in the very
nature of things, be "saved" or "delivered." Ever since the
eighteenth century many philosophers have argued, and many
non-philosophers have more or less passionately believed, that
Mankind will somehow be redeemed by progressive History.
In his book *Faith and History*, Dr. Reinhold Niebuhr has
rightly insisted that, in itself, history is not, and cannot be,
a redemptive process. But he goes on airily to dismiss the
age-old revelation that man's Final End is the unitive knowledge of God here and now, at any time and in any place,
and proclaims that, though history is not redemptive in any
ordinary sense of the word, it is yet supremely important for
salvation in some Pickwickian sense—because of the General
Resurrection and the Last Judgment. "These eschatological
expectations in New Testament faith, however embarrassing
when taken literally, are necessary," he insists, "for a Christian interpretation of history." So far as I am able to understand him, Dr. Niebuhr seems to imply that the meaning of
life will be clarified only in the future, through a history
culminating in "the end of history, in which historical existence will be transfigured."

This seems to imply that all persons living in the past,
present and pre-millennial future are in some sort mere means
and instruments, and that their redemption depends, not upon
a personal relationship, here and now, with the divine Spirit,

but upon future events in which it is impossible for them to participate. Dr. Niebuhr rejects the classical and oriental conceptions of history on the ground that they reduce historical events to the "inferior realm of coming-to-be and passing away." They offer no hope for the fulfillment of the unique capacities of human personality. But "human personality" is an abstraction. In reality there are only individual personalities. Between personalities existing today and personalities existing in 3000 B.C. there is no continuity of experience. Fulfillments of persons living now are not fulfillments of persons living then; nor will fulfillments of persons living during the millennium be fulfillments of persons living in the twentieth century. Dr. Niebuhr obscures this obvious fact by speaking of societies as though they possessed the characteristics of persons. Thus "mankind will continue to 'see through a glass darkly.' " Again, "collective organisms," like individuals, have a "sense of the contingent and insecure character of social existence." But it is very doubtful whether a society is an organism; and it is certain that it can know nothing about the character of human existence. Individuals may make true statements about large groups; but large groups can say nothing about either individuals or themselves. Or consider the following: "Man in his individual life and in his total enterprise, moves from a limited to a more extensive expression of freedom over nature." Here everything depends upon an ambiguity of language. By a simple trick of sentence construction "man in his individual life" is assimilated to "man in his total enterprise." But the first phrase stands for Smith and Jones, for all the Smiths and Joneses since the Ice Age, each considered as an experiencing person; the second stands for those very large groups with which actuaries, sociologists and historians are accustomed to deal. Gas laws are not the same as the laws governing molecules. What is true of large numbers is not true of individuals. From the fact that a society has achieved some measure of control over its natural environment it does not follow that the individuals who at any given moment constitute that society enjoy an analogous freedom in regard to *their* environment—an environment consisting of Nature, their neighbors and their own thoughts, passions and organic processes. In the history of societies novelty is constantly emerging; but within the framework of these novelties the problems with which individuals have to deal remain fundamentally the same. The fact that one can travel in a jet plane rather than on foot does not, of itself, make the solution of those problems any easier.

"I show you sorrow," said the Buddha, "and the ending of sorrow." Sorrow is the unregenerate individual's life in time, the life of craving and aversion, pleasure and pain, organic growth and decay. The ending of sorrow is the awareness of eternity—a knowledge that liberates the knower and transfigures the temporal world of his or her experience. Every individual exists within the fields of a particular history, culture and society. Sorrow exists within all fields and can be ended within all fields. Nevertheless it remains true that some fields put more obstacles in the way of individual development and individual enlightenment than do others. Our business, as politicians and economists, is to create and maintain the social field which offers the fewest possible impediments to the ending of sorrow. It is a fact of experience that if we are led into powerful and prolonged temptations, we generally succumb. Social, political and economic reforms can accomplish only two things: improvement in the conditions of organic life, and the removal of certain temptations to which individuals are all too apt to yield—with disastrous results for themselves and others. For example, a centralized and hierarchical organization in State or Church constitutes a standing temptation to abuse of power by the few and to subservient irresponsibility and imbecility on the part of the many. These temptations may be reduced or even eliminated by reforms aiming at the decentralization of wealth and power and the creation of a federated system of self-governing co-operatives.

Getting rid of these and other temptations by means of social reforms will not, of course, guarantee that there shall be an ending of sorrow for all individuals within the reformed society. All we can say is that in a society which does not constantly tempt individuals to behave abominably the obstacles to personal deliverance will probably be fewer than in a society whose structure is such that men and women are all the time encouraged to indulge their worst propensities.

Of all possible fields, about the worst, so far as persons are concerned, is that within which ever greater numbers of our contemporaries are being forced to live—the field of militaristic and industrialized totalitarianism. Within this field, persons are treated as means to non-personal ends. Their right to a private existence, unconditioned by history and society, is denied on principle; and whereas the old tyrannies found it hard to make this denial universally effective, their modern counterparts, thanks to applied science and the improved techniques of inquisition and coercion, are able to translate their principles into practice on a scale and with a discriminatory precision unknown in the past.

"How small," Dr. Johnson could write two centuries ago,

> How small of all that human hearts endure
> The part which kings or laws can cause or cure!

In the eighteenth century it was still perfectly true that "public affairs vex no man"; that the news of a lost battle caused "no man to eat his dinner the worse"; that "when a butcher tells you that *his heart bleeds for his country,* he has, in fact, no uneasy feeling." And even in the bloody sixteenth century Montaigne "doubts if he can honestly enough confess with how very mean a sacrifice of his peace of mind and tranquillity he has lived more than half his life, whilst his country was in ruins." But the progress of technology is rapidly changing this relatively happy state of things. The modern dictator has, not only the desire, but also the effective means to reduce the whole man to the mere citizen, to deprive individuals of all private life but the most rudimentarily physical and to convert them at last into unquestioning instruments of a social organization whose ends and purposes are different from, and indeed incompatible with, the purposes and ends of personal existence.

(From "Variations on a Philosopher,"
Themes and Variations)

Usually Destroyed

Our guide through the labyrinthine streets of Jerusalem was a young Christian refugee from the other side of the wall which now divides the ancient city from the new, the non-viable state of Jordan from the non-viable state of Israel. He was a sad, embittered young man—and well he might be. His prospects had been blighted, his family reduced from comparative wealth to the most abject penury, their house and land taken away from them, their bank account frozen and devaluated. In the circumstances, the surprising thing was not his bitterness, but the melancholy resignation with which it was tempered.

He was a good guide—almost too good, indeed; for he was quite remorseless in his determination to make us visit all those deplorable churches which were built, during the nineteenth century, on the ruins of earlier places of pilgrimage. There are tourists whose greatest pleasure is a trip through historical associations and their own fancy. I am not one of them. When I travel, I like to move among intrinsically significant objects, not through an absence peopled only by literary references, Victorian monuments and the surmises of archaeologists. Jerusalem, of course, contains much more than ghosts and architectural monstrosities. Besides being one of the most profoundly depressing of the earth's cities, it is one

of the strangest and, in its own way, one of the most beautiful. Unfortunately our guide was far too conscientious to
spare us the horrors and the unembodied, or ill-embodied,
historical associations. We had to see everything—not merely
St. Anne's and St. James's and the Dome of the Rock, but
the hypothetical site of Caiaphas's house and what the
Anglicans had built in the seventies, what the Tsar and the
German Emperor had countered with in the eighties, what had
been considered beautiful in the early nineties by the Copts
or the French Franciscans. But, luckily, even at the dreariest
moments of our pilgrimage there were compensations. Our
sad young man spoke English well and fluently, but spoke it as
eighteenth-century virtuosi played music—with the addition
of *fioriture* and even whole cadenzas of their own invention.
His most significant contribution to colloquial English (and,
at the same time, to the science and art of history) was the
insertion into almost every sentence of the word "usually."
What he actually meant by it, I cannot imagine. It may be,
of course, that he didn't mean anything at all, and that what
sounded like an adverb was in fact no more than one of those
vocalized tics to which nervous persons are sometimes subject.
I used to know a professor whose lectures and conversations
were punctuated, every few seconds, by the phrase, "With a
thing with a thing." "With a thing with a thing" is manifestly
gibberish. But our young friend's no less compulsive "usually"
had a fascinating way of making a kind of sense—much more
sense, very often, than the speaker had intended. "This area,"
he would say as he showed us one of the Victorian monstrosities, "this area" [it was one of his favorite words] "is
very rich in antiquity. St. Helena built here a very vast
church, but the area was usually destroyed by the Samaritans
in the year 529 after Our Lord Jesus Christ. Then the Crusaders came to the area, and built a new church still more vast.
Here were mosaics the most beautiful in the world. In the
seventeenth century after Our Lord Jesus Christ the Turks
usually removed the lead from the roof to make ammunition;
consequently rain entered the area and the church was thrown
down. The present area was erected by the Prussian Government in the year 1879 after Our Lord Jesus Christ and all
these broken-down houses you see over there were usually
destroyed during the war with the Jews in 1948."

Usually destroyed and then usually rebuilt, in order, of
course, to be destroyed again and then rebuilt, *da capo ad
infinitum*. That vocalized tic had compressed all history into
a four-syllabled word. Listening to our young friend, as we
wandered through the brown, dry squalor of the Holy City, I
felt myself overwhelmed, not by the mere thought of man's

enduring misery, but by an obscure, immediate sense of it, an organic realization. These pullulations among ruins and in the dark of what once were sepulchers; these hordes of sickly children; these galled asses and the human beasts of burden bent under enormous loads; these mortal enemies beyond the dividing wall; these priest-conducted groups of pilgrims befuddling themselves with the vain repetitions, against which the founder of their religion had gone out of his way to warn them—they were dateless, without an epoch. In this costume or that, under one master or another, praying to whichever God was temporarily in charge, they had been here from the beginning. Had been here with the Egyptians, been here with Joshua, been here when Solomon in all his glory ordered his slaves in all their misery to build the temple, which Nebuchadnezzar had usually demolished and Zedekiah, just as usually, had put together again. Had been here during the long pointless wars between the two kingdoms, and at the next destruction under Ptolemy, the next but one under Antiochus and the next rebuilding under Herod and the biggest, best destruction of all by Titus. Had been here when Hadrian abolished Jerusalem and built a brand-new Roman city, complete with baths and a theater, with a temple of Jupiter, and a temple of Venus, to take its place. Had been here when the insurrection of Bar Cocheba was drowned in blood. Had been here while the Roman Empire declined and turned Christian, when Chosroes the Second destroyed the churches and when the Caliph Omar brought Islam and, most unusually, destroyed nothing. Had been here to meet the Crusaders and then to wave them good-by, to welcome the Turks and then to watch them retreat before Allenby. Had been here under the Mandate and through the troubles of '48, and were here now and would be here, no doubt, in the same brown squalor, alternately building and destroying, killing and being killed, indefinitely.

"I do not think," Lord Russell has recently written, "that the sum of human misery has ever in the past been so great as it has been in the last twenty-five years." One is inclined to agree. Or are we, on second thoughts, merely flattering ourselves? At most periods of history moralists have liked to boast that theirs was the most iniquitous generation since the time of Cain—the most iniquitous and therefore, since God is just, the most grievously afflicted. Today, for example, we think of the thirteenth century as one of the supremely creative periods of human history. But the men who were actually contemporary with the cathedrals and Scholastic Philosophy regarded their age as hopelessly degenerate, uniquely bad and condignly punished. Were they right, or are we? The

answer, I suspect is: Both. Too much evil and too much suffering can make it impossible for men to be creative; but within
very wide limits greatness is perfectly compatible with organized insanity, sanctioned crime and intense, chronic unhappiness for the majority. Every one of the great religions preaches
a mixture of profound pessimism and the most extravagant
optimism. "I show you sorrow," says the Buddha, pointing to
man in his ordinary unregenerate condition. And in the same
context Christian theologians speak of the Fall, of Original
Sin, of the Vale of Tears, while Hindus refer to the workings
of man's home-made destiny, his evil karma. But over against
the sorrow, the tears, the self-generated, self-inflicted disasters,
what superhuman prospects! If he so wishes, the Hindu affirms,
a man can realize his identity with Brahman, the Ground of
all being; if he so wishes, says the Christian, he can be filled
with God; if he so wishes, says the Buddhist, he can live in
a transfigured world where nirvana and samsara, the eternal
and the temporal, are one. But, alas—and from optimism
based on the experience of the few, the saints and sages
return to the pessimism forced upon them by their observation
of the many—the gate is narrow, the threshold high, few are
chosen because few choose to be chosen. In practice man
usually destroys himself—but has done so up till now a little
less thoroughly than he has built himself up. In spite of
everything, we are still here. The spirit of destruction has
been willing enough, but for most of historical time its technological flesh has been weak. The Mongols had only horses
as transport, only bows and spears and butchers' knives for
weapons; if they had possessed our machinery, they could
have depopulated the planet. As it was, they had to be content
with small triumphs—the slaughter of only a few millions, the
stamping out of civilization only in Western Asia.

In this universe of ours nobody has ever succeeded in
getting anything for nothing. In certain fields, progress in the
applied sciences and the arts of organization has certainly
lessened human misery; but it has done so at the cost of
increasing it in others. The worst enemy of life, freedom and
the common decencies is total anarchy; their second worst
enemy is total efficiency. Human interests are best served
when society is tolerably well organized and industry moderately advanced. Chaos and ineptitude are anti-human; but so
too is a superlatively efficient government, equipped with all
the products of a highly developed technology. When such a
government goes in for usually destroying, the whole race is
in danger.

The Mongols were the aesthetes of militarism; they believed
in gratuitous massacre, in destruction for destruction's sake.

Our malice is less pure and spontaneous; but, to make up for this deficiency, we have ideals. The end proposed, on either side of the Iron Curtain, is nothing less than the Good of Humanity and its conversion to the Truth. Crusades can go on for centuries, and wars in the name of God or Humanity are generally diabolic in their ferocity. The unprecedented depth of human misery in our time is proportionate to the unprecedented height of the social ideals entertained by the totalitarians on the one side, the Christians and the secularist democrats on the other.

And then there is the question of simple arithmetic. There are far more people on the earth today than there were in any earlier century. The miseries which have been the usual consequence of the usual course of nature and the usual behavior of human beings are the lot today, not of the three hundred millions of men, women and children who were contemporary with Christ, but of more than two and a half billions. Obviously, then, the sum of our present misery cannot fail to be greater than the sum of misery in the past. Every individual is the center of a world, which it takes very little to transform into a world of unadulterated suffering. The catastrophes and crimes of the twentieth century can transform almost ten times as many human universes into private hells as did the catastrophes and crimes of two thousand years ago. Moreover, thanks to improvements in technology, it is possible for fewer people to do more harm to greater numbers than ever before.

After the capture of Jerusalem by Nebuchadnezzar, how many Jews were carried off to Babylon? Jeremiah puts the figure at four thousand six hundred, the compiler of the Second Book of Kings at ten thousand. Compared with the forced migrations of our time, the Exile was the most trivial affair. How many millions were uprooted by Hitler and the Communists? How many more millions were driven out of Pakistan into India, out of India into Pakistan? How many hundreds of thousands had to flee, with our young guide, from their homes in Israel? By the waters of Babylon ten thousand at the most sat down and wept. In the single refugee camp at Bethlehem there are more exiles than that. And Bethlehem's is only one of dozens of such camps scattered far and wide over the Near East.

So it looks, all things considered, as though Lord Russell were right—that the sum of misery is indeed greater today than at any time in the past. And what of the future? Germ warfare and the H-bomb get all the headlines and, for that very reason, may never be resorted to. Those who talk a great deal about suicide rarely commit it. The greatest threat to happiness is biological. There were about twelve hundred million people on the planet when I was born, six years before the turn of the century. Today there are two thousand seven hundred millions; thirty years from now there will probably be four thousand millions. At present about sixteen hundred million people are underfed. In the nineteen-eighties the total may well have risen to twenty-five hundred millions, of whom a considerable number may actually be starving. In many parts of the world famine may come even sooner. In his Report on the Census of 1951 the Registrar General of India has summed up the biological problem as it confronts the second most populous country of the world. There are now three hundred and seventy-five million people living within the borders of India, and their numbers increase by five millions annually. The current production of basic foods is seventy million tons a year, and the highest production that can be achieved in the foreseeable future is ninety-four million tons. Ninety-four million tons will support four hundred and fifty million people at the present substandard level, and the population of India will pass the four hundred and fifty million mark in 1969. After that, there will be a condition of what the Registrar General calls "catastrophe."

In the index at the end of the sixth volume of Dr. Toynbee's *A Study of History*, Popilius Laenas gets five mentions and Porphyry of Batamaea, two; but the word you would expect to find between these names, Population, is conspicuous by its absence. In his second volume, Mr. Toynbee has written at length on "the stimulus of pressures"—but without ever mentioning the most important pressure of them all, the pressure of population on available resources. And here is a note in which the author describes his impressions of the Roman Campagna after twenty years of absence. "In 1911 the student who made the pilgrimage of the Via Appia Antica found himself walking through a wilderness almost from the moment when he passed beyond the City Walls. . . . When he repeated the pilgrimage in 1931, he found that, in the interval, Man had been busily reasserting his mastery over the whole stretch of country that lies between Rome and the Castelli Romani. . . . The tension of human energy on the Roman Campagna is now beginning to rise again for the first time since the end of the third century B.C." And there the matter is left, without any reference to the compelling reason for this "rise of tension." Between 1911 and 1931 the population of Italy had increased by the best part of eight millions. Some of these eight millions went to live in the Roman Campagna. And they did so, not because Man with a large M had in some mystical way increased the tension of human energy, but for the sufficiently obvious reason that there was nowhere else for them to go. In terms of a history that takes no cognizance of demographical facts, the past can never be fully understood, the present is quite incomprehensible and the future entirely beyond prediction.

Thinking, for a change, in demographic as well as in merely cultural, political and religious terms, what kind of reasonable guesses can we make about the sum of human misery in the years to come? First, it seems pretty certain that more people will be hungrier and that, in many parts of the world, malnutrition will modulate into periodical or chronic famine. (One would like to know something about the Famines of earlier ages, but the nearest one gets to them in Mr. Toynbee's index is a blank space between Muhammad Falak-al-Din and Gaius Fannius.) Second, it seems pretty certain that, though they may help in the long run, remedial measures aimed at reducing the birthrate will be powerless to avert the miseries lying in wait for the next generation. Third, it seems pretty certain that improvements in Agriculture (not referred to in Mr. Toynbee's index, though Agrigentum gets two mentions and Agis IV, King of Sparta, no less than forty-seven) will be unable to catch up with current and foreseeable increases in population. If the standard of living in industrially backward countries is to be improved, agricultural production will have to go up every single year by at least two and a half per cent, and preferably by three and a half per cent. Instead of which, according to the FAO, Far Eastern food production per head of population will be ten per cent less in 1956 (and this assumes that the current Five-Year Plans will be fully realized) than it was in 1938.

Fourth, it seems pretty certain that, as a larger and hungrier population "mines the soil" in a desperate search for food, the destructive processes of erosion and deforestation will be speeded up. Fertility will therefore tend to go down as human numbers go up. (One looks up Erosion in Mr. Toynbee's index but finds only Esarhaddon, Esotericism and Esperanto; one hunts for Forests, but has to be content, alas, with Formosus of Porto.)

Fifth, it seems pretty certain that the increasing pressure of population upon resources will result in increasing political and social unrest, and that this unrest will culminate in wars, revolutions and counter-revolutions.

Sixth, it seems pretty certain that, whatever the avowed political principles and whatever the professed religion of the societies concerned, increasing pressure of population upon resources will tend to increase the power of the central government and to diminish the liberties of individual citizens. For, obviously, where more people are competing for less food, each individual will have to work harder and longer for his ration, and the central government will find it necessary to intervene more and more frequently in order to save the rickety economic machine from total breakdown, and at the same time to repress the popular discontent begotten by deepening poverty.

If Lord Russell lives to a hundred and twenty (and, for all our sakes, I hope most fervently that he will), he may find himself remembering these middle decades of the twentieth century as an almost Golden Age. In 1954, it is true, he decided that the sum of human misery had never been so great as it had been in the preceding quarter century. On the other hand, "you ain't seen nuthin' yet." Compared with the sum of four billion people's misery in the eighties, the sum of two billion miseries just before, during and after the Second World War may look like the Earthly Paradise.

But meanwhile here we were in Jerusalem, looking at the usually destroyed antiquities and rubbing shoulders with the usually poverty-stricken inhabitants, the usually superstitious pilgrims. Here was the Wailing Wall, with nobody to wail at it; for Israel is on the other side of a barrier, across which there is no communication except by occasional bursts of rifle fire, occasional exchanges of hand grenades. Here, propped up with steel scaffolding, was the Church of the Holy Sepulchre—that empty tomb to which, for three centuries, the early Christians paid no attention whatsoever, but which came, after the time of Constantine, to be regarded, throughout Europe, as the most important thing in the entire universe. And here was Siloam, here St. Anne's, here the Dome of the Rock and the site of the Temple, here, more ominous than Pompeii, the Jewish quarter, leveled, usually, in 1948 and not yet usually reconstructed. Here, finally, was St. James's, of the Armenians, gay with innumerable rather bad but charming paintings, and a wealth of gaudily colored tiles. The great church glowed like a dim religious merry-go-round. In all Jerusalem it was the only oasis of cheerfulness. And not alone of cheerfulness. As we came out into the courtyard, through which the visitor must approach the church's main entrance, we heard a strange and wonderful sound. High up, in one of the houses surrounding the court, somebody was playing the opening Fantasia of Bach's Partita in A Minor—playing it, what was more, remarkably well. From out of the open window, up there on the third floor, the ordered torrent of bright pure notes went streaming out over the city's immemorial squalor. Art and religion, philosophy and science, morals and politics—these are the instruments by means of which men have tried to discover a coherence in the flux of events, to impose an order on the chaos of experience. The most intractable of our experiences is the experience of Time—the intuition of duration, combined with the thought of perpetual perishing. Music is a device for working directly upon the experience of Time. The composer takes a piece of raw, undifferentiated duration and extracts from it, as the sculptor extracts the statue from his marble, a complex pattern of tones and silences, of harmonic sequences and contrapuntal interweavings. For the number of minutes it takes to play or listen to his composition, duration is transformed into something intrinsically significant, something held together by the internal logics of style and temperament, of personal feelings interacting with an artistic tradition, of creative insights expressing themselves within and beyond some given technical convention. This Fantasia, for example—with what a tireless persistence it drills its way through time! How effectively—and yet with no fuss, no self-conscious heroics—it transfigures the mortal lapse through time into the symbol, into the very fact, of a more than human life! A tunnel of joy and understanding had been driven through chaos and was demonstrating, for all to hear, that perpetual perishing is also perpetual creation. Which was precisely what our young friend had been telling us, in his own inimitable way, all the time. Usually destroyed—but also, and just as often, usually rebuilt. Like the rain, like sunshine, like the grace of God and the devastations of Nature, his verbalized tic was perfectly impartial. We walked out of the courtyard and down the narrow street. Bach faded, a donkey brayed, there was a smell of undisposed sewage. "In the year of Our Lord 1916," our guide informed us, "the Turkish Government usually massacred approximately seven hundred and fifty thousand Armenians."

(From *Tomorrow and Tomorrow and Tomorrow*)

POLITICS

Words and Behavior

Words form the thread on which we string our experiences. Without them we should live spasmodically and intermittently. Hatred itself is not so strong that animals will not forget it, if distracted, even in the presence of the enemy. Watch a pair of cats, crouching on the brink of a fight. Balefully the eyes glare; from far down in the throat of each come bursts of a strange, strangled noise of defiance; as though animated by a life of their own, the tails twitch and tremble. With aimed intensity of loathing! Another moment and surely there must be an explosion. But no; all of a sudden one of the two creatures turns away, hoists a hind leg in a more than fascist salute and, with the same fixed and focused attention as it had given a moment before to its enemy, begins to make a lingual toilet. Animal love is as much at the mercy of distractions as animal hatred. The dumb creation lives a life made up of discreet and mutually irrelevant episodes. Such as it is, the consistency of human characters is due to the words upon which all human experiences are strung. We are purposeful because we can describe our feelings in rememberable words, can justify and rationalize our desires in terms of some kind of argument. Faced by an enemy we do not allow an itch to distract us from our emotions; the mere word "enemy" is enough to keep us reminded of our hatred, to convince us that we do well to be angry. Similarly the word "love" bridges for us those chasms of momentary indifference and boredom which gape from time to time between even the most ardent lovers. Feeling and desire provide us with our motive

245

power; words give continuity to what we do and to a considerable extent determine our direction. Inappropriate and badly chosen words vitiate thought and lead to wrong or foolish conduct. Most ignorances are vincible, and in the greater number of cases stupidity is what the Buddha pronounced it to be, a sin. For, consciously, or subconsciously, it is with deliberation that we do not know or fail to understand—because incomprehension allows us, with a good conscience, to evade unpleasant obligations and responsibilities, because ignorance is the best excuse for going on doing what one likes, but ought not, to do. Our egotisms are incessantly fighting to preserve themselves, not only from external enemies, but also from the assaults of the other and better self with which they are so uncomfortably associated. Ignorance is egotism's most effective defense against that Dr. Jekyll in us who desires perfection; stupidity, its subtlest stratagem. If, as so often happens, we choose to give continuity to our experience by means of words which falsify the facts, this is because the falsification is somehow to our advantage as egotists.

Consider, for example, the case of war. War is enormously discreditable to those who order it to be waged and even to those who merely tolerate its existence. Furthermore, to developed sensibilities the facts of war are revolting and horrifying. To falsify these facts, and by so doing to make war seem less evil than it really is, and our own responsibility in tolerating war less heavy, is doubly to our advantage. By suppressing and distorting the truth, we protect our sensibilities and preserve our self-esteem. Now, language is, among other things, a device which men use for suppressing and distorting the truth. Finding the reality of war too unpleasant to contemplate, we create a verbal alternative to that reality, parallel with it, but in quality quite different from it. That which we contemplate thenceforward is not that to which we react emotionally and upon which we pass our moral judgments, is not war as it is in fact, but the fiction of war as it exists in our pleasantly falsifying verbiage. Our stupidity in using inappropriate language turns out, on analysis, to be the most refined cunning.

The most shocking fact about war is that its victims and its instruments are individual human beings, and that these individual human beings are condemned by the monstrous conventions of politics to murder or be murdered in quarrels not their own, to inflict upon the innocent and, innocent themselves of any crime against their enemies, to suffer cruelties of every kind.

The language of strategy and politics is designed, so far as it is possible, to conceal this fact, to make it appear as though wars were not fought by individuals drilled to murder one another in cold blood and without provocation, but either by impersonal and therefore wholly non-moral and impassible forces, or else by personified abstractions.

Here are a few examples of the first kind of falsification. In place of "cavalrymen" or "foot-soldiers" military writers like to speak of "sabres" and "rifles." Here is a sentence from a description of the Battle of Marengo: "According to Victor's report, the French retreat was orderly; it is certain, at any rate, that the regiments held together, for the six thousand Austrian sabres found no opportunity to charge home." The battle is between sabres in line and muskets in échelon—a mere clash of ironmongery.

On other occasions there is no question of anything so vulgarly material as ironmongery. The battles are between Platonic ideas, between the abstractions of physics and mathematics. Forces interact; weights are flung into scales; masses are set in motion. Or else it is all a matter of geometry. Lines swing and sweep; are protracted or curved; pivot on a fixed point.

Alternatively the combatants are personal, in the sense that they are personifications. There is "the enemy," in the singular, making "his" plans, striking "his" blows. The attribution of personal characteristics to collectivities, to geographical expressions, to institutions, is a source, as we shall see, of endless confusions in political thought, of innumerable political mistakes and crimes. Personification in politics is an error which we make because it is to our advantage as egotists to be able to feel violently proud of our country and of ourselves as belonging to it, and to believe that all the misfortunes due to our own mistakes are really the work of the Foreigner. It is easier to feel violently toward a person than toward an abstraction; hence our habit of making political personifications. In some cases military personifications are merely special instances of political personifications. A particular collectivity, the army or the warring nation, is given the name and, along with the name, the attributes of a single person, in order that we may be able to love or hate it more intensely than we could do if we thought of it as what it really is: a number of diverse individuals. In other cases personification is used for the purpose of concealing the fundamental absurdity and monstrosity of war. What is absurd and monstrous about war is that men who have no personal quarrel should be trained to murder one another in cold blood. By personifying opposing armies or countries, we are able to think of war as a conflict between individuals. The same result is obtained by writing of war as though it were carried on exclusively by the generals in command and not by the private soldiers in their armies. ("Rennenkampf had pressed back von Schubert.") The implication in both cases is that war is indistinguishable from a bout of fisticuffs in a bar room. Whereas in reality it is profoundly different. A scrap between two individuals is forgivable; mass murder, deliberately organized, is a monstrous iniquity. We still choose to use war as an instrument of policy; and to comprehend the full wickedness and absurdity of war would therefore be inconvenient. For, once we understood, we should have to make some effort to get rid of the abominable thing. Accordingly, when we talk about war, we use a language which conceals or embellishes its reality. Ignoring the facts, so far as we possibly can, we imply that battles are not fought by soldiers, but by things, principles, allegories, personified collectivities, or (at the most human) by opposing commanders, pitched against one another in single combat. For the same reason, when we have to describe the processes and the results of war, we employ a rich variety of euphemisms. Even the most violently patriotic and militaristic are reluctant to call a spade by its own name. To conceal their intentions even from themselves, they make use of picturesque metaphors. We find them, for example, clamoring for war planes numerous and powerful enough to go and "destroy the hornets in their nests"—in other words, to go and throw thermite, high explosives and vesicants upon the inhabitants of neighboring countries before they have time to come and do the same to us. And how reassuring is the language of historians and strategists! They write admiringly of those military geniuses who know "when to strike at the enemy's line" (a single combatant deranges the geometrical constructions of a personification); when to "turn his flank"; when to "execute an enveloping movement." As though they were engineers discussing the strength of materials and the distribution of stresses, they talk of abstract entities called "man power" and "fire power." They sum up the long-drawn sufferings and atrocities of trench warfare in the phrase, "a war of attrition"; the massacre and mangling of human beings is assimilated to the grinding of a lens.

A dangerously abstract word, which figures in all discussions about war, is "force." Those who believe in organizing collective security by means of military pacts against a possible aggressor are particularly fond of this word. "You cannot," they say, "have international justice unless you are prepared to impose it by force." "Peace-loving countries must unite to use force against aggressive dictatorships." "Democratic institutions must be protected, if need be, by force." And so on.

Now, the word "force," when used in reference to human relations, has no single, definite meaning. There is the "force" used by parents when, without resort to any kind of physical violence, they compel their children to act or refrain from acting in some particular way. There is the "force" used by attendants in an asylum when they try to prevent a maniac from hurting himself or others. There is the "force" used by the police when they control a crowd, and that other "force" which they used in a baton charge. And finally there is the "force" used in war. This, of course, varies with the technological devices at the disposal of the belligerents, with the policies they are pursuing, and with the particular circumstances of the war in question. But in general it may be said that, in war, "force" connotes violence and fraud used to the limit of the combatants' capacity. .

Variations in quantity, if sufficiently great, produce variations in quality. The "force" that is war, particularly modern war, is very different from the "force" that is police action, and the use of the same abstract word to describe the two dissimilar processes is profoundly misleading. (Still more misleading, of course, is the explicit assimilation of a war, waged by allied League-of-Nations powers against an aggressor, to police action against a criminal. The first is the use of violence and fraud without limit against innocent and guilty alike; the second is the use of strictly limited violence and a minimum of fraud exclusively against the guilty.)

Reality is a succession of concrete and particular situations. When we think about such situations we should use the particular and concrete words which apply to them. If we use abstract words which apply equally well (and equally badly) to other, quite dissimilar situations, it is certain that we shall think incorrectly.

Let us take the sentences quoted above and translate the abstract word "force" into language that will render (however inadequately) the concrete and particular realities of contemporary warfare.

"You cannot have international justice, unless you are prepared to impose it by force." Translated, this becomes: "You cannot have international justice unless you are prepared, with a view to imposing a just settlement, to drop thermite, high explosives and vesicants upon the inhabitants of foreign cities and to have thermite, high explosives and vesicants dropped in return upon the inhabitants of your cities." At the end of this proceeding, justice is to be imposed by the victorious party—that is, if there is a victorious party. It should be remarked that justice was to have been imposed by the victorious party at the end of the last war. But, unfor-

tunately, after four years of fighting, the temper of the victors
was such that they were quite incapable of making a just
settlement. The Allies are reaping in Nazi Germany what they
sowed at Versailles. The victors of the next war will have
undergone intensive bombardments with thermite, high explosives and vesicants. Will their temper be better than that of
the Allies in 1918? Will they be in a fitter state to make a
just settlement? The answer, quite obviously, is: No. It is
psychologically all but impossible that justice should be
secured by the methods of contemporary warfare.

The next two sentences may be taken together. "Peace-
loving countries must unite to use force against aggressive
dictatorships. Democratic institutions must be protected, if
need be, by force." Let us translate. "Peace-loving countries
must unite to throw thermite, high explosives and vesicants
on the inhabitants of countries ruled by aggressive dictators.
They must do this, and of course abide the consequences, in
order to preserve peace and democratic institutions." Two
questions immediately propound themselves. First, is it likely
that peace can be secured by a process calculated to reduce
the orderly life of our complicated societies to chaos? And,
second, is it likely that democratic institutions will flourish in
a state of chaos? Again, the answers are pretty clearly in the
negative.

By using the abstract word "force," instead of terms which
at least attempt to describe the realities of war as it is today,
the preachers of collective security through military collaboration disguise from themselves and from others, not only the
contemporary facts, but also the probable consequences of
their favorite policy. The attempt to secure justice, peace and
democracy by "force" seems reasonable enough until we realize, first, that this noncommittal word stands, in the circumstances of our age, for activities which can hardly fail to
result in social chaos; and second, that the consequences of
social chaos are injustice, chronic warfare and tyranny. The
moment we think in concrete and particular terms of the
concrete and particular process called "modern war," we see
that a policy which worked (or at least didn't result in complete disaster) in the past has no prospect whatever of working in the immediate future. The attempt to secure justice,
peace and democracy by means of a "force," which means, at
this particular moment of history, thermite, high explosives
and vesicants, is about as reasonable as the attempt to put out
a fire with a colorless liquid that happens to be, not water, but
petrol.

What applies to the "force" that is war applies in large

measure to the "force" that is revolution. It seems inherently
very unlikely that social justice and social peace can be
secured by thermite, high explosives and vesicants. At first,
it may be, the parties in a civil war would hesitate to use
such instruments on their fellow-countrymen. But there can
be little doubt that, if the conflict were prolonged (as it
probably would be between the evenly balanced Right and
Left of a highly industrialized society), the combatants would
end by losing their scruples.

The alternatives confronting us seem to be plain enough.
Either we invent and conscientiously employ a new technique
for making revolutions and settling international disputes; or
else we cling to the old technique and, using "force" (that is
to say, thermite, high explosives and vesicants), destroy ourselves. Those who, for whatever motive, disguise the nature
of the second alternative under inappropriate language, render
the world a grave disservice. They lead us into one of the
temptations we find it hardest to resist—the temptation to run
away from reality, to pretend that facts are not what they are.
Like Shelley (but without Shelley's acute awareness of what
he was doing) we are perpetually weaving

> A shroud of talk to hide us from the sun
> Of this familiar life.

We protect our minds by an elaborate system of abstractions,
ambiguities, metaphors and similes from the reality we do not
wish to know too clearly; we lie to ourselves, in order that we
may still have the excuse of ignorance, the alibi of stupidity
and incomprehension, possessing which we can continue with
a good conscience to commit and tolerate the most monstrous
crimes:

> The poor wretch who has learned his only prayers
> From curses, who knows scarcely words enough
> To ask a blessing from his Heavenly Father,
> Becomes a fluent phraseman, absolute
> And technical in victories and defeats,
> And all our dainty terms for fratricide;
> Terms which we trundle smoothly o'er our tongues
> Like mere abstractions, empty sounds to which
> We join no meaning and attach no form!
> As if the soldier died without a wound:
> As if the fibers of this godlike frame
> Were gored without a pang: as if the wretch
> Who fell in battle, doing bloody deeds,
> Passed off to Heaven translated and not killed;
> As though he had no wife to pine for him,
> No God to judge him.

The language we use about war is inappropriate, and its inappropriateness is designed to conceal a reality so odious that we do not wish to know it. The language we use about politics is also inappropriate; but here our mistake has a different purpose. Our principal aim in this case is to arouse and, having aroused, to rationalize and justify such intrinsically agreeable sentiments as pride and hatred, self-esteem and contempt for others. To achieve this end we speak about the facts of politics in words which more or less completely misrepresent them.

The concrete realities of politics are individual human beings, living together in national groups. Politicians—and to some extent we are all politicians—substitute abstractions for these concrete realities, and having done this, proceed to invest each abstraction with an appearance of concreteness by personifying it. For example, the concrete reality of which "Britain" is the abstraction consists of some forty-odd millions of diverse individuals living on an island off the west coast of Europe. The personification of this abstraction appears, in classical fancy-dress and holding a very large toasting fork, on the backside of our copper coinage; appears in verbal form, every time we talk about international politics. "Britain," the abstraction from forty millions of Britons, is endowed with thoughts, sensibilities and emotions, even with a sex—for, in spite of John Bull, the country is always a female.

Now, it is of course possible that "Britain" is more than a mere name—is an entity that possesses some kind of reality distinct from that of the individuals constituting the group to which the name is applied. But this entity, if it exists, is certainly not a young lady with a toasting fork; nor is it possible to believe (though some eminent philosophers have preached the doctrine) that it should possess anything in the nature of a personal will. One must agree with T. H. Green that "there can be nothing in a nation, however exalted its mission, or in a society however perfectly organized, which is not in the persons composing the nation or the society.... We cannot suppose a national spirit and will to exist except as the spirit and will of individuals." But the moment we start resolutely thinking about our world in terms of individual persons we find ourselves at the same time thinking in terms of universality. "The great rational religions," writes Professor Whitehead, "are the outcome of the emergence of a religious consciousness that is universal, as distinguished from tribal, or even social. Because it is universal, it introduces the note of solitariness." (And he might have added that, because it is solitary, it introduces the note of universality.) "The reason of this connection between universality and solitude is that

universality is a disconnection from immediate surroundings."
And conversely the disconnection from immediate surroundings, particularly such social surrounding as the tribe or
nation, the insistence on the person as the fundamental reality,
leads to the conception of an all-embracing unity.

A nation, then, may be more than a mere abstraction, may
possess some kind of real existence apart from its constituent
members. But there is no reason to suppose that it is a
person; indeed, there is every reason to suppose that it isn't.
Those who speak as though it were a person (and some go
further than this and speak as though it were a personal god)
do so, because it is to their interest as egotists to make precisely this mistake.

In the case of the ruling class these interests are in part
material. The personification of the nation as a sacred being,
different from and superior to its constituent members, is
merely (I quote the words of a great French jurist, Léon
Duguit) "a way of imposing authority by making people
believe it is an authority *de jure* and not merely *de facto.*"
By habitually talking of the nation as though it were a person
with thoughts, feelings and a will of its own, the rulers of a
country legitimate their own powers. Personification leads
easily to deification; and where the nation is deified, its government ceases to be a mere convenience, like drains or a
telephone system, and, partaking in the sacredness of the
entity it represents, claims to give orders by divine right and
demands the unquestioning obedience due to a god. Rulers
seldom find it hard to recognize their friends. Hegel, the man
who elaborated an inappropriate figure of speech into a complete philosophy of politics, was a favorite of the Prussian
government. *"Es ist,"* he had written, *"es ist der Gang Gottes
in der Welt, das der Staat ist."* The decoration bestowed on
him by Frederick William III was richly deserved.

Unlike their rulers, the ruled have no material interest in
using inappropriate language about states and nations. For
them, the reward of being mistaken is psychological. The
personified and deified nation becomes, in the minds of the
individuals composing it, a kind of enlargement of themselves.
The superhuman qualities which belong to the young lady
with the toasting fork, the young lady with plaits and a brass
soutien-gorge, the young lady in a Phrygian bonnet, are
claimed by individual Englishmen, Germans and Frenchmen
as being, at least in part, their own. *Dulce et decorum est pro
patria mori.* But there would be no need to die, no need of
war, if it had not been even sweeter to boast and swagger
for one's country, to hate, despise, swindle and bully for it.
Loyalty to the personified nation, or to the personified class

or party, justifies the loyal in indulging all those passions
which good manners and the moral code do not allow them
to display in their relations with their neighbors. The personified entity is a being, not only great and noble, but also
insanely proud, vain and touchy; fiercely rapacious; a brag-
gart; bound by no considerations of right and wrong. (Hegel
condemned as hopelessly shallow all those who dared to
apply ethical standards to the activities of nations. To condone
and applaud every iniquity committed in the name of the
State was to him a sign of philosophical profundity.) Identifying themselves with this god, individuals find relief from the
constraints of ordinary social decency, feel themselves justified
in giving rein, within duly prescribed limits, to their criminal
proclivities. As a loyal nationalist or party-man, one can
enjoy the luxury of behaving badly with a good conscience.

The evil passions are further justified by another linguistic
error—the error of speaking about certain categories of persons as though they were mere embodied abstractions. Foreigners and those who disagree with us are not thought of as
men and women like ourselves and our fellow-countrymen;
they are thought of as representatives and, so to say, symbols
of a class. In so far as they have any personality at all, it is
the personality we mistakenly attribute to their class—a personality that is, by definition, intrinsically evil. We know that
the harming or killing of men and women is wrong, and we
are reluctant consciously to do what we know to be wrong.
But when particular men and women are thought of merely
as representatives of a class, which has previously been defined
as evil and personified in the shape of a devil, then the reluctance to hurt or murder disappears. Brown, Jones and Robinson are no longer thought of as Brown, Jones and Robinson,
but as heretics, gentiles, Yids, niggers, barbarians, Huns,
communists, capitalists, fascists, liberals—whichever the case
may be. When they have been called such names and assimilated to the accursed class to which the names apply, Brown,
Jones and Robinson cease to be conceived as what they really
are—human persons—and become for the users of this fatally
inappropriate language mere vermin or, worse, demons whom
it is right and proper to destroy as thoroughly and as painfully
as possible. Wherever persons are present, questions of morality arise. Rulers of nations and leaders of parties find
morality embarrassing. That is why they take such pains to
depersonalize their opponents. All propaganda directed against
an opposing group has but one aim: to substitute diabolical
abstractions for concrete persons. The propagandist's purpose
is to make one set of people forget that certain other sets of
people are human. By robbing them of their personality, he

puts them outside the pale of moral obligation. Mere symbols can have no rights—particularly when that of which they are symbolical is, by definition, evil.

Politics can become moral only on one condition: that its problems shall be spoken of and thought about exclusively in terms of concrete reality; that is to say, of persons. To depersonify human beings and to personify abstractions are complementary errors which lead, by an inexorable logic, to war between nations and to idolatrous worship of the State, with consequent governmental oppression. All current political thought is a mixture, in varying proportions, between thought in terms of concrete realities and thought in terms of depersonified symbols and personified abstractions. In the democratic countries the problems of internal politics are thought about mainly in terms of concrete reality; those of external politics, mainly in terms of abstractions and symbols. In dictatorial countries the proportion of concrete to abstract and symbolic thought is lower than in democratic countries. Dictators talk little of persons, much of personified abstractions, such as the Nation, the State, the Party, and much of depersonified symbols, such as Yids, Bolshies, Capitalists. The stupidity of politicians who talk about a world of persons as though it were not a world of persons is due in the main to self-interest. In a fictitious world of symbols and personified abstractions, rulers find that they can rule more effectively, and the ruled, that they can gratify instincts which the conventions of good manners and the imperatives of morality demand that they should repress. To think correctly is the condition of behaving well. It is also in itself a moral act; those who would think correctly must resist considerable temptations.

(From *The Olive Tree*)

Decentralization and Self-Government

The Anarchists propose that the state should be abolished; and in so far as it serves as the instrument by means of which the ruling class preserves its privileges; in so far as it is a device for enabling paranoiacs to satisfy their lust for power and carry out their crazy dreams of glory, the state is obviously worthy of abolition. But in complex societies like our own the state has certain other and more useful functions to perform. It is clear, for example, that in any such society

there must be some organization responsible for co-ordinating
the activities of the various constituent groups; clear, too, that
there must be a body to which is delegated the power of acting
in the name of the society as a whole. If the word "state" is
too unpleasantly associated with ideas of domestic oppression
and foreign war, with irresponsible domination and no less
irresponsible submission, then by all means let us call the
necessary social machinery by some other name. For the
present there is no general agreement as to what that name
should be; I shall therefore go on using the bad old word,
until some better one is invented.

No economic reform, however intrinsically desirable, can
lead to desirable changes in individuals and the society they
constitute, unless it is carried through in a desirable context
and by desirable methods. So far as the state is concerned,
the desirable context for reform is decentralization and self-
government all round. The desirable methods for enacting
reform are the methods of non-violence.

Passing from the general to the particular and the concrete,
the rational idealist finds himself confronted by the following
questions. First, by what means can the principle of self-
government be applied to the daily lives of men and women?
Second, to what extent is the self-government of the component parts of a society compatible with its efficiency as a
whole? And, thirdly, if a central organization is needed to co-
ordinate the activities of the self-governing parts, what is to
prevent this organization from becoming a ruling oligarchy
of the kind with which we are only too painfully familiar?

The technique for self-government all round, self-government for ordinary people in their ordinary avocation, is a
matter which we cannot profitably discuss unless we have a
clear idea of what may be called the natural history and
psychology of groups. Quantitatively, a group differs from a
crowd in size; qualitatively, in the kind and intensity of the
mental life of the constituent individuals. A crowd is a lot of
people; a group is a few. A crowd has a mental life inferior
in intellectual quality and emotionally less under voluntary
control than the mental life of each of its members in isolation. The mental life of a group is not inferior, either intellectually or emotionally, to the mental life of the individual
composing it and may, in favorable circumstances, actually be
superior.

The significant psychological facts about the crowd are as
follows. The tone of crowd emotion is essentially orgiastic and
dionysiac. In virtue of his membership of the crowd, the
individual is released from the limitations of his personality,
made free of the sub-personal, sub-human world of unre-

strained feeling and uncriticized belief. To be a member of a crowd is an experience closely akin to alcoholic intoxication. Most human beings feel a craving to escape from the cramping limitations of their ego, to take periodical holidays from their all too familiar, all too squalid little selves. As they do not know how to travel upwards from personality into a region of super-personality and as they are unwilling, even if they do know, to fulfill the ethical, psychological and physiological conditions of self-transcendence, they turn naturally to the descending road, the road that leads down from personality to the darkness of sub-human emotionalism and panic animality. Hence the persistent craving for narcotics and stimulants, hence the never failing attraction of the crowd. The success of the dictators is due in large measure to their extremely skillful exploitation of the universal human need for escape from the limitations of personality. Perceiving that people wished to take holidays from themselves in sub-human emotionality, they have systematically provided their subjects with the occasions for doing so. The Communists denounce religion as the opium of the people; but all they have done is to replace this old drug by a new one of similar composition. For the crowd round the relic of the saint they have substituted the crowd at the political meeting; for religious processions, military reviews and May Day parades. It is the same with Fascist dictators. In all the totalitarian states the masses are persuaded, and, even compelled, to take periodical holidays from themselves in the sub-human world of crowd emotion. It is significant that while they encourage and actually command the descent into sub-humanity, the dictators do all they can to prevent men from taking the upward road from personal limitation, the road that leads toward non-attachment to the "things of this world" and attachment to that which is super-personal. The higher manifestations of religion are far more suspect to the tyrants than the lower—and with reason. For the man who escapes from egotism into super-personality has transcended his old idolatrous loyalty, not only to himself, but also to the local divinities—nation, party, class, deified boss. Self-transcendence, escape from the prison of the ego into union with what is above personality, is generally accomplished in solitude. That is why the tyrants like to herd their subjects into those vast crowds, in which the individual is reduced to a state of intoxicated sub-humanity.

It is time now to consider the group. The first question we must ask ourselves is this: when does a group become a crowd? This is not a problem in verbal definition; it is a matter of observation and experience. It is found empirically that group activities and characteristic group feeling become increasingly difficult when more than about twenty or less than about five individuals are involved. Groups which come together for the purpose of carrying out a specific job of manual work can afford to be larger than groups which meet for the purpose of pooling information and elaborating a common policy, or which meet for religious exercises, or for mutual comfort, or merely for the sake of convivially "getting together." Twenty or even as many as thirty people can work together and still remain a group. But these numbers would be much too high in a group that had assembled for the other purposes I have mentioned. It is significant that Jesus had only twelve apostles; that the Benedictines were divided into groups of ten under a dean (Latin *decanus* from Greek δεκα ten); that ten is the number of individuals constituting a Communist cell. Committees of more than a dozen members are found to be unmanageably large. Eight is the perfect number for a dinner party. The most successful Quaker meetings are generally meetings at which few people are present. Educationists agree that the most satisfactory size for a class is between eight and fifteen. In armies, the smallest unit is about ten. The witches' "coven" was a group of thirteen. And so on. All evidence points clearly to the fact that there is an optimum size for groups and that this optimum is round about ten for groups meeting for social, religious or intellectual purposes and from ten to thirty for groups engaged in manual work. This being so, it is clear that the units of self-government should be groups of the optimum size. If they are smaller than the optimum, they will fail to develop that emotional field which gives to group activity its characteristic quality, while the available quantity of pooled information and experience will be inadequate. If they are larger than the optimum, they will tend to split into sub-groups of the optimum size or, if the constituent individuals remain together in a crowd there will be a danger of their relapsing into the crowd's sub-human stupidity and emotionality.

The technique of industrial self-government has been discussed with a wealth of concrete examples in a remarkable book by the French economist Hyacinthe Dubreuil, entitled, *A Chacun sa Chance*. Among the writers on industrial organization Dubreuil occupies a place apart; for he is almost the only one of them who has himself had experience of factory conditions as a workman. Accordingly, what he writes on the subject of industrial organization carries an authority denied to the utterances of those who rely on second-hand information as a basis for their theories. Dubreuil points out that even the largest industries can be organized so as to consist of a series of self-governing, yet co-ordinated, groups of, at the outside, thirty members. Within the industry each one of such groups can act as a kind of sub-contractor, undertaking to perform so much of such and such a kind of work for such and such a sum. The equitable division of this sum among the constituent members is left to the group itself, as is also the preservation of discipline, the election of representatives and leaders. The examples which Dubreuil quotes from the annals of industrial history and from his own experience as a workman tend to show that this form of organization is appreciated by the workers, to whom it gives a measure of independence even within the largest manufacturing concern, and that in most cases it results in increased efficiency of working. It possesses, as he points out, the further merit of being a form of organization that educates those who belong to it in the practice of co-operation and mutual responsibility.

Under the present dispensation, the great majority of factories are little despotisms, benevolent in some cases, malevolent in others. Even where benevolence prevails, passive obedience is demanded of the workers, who are ruled by overseers, not of their own election, but appointed from above. In theory, they may be the subjects of a democratic state; but in practice they spend the whole of their working lives as the subjects of a petty tyrant. Dubreuil's scheme, if it were generally acted upon, would introduce genuine democracy into the factory. And if some such scheme is not acted upon, it is of small moment to the individual whether the industry in which he is working is owned by the state, by a co-operative society, by a joint stock company or by a private individual. Passive obedience to officers appointed from above is always passive obedience, whoever the general in ultimate control may be. Conversely, even if the ultimate control is in the wrong hands, the man who voluntarily accepts rules in the making of which he has had a part, who obeys leaders he himself has chosen, who has helped to decide how much and in what conditions he himself and his companions shall be paid, is to that extent the free and responsible subject of a genuinely democratic government, and enjoys those psychological advantages which only such a form of government can give.

Of modern wage-slaves, Lenin writes that they "remain to such an extent crushed by want and poverty that they 'can't be bothered with democracy,' have 'no time for politics,' and in the ordinary peaceful course of events, the majority of the population is debarred from participating in public political life." This statement is only partially true. Not all those who can't be bothered with democracy are debarred from political life by want and poverty. Plenty of well-paid workmen and, for that matter, plenty of the wealthiest beneficiaries of the capitalistic system, find that they can't be bothered with politics. The reason is not economic, but psychological; has its source, not in environment, but in heredity. People belong to different psycho-physiological types and are endowed with different degrees of general intelligence. The will and ability to take an effective interest in large-scale politics do not belong to all, or even a majority of, men and women. Preoccupation with general ideas, with things and people distant in space, with contingent events remote in future time, is something which it is given to only a few to feel. "What's Hecuba to him or he to Hecuba?" The answer in most cases is: Nothing whatsoever. An improvement in the standard of living might perceptibly increase the number of those for whom Hecuba meant something. But even if all were rich, there would still be many congenitally incapable of being bothered with anything so far removed from the warm, tangible facts of everyday experience. As things are at present, millions of men and women come into the world disfranchised by nature. They have the privilege of voting on long-range, large-scale political issues; but they are congenitally incapable of taking an intelligent interest in any but short-range, small-scale problems. Too often the framers of democratic constitutions have acted as though man were made for democracy, not democracy for man. The vote has been a kind of bed of Procrustes upon which, however long their views, however short their ability, all human beings were expected to stretch themselves. Not unnaturally, the results of this kind of democracy have proved disappointing. Nevertheless, it remains true that democratic freedom is good for those who enjoy it and that practice in self-government is an almost indispensable element in the curriculum of man's moral and psychological education. Human beings belong to different types; it is therefore necessary to create different types of democratic and self-governing institutions, suitable for the various kinds of men and women. Thus, people with short-range, small-scale interests can find scope for their kind of political abilities in self-governing groups within an industry, within a consumer or producer co-operative, within the administrative machinery of the parish, borough or county. By means of comparatively small changes in the existing systems of local and professional organization it would be possible to make almost every individual a member of some self-governing group. In this way the curse of merely passive obedience could be got rid of, the vice of political indolence cured and the advantages of responsible and active freedom brought to all. In this context it is worth remarking on a very significant change which has recently taken place in our social habits. Materially, this change may be summed up as the decline of the community; psychologically, as the decline of the community sense. The reasons for this double change are many and of various kinds. Here are a few of the more important.

Birth control has reduced the size of the average family and, for various reasons which will be apparent later, the old habits of patriarchal living have practically disappeared. It is very rare nowadays to find parents, married children, and grandchildren living together in the same house or in close association. Large families and patriarchal groups were communities in which children and adults· had to learn (often by very painful means) the art of co-operation and the need to accept responsibility for others. These admittedly rather crude schools of community sense have now disappeared.

New methods of transport have profoundly modified the life in the village and small town. Up to only a generation ago most villages were to a great extent self-sufficing communities. Every trade was represented by its local technician; the local produce was consumed or exchanged in the neighborhood; the inhabitants worked on the spot. If they desired instruction or entertainment or religion, they had to mobilize the local talent and produce it themselves. Today all this is changed. Thanks to improved transport, the village is now closely bound up with the rest of the economic world. Supplies and technical services are obtained from a distance. Large numbers of the inhabitants go out to work in factories and offices in far-off cities. Music and the drama are provided, not by local talent, but over the ether and in the picture theater. Once all the members of the community were always on the spot; now, thanks to cars, motor cycles and buses the villagers are rarely in their village. Community fun, community worship, community efforts to secure culture have tended to decline for the simple reason that, in leisure hours, a large part of the community's membership is always somewhere else. Nor is this all. The older inhabitants of Middletown, as readers of the Lynds' classical study of American small-town life will remember, complained that the internal combustion engine had led to a decline of neighborliness. Neighbors have Fords and Chevrolets, consequently are no longer there to be neighborly; or if by chance they should be at home, they content themselves with calling up on the telephone. Technological progress has reduced the number of physical contacts, and thus impoverished the spiritual relations between the members of a community.

Centralized professionalism has not only affected local entertainment; it had also affected the manifestations of local charity and mutual aid. State-provided hospitals, state-provided medical and nursing services are certainly much more efficient than the ministrations of the neighbors. But this increased efficiency is purchased at the price of a certain tendency on the part of neighbors to disclaim liability for one another and throw their responsibilities entirely upon the central authority. Under a perfectly organized system of state socialism charity would be, not merely superfluous, but actually criminal. Good Samaritans would be prosecuted for daring to interfere in their bungling amateurish way with what was obviously a case for state-paid professionals.

The last three generations have witnessed a vast increase in the size and number of large cities. Life is more exciting and more money can be earned in the cities than in villages and small towns. Hence the migration from country to city. In the van of this migrating host have marched the ambitious, the talented, the adventurous. For more than a century, there has been a tendency for the most gifted members of small rural communities to leave home and seek their fortune in the towns. Consequently what remains in the villages and country towns of the industrialized countries is in the nature of a residual population, dysgenically selected for its lack of spirit and intellectual gifts. Why is it so hard to induce peasants and small farmers to adopt new scientific methods? Among other reasons, because almost every exceptionally intelligent child born into a rural family for a century past has taken the earliest opportunity of deserting the land for the city. Community life in the country is thus impoverished; but (and this is the important point) the community life of the great urban centers is not correspondingly enriched. It is not enriched for the good reason that, in growing enormous, cities have also grown chaotic. A metropolitan "wen," as Cobbett was already calling the relatively tiny London of his day, is no longer an organic whole, no longer exists as a community, in whose life individuals can fruitfully participate. Men and women rub shoulders with other men and women; but the contact is external and mechanical. Each one of them can say, in the words of the Jolly Miller of the song, "I care for nobody, no, not I, and nobody cares for me." Metropolitan life is atomistic. The city, as a city, does nothing to correlate its human particles into a pattern of responsible, communal living. What the country loses on the swings, the city loses all over again on the roundabouts.

In the light of this statement of the principal reasons for the recent decline of the community and of the community sense in individuals, we can suggest certain remedies. Schools and colleges can be transformed into organic communities and used to offset, during a short period of the individual's career, the decay in family and village life. (A very interesting experiment in this direction is being made at Black Mountain College in North Carolina.) To some extent, no doubt, the old, "natural" life of villages and small towns, the life that the economic, technological and religious circumstances of the past conspired to impose upon them, can be replaced by a consciously designed synthetic product—a life of associations organized for local government, for sport, for cultural activities and the like. Such associations already exist, and there should be no great difficulty in opening them to larger numbers and, at the same time, in making their activities so interesting that people will wish to join them instead of taking the line of least resistance, as they do now, and living unconnected, atomistic lives, passively obeying during their working hours and passively allowing themselves to be entertained by machinery during their hours of leisure. The existence of associations of this kind would serve to make country life less dull and so do something to arrest the flight toward the city. At the same time, the decentralization of industry and its association with agriculture should make it possible for the countryman to earn as much as the city dweller. In spite of the ease with which electric power can now be distributed, the movement toward the decentralization of industry is not yet a very powerful one. Great centers of population, like London and Paris, possess an enormous power of attraction to industries. The greater the population, the greater the market; and the greater the market, the stronger the gravitational pull exercised upon the manufacturer. New industries establish themselves on the outskirts of large cities and make them become still larger. For the sake of slight increased profits, due to lower distributing costs, the manufacturers are busily engaged in making London chaotically large, hopelessly congested, desperately hard to enter or leave, and vulnerable to air attacks as no other city of Europe is vulnerable. To compel a rational and planned decentralization of industry is one of the legitimate, the urgently necessary functions of the state.

Life in the great city is atomistic. How shall it be given a communal pattern? How shall the individual be incorporated in a responsible, self-governing group? In a modern city, the problem of organizing responsible community life on a local basis is not easily solved. Modern cities have been created and are preserved by the labors of highly specialized technicians. The massacre of a few thousands of engineers, administrators and doctors would be sufficient to reduce any of the great metropolitan centers to a state of plague-stricken, starving chaos. Accordingly, in most of its branches, the local government of a great city has become a highly technical affair, a business of the kind that must be centrally planned and carried out by experts. The only department in which there would seem to be a possibility of profitably extending the existing institutions of local self-government is the department concerned with police-work and the observance of laws. I have read that in Japan, the cities were, and perhaps still are, divided into wards of about a hundred inhabitants apiece. The people in each ward accepted a measure of liability for one another and were to some extent responsible for good behavior and the observance of law within their own small unit. That such a system lends itself to the most monstrous abuses under a dictatorial government is obvious. Indeed, it is reported that the Nazis have already organized their cities in this way. But there is no governmental institution that cannot be abused. Elected parliaments have been used as instruments of oppression; plebiscites have served to confirm and strengthen tyranny; courts of justice have been transformed into Star Chambers and military tribunals. Like all the rest, the ward system may be a source of good in a desirable context and a source of unmitigated evil in an undesirable context. It remains in any case a device worth considering by those who aspire to impose a communal pattern upon the atomistic, irresponsible life of modern city dwellers. For the rest, it looks as though the townsman's main experience of democratic institutions and responsible self-government would have to be obtained, not in local administrations, but in the fields of industry and economics, of religious and cultural activity, of athletics and entertainment.

In the preceding paragraphs I have tried to answer the first of our questions and have described the methods by which the principle of self-government can be applied to the daily lives of ordinary men and women. Our second question concerns the compatibility of self-government all round with the efficiency of industry in particular and society as a whole. In Russia self-government in industry was tried in the early years of the revolution and was abandoned in favor of authoritarian management. Within the factory discipline is no longer enforced by elected representatives of the Soviet or worker's committee, but by appointees of the Communist Party. The new conception of management current in Soviet Russia was summed up by Kaganovitch in a speech before the seventeenth congress of the Communist Party. "Management," he said, "means the power to distribute material things, to appoint and discharge subordinates, in a word, to be master of the particular enterprise." This is a definition of management to which every industrial dictator in the capitalist countries would unhesitatingly subscribe.

By supporters of the present Russian government it is said that the change over from self-government to authoritarian management had to be made in the interests of efficiency. That extremely inexperienced and ill-educated workers should have been unable to govern themselves and keep up industrial efficiency seems likely enough. But in Western Europe and the United States such a situation is not likely to arise. Indeed, Dubreuil has pointed out that, as a matter of historical fact, self-government within factories has often led to increased efficiency. It would seem, then, that in countries where all men and women are relatively well educated and have been accustomed for some time to the working of democratic institutions, there is no danger that self-government will lead to a breakdown of discipline within the factory or a decline in output. But, like "liberty" the word "efficiency" covers a multitude of sins. Even if it should be irrefragably demonstrated that self-government in industry invariably led to a greater contentment and increased output, even if it could be proved experimentally that the best features of individualism and collectivism could be combined if the state were to co-ordinate the activities of self-governing industries, there would still be complaints of "inefficiency." And by their own lights, the complainers would be quite right. For to the ruling classes, not only in the totalitarian, but also in the democratic countries, "efficiency" means primarily "military efficiency." Now, a society in which the principle of self-government has been applied to the ordinary activities of all its members, is a society which, for purely military purposes, is probably decidedly inefficient. A militarily efficient society is one whose members have been brought up in habits of passive obedience and at the head of which there is an individual exercising absolute authority through a perfectly trained hierarchy of administrators. In time of war, such a society can be manipulated as a single unit and with extraordinary rapidity and precision. A society composed of men and women habituated to working in self-governing groups is not a perfect war-machine. Its members may think and have wills of their own. But soldiers must not think nor have wills. "Theirs not to reason why; theirs but to do and die." Furthermore a society in which authority is decentralized, a society composed of co-ordinated but self-governing parts, cannot be manipulated so swiftly and certainly as a totalitarian society under a dictator. Self-government all round is not compatible with military efficiency. So long as nations persist in using war as an instrument of policy, military efficiency will be prized above all else.

Therefore schemes for extending the principle of self-government will either not be tried at all or, if tried, as in Russia,
will be speedily abandoned. Inevitably, we find ourselves
confronted, yet once more, by the central evil of our time,
the overpowering and increasing evil of war.

I must now try to answer our questions concerning the
efficiency of a society made up of co-ordinated self-governing
units and the nature of the co-ordinating body.

Dubreuil has shown that even the largest industrial undertakings can be organized so as to consist of a number of
co-ordinated but self-governing groups; and he has produced
reasons for supposing that such an organization would not
reduce the efficiency of the businesses concerned and might
even increase it. This small-scale industrial democracy is
theoretically compatible with any kind of large-scale control
of the industries concerned. It can be (and in certain cases
actually has been) applied to industries working under the
capitalist system; to businesses under direct state control; to
co-operative enterprises; to mixed concerns, like the Port of
London Authority, which are under state supervision, but
have their own autonomous, functional management. In practice this small-scale industrial democracy, this self-government
for all, is intrinsically most compatible with business organizations of the last two kinds—co-operative and mixed. It is
almost equally incompatible with capitalism and state socialism. Capitalism tends to produce a multiplicity of petty dictators, each in command of his own little business kingdom.
State socialism tends to produce a single, centralized, totalitarian dictatorship, wielding absolute authority over all its
subjects through a hierarchy of bureaucratic agents.

Co-operatives and mixed concerns already exist and work
extremely well. To increase their numbers and to extend their
scope would not seem a revolutionary act, in the sense that
it would probably not provoke the violent opposition which
men feel toward projects involving an entirely new principle.
In its effects, however, the act would *be* revolutionary; for
it would result in a profound modification of the existing
system. This alone is a sufficient reason for preferring these
forms of ultimate industrial control to all others. The intrinsic
compatibility of the co-operative enterprise and mixed concern with small-scale democracy and self-government all
round constitutes yet another reason for the preference. To
discuss the arrangements for co-ordinating the activities of
partially autonomous co-operative and mixed concerns is not
my business in this place. For technical details, the reader is
referred once again to the literature of social and economic
planning. I will confine myself here to quoting a relevant

passage from the admirable essay contributed by Professor David Mitrany to the Yale Review in 1934. Speaking of the need for comprehensive planning, Professor Mitrany writes that "this does not necessarily mean more centralized government and bureaucratic administration. Public control is just as likely to mean decentralization—as, for instance, the taking over from a nation-wide private corporation of activities and services which could be performed with better results by local authorities. Planning, in fact, if it is intelligent, should allow for a great variety of organization, and should adapt the structure and working of its parts to the requirements of each case."

A striking change of view on this point is evident in the paradox that the growing demand for state action comes together with a growing distrust of the state's efficiency. Hence, even among socialists, as may be seen from the more recent Fabian tracts, the old idea of the nationalization of an industry under a government department, responsible to Parliament for both policy and management, has generally been replaced by schemes which even under public ownership provide for autonomous functional managements. After describing the constitution of such mixed concerns as the Central Electricity Board (set up in England by a Conservative government), the British Broadcasting Corporation and the London Transport Board, Professor Mitrany concludes that it is only "by some such means that the influence both of politics and of money can be eliminated. Radicals and conservatives now agree on the need for placing the management of such public undertakings upon a purely functional basis, which reduces the role of Parliament or of any other representative body to a distant, occasional and indirect determination of general policy."

Above these semi-autonomous "functional managers" there will have to be, it is clear, an ultimate co-ordinating authority —a group of technicians whose business it will be to manage the managers. What is to prevent the central political executive from joining hands with these technical managers of managers to become the ruling oligarchy of a totalitarian state? The answer is that, so long as nations continue to prepare for the waging of scientific warfare, there is nothing whatever to prevent this from happening—there is every reason, indeed, to suppose that it will happen. In the context of militarism, even the most intrinsically desirable changes inevitably become distorted. In a country which is preparing for modern war, reforms intended to result in decentralization and genuine democracy will be made to serve the purpose of military efficiency—which means in practice that they will be used to strengthen the position of a dictator or a ruling oligarchy.

Where the international context is militaristic, dictators will use the necessity for "defense" as their excuse for seizing absolute power. But even where there is no threat of war, the temptation to abuse a position of authority will always be strong. How shall our hypothetical managers of managers and the members of the central political executive be delivered from this evil? Ambition may be checked, but cannot be suppressed by any kind of legal machinery. If it is to be scotched, it must be scotched at the source, by education in the widest sense of the word. In our societies men are paranoiacally ambitious, because paranoiac ambition is admired as a virtue and successful climbers are adored as though they were gods. More books have been written about Napoleon than about any other human being. The fact is deeply and alarmingly significant. What must be the day-dreams of people for whom the world's most agile social climber and ablest bandit is the hero they most desire to hear about? Duces and Fuehrers will cease to plague the world only when the majority of its inhabitants regard such adventurers with the same disgust as they now bestow on swindlers and pimps. So long as men worship the Caesars and Napoleons, Caesars and Napoleons will duly rise and make them miserable. The proper attitude toward the "hero" is not Carlyle's, but Bacon's. "He doth like the ape," wrote Bacon of the ambitious tyrant, "he doth like the ape that, the higher he clymbes, the more he shewes his ars." The hero's qualities are brilliant; but so is the mandril's rump. When all concur in the great Lord Chancellor's judgment of Fuehrers, there will be no more Fuehrers to judge. Meanwhile we must content ourselves by putting merely legal and administrative obstacles in the way of the ambitious. They are a great deal better than nothing; but they can never be completely effective.

(From *Ends and Means*)

Politics and Religion

About politics one can make only one completely unquestionable generalization, which is that it is quite impossible for statesmen to foresee, for more than a very short time, the results of any course of large-scale political action. Many of them, it is true, justify their actions by pretending to themselves and others that they can see a long way ahead; but the fact remains that they can't. If they were completely honest they would say, with Father Joseph,

> *J'ignore où mon dessein, qui surpasse ma vue,*
> *Si vite me conduit;*
> *Mais comme un astre ardent qui brille dans la nue,*
> *Il me guide en la nuit.*

If hell is paved with good intentions, it is, among other reasons, because of the impossibility of calculating consequences. Bishop Stubbs therefore condemns those historians who amuse themselves by fixing on individuals or groups of men responsibility for the remoter consequences of their actions. "It strikes me," he writes, "as not merely unjust, but as showing an ignorance of the plainest aphorisms of common sense, . . . to make an historical character responsible for evils and crimes, which have resulted from his actions by processes which he could not foresee." This is sound so far as it goes; but it does not go very far. Besides being a moralist, the historian is one who attempts to formulate generalizations about human events. It is only by tracing the relations between acts and their consequences that such generalizations can be made. When they have been made, they are available to politicians in framing plans of action. In this way past records of the relation between acts and consequences enter the field of ethics as relevant factors in a situation of choice. And here it may be pointed out that, though it is impossible to foresee the remoter consequences of any given course of action, it is by no means impossible to foresee, in the light of past historical experience, the sort of consequences that are likely, in a general way, to follow certain sorts of acts. Thus, from the records of past experience, it seems sufficiently clear that the consequences attendant on a course of action involving such things as large-scale war, violent revolution, unrestrained tyranny and persecution are likely to be bad. Consequently, any politician who embarks on such courses of action cannot plead ignorance as an excuse. Father Joseph, for example, had read enough history to know that policies like that which Richelieu and he were pursuing are seldom, even when nominally successful, productive of lasting good to the parties by whom they were framed. But his passionate ambition for the Bourbons made him cling to a voluntary ignorance, which he proceeded to justify by speculations about the will of God.

Here it seems worth while to comment briefly on the curious time sense of those who think in political terms. Courses of action are recommended on the ground that if carried out, they cannot fail to result in a solution to all outstanding prob-

lems—a solution either definitive and everlasting, like that
which Marx foresaw as the result of the setting up of a classless society, or else of very long duration, like the thousand-
year futures foretold for their regimes by Mussolini and
Hitler. Richelieu's admirers envisaged a Bourbon golden age
longer than the hypothetical Nazi or Fascist era, but shorter
(since it had a limit) than the final, classless stage of Communism. In a contemporary defense of the Cardinal's policy
against the Huguenots, Voiture justifies the great expenditures
involved by saying that "the capture of La Rochelle alone
has economized millions; for La Rochelle would have raised
rebellion at every royal minority, every revolt of the nobles
during the next two thousand years." Such are the illusions
cherished by the politically minded when they reflect on the
consequences of a policy immediately before or immediately
after it has been put in action. But when the policy has begun
to show its fruits, their time sense undergoes a radical change.
Gone are the calculations in terms of centuries or millennia.
A single victory is now held to justify a *Te Deum,* and if the
policy yields apparently successful results for only a few years,
the statesman feels satisfied and his sycophants are lavish in
their praise of his genius. Even sober historians writing long
after the event tend to express themselves in the same vein.
Thus, Richelieu is praised by modern writers as a very great
and far-sighted statesman, even though it is perfectly clear
that the actions he undertook for the aggrandizement of the
Bourbon dynasty created the social and economic and political
conditions, which led to the downfall of that dynasty, the rise
of Prussia and the catastrophes of the nineteenth and twentieth centuries. His policy is praised as if it had been eminently successful, and those who objected to it are blamed
for their short-sighted views. Here, for example, is what
Gustave Fagniez has to say of the French peasants and
burgesses who opposed the Cardinal's war policy—a policy
for which they had to pay with their money, their privations
and their blood. "Always selfish and unintelligent, the masses
cannot be expected to put up for a long time with hardships,
of which future generations are destined to reap the fruits."
And this immediately after a passage setting forth the nature
of these particular fruits—the union of all Europe against
Louis XIV and the ruin of the French people. Such extraordinary inconsistency can only be explained by the fact
that, when people come to talk of their nation's successes,
they think in terms of the very briefest periods of time. A
triumph is to be hymned and gloated over, even if it lasts no
more than a day. Retrospectively, men like Richelieu and
Louis XIV and Napoleon are more admired for the brief glory

they achieved than hated for the long-drawn miseries which were the price of that glory.

Among the sixteen hundred-odd ladies whose names were set down in the catalogue of Don Giovanni's conquests, there were doubtless not a few whose favors made it necessary for the hero to consult his physician. But pox or no pox, the mere fact that the favors had been given was a thing to feel proud of, a victory worth recording in Leporello's chronicle of successes. The history of the nations is written in the same spirit.

So much for the consequences of the policy which Father Joseph helped to frame and execute. Now for the questions of ethics. Ethically, Father Joseph's position was not the same as that of an ordinary politician. It was not the same because, unlike ordinary politicians, he was an aspirant to sanctity, a contemplative with a considerable working knowledge of mysticism, one who knew the nature of spiritual religion and had actually made some advance along the "way of perfection" toward union with God. Theologians agree that all Christians are called to union with God, but that few are willing to make the choice which qualifies them to be chosen. Father Joseph was one of those few. But having made the choice, he went on, some years later, to make another; he chose to go into politics, as Richelieu's collaborator. As we have seen, Father Joseph's intention was to combine the life of political activity with that of contemplation, to do what power politics demanded and to annihilate it in God's will even while it was being done. In practice, the things which had to be done proved unannihilatable, and with one part of his being Father Joseph came to be bitterly sorry that he had ever entered politics. But there was also another part of him, a part that craved for action, that yearned to do something heroic for the greater glory of God. Looking back over his life, Father Joseph, the contemplative, felt that he had done wrong, or at any rate been very unwise, to enter politics. But if he had not done so, if he had remained the evangelist, teacher and religious reformer, he would probably have felt to the end of his days that he had done wrong to neglect the opportunity of doing God's will in the great world of international politics—*gesta Dei per Francos.*

Father Joseph's dilemma is one which confronts all spirituals and contemplatives, all who aspire to worship God theocentrically and for his own sake, all who attempt to obey the commandment to be perfect as their Father in heaven is perfect. In order to think clearly about this dilemma, we must learn first of all to think clearly about certain matters of more general import. Catholic theologians had done a great deal of this necessary clear thinking, and, if he had cared to make use of them, Father Joseph could have found in the teachings of his predecessors and contemporaries most of the materials for a sound philosophy of action and a sound sociology of contemplation. That he did not make use of them was due to the peculiar nature of his temperament and talents and, above all, to his intense vicarious ambition for the French monarchy. He was lured away from the path of perfection by the most refined of all temptations—the baits of loyalty and self-sacrifice, but of a loyalty to a cause inferior to the supreme good, a sacrifice of self undertaken in the name of something less than God.

Let us begin by a consideration of the theory of action which was current in the speculative writings available to Father Joseph. The first thing we have to remember is that, when theologians speak of the active life as contrasted with that of contemplation, they do not refer to what contemporary, non-theological writers call by the same name. To us, "life of action" means the sort of life led by movie heroes, business executives, war correspondents, cabinet ministers and the like. To the theologians, all these are merely worldly lives, lived more or less unregenerately by people who have done little or nothing to get rid of their Old Adams. What *they* call active life, is the life of good works. To be active is to follow the way of Martha, who spent her time ministering to the material needs of the master, while Mary (who in all mystical literature stands for the contemplative) sat and listened to his words. When Father Joseph chose the life of politics, he knew very well that it was not the life of action in the theological sense, that the way of Richelieu was not identical with the way of Martha. True, France was, *ex hypothesi* and almost by definition, the instrument of divine providence. Therefore any policy tending to the aggrandizement of France must be good in its essence. But though its essence might be good and entirely accordant with God's will, its accidents were often questionable. This was where the practice of active annihilation came in. By means of it, Father Joseph hoped to be able to sterilize the rather dirty things he did and to make them harmless, at any rate to himself.

Most people at the present time probably take for granted the validity of the pragmatists' contention, that the end of thought is action. In the philosophy which Father Joseph had studied and made his own, this position is reversed. Here contemplation is the end and action (in which is included discursive thought) is valuable only as a means to the beatific vision of God. In the words of St. Thomas Aquinas, "action should be something added to the life of prayer, not something taken away from it." To the man of the world, this statement is almost totally devoid of meaning. To the contemplative, whose concern is with spiritual religion, with the kingdom of God rather than the kingdom of selves, it seems axiomatic. Starting from this fundamental principle of theocentric religion, the practical mystics have critically examined the whole idea of action and have laid down, in regard to it, a set of rules for the guidance of those desiring to follow the mystical path toward the beatific vision. One of the best formulations of the traditional mystical doctrine in regard to action was made by Father Joseph's contemporary, Louis Lallemant. Lallemant was a Jesuit, who, in spite of the prevailing anti-mystical tendencies of his order, was permitted to teach a very advanced (but entirely orthodox) kind of spirituality to the men entrusted to his care.

Whenever we undertake any action, Father Lallemant insists, we must model ourselves upon God himself, who creates and sustains the world without in any way modifying his essential existence. But we cannot do this unless we learn to practice formal contemplation and a constant awareness of God's presence. Both are difficult, especially the latter which is possible only to those very far advanced along the way of perfection. So far as beginners are concerned, even the doing of good works may distract the soul from God. Action is not safe, except for proficients in the art of mental prayer. "If we have gone far in orison," says Lallemant, "we shall give much to action; if we are but middlingly advanced in the inward life, we shall give ourselves only moderately to outward life; if we have only a very little inwardness, we shall give nothing at all to what is external, unless our vow of obedience commands the contrary." To the reasons already given for this injunction we may add others of a strictly utilitarian nature. It is a matter of experience and observation that actions undertaken by ordinary unregenerate people, sunk in their selfhood and without spiritual insight, seldom do much good. A generation before Lallemant, St. John of the Cross had put the whole matter in a single question and answer. Those who rush headlong into good works without having acquired through contemplation the power to act well—what do they accomplish? *"Poco mas que nada, y a veces nada, y aun a veces dano."* (Little more than nothing, and sometimes nothing at all, and sometimes even harm.) One reason for hell being paved with good intentions has already been mentioned, and to this, the impossibility of foreseeing the consequences of actions, we must now add another, the intrinsically unsatisfactory nature of actions performed by the ordinary run of average unregenerate men and women. This being so, Lallemant recommends the least possible external activity until such time as, by contemplation and the unremitting practice of the presence, the soul has been trained to give itself completely to God. Those who have traveled only a little way along the road to union, "should not go out of themselves for the service of their neighbors, except by way of trial and experiment. We must be like those hunting dogs that are still half held upon the leash. When we shall have come by contemplation to possess God, we shall be able to give greater freedom to our zeal." External activity causes no interruption in the orison of the proficient; on the contrary it is a means for bringing them nearer to reality. Those for whom it is not such a means should as far as possible refrain from action. Once again Father Lallemant justifies himself by the appeal to experience and a purely utilitarian consideration of consequences. In all that concerns the saving of souls and the improving of the quality of people's thoughts and feelings and behavior, "a man of orison will accomplish more in one year than another man in all his life."

What is true of good works is true, *a fortiori*, of merely worldly activity, particularly when it is activity on a large scale, involving the collaboration of great numbers of individuals in every stage of unenlightenment. Good is a product of the ethical and spiritual artistry of individuals; it cannot be mass-produced. All Catholic theologians were well aware of this truth, and the church has acted upon it since its earliest days. The monastic orders—and preeminently that to which Father Joseph himself belonged—were living demonstrations of the traditional doctrine of action. This doctrine affirmed that goodness of more than average quantity and quality could be practically realized only on a small scale, by self-dedicated and specially trained individuals. In his own work of religious reform and spiritual instruction, Father Joseph always acted on this same principle. The art of mental prayer was taught by him only to individuals or small groups; the Calvarian rule was given as a way of life to only a very few of the nuns of Fontevrault, the order as a whole being much too large to be capable of realizing that peculiar spiritual good which the reform was intended to produce. And yet, in spite of his theoretical and experimental knowledge that good cannot be mass-produced in an unregenerate society, Father Joseph went into power politics, convinced not only that by so doing he was fulfilling the will of God, but also that great and lasting material and spiritual benefits would result from the war which he did his best to prolong and exacerbate. He knew that it was useless to try to compel the good ladies of Fontevrault to be more virtuous and spiritual than they wanted to be; and yet he believed that active French intervention in the

Thirty Years' War would result in "a new golden age." This strange inconsistency was, as we have often insisted, mainly a product of the will—that will which Father Joseph thought he had succeeded in subordinating to the will of God, but which remained, in certain important respects, unregenerately that of the natural man. In part, however, it was also due to intellectual causes, specifically to his acceptance of a certain theory of providence, widely held in the church and itself inconsistent with the theories of action and the good outlined above. According to this theory, all history is providential and its interminable catalogue of crimes and insanities is an expression of the divine will. As the most spectacular crimes and insanities of history are perpetrated at the orders of governments, it follows that these and the states they rule are also embodiments of God's will. Granted the truth of this providential theory of history and the state, Father Joseph was justified in believing that the Thirty Years' War was a good thing and that a policy which disseminated cannibalism, and universalized the practice of torture and murder, might be wholly accordant with God's will, provided only that it was advantageous to France. This condition was essential; for as a politician, one was justified by the providential theory of history in believing that God performs his *gesta per Francos*, even though, as a practical reformer and spiritual director one knew very well that the deeds of God get done, not by the Franks at large, but by one Frank here and another there, even by occasional Britons, such as Benet Fitch, and occasional Spaniards, such as St. Teresa.

Mystical philosophy can be summed up in a single phrase: "The more of the creature, the less of God." The large-scale activities of unregenerate men and women are almost wholly creaturely; therefore they almost wholly exclude God. If history is an expression of the divine will, it is so mainly in a negative sense. The crimes and insanities of large-scale human societies are related to God's will only in so far as they are acts of disobedience to that will, and it is only in this sense that they and the miseries resulting from them can properly be regarded as providential. Father Joseph justified the campaigns he planned by an appeal to the God of Battles. But there is no God of Battles; there is only an ultimate reality, expressing itself in a certain nature of things, whose harmony is violated by such events as battles, with consequences more or less disastrous for all directly or indirectly concerned in the violation.

This brings us to the heart of that great paradox of politics —the fact that political action is necessary and at the same time incapable of satisfying the needs which called it into existence.

Only static and isolated societies, whose way of life is determined by an unquestioned tradition, can dispense with politics. In unstable, unisolated, technologically progressive societies, such as ours, large-scale political action is unavoidable. But even when it is well-intentioned (which it very often is not) political action is always foredoomed to a partial, sometimes even a complete, self-stultification. The intrinsic nature of the human instruments with which, and the human materials upon which, political action must be carried out, is a positive guarantee against the possibility that such action shall yield the results that were expected from it. This generalization could be illustrated by an indefinite number of instances drawn from history. Consider, for example, the results actually achieved by two reforms upon which well-intentioned people have placed the most enormous hopes— universal education and public ownership of the means of production. Universal education has proved to be the state's most effective instrument of universal regimentation and militarization, and has exposed millions, hitherto immune, to the influence of organized lying and the allurements of incessant, imbecile and debasing distractions. Public ownership of the means of production has been put into effect on a large scale only in Russia, where the results of the reform have been, not the elimination of oppression, but the replacement of one kind of oppression by another—of money power by political and bureaucratic power, of the tyranny of rich men by a tyranny of the police and the party.

For several thousands of years now men have been experimenting with different methods for improving the quality of human instruments and human material. It has been found that a good deal can be done by such strictly humanistic methods as the improvement of the social and economic environment, and the various techniques of character training. Among men and women of a certain type, startling results can be obtained by means of conversion and catharsis. But though these methods are somewhat more effective than those of the purely humanistic variety, they work only erratically and they do not produce the radical and permanent transformation of personality, which must take place, and take place on a very large scale, if political action is ever to produce the beneficial results expected from it. For the radical and permanent transformation of personality only one effective method has been discovered—that of the mystics. It is a difficult method, demanding from those who undertake it a great deal more patience, resolution, self-abnegation and awareness than most people are prepared to give, except perhaps in times of crisis, when they are ready for a short while to make the most enormous sacrifices. But unfortunately the amelioration of the world cannot be achieved by sacrifices in moments of crisis; it depends on the efforts made and constantly repeated during the humdrum, uninspiring periods, which separate one crisis from another, and of which normal lives mainly consist. Because of the general reluctance to make such efforts during uncritical times, very few people are prepared, at any given moment of history, to undertake the method of the mystics. This being so, we shall be foolish if we expect any political action, however well-intentioned and however nicely planned, to produce more than a fraction of the general betterment anticipated.

The history of any nation follows an undulatory course. In the trough of the wave we find more or less complete anarchy; but the crest is not more or less complete Utopia, but only, at best, a tolerably humane, partially free and fairly just society that invariably carries within itself the seeds of its own decadence. Large-scale organizations are capable, it would seem, of going down a good deal further than they can go up. We may reasonably expect to reach the upper limit once again; but unless a great many more people than in the past are ready to undertake the only method capable of transforming personality, we may not expect to rise appreciably above it.

What can the politicians do for their fellows by actions within the political field, and without the assistance of the contemplatives? The answer would seem to be: not very much. Political reforms cannot be expected to produce much general betterment, unless large numbers of individuals undertake the transformation of their personality by the only known method which really works—that of the contemplatives. Moreover, should the amount of mystical, theocentric leaven in the lump of humanity suffer a significant decrease, politicians may find it impossible to raise the societies they rule even to the very moderate heights realized in the past.

Meanwhile, politicians can do something to create a social environment favorable to contemplatives. Or perhaps it is better to put the matter negatively and say that they can refrain from doing certain things and making certain arrangements which are specially unfavorable.

The political activity that seems to be least compatible with theocentric religion is that which aims at increasing a certain special type of social efficiency—the efficiency required for waging or threatening large-scale war. To achieve this kind of efficiency, politicians always aim at some kind of totalitarian-

ism. Acting like the man of science who can only deal with
the complex problems of real life by arbitrarily simplifying
them for experimental purposes, the politician in search of
military efficiency arbitrarily simplifies the society with which
he has to deal. But whereas the scientist simplifies by a
process of analysis and isolation, the politician can only simplify by compulsion, by a Procrustean process of chopping and
stretching designed to make the living organism conform to
a certain easily understood and readily manipulated mechanical pattern. Planning a new kind of national, military efficiency, Richelieu set himself to simplify the complexity of
French society. That complexity was largely chaotic, and a
policy of simplification, judiciously carried out by desirable
means would have been fully justified. But Richelieu's policy
was not judicious and, when continued after his death, resulted in the totalitarianism of Louis XIV—a totalitarianism
which was intended to be as complete as anything we see in
the modern world, and which only failed to be so by reason
of the wretched systems of communication and organization
available to the Grand Monarque's secret police. The tyrannical spirit was very willing, but, fortunately for the French,
the technological flesh was weak. In an era of telephones,
finger printing, tanks and machine guns, the task of a totalitarian government is easier than it was.

Totalitarian politicians demand obedience and conformity in
every sphere of life, including, of course, the religious. Here,
their aim is to use religion as an instrument of social consoli-
dation, an increaser of the country's military efficiency. For
this reason, the only kind of religion they favor is strictly
anthropocentric, exclusive and nationalistic. Theocentric religion, involving the worship of God for his own sake, is
inadmissible in a totalitarian state. All the contemporary
dictators, Russian, Turkish, Italian and German, have either
discouraged or actively persecuted any religious organization
whose members advocate the worship of God, rather than the
worship of the deified state or the local political boss. Louis
XIV was what is called "a good Catholic"; but his attitude
toward religion was characteristically totalitarian. He wanted
religious unity, therefore he revoked the Edict of Nantes and
persecuted the Huguenots. He wanted an exclusive, nationalistic religion; therefore he quarreled with the Pope and insisted on his own spiritual supremacy in France. He wanted
state-worship and king-worship; therefore he sternly discouraged those who taught theocentric religion, who advocated
the worship of God alone and for his own sake. The decline of
mysticism at the end of the seventeenth century was due in part
to the fatal over-orthodoxy of Bérulle and his school, but partly

also to a deliberate persecution of mystics at the hands of ecclesiastics, who could say, with Bossuet, that they worshiped God under the forms of the King, Jesus Christ and the Church. The attack on quietism was only partly the thing it professed to be—a punitive expedition against certain rather silly heretical views and certain rather undesirable practices. It was also and more significantly a veiled assault upon mysticism itself. The controversial writings of Nicole, who worked in close collaboration with Bossuet, make it quite clear that the real enemy was spiritual religion as such. Unfortunately for Nicole, the church had given its approval to the doctrines and practices of earlier mystics, and it was therefore necessary to proceed with caution; but this caution was not incompatible with a good deal of anti-mystical violence. Consciously, or unconsciously, Nicole and the other enemies of contemplation and theocentric religion were playing the game of totalitarianism.

The efficiency of a pre-industrial totalitarian state, such as that which Richelieu planned and Louis XIV actually realized, can never be so high as that of an industrial state, possessed of modern weapons, communications and organizing methods. Conversely, it does not need to be so high. A national industrial system is something so complicated that, if it is to function properly and compete with other national systems, it must be controlled in all its details by a centralized state authority. Even if the intentions of the various centralized state authorities were pacific, which they are not, industrialism would tend of its very nature to transform them into totalitarian governments. When the need for military efficiency is added to the need for industrial efficiency, totalitarianism becomes inevitable. Technological progress, nationalism and war seem to guarantee that the immediate future of the world shall belong to various forms of totalitarianism. But a world made safe for totalitarianism is a world, in all probability, made very unsafe for mysticism and theocentric religion. And a world made unsafe for mysticism and theocentric religion is a world where the only proved method of transforming personality will be less and less practiced, and where fewer and fewer people will possess any direct, experimental knowledge of reality to set up against the false doctrine of totalitarian anthropocentrism and the pernicious ideas and practices of nationalistic pseudo-mysticism. In such a world there seems little prospect that any political reform, however well intentioned, will produce the results expected of it.

The quality of moral behavior varies in inverse ratio to the number of human beings involved. Individuals and small groups do not always and automatically behave well. But at least they *can* be moral and rational to a degree unattainable by large groups. For, as numbers increase, personal relations between members of the group, and between its members and those of other groups, become more difficult and finally, for the vast majority of the individuals concerned, impossible. Imagination has to take the place of direct acquaintance, behavior motivated by a reasoned and impersonal benevolence, the place of behavior motivated by personal affection and a spontaneous and unreflecting compassion. But in most men and women reason, sympathetic imagination and the impersonal view of things are very slightly developed. That is why, among other reasons, the ethical standards prevailing within large groups, between large groups, and between the rulers and the ruled in a large group, are generally lower than those prevailing within and among small groups. The art of what may be called "goodness politics," as opposed to power politics, is the art of organizing on a large scale without sacrificing the ethical values which emerge only among individuals and small groups. More specifically, it is the art of combining decentralization of government and industry, local and functional autonomy and smallness of administrative units with enough over-all efficiency to guarantee the smooth running of the federated whole. Goodness politics have never been attempted in any large society, and it may be doubted whether such an attempt, if made, could achieve more than a partial success, so long as the majority of individuals concerned remain unable or unwilling to transform their personalities by the only method known to be effective. But though the attempt to substitute goodness politics for power politics may never be completely successful, it still remains true that the methods of goodness politics combined with individual training in theocentric theory and contemplative practice alone provide the means whereby human societies can become a little less unsatisfactory than they have been up to the present. So long as they are not adopted, we must expect to see an indefinite continuance of the dismally familiar alternations between extreme evil and a very imperfect, self-stultifying good, alternations which constitute the history of all civilized societies. In a world inhabited by what the theologians call unregenerate, or natural men, church and state can probably never become appreciably better than the best of the states and churches, of which the past has left us the record. Society can never be greatly improved, until such time as most of its members choose to become theocentric saints. Meanwhile, the few theocentric saints which exist at any given moment are able in some slight measure to qualify and mitigate the poisons which society generates within itself by its political and economic activities. In the gospel phrase, theocentric saints are the salt which preserves the social world from breaking down into irremediable decay.

This antiseptic and antidotal function of the theocentric is performed in a variety of ways. First of all, the mere fact that he exists is profoundly salutary and important. The potentiality of knowledge of, and union with, God is present in all men and women. In most of them, however, it is covered, as Eckhart puts it, "by thirty or forty skins or hides, like an ox's or a bear's, so thick and hard." But beneath all this leather, and in spite of its toughness, the divine more-than-self, which is the quick and principle of our being, remains alive, and can and does respond to the shining manifestation of the same principle in the theocentric saint. The "old man dressed all in leather" meets the new man, who has succeeded in stripping off the carapace of his thirty or forty ox-hides, and walks through the world, a naked soul, no longer opaque to the radiance immanent within him. From this meeting, the old man is likely to come away profoundly impressed by the strangeness of what he has seen, and with the nostalgic sense that the world would be a better place if there were less leather in it. Again and again in the course of history, the meeting with a naked and translucent spirit, even the reading about such spirits, has sufficed to restrain the leather men who rule over their fellows from using their power to excess. It is respect for theocentric saints that prompts the curious hypocrisy which accompanies and seeks to veil the brutal facts of political action. The preambles of treaties are always drawn up in the choicest Pecksniffian style, and the more sinister the designs of a politician, the more high-flown, as a rule, becomes the nobility of his language. Cant is always rather nauseating; but before we condemn political hypocrisy, let us remember that it is the tribute paid by men of leather to men of God, and that the acting of the part of someone better than oneself may actually commit one to a course of behavior perceptibly less evil than what would be normal and natural in an avowed cynic.

The theocentric saint is impressive, not only for what he is, but also for what he does and says. His actions and all his dealings with the world are marked by disinterestedness and serenity, invariable truthfulness and a total absence of fear. These qualities are the fruits of the doctrine he preaches, and their manifestation in his life enormously reinforces that doctrine and gives him a certain strange kind of uncoercive but none the less compelling authority over his fellow men. The essence of this authority is that it is purely spiritual and moral, and is associated with none of the ordinary social sanctions of power, position or wealth. It was here, of course, that Father Joseph made his gravest and most fatal mistake. Even if his mysticism had proved to be compatible with his power politics, which it did not, he would still have been wrong to accept the position of Richelieu's collaborator; for by accepting it he automatically deprived himself of the power to exercise a truly spiritual authority, he cut himself off from the very possibility of being the apostle of mysticism.

True, he could still be of use to his Calvarian nuns, as a teacher of contemplation; but this was because he entered their convent, not as the foreign minister of France, but as a simple director. Outside the convent, he was always the Grey Eminence. People could not speak to him without remembering that he was a man from whom there was much to hope or fear; between themselves and this friar turned politician, there could no longer be the direct contact of soul with naked soul. For them, his authority was temporal, not spiritual. Moreover, they remembered that this was the man who had organized the secret service, who gave instructions to spies, who had outwitted the Emperor at Ratisbon, who had worked his hardest to prolong the war; and remembering these things, they could be excused for having their doubts about Father Joseph's brand of religion. The tree is known by its fruits, and if *these* were the fruits of mental prayer and the unitive life—why, then they saw no reason why they shouldn't stick to wine and women, tempered by church on Sundays, confession once a quarter and communion at Christmas and Easter.

It is a fatal thing, say the Indians, for the members of one caste to usurp the functions that properly belong to another. Thus when the merchants trespass upon the ground of the *kshatriyas* and undertake the business of ruling, society is afflicted by all the evils of capitalism; and when the *kshatriyas* do what only the theocentric *brahmin* has a right to do, when they presume to lay down the law on spiritual matters, there is totalitarianism, with its idolatrous religions, its deifications of the nation, the party, the local political boss. Effects no less disastrous occur when the *brahmins* go into politics or business; for then they lose their spiritual insight and authority, and the society which it was their business to enlighten remains wholly dark, deprived of all communication with divine reality, and consequently an easy victim to preachers of false doctrines. Father Joseph is an eminent example of this last confusion of the castes. Abandoning seership for rulership, he gradually, despite his most strenuous efforts to retain it, lost the mystical vision which had given him his spiritual authority—but not, unfortunately, before he had covered with that authority many acts and policies of the most questionable nature. (Richelieu was a good psychologist, and it will be remembered that "whenever he wanted to perform some piece of knavery, he always made use of men of piety.") In a very little while, the last vestiges of Father Joseph's spiritual authority disappeared, and he came, as we have seen, to be regarded with general horror, as a man capable of every crime and treachery.

The politically minded Jesuits, who practiced the same disastrous confusion of castes, came to have a reputation as bad as Father Joseph's. The public was wrong in thinking of these generally virtuous and well-intentioned men as fairy-tale monsters; but in condemning the fundamental principle of their work in the world, it was profoundly right. The business of a seer is to see, and if he involves himself in the kind of God-eclipsing activities which make seeing impossible, he betrays the trust which his fellows have tacitly placed in him. Mystics and theocentrics are not always loved or invariably listened to; far from it. Prejudice and the dislike of what is unusual, may blind their contemporaries to the virtues of these men and women of the margin, may cause them to be persecuted as enemies of society. But should they leave their margin, should they take to competing for place and power within the main body of society, they are certain to be generally hated and despised as traitors to their seership.

To be a seer is not the same thing as to be a mere spectator. Once the contemplative has fitted himself to become, in Lallemant's phrase, "a man of much orison," he can undertake work in the world with no risk of being thereby distracted from his vision of reality, and with fair hope of achieving an appreciable amount of good. As a matter of historical fact, many of the great theocentrics have been men and women of enormous and beneficent activity.

The work of the theocentrics is always marginal, is always started on the smallest scale and, when it expands, the resulting organization is always subdivided into units sufficiently small to be capable of a shared spiritual experience and of moral and rational conduct.

The first aim of the theocentrics is to make it possible for any one who desires it to share their own experience of ultimate reality. The groups they create are organized primarily for the worship of God for God's sake. They exist in order to disseminate various methods (not all of equal value) for transforming the "natural man," and for learning to know the more-than-personal reality immanent within the leathery casing of selfhood. At this point, many theocentrics are content to stop. They have their experience of reality and they proceed to impart the secret to a few immediate disciples, or commit it to writing in a book that will be read by a wider circle removed from them by great stretches of space and time. Or else, more systematically, they establish small organized groups, a self-perpetuating order of contemplatives living under a rule. In so far as they may be expected to maintain or possibly increase the number of seers and theocentrics in a given community, these proceedings have a considerable social importance. Many theocentrics, however, are not content with this, but go on to employ their organizations to make a direct attack upon the thorniest social problems. Such attacks are always launched from the margin, not the center, always (at any rate in their earlier phases) with the sanction of a purely spiritual authority, not with the coercive power of the state. Sometimes the attack is directed against economic evils, as when the Benedictines addressed themselves to the revival of agriculture and the draining of swamps. Sometimes, the evils are those of ignorance and the attack is through various kinds of education. Here again the Benedictines were pioneers. (It is worth remarking that the Benedictine order owed its existence to the apparent folly of a young man who, instead of doing the proper, sensible thing, which was to go through the Roman schools and become an administrator under the Gothic emperors, went away and, for three years, lived alone in a hole in the mountains. When he had become "a man of much orison," he emerged, founded monasteries and composed a rule to fit the needs to a self-perpetuating order of hard-working contemplatives. In the succeeding centuries, the order civilized northwestern Europe, introduced or re-established the best agricultural practice of the time, provided the only educational facilities then available, and preserved and disseminated the treasures of ancient literature. For generations Benedictinism was the principal antidote to barbarism. Europe owes an incalculable debt to the young man who, because he was more interested in knowing God than in getting on, or even "doing good," in the world, left Rome for that burrow in the hillside above Subiaco.)

Work in the educational field has been undertaken by many theocentric organizations other than the Benedictine order—all too often, unhappily, under the restrictive influence of the political, state-supported and state-supporting church. More recently the state has everywhere assumed the role of universal educator—a position that exposes governments to peculiar temptations, to which sooner or later they all succumb, as we see at the present time, when the school system is used in almost every country as an instrument of regimentation, militarization and nationalistic propaganda. In any state that pursued goodness politics rather than power politics, education would remain a public charge, paid for out of the taxes, but would be returned, subject to the fulfillment of certain conditions, to private hands. Under such an arrangement, most schools would probably be little or no better than they are at present; but at least their badness would be variegated, while educators of exceptional originality or possessed of the gift of seership would be given opportunities for teaching at present denied them.

Philanthropy is a field in which many men and women of the margin have labored to the great advantage of their fellows. We may mention the truly astounding work accomplished by Father Joseph's contemporary, St. Vincent de Paul, a great theocentric, and a great benefactor to the people of seventeenth-century France. Small and insignificant in its beginnings, and carried on, as it expanded, under spiritual authority alone and upon the margin of society, Vincent's work among the poor did something to mitigate the sufferings imposed by the war and by the ruinous fiscal policy which the war made necessary. Having at their disposal all the powers and resources of the state, Richelieu and Father Joseph were able, of course, to do much more harm than St. Vincent and his little band of theocentrics could do good. The antidote was sufficient to offset only a part of the poison.

It was the same with another great seventeenth-century figure, George Fox. Born at the very moment when Richelieu was made president of the council and Father Joseph finally committed himself to the political life, Fox began his ministry the year before the Peace of Westphalia was signed. In the course of the next twenty years the Society of Friends gradually crystallized into its definitive form. Fanatically marginal —for when invited, he refused even to dine at Cromwell's table, for fear of being compromised—Fox was never corrupted by success, but remained to the end the apostle of the inner light. The society he founded has had its ups and downs, its long seasons of spiritual torpor and stagnation, as well as its times of spiritual life; but always the Quakers have clung to Fox's intransigent theocentrism and, along with it, to his conviction that, if it is to remain at all pure and unmixed, good must be worked for upon the margin of society, by individuals and by organizations small enough to be capable of moral, rational and spiritual life. That is why, in the two hundred and seventy-five years of its existence, the Society of Friends has been able to accomplish a sum of useful and beneficent work entirely out of proportion to its numbers. Here again the antidote has always been insufficient to offset more than a part of the poison injected into the body politic by the statesmen, financiers, industrialists, ecclesiastics and all the undistinguished millions who fill the lower ranks of the social hierarchy. But though not enough to counteract more than some of the effects of the poison, the leaven of theocentrism is the one thing which, hitherto, has saved the civilized world from total self-destruction. Father Joseph's hope of leading a whole national community along a political short cut into the kingdom of heaven on earth is illusory, so long as the human instruments and material of political action remain untransformed. His place was with the antidote-makers, not with those who brew the poisons.

(From *Grey Eminence*)

The Scientist's Role

It is fashionable nowadays to say that Malthus was wrong, because he did not foresee that improved methods of transportation can now guarantee that food surpluses produced in one area shall be quickly and cheaply transferred to another, where there is a shortage. But first of all, modern transportation methods break down whenever the power politicians resort to modern war, and even when the fighting stops they are apt to remain disrupted long enough to guarantee the starvation of millions of persons. And, secondly, no country in which population has outstripped the local food supply can, under present conditions, establish a claim on the surpluses of other countries without paying for them in cash or exports. Great Britain and the other countries in western Europe, which cannot feed their dense populations, have been able, in times of peace, to pay for the food they imported by means of the export of manufactured goods. But industrially back-ward India and China—countries in which Malthus' night-mare has come true with a vengeance and on the largest scale—produce few manufactured goods, consequently lack the means to buy from underpopulated areas the food they need. But when and if they develop mass-producing industries to the point at which they are able to export enough to pay for the food their rapidly expanding populations require, what will be the effect upon world trade and international politics? Japan had to export manufactured goods in order to pay for the food that could not be produced on the over-crowded home islands. Goods produced by workers with a low standard of living came into competition with goods produced by the better paid workers of the West, and under-

sold them. The West's retort was political and consisted of
the imposition of high tariffs, quotas and embargoes. To
these restrictions on her trade Japan's answer was the plan
for creating a vast Asiatic empire at the expense of China
and of the Western imperialist powers. The result was war.
What will happen when India and China are as highly industrialized as prewar Japan and seek to exchange their low-
priced manufactured goods for food, in competition with
Western powers, whose standard of living is a great deal
higher than theirs? Nobody can foretell the future; but undoubtedly the rapid industrialization of Asia (with equipment,
let it be remembered, of the very latest and best postwar
design) is pregnant with the most dangerous possibilities.

It is at this point that internationally organized scientists
and technicians might contribute greatly to the cause of peace
by planning a world-wide campaign, not merely for greater
food production, but also (and this is the really important
point) for regional self-sufficiency in food production. Greater
food production can be obtained relatively easily by the
opening up of the earth's vast subarctic regions at present
almost completely sterile. Spectacular progress has recently
been made in this direction by the agricultural scientists of
the Soviet Union; and presumably what can be done in Siberia
can also be done in northern Canada. Powerful ice-breakers
are already being used to solve the problems of transportation
by sea and river; and perhaps commercial submarines, specially equipped for traveling under the ice may in the future
insure a regular service between arctic ports and the rest of
the world. Any increase of the world's too scanty food supply
is to be welcomed. But our rejoicings must be tempered by
two considerations. First, the surpluses of food produced by
the still hypothetical arctic granaries of Siberia and Canada
will have to be transferred by ship, plane and rail to the
overpopulated areas of the world. This means that no supplies
would be available in wartime. Second, possession of food-
producing arctic areas constitutes a natural monopoly, and
this natural monopoly will not, as in the past, be in the hands
of politically weak nations, such as Argentina and Australia,
but will be controlled by the two great power systems of the
postwar period—the Russian power system and the Anglo-
American power system. That their monopolies of food surpluses will be used as weapons in the game of power politics
seems more than probable. "Lead us not into temptation."
The opening up of the Arctic will be undoubtedly a great
good. But it will also be a great temptation for the power
politicians—a temptation to exploit a natural monopoly in
order to gain influence and finally control over hitherto inde-

pendent countries, in which population has outstripped the
food supply.

It would seem, then, that any scientific and technological
campaign aimed at the fostering of international peace and
political and personal liberty must, if it is to succeed, increase
the total planetary food supply by increasing the various
regional supplies to the point of self-sufficiency. Recent history
makes it abundantly clear that nations, as at present constituted, are quite unfit to have extensive commercial dealings
with one another. International trade has always, hitherto,
gone hand in hand with war, imperialism and the ruthless
exploitation of industrially backward peoples by the highly
industrialized powers. Hence the desirability of reducing
international trade to a minimum, until such time as nationalist passions lose their intensity and it becomes possible to
establish some form of world government. As a first step in
this direction, scientific and technical means must be found
for making it possible for even the most densely populated
countries to feed their inhabitants. The improvement of existing food plants and domestic animals; the acclimatization in
hitherto inhospitable regions of plants that have proved useful
elsewhere; the reduction of the present enormous wastes of
food by the improvement of insect controls and the multiplica-
tion of refrigerating units; the more systematic exploitation
of seas and lakes as sources of food; the development of
entirely new foods, such as edible yeasts; the synthesizing
of sugars as a food for such edible yeasts; the synthesizing of
chlorophyll so as to make direct use of solar energy in food
production—these are a few of the lines along which important advances might be made in a relatively short time.

Hardly less important than regional self-sufficiency in food
is self-sufficiency in power for industry, agriculture and transportation. One of the contributing causes of recent wars has
been international competition for the world's strictly localized sources of petroleum, and the current jockeying for
position in the Middle East, where all the surviving great
powers have staked out claims to Persian, Mesopotamian and
Arabian oil, bodes ill for the future. Organized science could
diminish these temptations to armed conflict by finding means
for providing all countries, whatever their natural resources,
with a sufficiency of power. Water power has already been
pretty well exploited. Besides, over large areas of the earth's
surface there are no mountains and therefore no sources of
hydroelectric power. But across the plains where water stands
almost still, the air often moves in strong and regular currents.
Small windmills have been turning for centuries; but the use
of large-scale wind turbines is still, strangely enough, only in

the experimental stage. Until recently the direct use of solar power has been impracticable, owing to the technical difficulty of constructing suitable reflectors. A few months ago, however, it was announced that Russian engineers had developed a cheap and simple method for constructing paraboloid mirrors of large size, capable of producing superheated steam and even of melting iron. This discovery could be made to contribute very greatly to the decentralization of production and population and the creation of a new type of agrarian society making use of cheap and inexhaustible power for the benefit of individual small holders or self-governing, co-operative groups. For the peoples of such tropical countries as India and Africa the new device for directly harnessing solar power should be of enormous and enduring benefit—unless, of course, those at present possessing economic and political power should choose to build mass-producing factories around enormous mirrors, thus perverting the invention to their own centralistic purposes, instead of encouraging its small-scale use for the benefit of individuals and village communities. The technicians of solar power will be confronted with a clearcut choice. They can work either for the completer enslavement of the industrially backward peoples of the tropics, or for their progressive liberation from the twin curses of poverty and servitude to political and economic bosses.

The storage of the potentialities of power is almost as important as the production of power. One of the most urgent tasks before applied science is the development of some portable source of power to replace petroleum—a most undesirable fuel from the political point of view, since deposits of it are rare and unevenly distributed over the earth's surface, thus constituting natural monopolies which, when in the hands of strong nations, are used to increase their strength at the expense of their neighbors and, when possessed by weak ones, are coveted by the strong and constitute almost irresistible temptations to imperialism and war. From the political and human point of view, the most desirable substitute for petroleum would be an efficient battery for storing the electric power produced by water, wind or the sun. Further research into atomic structure may perhaps suggest new methods for the construction of such a battery.

Meanwhile it is possible that means may be devised, within the next few years, for applying atomic energy to the purposes of peace, as it is now being applied to those of war. Would not this technological development solve the whole problem of power for industry and transportation? The answer to this question may turn out to be simultaneously affirmative and negative. The problems of power may indeed be solved—but solved in the wrong way, by which I mean in a way favorable to centralization and the ruling minority, not for the benefit of individuals and co-operative, self-governing groups. If the raw material of atomic energy must be sought in radioactive deposits, occurring sporadically, here and there, over the earth's surface, then we have natural monopoly with all its undesirable political consequences, all its temptations to power politics, war, imperialistic aggression and exploitation. But of course it is always possible that other methods of releasing atomic energy may be discovered—methods that will not involve the use of uranium. In this case there will be no natural monopoly. But the process of releasing atomic energy will always be a very difficult and complicated affair, to be accomplished only on the largest scale and in the most elaborately equipped factories. Furthermore, whatever political agreements may be made, the fact that atomic energy possesses unique destructive potentialities will always constitute a temptation to the boy gangster who lurks within every patriotic nationalist. And even if a world government should be set up within a fairly short space of time, this will not necessarily guarantee peace. The Pax Romana was a very uneasy affair, troubled at almost every imperial death by civil strife over the question of succession. So long as the lust for power persists as a human trait—and in persons of a certain kind of physique and temperament this lust is over-masteringly strong—no political arrangement, however well contrived, can guarantee peace. For such men the instruments of violence are as fearfully tempting as are, to others, the bodies of women. Of all instruments of violence, those powered by atomic energy are the most decisively destructive; and for power lovers, even under a system of world government, the temptation to resort to these all too simple and effective means for gratifying their lust will be great indeed. In view of all this, we must conclude that atomic energy is, and for a long time is likely to remain, a source of industrial power that is, politically and humanly speaking, in the highest degree undesirable.

It is not necessary in this place, nor am I competent, to enter any further into the hypothetical policy of internationally organized science. If that policy is to make a real contribution toward the maintenance of peace and the spread of political and personal liberty, it must be patterned throughout along the decentralist lines laid down in the preceding discussion of the two basic problems of food and power. Will scientists and technicians collaborate to formulate and pursue some such policy as that which has been adumbrated here? Or will they permit themselves, as they have done only too often in the past, to become the conscious or unconscious instruments of militarists, imperialists and a ruling oligarchy of capitalistic or governmental bosses? Time alone will show. Meanwhile, it is to be hoped that all concerned will carefully consider a suggestion made by Dr. Gene Weltfish in the September, 1945, issue of the *Scientific Monthly*. Before embarking upon practice, all physicians swear a professional oath— the oath of Hippocrates—that they will not take improper advantage of their position, but always remember their responsibilities toward suffering humanity. Technicians and scientists, proposes Dr. Weltfish, should take a similar oath in some such words as the following: "I pledge myself that I will use my knowledge for the good of humanity and against the destructive forces of the world and the ruthless intent of men; and that I will work together with my fellow scientists of whatever nation, creed or color for these our common ends."

(From *Science, Liberty and Peace*)

Tomorrow and Tomorrow and Tomorrow

Between 1800 and 1900 the doctrine of Pie in the Sky gave place, in a majority of Western minds, to the doctrine of Pie on the Earth. The motivating and compensatory Future came to be regarded, not as a state of disembodied happiness, to be enjoyed by me and my friends after death, but as a condition of terrestrial well-being for my children or (if that seemed a bit too optimistic) my grandchildren, or maybe my great-grandchildren. The believers in Pie in the Sky consoled themselves for all their present miseries by the thought of posthumous bliss, and whenever they felt inclined to make other people more miserable than themselves (which was most of the time), they justified their crusades and persecutions by proclaiming, in St. Augustine's delicious phrase, that they were practicing a "benignant asperity," which would ensure the eternal welfare of souls through the destruction or torture of mere bodies in the inferior dimensions of space and time. In our days, the revolutionary believers in Pie on the Earth console themselves for *their* miseries by thinking of the wonderful time people will be having a hundred years from now, and then go on to justify wholesale liquidations and enslavements by pointing to the nobler, humaner world which these atrocities will somehow or other call into existence.

Not all the believers in Pie on the Earth are revolutionaries, just as not all believers in Pie in the Sky were persecutors. Those who think mainly of other people's future life tend to become proselytisers, crusaders and heresy hunters. Those who think mainly of their own future life become resigned. The preaching of Wesley and his followers had the effect of reconciling the first generations of industrial workers to their intolerable lot and helped to preserve England from the horrors of a full-blown political revolution.

Today the thought of their great-grandchildren's happiness in the twenty-first century consoles the disillusioned beneficiaries of progress and immunizes them against Communist propaganda. The writers of advertising copy are doing for this generation what the Methodists did for the victims of the first Industrial Revolution.

The literature of the Future and of that equivalent of the Future, the Remote, is enormous. By now the bibliography of Utopia must run into thousands of items. Moralists and political reformers, satirists and science fictioneers—all have contributed their quota to the stock of imaginary worlds. Less picturesque, but more enlightening, than these products of phantasy and idealistic zeal are the forecasts made by sober and well-informed men of science. Three very important prophetic works of this kind have appeared within the last two or three years—*The Challenge of Man's Future* by Harrison Brown, *The Foreseeable Future* by Sir George Thomson, and *The Next Million Years* by Sir Charles Darwin. Sir George and Sir Charles are physicists and Mr. Brown is a distinguished chemist. Still more important, each of the three is something more and better than a specialist.

Let us begin with the longest look into the future—*The Next Million Years*. Paradoxically enough, it is easier, in some ways, to guess what is going to happen in the course of ten thousand centuries than to guess what is going to happen in the course of one century. Why is it that no fortune tellers are millionaires and that no insurance companies go bankrupt? Their business is the same—foreseeing the future. But whereas the members of one group succeed all the time, the members of the other group succeed, if at all, only occasionally. The reason is simple. Insurance companies deal with statistical averages. Fortune tellers are concerned with particular cases. One can predict with a high degree of precision what is going to happen in regard to very large numbers of things or people. To predict what is going to happen to any particular thing or person is for most of us quite impossible and even for the specially gifted minority, exceedingly difficult. The history of the next century involves very large numbers; consequently it is possible to make certain predictions about it with a fairly high degree of certainty. But though we can pretty confidently say that there will be revolutions, battles, massacres, hurricanes, droughts, floods, bumper crops and bad harvests, we cannot specify the dates of these events nor the exact locations, nor their immediate, short-range consequences. But when we take the longer view and consider the much greater numbers involved in the history of the next ten thousand centuries, we find that these ups and downs of human and natural happenings tend to cancel out, so that it becomes possible to plot a curve representing the average of future history, the mean between ages of creativity and ages of decadence, between propitious and unpropitious circumstances, between fluctuating triumph and disaster. This is the actuarial approach to prophecy—sound on the large scale and reliable on the average. It is the kind of approach which permits the prophet to say that there will be dark handsome men in the lives of x per cent of women, but not which particular woman will succumb.

A domesticated animal is an animal which has a master who is in a position to teach it tricks, to sterilize it or compel it to breed as he sees fit. Human beings have no masters. Even in his most highly civilized state, Man is a wild species, breeding at random and always propagating his kind to the limit of available food supplies. The amount of available food may be increased by the opening up of new land, by the sudden disappearance, owing to famine, disease or war, of a considerable fraction of the population, or by improvements in agriculture. At any given period of history there is a practical limit to the food supply currently available. Moreover, natural processes and the size of the planet being what they are, there is an absolute limit, which can never be passed. Being a wild species, Man will always tend to breed up to the limits of the moment. Consequently very many members of the species must always live on the verge of starvation. This has happened in the past, is happening at the present time, when about sixteen hundred millions of men, women and children are more or less seriously undernourished, and will go on happening for the next million years—by which time we may expect that the species Homo sapiens will have turned into some other species, unpredictably unlike ourselves but still, of course, subject to the laws governing the lives of wild animals.

We may not appreciate the fact; but a fact nevertheless it remains: we are living in a Golden Age, the most gilded Golden Age of human history—not only of past history, but of future history. For, as Sir Charles Darwin and many others before him have pointed out, we are living like drunken sailors, like the irresponsible heirs of a millionaire uncle. At an ever accelerating rate we are now squandering the capital of metallic ores and fossil fuels accumulated in the earth's crust during hundreds of millions of years. How long can this spending spree go on? Estimates vary. But all are agreed that within a few centuries or at most a few millennia, Man will have run through his capital and will be compelled to live, for the remaining nine thousand nine hundred and seventy or eighty centuries of his career as Homo sapiens, strictly on income. Sir Charles is of the opinion that Man will successfully make the transition from rich ores to poor ores and even sea water, from coal, oil, uranium and thorium to solar energy and alcohol derived from plants. About as much energy as is now available can be derived from the new sources—but with a far greater expense in man hours, a much larger capital investment in machinery. And the same holds true of the raw materials on which industrial civilization depends. By doing a great deal more work than they are doing now, men will contrive to extract the diluted dregs of the planet's metallic wealth or will fabricate non-metallic substitutes for the elements they have completely used up. In such an event, some human beings will still live fairly well, but not in the style to which we, the squanderers of planetary capital, are accustomed.

Mr. Harrison Brown has his doubts about the ability of the human race to make the transition to new and less concentrated sources of energy and raw materials. As he sees it, there are three possibilities. "The first and by far the most likely pattern is a return to agrarian existence." This return, says Mr. Brown, will almost certainly take place unless Man is able not only to make the technological transition to new energy sources and new raw materials, but also to abolish war and at the same time stabilize his population. Sir Charles, incidentally, is convinced that Man will never succeed in stabilizing his population. Birth control may be practiced here and there for brief periods. But any nation which limits its population will ultimately be crowded out by nations which have not limited theirs. Moreover, by reducing cut-throat competition within the society which practices it, birth control restricts the action of natural selection. But wherever natural selection is not allowed free play, biological degeneration rapidly sets in. And then there are the short-range, practical difficulties. The rulers of sovereign states have never been able to agree on a common policy in relation to economics, to disarmament, to civil liberties. Is it likely, is it even conceivable, that they will agree on a common policy in relation to the much more ticklish matter of birth control?

The answer would seem to be in the negative. And if, by a miracle, they should agree, or if a world government should someday come into existence, how could a policy of birth control be enforced? Answer: only by totalitarian methods and, even so, pretty ineffectively.

Let us return to Mr. Brown and the second of his alternative futures. "There is a possibility," he writes, "that stabilization of population can be achieved, that war can be avoided, and that the resource transition can be successfully negotiated. In that event mankind will be confronted with a pattern which looms on the horizon of events as the second most likely possibility—the completely controlled, collectivized industrial society." (Such a future society was described in my own fictional essay in Utopianism, *Brave New World*.)

"The third possibility confronting mankind is that of a world-wide free industrial society, in which human beings can live in reasonable harmony with their environment." This is a cheering prospect; but Mr. Brown quickly chills our optimism by adding that "it is unlikely that such a pattern can exist for long. It certainly will be difficult to achieve, and it clearly will be difficult to maintain once it is established."

From these rather dismal speculations about the remoter future it is a relief to turn to Sir George Thomson's prophetic view of what remains of the present Golden Age. So far as easily available power and raw materials are concerned, Western man never had it so good as he has it now and, unless he should choose in the interval to wipe himself out, as he will go on having it for the next three, or five, or perhaps even ten generations. Between the present and the year 2050, when the population of the planet will be at least five billions and perhaps as much as eight billions, atomic power will be added to the power derived from coal, oil and falling water, and Man will dispose of more mechanical slaves than ever before. He will fly at three times the speed of sound, he will travel at seventy knots in submarine liners, he will solve hitherto insoluble problems by means of electronic thinking machines. High-grade metallic ores will still be plentiful, and research in physics and chemistry will teach men how to use them more effectively and will provide at the same time a host of new synthetic materials. Meanwhile the biologists will not be idle. Various algae, bacteria and fungi will be domesticated, selectively bred and set to work to produce various kinds of food and to perform feats of chemical synthesis, which would otherwise be prohibitively expensive. More picturesquely (for Sir George is a man of imagination), new breeds of monkeys will be developed, capable of performing the more troublesome kinds of agricultural work, such as picking fruit, cotton and coffee. Electron beams will be directed onto particular areas of plant and animal chromosomes and, in this way, it may become possible to produce controlled mutations. In the field of medicine, cancer may finally be prevented, while senility ("the whole business of old age is odd and little understood") may be postponed, perhaps almost indefinitely. "Success," adds Sir George, "will come, when it does, from some quite unexpected directions; some discovery in physiology will alter present ideas as to how and why cells grow and divide in the healthy body, and with the right fundamental knowledge, enlightenment will come. It is only the rather easy superficial problems that can be solved by working on them directly; others depend on still undiscovered fundamental knowledge and are hopeless till this has been acquired."

All in all, the prospects for the industrialized minority of mankind are, in the short run, remarkably bright. Provided we refrain from the suicide of war, we can look forward to very good times indeed. That we shall be discontented with our good time goes without saying. Every gain made by individuals or societies is almost instantly taken for granted. The luminous ceiling toward which we raise our longing eyes becomes, when we have climbed to the next floor, a stretch of disregarded linoleum beneath our feet. But the right to disillusionment is as fundamental as any other in the catalogue. (Actually the right to the pursuit of happiness is nothing else than the right to disillusionment phrased in another way.)

Turning now from the industrialized minority to that vast majority inhabiting the underdeveloped countries, the immediate prospects are much less reassuring. Population in these countries is increasing by more than twenty millions a year and in Asia at least, according to the best recent estimates, the production of food per head is now ten per cent less than it used to be in 1938. In India the average diet provides about two thousand calories a day—far below the optimum figure. If the country's food production could be raised by forty per cent—and the experts believe that, given much effort and a very large capital investment, it could be increased to this extent within fifteen or twenty years—the available food would provide the present population with twenty-eight hundred calories a day, a figure still below the optimum level. But twenty years from now the population of India will have increased by something like one hundred millions, and the additional food, produced with so much effort and at such great expense, will add little more than a hundred calories to the present woefully inadequate diet. And meanwhile it is not at all probable that a forty per cent increase in food production will in fact be achieved within the next twenty years.

The task of industrializing the underdeveloped countries, and of making them capable of producing enough food for their peoples, is difficult in the extreme. The industrialization of the West was made possible by a series of historical accidents. The inventions which launched the Industrial Revolution were made at precisely the right moment. Huge areas of empty land in America and Australia were being opened up by European colonists or their descendants. A great surplus of cheap food became available, and it was upon this surplus that the peasants and farm laborers, who migrated to the towns and became factory hands, were enabled to live and multiply their kind. Today there are no empty lands—at any rate none that lend themselves to easy cultivation—and the over-all surplus of food is small in relation to present populations. If a million Asiatic peasants are taken off the land and set to work in factories, who will produce the food which their labor once provided? The obvious answer is: machines. But how can the million new factory workers make the necessary machines if, in the meanwhile, they are not fed? Until they make the machines, they cannot be fed from the land they once cultivated; and there are no surpluses of cheap food from other, emptier countries to support them in the interval.

And then there is the question of capital. "Science," you often hear it said, "will solve all our problems." Perhaps it will, perhaps it won't. But before science can start solving any practical problems, it must be applied in the form of usable technology. But to apply science on any large scale is extremely expensive. An underdeveloped country cannot be industrialized, or given an efficient agriculture, except by the investment of a very large amount of capital. And what is capital? It is what is left over when the primary needs of a society have been satisfied. In most of Asia the primary needs of most of the population are never satisfied; consequently almost nothing is left over. Indians can save about one hundredth of their per capita income. Americans can save between one tenth and one sixth of what they make. Since the income of Americans is much higher than that of Indians, the amount of available capital in the United States is about seventy times as great as the amount of available capital in India. To those who have shall be given and from those who have not shall be taken away even that which they have. If the underdeveloped countries are to be industrialized, even partially, and made self-supporting in the matter of food, it will be necessary to establish a vast international Marshall

Plan providing subsidies in grain, money, machinery, and trained manpower. But all these will be of no avail, if the population in the various underdeveloped areas is permitted to increase at anything like the present rate. Unless the population of Asia can be stabilized, all attempts at industrialization will be doomed to failure and the last state of all concerned will be far worse than the first—for there will be many more people for famine and pestilence to destroy, together with much more political discontent, bloodier revolutions and more abominable tyrannies.

(From *Tomorrow and Tomorrow and Tomorrow*)

PSYCHOLOGY

Madness, Badness, Sadness

Goering and Hitler displayed an almost maudlin concern for the welfare of animals; Stalin's favorite work of art was a celluloid musical about Old Vienna, called *The Great Waltz*. And it is not only dictators who divide their thoughts and feelings into unconnected, logic-tight compartments; the whole world lives in a state of chronic and almost systematic inconsistency. Every society is a case of multiple personality and modulates, without a qualm, without even being aware of what it is up to, from Jekyll to Hyde, from the scientist to the magician, from the hardheaded man of affairs to the village idiot. Ours, for example, is the age of unlimited violence; but it is also the age of the welfare state, of bird sanctuaries, of progressive education, of a growing concern for the old, the physically handicapped, the mentally sick. We build orphanages, and at the same time we stockpile the bombs that will be dropped on orphanages. "A foolish consistency," says Emerson, "is the hobgoblin of little minds, adored by little statesmen, philosophers and divines." In that case, we must be very great indeed.

That all, or even most, human beings will ever be consistently humane seems very unlikely. We must be content with the smaller mercies of unemployment benefits and school lunches in the midst and in spite of an armament race. We must console ourselves with the thought that our inky darks are relieved by quite a number of lights.

Between Los Angeles and Long Beach, California, there stands a mental hospital which admirably illustrates our

blessed inconsistency. Bomber plants and guided-missile laboratories surround it on every side, but have not succeeded
in obliterating this oasis of organized and instructed benevolence. With their wide lawns, their tree-lined walks, their
scattering of nondescript buildings, the hospital grounds look
like the campus of an unpretentious college. The inmates,
unfortunately, could never be mistaken for undergraduates and
co-eds. The mind is its own place, and their gait, their posture,
the distressed or remotely preoccupied expression of their
faces reveal them as the inhabitants of dark worlds, full of
confusion, fertile in private terrors. But at least nothing is
being done in this green oasis among the jets and the rockets
to deepen the confusion or intensify the terrors. On the contrary, much good will and intelligence, much knowledge and
skill are going into a concerted effort to transform their isolated, purgatorial universes into something happier and more
accessible.

Not long ago a psychiatrist friend took me with him to this
oasis. Walking through one of the Disturbed Wards, I found
myself suddenly remembering the first occasion on which I
had visited a mental hospital. The place was Kashmir, the
time more than thirty years ago, and the hospital was actually
no hospital, but that part of the local prison which was used
for the confinement of maniacs. Naked, unkempt, horribly
unwashed, these unfortunates were shut up in cages. Not the
spacious enclosures reserved, in zoos, for gibbons and orangu-
tans, but filthy little pens, in which a couple of steps in any
direction would bring their occupants to the confining bars.
Kashmir is remote, "uncivilized," non-Christian. But let us
be in no hurry to flatter ourselves. The horrors I witnessed
there, among the Himalayas, were of exactly the same kind
as the horrors which my grandfather and his contemporaries
could see in any asylum in civilized and Christian England,
France or Germany, in civilized and Christian America. Of
the many dark and hideous pages of our history, few are more
shameful than the record of Western man's treatment of the
mentally ill. The story has been told at length in Doctor
Gregory Zilboorg's *History of Medical Psychology* and there
are whole libraries of books dealing with special periods and
particular aspects of the long martyrdom of the insane.

The tormentors of the insane have been drawn, in the main,
from two professions—the medical and the clerical. To which
shall we award the palm? Have clergymen been responsible
for more gratuitous suffering than doctors? Or have doctors
made up for a certain lack of intensity in their brand of torture (after all, they never went so far as to burn anyone alive
for being mad) by its longer duration and the greater number

of the victims to whom it was applied? It is a nice point. To prevent hard feelings, let us divide the prize equally between the contenders.

So far as the mentally sick are concerned, Western history has had only two golden ages. The first lasted from about fifty years before the birth of Christ into the second century of our era; the second began, very hesitantly, in the early years of the nineteenth century and is still continuing. During these golden ages the mentally sick, or at least the more fortunate of them in the more civilized parts of the classical and modern world, were treated with a measure of common decency, as though they were unfortunate human beings. During the intervening centuries they were either ignored, or else systematically tormented, first (on the highest theological grounds) by the clergy, later (for the soundest of medical reasons) by the doctors.

Let us ask ourselves a question. If I had lived in the eighteenth century, and if I had been afflicted by some mental illness, what would have happened to me?

What happened to you in those days depended, first of all, on the financial situation of your family. People with money either locked up their insane relatives in some remote corner of the family mansion, or banished them, with a staff of attendants, to an isolated cottage in the country, or else boarded them out, at considerable expense, in a private madhouse run for profit by a doctor or, under medical supervision, by some glorified jailer. Lunatics confined in the attics (like Mr. Rochester's wife in *Jane Eyre*) or in a country cottage were spared the rigors of medical treatment, which could only be administered in an institution staffed by brawny attendants and equipped with the instruments of coercion. Those who were sent to such an institution were first stripped naked. Mad people were generally kept in a state of partial or complete nudity. Nakedness solved the problem of soiled clothes and contributed, in what was felt to be a most salutary way, to the patient's sense of degradation and inferiority. After being stripped, the patient was shaved, so as to prepare him or her for that part of the treatment which consisted in rubbing various salves into the scalp with a view to soothing or stimulating the brain. Then he or she was taken to a cell, tied down to the bed and locked in for the night. If the patient struggled and screamed, that was a sign of mania; if he reacted with silent resignation, he was obviously suffering from some form of melancholy. In either case he needed treatment and, duly, next morning the treatment was commenced. In the medical literature of the time it was referred to as "Reducing the Patient by Physic." Over a period of eight

or ten weeks the victim was repeatedly bled, at least one
pound of blood being taken on each occasion. Once a week,
or if the doctor thought it advisable at shorter intervals, he
or she was given an emetic—a "Brisk Vomit" as our ancestors,
with their admirable command of English, liked to call it.
The favorite Brisk Vomit was a concoction of the roots of
black hellebore. Hellebore had been used in the treatment
of the insane since the time of Melampus, a legendary sooth-
sayer, first mentioned by Homer. Taken internally, the toxi-
cologists tell us, hellebore "occasions ringing in the ears,
vertigo, stupor, thirst, with a feeling of suffocation, swelling
of the tongue and fauces, emesis and catharsis, slowing of the
pulse and finally collapse and death from cardiac paralysis.
Inspection after death reveals much inflammation of the
stomach and intestines, more especially the rectum." The doses
prescribed by the old psychiatrists were too small to be fatal,
but quite large enough to produce a dangerous syndrome,
known in medical circles as "helleborism." Every administration of the drug resulted in an iatrogenic (doctor-induced)
disease of the most distressing and painful kind. One Brisk
Vomit was more than enough; there were no volunteers for
a second dose. All the later administrations of hellebore had
to be forcible. After five or six bouts of helleborism, the time
was ripe for purgatives. Senna, rhubarb, sulphur, colocynth,
antimony, aloes—blended into Black Draughts or worked up
into enormous boluses, these violent cathartics were forced,
day after day, down the patient's throat. At the end of the
two-month course of bloodlettings, vomits and purges, most
psychotics were "reduced by physic" to a point where they
were in no condition to give trouble. These reductions were
repeated every spring during the patient's incarceration and
in the meantime he was kept on a low diet, deficient in
proteins, vitamins and even calories. It is a testimony to the
amazing toughness of the human species that many psychotics
survived under this treatment for decades. Indeed, they did
more than survive; in spite of chronic undernourishment and
periodical reductions by physic, some of them still found the
strength to be violent. The answer to violence was mechanical
restraint and corporal punishment. "I have seen," wrote Dorothea Dix in 1848, "more than nine thousand idiots, epileptics
and insane in the United States, destitute of appropriate care
and protection, bound with galling chains, bowed beneath
fetters and heavy iron balls attached to drag chains, lacerated
with ropes, scourged with rods and terrified beneath storms of
execration and cruel blows." The armamentarium of an English asylum of the Early Victorian period comprised "strait-
waistcoats, handcuffs, leg locks, various coarse devices of

leather and iron, including gags and horrible screws to force open the mouths of patients who were unwilling or even unable to take food." In the Lancaster Asylum good old-fashioned chains had been ingeniously combined with the very latest in plumbing. In 1840 its two Restraint Rooms were fitted up with "rows of stalled seats serving the double purpose of a water closet and an ordinary seat. The patients were secured by hand locks to the upper portion of the stalls and by leg locks to the lower portion." The Lancaster lunatics were relatively well off. The toilets to which they were chained guaranteed a certain cleanliness and the newly installed heating system, of which the asylum was justly proud, preserved them from the long-drawn torture-by-freezing, which was the lot, each winter, of the overwhelming majority of mentally sick paupers. For while the private madhouses provided a few of the rudimentary creature comforts, the public asylums and workhouses, in which the psychotic "Objects of Charity" were confined, were simply dungeons. (In official documents the phrase, "Objects of Charity" is abbreviated, and the insane poor are regularly referred to as "Objects.") "I have seen them naked," wrote Esquirol of the Objects in French asylums, "and protected only by straw from the damp, cold pavement on which they were lying." And here is William Tuke's account of what he saw in the lunatic ward of an English workhouse in 1811: "The poor women were absolutely without any clothes. The weather was intensely cold, and the evening previous to our visit the thermometer had been sixteen degrees below freezing. One of these forlorn Objects lay buried under a miserable covering of straw, without a blanket or even a horsecloth to defend her from the cold." The feet of chained lunatics often became frostbitten. From frostbite to gangrene was a short step, and from gangrene through amputation to death was only a little longer.

Lunatics were not merely confined. Attempts were even made to cure them. The procedures by which patients were reduced to physical exhaustion were also supposed to restore them to sanity. Psychoses were thought to be due to an imbalance between the four humors of the body, together with a local excess or deficiency of the vital and animal spirits. The bloodlettings, the vomits and the purges were intended to rid the viscera and the circulatory system of peccant humors, and at the same time to relieve the pressure of the animal spirits upon the brain. Physical treatment was supplemented by psychological treatment. This last was based upon the universally accepted principle that the most effective cure for insanity is terror. Boerhaave, the most influential medical teacher of the first half of the eighteenth century, instructed his pupils "to throw the Patient into the Sea, and to keep him under for as long as he can possibly bear without being stifled." In the intervals between duckings the mentally sick were to be kept in constant fear by the threat of punishment. The simplest and handiest form of punishment is beating, and beating, in consequence, was regularly resorted to. During his psychotic episodes even George III was beaten—with the permission, of course, of his Privy Council and both Houses of Parliament. But beating "was only one form, and that the slightest, of cruelty toward the insane." (I quote the words of the great French reformer, Doctor Pinel.) "The inventions to give pain were truly marvelous." Thus an eminent German doctor had devised a therapeutic punishment, which consisted in tying a rope about the patient's middle, hoisting him to a great height and then lowering him very rapidly, so that he should have the sensation of falling, into a dark cellar, "which was to be all the better if it could be stocked with serpents." A very similar torture is minutely described by the Marquis de Sade, the heroine of whose novel, *Justine,* is punished for being virtuous (among many other ways) by being dangled halfway down a shaft opening into a cavern full of rats and corpses, while her tormentor of the moment keeps threatening, from above, to cut the rope. That this fiendish notion should have occurred not only to the most famous psychotic of the period, but also to one of its leading psychiatrists, throws a revealing light on our ancestors' attitude toward the mentally sick. In relation to these predestined victims sadistic behavior was right and proper, so much so that it could be publicly avowed and rationalized in terms of current scientific theories.

So much for what would have happened to me, if I had become mentally sick in the eighteenth, or even the first half of the nineteenth, century. If I had lived in the sixteenth century, my fate might have been even worse. For in the sixteenth century most of the symptoms of mental illness were regarded as supernatural in origin. For example, the pathological refusal or inability to speak was held to be a sure sign of diabolic possession. Mutism was frequently punished by the infliction of torture and death at the stake. Dumb devils are mentioned in the Gospels; but the evangelists made no mention of another hysterical symptom, localized insensibility to pain. Unfortunately for the mentally ill, the Early Fathers noticed this curious phenomenon. For them, the insensitive spots on the body of a mentally sick person were "the Devil's stigmata," the marks with which Satan branded his human cattle. In the sixteenth century anyone suspected of witchcraft would be systematically pricked with an awl or bodkin. If an insensitive spot were found, it was clear that the victim was allied with the devil and must therefore be tortured and burned alive. Again, some mentally sick persons hear voices, see visions of sinister figures, have phantasies of omnipotence or alternatively of persecution, believe themselves to be capable of flying, of being subject to metamorphosis into animals. In the sixteenth century these common symptoms of mental derangement were treated as so many statements of objective fact, so many confessions, explicit or implicit, of collaboration with the Enemy. But, obviously, anyone who collaborated with the Devil had to 'be tortured and burned alive. And what about the neurotics, particularly the female neurotics, who suffer from sexual illusions. "All witchcraft," proclaim the learned clerical authors of the *Malleus Maleficarum,* the standard textbook for sixteenth-century inquisitors and magistrates, "all witchcraft comes from carnal lust, which in women is insatiable." From this it followed that any disturbed woman, whose sexual daydreams were more than ordinarily vivid, was having relations with an Incubus. But an Incubus is a devil. Therefore she too must be tortured and burned alive.

Doctor Johann Weier, who has been called the Father of Psychiatry, had the humanity, courage and common sense to assail the theories and hellish practices of the Catholic theologians and magistrates, and the no-less-ferocious Protestant witch-hunters of his time. But the majority even of well-educated men approved the crimes and follies of the Church. For having ventured to treat the witches' confessions as symptoms of mental illness, Weier was regarded as a diabolical fellow traveler, even a full-blown sorcerer. That he was not arrested, tortured and burned was due to the fact that he was the personal physician of a ruling prince. Weier died in his bed; but his book was placed on the Index, and the persecution of the mentally ill continued, unabated, for another century. How many witches were tortured and burned during the sixteenth century is not exactly known. The total number is variously estimated at anything from one hundred thousand to several millions. Many of the victims were perfectly sane adherents of the old fertility cult which still lingered on in every part of Europe. Of the rest, some were persons incriminated by informers, some the unhappy victims of a mental illness. "If we took the whole of the population of our present-day hospitals for mental diseases," writes Dr. Zilboorg, "and if we sorted out the cases of dementia praecox, some of the senile psychoses, some of those afflicted with general paralysis, and some of the so-called involution melancholies, we should see that Bodin (the great French jurist, who de-

nounced Dr. Weier as a sorcerer and heretic) would not have
hesitated to plead for their death at the stake, so similar and
characteristic are their trends to those he describes. It is
truly striking that the ideational contents of the mental diseases of four hundred years ago are so similar to those of
today."

In the second half of the seventeenth century the mentally
sick ceased to be the prey of the clergy and the theologically
minded lawyers, and were left instead to the tender mercies
of the doctors. The crimes and follies committed in the name
of Galen were, as we have seen, almost as monstrous as those
committed at an earlier period in the name of God. Improvement came at last in the closing years of the eighteenth
century, and was due to the efforts of a few nonconforming
individuals, some of them doctors, others outside the pale of
medicine. These nonconformists did their work in the teeth of
official indifference, sometimes of active official resistance. As
corporations, neither the Church nor the medical profession
ever initiated any reform in the treatment of the mentally sick.
Obscure priests and nuns had often cared for the insane with
kindness and understanding; but the theological bigwigs
thought of mental illness in terms of diabolic possession, heresy
and apostasy. It was the same with the medical bigwigs. Strait
jackets, Brisk Vomits and systematic terrorism remained the
official medical policy until well into the nineteenth century.
It was only tardily and reluctantly that the bigwigs accepted
the reforms initiated by heroic nonconformists, and officially
changed their old, bad tune.

Reform began almost simultaneously on either side of the
Channel. In England a Quaker merchant, William Tuke, set
up the York Retreat, a hospital for the mentally sick, in which
restraint was never used and the psychological treatment was
aimed, not at frightening the patients, but at bringing them
back from their isolation by persuading them to work, play,
eat, talk and worship together. In France the pioneer in
reform was Doctor Philippe Pinel, who was appointed to the
direction of the Bicêtre Asylum in Paris at the height of the
French Revolution. Many of the patients were kept permanently chained in unlighted cells. Pinel asked permission of
the revolutionary government to set them free. It was refused.
Liberty, Equality and Fraternity were not for lunatics. Pinel
insisted, and at last permission was grudgingly given. The
account of what followed is touching in the extreme. "The
first man on whom the experiment was tried was an English
captain, whose history no one knew, as he had been in chains
for forty years. He was thought to be one of the most furious
among them. His keepers approached him with caution, as

he had in a fit of fury killed one of them on the spot with a
blow from his manacles. He was chained more rigorously than
any of the others. Pinel entered his cell unattended and calmly
said to him, 'Captain, I will order your chains to be taken off
and give you liberty to walk in the court, if you will promise
me to behave well and injure no one.' 'Yes, I promise,' said
the maniac. 'But you are laughing at me. . . .' His chains were
removed and the keepers retired, leaving the door of his cell
open. He raised himself many times from the seat, but fell
again on it; for he had been in a sitting posture so long that
he had lost the use of his legs. In a quarter of an hour he
succeeded in maintaining his balance and with tottering steps
came to the door of his dark cell. His first look was at the
sky, and he exclaimed, 'How beautiful, how beautiful!' During
the rest of the day he was constantly in motion, uttering
exclamations of delight. In the evening he returned of his
own accord to his cell and slept tranquilly."

In Europe the pioneer work of Tuke and Pinel was continued by Conolly, Esquirol and a growing number of their
followers in every country. In America, the standard bearer of
reform was a heroic woman, Dorothea Dix. By the middle of
the century many of the worst abominations of the old regime
were things of the past. The mentally ill began to be treated
as unfortunate human beings, not as Objects. It was an immense advance; but it was not yet enough. Reform had produced institutional care, but still no adequate treatment. For
most nineteenth-century doctors, things were more real than
thoughts and the study of matter seemed more scientific than
the study of mind. The dream of Victorian medicine was, in
Zilboorg's phrase, to develop a psychiatry that should be
completely independent of psychology. Hence the widespread
and passionate rejection of the procedures lumped under the
names of Animal Magnetism and Hypnotism. In France,
Charcot, Liébault and Bernheim achieved remarkable results
with hypnosis; but the intellectually respectable psychiatrists
of Europe and America turned their backs on this merely
psychological treatment of mental illness and concentrated
instead on the more "objective," the more "scientific" methods
of surgery.

It had all happened before, of course. Cutting holes in the
skull was an immemorially ancient form of psychiatry. So was
castration, as a cure for epilepsy. Continuing this grand old
tradition, the Victorian doctors removed the ovaries of their
hysterical patients and treated neurosis in young girls by the
gruesome operation known to ethnologists as "female circum-
cision." In the early years of the present century Metchnikoff
was briefly a prophet, and autointoxication was all the rage

in medical circles. Along with practically every other disease, neuroses were supposed to be due to intestinal stasis. No intestine, no stasis—what could be more logical? The lucky neurotics who could afford a major operation went to hospital, had their colons cut out and the end of their small intestines stitched to the stump. Those who recovered found themselves with yet another reason for being neurotic: they had to hurry to the bathroom six or eight times a day. Intestinal stasis went out with the hobble skirt, and the new vogue was focal infection. According to the surgical psychiatrists, people were neurotic not because of conflicts in their unconscious mind, but because of inflammation in their tonsils or abscesses at the roots of their teeth. The dentists, the nose-and-throat men set to work with a will. Toothless and tonsilectomized, the neurotics, needless to say, went on behaving just as neurotically as ever. Focal infections followed intestinal stasis into oblivion, and the surgical psychiatrists now prefer to make a direct assault upon the brain. The current fashion is shock treatment or, on great occasions, prefrontal lobotomy. Meanwhile the pharmacologists have not been idle. The barbiturates, hailed not so long ago as panaceas, have given place to Chlorpromazine, Reserpine, Frenquel and Miltown. Insofar as they facilitate the specifically psychological treatment of mental disorders, these tranquilizers may prove to be extremely valuable. Even as symptom stoppers they have their uses.

The green oasis among the jets and the rockets is crammed to overflowing. So are all the other mental hospitals of the Western world. Technological and economic progress seems to have been accompanied by psychological regress. The incidence of neuroses and psychoses is apparently on the increase. Still larger hospitals, yet kinder treatment of patients, more psychiatrists and better pills—we need them all and need them urgently. But they will not solve our problem. In this field prevention is incomparably more important than cure; for cure merely returns the patient to an environment which begets mental illness. But how is prevention to be achieved? That is the sixty-four-billion-dollar question.

(From *Esquire* Magazine)

A Case of Voluntary Ignorance

That men do not learn very much from the lessons of history is the most important of all the lessons that history has to teach. *Si vis pacem,* the Romans liked to say, *para bellum—*

if you want peace prepare for war. For the last few thousand years the rulers of all the world's empires, kingdoms and republics have acted upon this maxim—with the result, as Professor Sorokin has laboriously shown, that every civilized nation has spent about half of every century of its existence waging war with its neighbors. But has mankind learned this lesson of history? The answer is emphatically in the negative. *Si vis pacem, para bellum* still is the watchword of every sovereign state, with the possible exception of Monaco. Again, what happens when economic power is concentrated in a few hands? History's answer to that question is that, whatever else it may be, that which happens is most certainly not democracy. But while politicians everywhere proclaim the virtues of democracy (even the totalitarian states are People's Republics), advancing technology is everywhere allowed and even encouraged to work for the concentration of economic power. Small-scale operators in agriculture and industry are progressively eliminated, and in their place advancing technology installs an oligarchy of giant concerns, owned and operated either by private corporations and their managers, or by the state and its bureaucrats.

It is interesting to note that the men who, in the teeth of history, proclaimed that, if you want peace, you must prepare for war, were the self-same men who solemnly declared that Experience teaches, *experientia docet*—or, as Mrs. Micawber more aptly put it, *"Experientia* does it." But as a matter of brute historical fact, *Experientia* generally doesn't. We got on doing what our own and our father's experience has demonstrated, again and again, to be inappropriate or downright disastrous; and we go on hoping (this time like *Mr.* Micawber) that "something will turn up"—something completely different from anything which, on the basis of experience, we have any right to expect. Needless to say, it does not turn up. The same old mistakes have the same old consequences and we remain in the same old mess.

And even when we do permit ourselves to be taught by experience, as embodied in our own or our society's history, how slow, in all too many cases, how grudging and reluctant is the process of learning! True, we learn very quickly the things we really want to learn. But the only things we *really* want to learn are the things which satisfy our physical needs, the things which arouse and justify our darling passions, and the things which confirm us in our intellectual prejudices. Thus, in any field of science, new facts and new hypotheses are accepted quickly and easily by those whose metaphysical beliefs happen to be compatible with the new material. They are rejected (or, if accepted, accepted very slowly and grudg-

ingly) by those into whose philosophy the new material cannot be fitted—those, in a word, whose intellectual presupposi-
tions are outraged by the facts and hypotheses in question.
To take an obvious example, the evolutionary hypothesis and
the factual evidence on which it was based were rejected by
the Fundamentalists, or accepted only in a Pickwickian sense
and after years of stubborn resistance. In precisely the same
way the dogmatic materialists of our own day refuse to accept
the factual evidence for ESP, or to consider the hypotheses
based upon that evidence. From their own experience or from
the recorded experience of others (history), men learn only
what their passions and their metaphysical prejudices allow
them to learn.

   A wonderfully instructive example of this truth is provided
by the history of hypnotism in its relations with orthodox
medicine—the history, that is to say, of an extremely odd and
still unexplained phenomenon in its relations with a body of
anatomical and physiological facts, with certain officially
sanctioned methods of treatment, with a system (in part
explicit, in part tacit and unexpressed) of metaphysical beliefs, and with the men who have held the beliefs and used
the methods. At the time of writing (the Summer of 1956)
hypnotism is in fairly good odor among medical men. During
World War II it was extensively used in the treatment of the
psychosomatic symptoms produced by so-called "battle fatigue." And at the present time it is being used by a growing
number of obstetricians to prepare expectant mothers for
childbirth and to make that blessed event more bearable, and
by a growing number of dentists to eliminate the pain of
probing and drilling. Most psychiatrists, it is true, fight shy of
it; but for that overwhelming majority of neurotics who cannot afford to spend two or three years and seven or eight
thousand dollars on a conventional analysis, hypnotic treatment, mainly at the hands of lay therapists, is being made
increasingly available. And now let us listen to what a distinguished anesthesiologist, Doctor Milton J. Marmer of Los
Angeles, has to say about the value of hypnotism in his special
field. "Hypnotism is the best way to make a patient fearless
before surgery, painless during it and comfortable after it."
Dr. Marmer adds that, in severe operations, "perfect anesthesia should be attained by employing hypnotism in conjunction with chemical agents. It can then be a pleasant
experience, involving no tension or apprehension." But, it
may be asked, why bother with hypnotism, when so many and
such excellent chemical anesthetics lie ready to hand? For the
good reason, says Dr. Marmer, that hypnotism "places no
extra load on circulation, breathing, or on the liver and kidney

systems." In a word, it is entirely non-toxic. Hypnotism, he
adds, is epecially valuable in operations on children. Children
who have been hypnotized into unconsciousness are more
cheerful after surgery, "more alert, more responsive, more
comfortable and more co-operative than those who undergo
anesthesia produced by chemicals alone." Patients who have
suffered severe burns are in constant pain, greatly depressed
and without appetite. Hypnotism will relieve pain, improve
morale and restore appetite, thereby greatly accelerating the
process of healing. Alone or in conjunction with relatively
small amounts of chemical anesthetics, hypnotism has been
used by Dr. Marmer in every kind of surgical situation, including even the removal of a tumor from the lung. Every
anesthesiologist, Dr. Marmer concludes, should also be a
hypnotist.

So much for hypnotism today. Now let us turn back to
the past and see what lessons the history of hypnotism has to
teach. Among the books in my library are two rather battered
volumes—*Mesmerism in India,* by James Esdaile, M.D., first
published in 1846, and *Mesmerism, in its Relation to Health
and Disease, and the Present State of Medicine,* by William
Neilson, published at Edinburgh in 1855. Esdaile was a Scottish physician and surgeon, who went out to India as a young
man and was put in charge of two hospitals in Bengal—one a
hospital for prisoners in the local jail, the other a charity hospital for the general public. In these hospitals and, later, in a
hospital at Calcutta, Esdaile performed more than three hundred major operations on patients in a state of hypnotic (or
as it was then called, "mesmeric" or "magnetic") anesthesia.
These operations included amputations of limbs, removals of
cancerous breasts, numerous operations for varicocele, cataract and chronic ulcers, removals of tumors in the throat and
mouth, and of the enormous tumors, weighing from thirty
to more than a hundred pounds apiece, caused by elephantiasis, then exceedingly prevalent in Bengal. Esdaile's Indian
patients felt no pain, even during the most drastic operations.
What was still more remarkable, they survived. In 1846—the
year in which Esdaile published his book—Semmelweiss had
not yet taught his students to wash their hands when they
came from the dissecting room to the maternity ward, Pasteur
was years away from his discovery of bacterial infection,
Lister, a mere boy in his teens. Surgery was strictly septic.
In the words of a historian of medicine, "suppuration and
septic poisonings of the system carried away even the most
promising patients and followed even trifling operations. Often,
too, these diseases rose to the height of epidemic pestilences,
so that patients, however extreme their need, feared the very

name of hospital, and the most skillful surgeons distrusted
their own craft." Before the advent of ether and chloroform
(which began to be used about 1847), the mortality of patients
after surgery averaged twenty-nine per cent in a well-run
hospital and would rise, when the streps and staphs were more
than usually active, to over fifty per cent. Chloroform changed
the techniques of surgery, but not, to any marked extent, its
results. The agonies of the fully conscious patient "had
naturally and rightly compelled the public to demand rapid
if not slapdash surgery, and the surgeon to pride himself on
it. Within decent limits of precision, the quickest craftsman
was the best." (There were famous specialists who could perform an operation for stone in fifty-eight seconds flat.) Thanks
to chloroform, "the surgeon was enabled to be not only as
cautious and sedulous as he was dexterous, but also to venture
on long, profound and intricate operations which, before the
coming of anesthetics, had been out of the question. But unfortunately this new enfranchisement seemed to be but an
ironic liberty of Nature, who with the other hand took away
what she had given." Bigger and better operations were performed under chemical anesthesia, but the patients went
on dying at almost the same ghastly rate. In the twenty years
following the introduction of chloroform and preceding Lister's advocacy of aseptic surgery, the death rate from post-
operative infections fell by only six percentage points—from
twenty-nine in every hundred cases to twenty-three. In other
words, almost a quarter of every Early Victorian surgeon's
clients were still regularly slaughtered. Chloroform had abolished the pain of operations, but not the virtual certainty of
infection afterwards, nor the one-in-four chance of a lingering
and unpleasant death.

Meanwhile, what was happening in Bengal? The answer is
startling in the extreme. In a debilitating climate and among
sickly and undernourished patients, Doctor Esdaile was performing major surgery without any deaths on the operating
table (a distressingly frequent event in the early days of badly
administered chloroform) and with a mortality from post-
operative infection of only five per cent. How are we to account for this extraordinary state of affairs? First of all,
Esdaile never allowed his patients' morale to be undermined
by apprehension. The men and women who came to him were
not told in advance when they were to be operated, nor even,
in many cases, that an operation would be necessary. After
examination by the surgeon, they were taken into a dark
room, asked to lie down on a couch, and then put to sleep by
"magnetic passes," which were made by relays of orderlies,
who would work on the patient, if it seemed necessary, for

three and four hours at a stretch. When the passes had taken effect and the patient was in a deep hypnotic coma, he would be taken into the operating room, have his leg cut off, or his forty-pound elephantiasis tumor removed, be stitched up and carried, still unconscious, to his bed. In most cases patients remained in trance for several hours after being operated, and would wake up unaware of what had happened and feeling no pain whatever. In the days that followed they were frequently re-mesmerized, and so spent most of their time in a state of trance. But in trance, as in natural sleep, the *vis medicatrix naturae*, nature's healing power, is able to do its work with the greatest possible effectiveness. The agitated and anxious ego is put to sleep and can make no trouble; left to its own devices, the autonomic system or Vegetative Soul (as it used to be called) goes about its business with infallible skill. In order to be freed from pain and self-consciousness, Esdaile's patients did not have to be poisoned by narcotics and analgesics; thanks to hypnotism, they were spared most of the miseries that normally follow an operation, and, thanks to hypnotism, their resistance was raised to such an extent that they could easily get the better of the deadly microorganisms associated with septic surgery.

Five deaths to every hundred operations—it was the biggest medical news since the days of Hippocrates! But when Esdaile published the facts, what happened? Were his colleagues delighted? Did they hasten in a body to follow his example? Not at all. Most of them were extremely angry when they heard of his achievement, and the bigwigs of the faculty did everything in their power to prevent Dr. Esdaile from continuing his beneficent work and, when that proved impossible (for Esdaile was backed up by the Governor General of India), to suppress the, to them, embarrassing and distasteful facts.

Doctor James Simpson, the first surgeon to advocate the use of chloroform and a most courageous crusader, in the teeth of Fundamentalist opposition, for painless childbirth, was at first intensely interested in mesmeric anesthesia. In a letter to Esdaile he wrote that he had "always considered the few deaths out of so many formidable operations one of the most remarkable things in the history of surgery." Furthermore, says Esdaile, "Dr. Simpson sent me a message that I owed it to myself and my profession to let my proceedings be known in England, and that, if I wrote an article, he would get it published in the journal he was connected with. I therefore sent him an account of one hundred and sixty-one scrotal tumors removed in the mesmeric trance." This paper was rejected on the ground that parts of it had appeared (in a greatly garbled form) in another medical journal. "A more general paper was offered; but after some compliments and considerable delay," Esdaile was informed that Dr. Simpson's brother editors had declined it as "not being sufficiently practical." "One of the most remarkable things in the history of surgery!" is Neilson's justifiably bitter comment. "Namely, how to reduce 23 per cent of deaths to 5 per cent—*not practical.*" And he adds that "it is very curious that, when Dr. Simpson professed to publish an account of all the means that have ever been used to prevent the pain of operations, he quite forgot to mention mesmerism."

This sort of thing had happened before Esdaile's day and was destined to happen again, and yet again, thereafter. Doctor John Elliotson, an eminent physician and Professor of Physiology at the University of London, had been derided and boycotted for his advocacy of mesmerism in surgery and general practice. Some of his critics had gone so far as to assert that a mesmerized man who had a leg amputated without showing the slightest sign of discomfort was a mere impostor —pretending that he felt no pain just to annoy the orthodox doctors. And one of them, Doctor Copland, solemnly declared that "pain is a wise provision of Nature; and patients *ought* to suffer pain, while their surgeon is operating; they are all the better for it and recover better." Later on, when the anesthetic properties of ether and chloroform had been discovered, the first reaction of many doctors was not to give thanks that the pain of operations had been abolished. No, their first reaction was to gloat over the discomfiture of the mesmerists. "Hurrah!" wrote Robert Liston, the first surgeon to perform an operation under ether. "Rejoice! Mesmerism and its professors have met with a heavy blow and great discouragement." More soberly, but with equal satisfaction, the official *Lancet* smugly editorialized: "We suppose that we shall hear no more of mesmerism and its absurdities." And, in effect, the absurdity of a five per cent death rate was not heard of again until Lister discovered that, if the surgeon used aseptic methods, the patient could survive in spite of lowered resistance and systematic poisoning by chemical anesthetics, narcotics and analgesics.

But mesmerism and its absurdities were observable facts and, in spite of everything, they refused to disappear. It therefore became necessary to legislate against them. For almost half a century after the publication of Esdaile's book, any English doctor who made use of hypnotism ran the risk of being hounded out of his profession. It was not until 1892 that the British Medical Association officially admitted the reality of hypnosis and officially sanctioned hypnotic treatment.

In France hypnotism fared better than in England. The first Royal Commission on Mesmerism (of which Benjamin Franklin was a member) had denied the existence of the "magnetic fluid," which was supposed to account for the phenomena of hypnotism, but had not pronounced on the reality of the physical and psychological phenomena induced by mesmeric procedures. The second commission pronounced in favor of mesmeric treatment. The third, dominated by the orthodox party, pronounced against mesmerism. Later, Charcot tried to prove that hypnosis was a form of hysterical epilepsy. But in spite of everything the practice of hypnotism continued and, at the close of the nineteenth century, was being extensively used for the relief of pain and the cure of sickness. Today, strangely enough, hypnotism is almost unknown among medical circles in France. It is as though such pioneers as Liébault and Bernheim had lived and labored in vain. The remarkable successes achieved by those men and their followers have been more or less completely forgotten.

These ups and downs in the popularity of hypnotism are characteristic of its history in every country. At one moment hypnotism seems to be on the point of entering medicine as a widely used form of therapy; then, a few years later, the public and the professional men seem to lose interest in this kind of treatment, which is either quietly ignored or else denounced as dangerous or vaguely immoral. In the United States, for example, hypnotism enjoyed wide popularity in the years following the Civil War. Three quarters of a century ago the editor of the American edition of *Deleuze's Treatise on Animal Magnetism* could write as follows: "Probably there is not a city nor village in North America where there could not be found at this time—1878—one or more magnetizers. Usually one is to be found in every family." Very few of these magnetizers were medical men; for most American doctors disapproved of hypnotism almost as heartily as did their British colleagues. But, medical or non-medical, the hypnotists existed and were evidently plentiful. By the turn of the century, however, the American magnetizer was already a rare bird, and by the early Twenties the species was almost extinct. Today, it seems to be on its way back. Within a few years, if present trends persist, every city and village in North America may have its medical or dental hypnotist, every family its practitioners of autohypnotism and mutual suggestion.

Why has the history of hypnotism been so strangely checkered? Why is it that, in the words of a great psychologist, the late William McDougall, "in spite of the frequent occurrence of states identical with or closely allied to hypnosis, some three centuries of enthusiastic investigation and of bitter controversy were required to establish the hypnotic state among the facts accepted by the world of European science"? The answer, as I have already suggested, is that most of us believe only what our interests, our passions and our metaphysical prejudices permit us to believe. "As Hobbes has well observed, if it were for the *profit* of a governing body that the three angles of a triangle should not be equal to two right angles, the doctrine that they were would, by that body, inevitably be denounced as false and pernicious. The most curious examples of this truth have been found in the history of medicine. This, on the one hand, is nothing more than a history of variations and, on the other, a still more wonderful history of how every successive variation has, by medical bodies, been first furiously denounced and then bigotedly adopted." So wrote an older contemporary of the persecuted mesmerists, the Scottish philosopher and essayist, Sir William Hamilton (who, like every intelligent man of the period outside the medical profession, took a lively interest in the phenomena of hypnotism). It should be added that the "profit" of a professional body is not to be measured exclusively in terms of money and power, or even of prestige. There are vested interests not only in the fields of economics and social position, but also in the field of pure ideas. That a beautiful and genuinely antique theory should be ruined by some new, coarse, essentially vulgar fact of mere observation seems quite intolerable to a mind brought up in a proper reverence for words and consecrated notions. And it goes without saying that, if the threat to a beloved theory should at the same time be a threat to personal reputation, this resentment will be raised to the pitch of outraged disapproval and a burning, righteous indignation. This was clearly recognized by one of the early historians of science, John Playfair, who noted that new ideas, new observations and new methods "must often change the relative place of men engaged in scientific pursuits, and must oblige many, after descending from the stations they formerly occupied, to take a lower place in the scale of intellectual improvement. The enmity of such men, if they be not animated by a spirit of real candor and the love of truth, is likely to be directed against the methods, observations and ideas by which their vanity is mortified and their importance lessened."

If the Early Victorian doctors hated mesmerism, it was because it threatened their vested interests in such time-hallowed therapeutic methods as blood-letting and pill-prescribing, and at the same time their vested interests in a time-hallowed philosophy of man and the universe, which had no place in it for the odder phenomena of human psychology. Moreover, they felt that they could not give up these methods or modify this philosophy without gravely injuring their professional dignity. "If mesmerism be true," wrote Esdaile, "the doctors, old and young, will have to go to school again; and this is what constitutes the bitterness of the mesmeric pill." (Substitute "parapsychology" for "mesmerism" and "parapsychological" for "mesmeric"—and you have here an explanation of the refusal, on the part of some contemporary scientists, to consider the vast accumulations of evidence in favor of the reality of ESP.)

The extreme bitterness of the pill accounts for the extreme violence of the medical diatribes against the new observations and the new methods of treatment, along with all those who had had anything to do with them. It is a violence comparable to that which, all too frequently, has characterized the controversies of clergymen. The doctors loathed the mesmerists with a full-blown *odium theologicum,* a theological hatred. In his volume of 1855, William Neilson quotes many examples of this truly religious intemperance of language. Disdaining argument and paying no attention to facts, the anti-mesmeric contributors to the *Lancet* and the *Medical Times* confined themselves exclusively to abuse. "While pursuing their frauds among lunatics and fools, mesmerists give us neither umbrage nor disquiet; but within the walls of our colleges (there were mesmerists of the highest scientific eminence at the Universities of Edinburgh and London) they are scandalous nuisances and an insufferable disgrace." Elliotson and his followers practice "a harlotry which they call science." Worse still, they refuse to bow to the authority of those licensed repositories of ultimate truth, the doctors. Instead, they make their appeal to mere reason and uncensored experience, with the shocking result that they have found enthusiastic supporters in every class of society—"the pert folly of the nobility, the weakest among the literary people, high and low ladies, quack clergymen (among whom, it may be remarked, were several bishops and even an archbishop), itinerant lecturers and exhibiting buffoons." To sum up, mesmerism is merely a compound of "quackery, obscenity and imposture, and its advocates are at the best deluded idiots, at the worst swindling knaves."

In one of its aspects, as we have seen, the history of medicine is the history of variations—the history of fads pursued and then rejected, of fashions adopted with enthusiasm and then quietly dropped in favor of some more modish style of diagnosis or of treatment. When all these fads and fashions are strictly physiological, the change from one to another can be made without difficulty and without any feeling of mental distress. But where non-physiological factors are involved—factors which cannot be explained in terms of the prevailing medical philosophy—changes of fashion are painful and the resistance to change is stubborn and often violent. Hypnotism involves non-physiological factors; consequently the reality of hypnosis and the value of hypnotic treatment were vehemently denied by the official spokesmen of the medical profession. That the ban upon hypnotism ever came to be lifted was due to a variety of causes. First of all, the metaphysical susceptibilities of the doctors were soothed by the work of Professor Heidenhain. This German researcher was able to convince himself and his colleagues that hypnosis was always the result of strictly physiological causes. It didn't happen to be true; but, to use the religious phraseology which seems appropriate to the case, it was highly edifying, it brought comfort to the troubled spirit of the doctors, and it helped, incidentally, to make hypnotism respectable. Meanwhile intensive research into the nature of mental illness was being carried on, especially in France and Germany, and the idea of subconscious mental activity gradually forced itself upon even the most physiologically minded psychiatrists. Within the enlarged framework of medical philosophy, hypnosis, though still unexplained, began to make a little more sense. But then—fortunately in some ways, unfortunately in others—the great Doctor Freud made his appearance. Freud banned hypnotism from his system of psychotherapy and, as an entirely illogical consequence of this ban, hypnotism came to be largely neglected in surgery and general medicine, where it is of such inestimable value as a nonpoisonous anesthetic, as a raiser of resistance to infection, as an improver of morale, as a promoter of healing and an accelerator of convalescence.

Wars tend to stimulate medical advance, at any rate in those countries which have escaped severe devastation. The current revival of interest in hypnotism is in part due to its successful employment in military hospitals. Medicine has now returned to the position once occupied by Esdaile and Elliotson. That it should have taken four generations to reconquer that position is certainly unfortunate. But better late than never.

(From *Esquire* Magazine)

The Oddest Science

The reading of yet another book about modern psychological theories is always, I find, a rather exasperating experience. Clothed in an ugly and hardly comprehensible jargon, the obvious is portentously enunciated, as though it were some kind of esoteric mystery. The immemorially ancient is presented, with fanfares, as a brand-new, epoch-making discovery. Instead of open-mindedness, we find dogmatism; instead of comprehensive views, we are given theories which ignore whole provinces of given reality, whole categories of the most significant kinds of facts. And instead of the concreteness so essential in a science of observation, instead of the principle of multiple causation which must govern all thinking about so complex a creature as man, we are treated to shameless displays of those gravest of intellectual sins, overabstraction, overgeneralization and oversimplification.

All this does not mean, of course, that treatises about modern psychological theories should not be read. These treatises are conspicuous facts in the life of our time and, as such, they must not be ignored. Besides, it goes without saying that, in spite of all their defects, the formulators of modern psychological theories have made substantial contributions to the sum of practical wisdom and have done something to deepen our understanding of human nature.

As a history of modern psychology in terms of "an integrative evaluation of Freud, Adler, Jung and Rank," Doctor Ira Progoff's recent book, *The Death and Rebirth of Psychology*, is clear and illuminating. So clear, indeed, and so illuminating that not only the virtues of modern psychology's founding fathers, but also their shortcomings stand out, in its pages, with glaring distinctness.

Let us begin with what is, I suppose, the most serious, as it is certainly the most conspicuous, shortcoming of them all—the absence from all these theories (with the partial exception of Adler's) of any mention of the body as a conditioning factor in the formation of a personality, or as a determinant of thoughts, feelings and behavior. Adler, it is true, made a number of penetrating remarks on the consequences of a sense of organic inferiority; but even Adler was very far from giving the body its due as a shaper of individual character and destiny. Freud, Jung and Rank seem to have imagined that they could understand human minds without taking into

account the bodies with which those minds are indissolubly
associated. Their one-sidedness is the mirror-image of the one-
sidedness of the exclusively physiological physician. But just
as it is perfectly clear that bodies cannot be understood or
successfully treated without reference to their minds, so too
it is perfectly clear that minds cannot be understood or successfully treated without reference to their bodies. Doctors are
at last reconciling themselves to the idea of psychosomatic
medicine. It is time for psychologists to reconcile themselves
to the complementary notion of a somato-psychic approach
to the problems of mind and character.

It was not only by psychology's founding fathers that the
body was neglected. The same absurd one-sidedness was and
still is observable in most of their successors. How rarely, in
recent books on psychology, do we come upon a passage like
the following from Doctor Erich Fromm's work on dreams,
The Forgotten Language. Commenting on the words of an
ancient Hindu writer, Dr. Fromm remarks that "he points
to a significant connection between temperament (*i.e.*, those
psychic qualities which are rooted in a constitutionally given
somatic basis) and dream content"—a connection "which has
found hardly any attention in contemporary dream interpretation, although it is a significant factor in dream interpretation,
as further research will undoubtedly show." After which
Dr. Fromm passes on to other, one-sidedly psychological
considerations. Let us hope that this passing reference to the
significance of temperament may serve as an opening wedge
to a new somato-psychic approach, not merely to dreaming,
but to *all* mental activities. It will not be difficult to make
such an approach; for all the really hard preparatory work has
already been done by Doctor William Sheldon and his colleagues. Using Sheldon's rigorous and powerful methods, it
is now possible for any psychologist or psychiatrist to make
an accurate assessment of the "constitutionally given somatic
basis," in which our "psychic qualities" are rooted. But
though the means are available, they are hardly ever used,
and psychologists continue to treat minds without reference to
bodies, and to publish what they are pleased to call "case
histories" without deigning to give the slightest indication of
what sort of people, somatically speaking, their patients were.
How much did Mrs. X weigh—ninety pounds or two hundred? Did Mr. Y have the physique of an ox or a daddy
longlegs, of a panther or a jellyfish? To these questions most
psychologists never vouchsafe an answer—presumably because, unlike the rest of mankind, they have never thought of
asking them. In his monumental *Atlas of Men*, Dr. Sheldon
has published several thousands of photographs showing the

continuous variation of masculine physique, and assessing those variations within a frame of reference having three co-ordinates, endomorphy, mesomorphy and ectomorphy. Turning over the pages of this book, one sees at a glance that it is obviously impossible for creatures so unlike one another as men at the extreme limits of possible variation to feel, think and behave in the same way. This is something which every one of normal intelligence has known for the last two or three hundred thousand years. It has remained for modern psychologists to ignore this self-evident fact and to talk, in their vague, rhetorical way, about "Man," "Modern Man," or even "Man in the Era of Sexuality," as though there were standardized objects corresponding to these words. But in fact, of course, nobody has ever encountered these mythical beings. Nobody has ever encountered anyone but Tom, Dick and Harry, Dolly, Molly and Polly. But, as everybody knows perfectly well, Tom is congenitally unlike Dick, and Harry is constitutionally different from both of the others. And the same is true of Dolly, Molly and Polly. They are profoundly different one from another, and many of their differences are built in, or (as Dr. Fromm would say), "rooted in a consti-tutionally given somatic basis." Why, one wonders, do the men and women whose profession it is to understand and treat people's minds neglect to study these constitutionally determined differences between individuals? Such voluntary ignorance can be accounted for, I suppose, partly by the force of inertia and ingrained habit; the one-sided approach is tra-ditional, time-hallowed, sanctioned by the bad example of the founding fathers. Nor must we forget that it is a great deal easier to be one-sided than to think and act realistically in terms of multiple causation. Wherever the line of least resist-ance *can* be followed, it generally *is* followed.

We see, then, that in their theories, as in their practice, the founding fathers completely neglected the "constitutionally given somatic basis," which determines so much of our think-ing, feeling and behavior. However, they did not neglect heredity altogether. Jung and, above all, Rank lightheartedly maintained that acquired characteristics are inherited—a doc-trine which all geneticists, even (since the fall of Lysenko) in Russia, now repudiate. It was assumed in their theorizing that notions popular in earlier periods of history are somehow built into the hereditary make-up of twentieth-century babies. According to Rank, "the meeting of the points of view of these two eras (the Spiritual Era and the Sexual Era) and the resulting tension that remained in man *ever afterwards* [italics mine] comprise the main source of those inner conflicts that a later age described as 'psychological.' " This, surely, is pure balderdash. Hardly less nonsensical is Jung's equation of a human culture-pattern with the built-in behavior of an insect. For the East African tribe of the Elgonyi, he writes, their morning ritual "is a part of the pattern of behavior that life requires, just as the leaf-cutting ant cannot do otherwise than live out the pattern inherent in the nature of its species." But in fact the behavior-pattern built into the cells of the leaf-cutting ant is of a radically different kind from the behavior-pattern acquired, during infancy and childhood, by an East African tribesman. Take a batch of ant's eggs from the tropics and hatch them out in a greenhouse in Stockholm; the adult leaf-cutters will behave precisely as adult leaf-cutters behave in Africa. But now take a new-born Elgonyi baby and bring him up in Stockholm. By the time he grows up, he will be thinking, feeling, speaking and behaving like any Swede of his particular physique and temperament. The morning ritual performed by the Elgonyi in Africa is no more built into them than are their table manners or their language. And now consider the following statement. "When Jung refers to Christ as a 'symbol of the Self,' he means to indicate the *fact* [italics mine] that for the western psyche some variation of the image of Jesus Christ is *inevitably* [italics mine] the center, around which the symbolism of individuation is expressed." But it is an observable fact that many people born and brought up in the West (and so, presumably, possessed of a "western psyche") do not experience the image of Christ as a central symbol. Its presence or absence depends on the nature of the conditioning to which the individual happens to have been subjected.

It is not only through their inherited make-up that bodies affect thoughts, feelings and behavior. Our moods, our general mental tone, our metaphysical theories and view of life, may be determined by faulty nutrition or a chronic infection. There is ample evidence that many undesirable mental states have their primary source, not in some traumatic event of child-hood or the more recent past, but in what the late F. M. Alexander aptly called "the improper use of the self"—in bad postural habits, resulting in impaired physiological and psychological functioning. If you teach an individual first to be aware of his physical organism and then to use it as it was meant to be used, you can often change his entire attitude to life and cure his neurotic tendencies. But this, of course, is something which no one-sided psychologist has been taught to do, or would approve of doing, even if he knew how. He just goes on with free association and dream analysis, and hopes for the best. And the best (as those who have tried to assess the effectiveness of psychoanalysis assure us) does not happen as often as one might hope or, given the exorbitant cost of the treatment, legitimately expect.

And here let us ask ourselves a question which is obviously of the highest importance. Why is it that, though practically every child has to endure large numbers of traumatic experiences, only some children grow up to be neurotics? This is a question to which neither the founding fathers, nor their successors, have paid the attention it deserves. Clearly, we are concerned here with one aspect of the more general problem of resistance. Why are some people so resistant to almost every kind of illness, while others go down like ninepins? There are doubtless many reasons for differences in individual resistance, some strictly environmental, others (more difficult, but perhaps not impossible, to control) built in and hereditary. Thus, extreme susceptibility to the common cold is probably due to a mutant gene. When the biochemical consequences of this mutation can be offset by pharmacological means, the problem of the common cold will be solved. (After which, no doubt, we shall have another, as yet unsuspected, problem to take its place!) And what extreme susceptibility of psychological traumas? Perhaps this too is genetic in origin. The number of psychotics in relation to the total population has remained, it would seem, remarkably constant. Presumably susceptibility to these severe mental illnesses is due to inherited metabolic anomalies, which result in enzyme disbalance and a special kind of self-poisoning. That some genetic factor may be responsible, at least in part, for susceptibility to the milder forms of mental illness seems perfectly possible. If this is the case, we may look forward to a time when the pharmacologists will achieve rapidly and certainly the results which present-day psychiatrists, with their one-sided methods, can achieve, if at all, only after years of analysis.

Dr. Progoff says of Freud that his psychological theories were too materialistic. My own view is that, like the theories of most other modern psychologists, they are not nearly materialistic enough. It is worthy of note that the most "spiritual" religions have been the ones to pay the closest, most scientific attention to the body. Hindu and Buddhist theology has a well-developed theory of inherited temperaments. According to this theory, a man is born to follow either the path of devotion, or the path of active duty, or the path of contemplation. And this is not all. If he is born with the capacity to unite himself with God through contemplation, he will be well advised to facilitate the contemplative process by paying special attention to his bodily posture and to such bodily functions as breathing, eating and excreting. Every Oriental philosophy is at bottom a treatise on transcendental psychotherapy. The aim of this therapy is to cure the (statistically speaking) normal of their complacent belief that they are sane, and to lead them on to a state of what may be called absolute, rather than statistical, normality—a state in which they realize who, at bottom, they are. There can be no spirituality except on a basis of well-informed materialism. Lacking completely such a basis, psychology as we know it at present is doomed to go on being theoretically unrealistic and, in practice, largely ineffective.

Hardly less amazing than the founding fathers' neglect of the body is their failure to pay any attention to language as a determinant of thought, feeling and behavior. We are human because we talk, and the universe in which we live is largely a homemade affair, carved out of the given world by our vocabulary and our syntax, and re-created by ourselves so as to conform in its structure to the structure of the language in which we happen to have been brought up. All the founding fathers, and especially Jung, were deeply interested in what Dr. Fromm calls "the forgotten language" of dreams, myths and fairy tales. But incomparably more important to every human being than this forgotten language is the well-remembered dialect in which he talks to other human beings, the native language—English, Chinese, Eskimo—in terms of which he does most of his learning, almost all his thinking and even much of his feeling and perceiving. (Our perceiving is hardly ever of events as they are immediately given; it is rather of our own ready-made, verbalized concepts projected by the perceiver into the outside world and super-imposed, so to speak, upon the objects of our immediate experience.) Our dependence on language is such that, for most of us, words no longer stand for things—rather things stand for words, and objects are treated as so many illustrations of our verbalized abstractions. No language is completely true to the inner and outer world, to which it is supposed to refer. Most languages, indeed, are so untrue to given reality that it has become necessary to supplement them with the special languages of mathematics. Thus, the world is unquestionably a continuum; there are in reality no separate substantial things, there are only merging events and interacting processes in space-time. But our languages (at any rate those of the Indo-European stock) do not permit us to speak about the world as a continuum, and whenever we want to discuss this aspect of reality, we must use such special, *ad hoc* languages as the calculus. Our linguistic troubles would be grave enough, even if we always used our language correctly, according to the rules of logic and the dictates of common sense. But in many circumstances of life, we use language incorrectly and with a total disregard for the rules. The result is unrealistic thinking, debauched feeling and distorted perception, leading to action of every degree of inappropriateness from the merely eccentric to the diabolic, from harmless Micawberism to such collective insanities as Hitlerism, heresy hunting and religious wars. Consistently bad language, as Korzybski and the Semanticists have pointed out, is a prime cause of delinquency in thinking, feeling and behaving. But most modern psychologists, as we have seen, are more interested in squabbling about the interpretation of the coded rigmarole of dreams than in studying the far more important subject of the language nobody ever forgets, and the ways in which, during our waking hours, we talk ourselves and one another out of all contact with cosmic reality and the elementary conventions of human decency.

And now let us briefly consider a few more of the shortcomings of the founding fathers. As Dr. Progoff has pointed out, all of them indulged in the intellectual sin of working up their private experiences into universal generalizations. Thus Freud, for psychological reasons of his own, extolled the extroverted life as "the way of health for every man." This conclusion is wholly unwarranted; for it is quite obvious that many people are congenitally introverted and that, for them, the extroverted life is the way of misery, neurosis and disease. And here is another curious example of the same kind of intellectual delinquency. Otto Rank broke with Freud by performing what was for him a great creative act—the writing of his book, *The Trauma of Birth*. Freud had been very kind to Rank, and, after the break, the latter felt severe pangs of remorse. Universalizing his private feelings, he proceeded to "make the acute observation that one of the aftermaths of a creative act is an attack of guilt feelings, remorse and anxiety." The only trouble with this "acute observation" is that it happens to be untrue to all the facts, except those of Rank's private experience in a very special situation. When Rank asserted that *all* creative acts are followed by guilt feelings, he was not making an acute observation; he was merely indulging in bad logic, egotism and voluntary ignorance. I have known many artists, and I have observed that their creative acts were sometimes followed by boredom and a sense of emptiness, due to the fact that they had finished their task and had nothing further, for the moment, to do. Occasionally, too, some of them would experience a feeling of disgust at the thought that they had put forth their best efforts and exposed their very souls for the amusement of an indifferent, uncomprehending and profoundly frivolous public. The artists of my acquaintance never suffered from guilt feelings after an act of creation—for the good reason that none was in the peculiar position, while creating, of having quarreled with a benefactor. Building up grandiose generalizations from a few cases, or even from a single case—this, among the psychologists, has been standard procedure.

No less characteristic, and no less deplorably unscientific, has been their tendency to dogmatize. The founding fathers quarreled with one another; for each was convinced of his own absolute rightness. Thus, in the matter of dream interpretations, "Freud," to quote the words of Dr. Fromm, "rigidly refused to accept any modification and insisted that the only possible interpretation of a dream was that of the wish-fulfillment theory. . . . Jung . . . equally dogmatically tended to interpret the dream as an expression of the wisdom of the unconscious." Some of the old *odium theologicum* (the theological hatred, the loathing on principle) tends to survive among their followers, and we are treated to the ludicrous spectacle—ludicrous, that is to say, in a field which is supposed to be scientific—of Freudianity pitted against Jungism, orthodoxy against orthodoxy, and both against the eclectic Modernism which is gradually taking their place. Perhaps the most ludicrous fact of all is that forty years of sectarian squabbling might have been avoided, if the combatants had taken the trouble to study a book, which appeared at the dawn of the "Psychological Era." I refer to F. W. H. Myers' *Human Personality,* first published in 1903. Myers set forth a theory of the unconscious far more comprehensive than Freud's narrow and one-sided hypothesis, and superior to Jung's in being better documented with concrete facts and less encumbered with those psycho-anthropologico-pseudo-genetic speculations which becloud the writings of the Sage of Zurich. Jung is like those German classical scholars, of whom Porson once said that "they dive deeper and come up muddier than any others." Myers has the immense merit of diving as deeply as Jung into that impersonal, spiritual world which transcends and interpenetrates our bodies, our conscious minds and our personal unconscious—of diving as deeply, but of coming up again with the minimum of mud on him. One of the oddest facts about the oddest of the sciences, is that this amazingly rich, wide-ranging and profound book should have been neglected in favor of description of psychological reality much less complete and realistic, and of explanatory theories much less adequate to the given facts.

(From *Esquire* Magazine)

RX FOR
SENSE AND PSYCHE

The Doors of Perception

It was in 1886 that the German pharmacologist, Ludwig
Lewin, published the first systematic study of the cactus, to
which his own name was subsequently given. *Anhalonium
Lewinii* was new to science. To primitive religion and the
Indians of Mexico and the American Southwest it was a
friend of immemorially long standing. Indeed, it was much
more than a friend. In the words of one of the early Spanish
visitors to the New World, "they eat a root which they call
peyote, and which they venerate as though it were a deity."

Why they should have venerated it as a deity became apparent when such eminent psychologists as Jaensch, Havelock
Ellis and Weir Mitchell began their experiments with mescalin,
the active principle of peyote. True, they stopped short at a
point well this side of idolatry; but all concurred in assigning
to mescalin a position among drugs of unique distinction.
Administered in suitable doses, it changes the quality of consciousness more profoundly and yet is less toxic than any
other substance in the pharmacologist's repertory.

Mescalin research has been going on sporadically ever since
the days of Lewin and Havelock Ellis. Chemists have not
merely isolated the alkaloid; they have learned how to synthe-
size it, so that the supply no longer depends on the sparse and
intermittent crop of a desert cactus. Alienists have dosed
themselves with mescalin in the hope thereby of coming to a
better, a first-hand, understanding of their patients' mental
processes. Working unfortunately upon too few subjects within
too narrow a range of circumstances, psychologists have ob-

served and catalogued some of the drug's more striking effects. Neurologists and physiologists have found out something about the mechanism of its action upon the central nervous system. And at least one professional philosopher has taken mescalin for the light it may throw on such ancient, unsolved riddles as the place of mind in nature and the relationship between brain and consciousness.

There matters rested until, two or three years ago, a new and perhaps highly significant fact was observed. Actually the fact had been staring everyone in the face for several decades; but nobody, as it happened, had noticed it until a young English psychiatrist, at present working in Canada, was struck by the close similarity, in chemical composition, between mescalin and adrenalin. Further research revealed that lysergic acid, an extremely potent hallucinogen derived from ergot, has a structural biochemical relationship to the others. Then came the discovery that adrenochrome, which is a product of the decomposition of adrenalin, can produce many of the symptoms observed in mescalin intoxication. But adrenochrome probably occurs spontaneously in the human body. In other words, each one of us may be capable of manufacturing a chemical, minute doses of which are known to cause profound changes in consciousness. Certain of these changes are similar to those which occur in that most characteristic plague of the twentieth century, schizophrenia. Is the mental disorder due to a chemical disorder? And is the chemical disorder due, in its turn, to psychological distresses affecting the adrenals? It would be rash and premature to affirm it. The most we can say is that some kind of a *prima facie* case has been made out. Meanwhile the clue is being systematically followed, the sleuths—biochemists, psychiatrists, psychologists—are on the trail.

By a series of, for me, extremely fortunate circumstances I found myself, in the spring of 1953, squarely athwart that trail. One of the sleuths had come on business to California. In spite of seventy years of mescalin research, the psychological material at his disposal was still absurdly inadequate, and he was anxious to add to it. I was on the spot and willing, indeed eager, to be a guinea pig. Thus it came about that, one bright May morning, I swallowed four-tenths of a gram of mescalin dissolved in half a glass of water and sat down to wait for the results. . . .

Half an hour after swallowing the drug I became aware of a slow dance of golden lights. A little later there were sumptuous red surfaces swelling and expanding from bright nodes of energy that vibrated with a continuously changing, patterned life. At another time the closing of my eyes revealed a complex of gray structures, within which pale bluish spheres kept emerging into intense solidity and, having emerged, would slide noiselessly upwards, out of sight. But at no time were there faces or forms of men or animals. I saw no landscapes, no enormous spaces, no magical growth and metamorphosis of buildings, nothing remotely like a drama or a parable. The other world to which mescalin admitted me was not the world of visions; it existed out there, in what I could see with my eyes open. The great change was in the realm of objective fact. What had happened to my subjective universe was relatively unimportant.

I took my pill at eleven. An hour and a half later, I was sitting in my study, looking intently at a small glass vase. The vase contained only three flowers—a full-blown Belle of Portugal rose, shell pink with a hint at every petal's base of a hotter, flamier hue; a large magenta and cream-colored carnation; and, pale purple at the end of its broken stalk, the bold heraldic blossom of an iris. Fortuitous and provisional, the little nosegay broke all the rules of traditional good taste. At breakfast that morning I had been struck by the lively dissonance of its colors. But that was no longer the point. I was not looking now at an unusual flower arrangement. I was seeing what Adam had seen on the morning of his creation— the miracle, moment by moment, of naked existence.

"Is it agreeable?" somebody asked. (During this part of the experiment, all conversations were recorded on a dictating machine, and it has been possible for me to refresh my memory of what was said.)

"Neither agreeable nor disagreeable," I answered. "It just *is*."

Istigkeit—wasn't that the word Meister Eckhart liked to use? "Is-ness." The Being of Platonic philosophy—except that Plato seems to have made the enormous, the grotesque mistake of separating Being from becoming and identifying it with the mathematical abstraction of the Idea. He could never, poor fellow, have seen a bunch of flowers shining with their own inner light and all but quivering under the pressure of the significance with which they were charged; could never have perceived that what rose and iris and carnation so intensely signified was nothing more, and nothing less, than what they were—a transience that was yet eternal life, a perpetual perishing that was at the same time pure Being, a bundle of minute, unique particulars in which, by some unspeakable and yet self-evident paradox, was to be seen the divine source of all existence.

I continued to look at the flowers, and in their living light I seemed to detect the qualitative equivalent of breathing—

but of a breathing without returns to a starting point, with no recurrent ebbs but only a repeated flow from beauty to heightened beauty, from deeper to ever deeper meaning. Words like "grace" and "transfiguration" came to my mind, and this, of course, was what, among other things, they stood for. My eyes traveled from the rose to the carnation, and from that feathery incandescence to the smooth scrolls of sentient amethyst which were the iris. The Beatific Vision, *Sat Chit Ananda,* Being-Awareness-Bliss—for the first time I understood, not on the verbal level, not by inchoate hints or at a distance, but precisely and completely what those prodigious syllables referred to. And then I remembered a passage I had read in one of Suzuki's essays. "What is the Dharma-Body of the Buddha?" ("The Dharma-Body of the Buddha" is another way of saying Mind, Suchness, the Void, the Godhead.) The question is asked in a Zen monastery by an earnest and bewildered novice. And with the prompt irrelevance of one of the Marx Brothers, the Master answers, "The hedge at the bottom of the garden." "And the man who realizes this truth," the novice dubiously inquires, "what, may I ask, is he?" Groucho gives him a whack over the shoulders with his staff and answers, "A golden-haired lion."

It had been, when I read it, only a vaguely pregnant piece of nonsense. Now it was all as clear as day, as evident as Euclid. Of course the Dharma-Body of the Buddha was the hedge at the bottom of the garden. At the same time, and no less obviously, it was these flowers, it was anything that I— or rather the blessed Not-I, released for a moment from my throttling embrace—cared to look at. The books, for example, with which my study walls were lined. Like the flowers, they glowed, when I looked at them, with brighter colors, a profounder significance. Red books, like rubies; emerald books; books bound in white jade; books of agate; of aquamarine, of yellow topaz; lapis lazuli books whose color was so intense, so intrinsically meaningful, that they seemed to be on the point of leaving the shelves to thrust themselves more insistently on my attention.

"What about spatial relationships?" the investigator inquired, as I was looking at the books.

It was difficult to answer. True, the perspective looked rather odd, and the walls of the room no longer seemed to meet in right angles. But these were not the really important facts. The really important facts were that spatial relationships had ceased to matter very much and that my mind was perceiving the world in terms of other than spatial categories. At ordinary times the eye concerns itself with such problems as *Where?—How far?—How situated in relation to what?* In

the mescalin experience the implied questions to which the
eye responds are of another order. Place and distance cease to
be of much interest. The mind does its perceiving in terms of
intensity of existence, profundity of significance, relationships
within a pattern. I saw the books, but was not at all concerned
with their positions in space. What I noticed, what impressed
itself upon my mind was the fact that all of them glowed with
living light and that in some the glory was more manifest
than in others. In this context position and the three dimensions were beside the point. Not, of course, that the category
of space had been abolished. When I got up and walked
about, I could do so quite normally, without misjudging the
whereabouts of objects. Space was still there; but it had lost
its predominance. The mind was primarily concerned, not with
measures and locations, but with being and meaning.

And along with indifference to space there went an even
more complete indifference to time.

"There seems to be plenty of it," was all I would answer,
when the investigator asked me to say what I felt about time.

Plenty of it, but exactly how much was entirely irrelevant.
I could, of course, have looked at my watch; but my watch,
I knew, was in another universe. My actual experience had
been, was still, of an indefinite duration or alternatively of a
perpetual present made up of one continually changing
apocalypse.

From the books the investigator directed my attention to
the furniture. A small typing table stood in the center of the
room; beyond it, from my point of view, was a wicker chair
and beyond that a desk. The three pieces formed an intricate
pattern of horizontals, uprights and diagonals—a pattern all
the more interesting for not being interpreted in terms of
spatial relationships. Table, chair and desk came together in
a composition that was like something by Braque or Juan
Gris, a still life recognizably related to the objective world,
but rendered without depth, without any attempt at photographic realism. I was looking at my furniture, not as the
utilitarian who has to sit on chairs, to write at desks and
tables, and not as the cameraman or scientific recorder, but
as the pure aesthete whose concern is only with forms and
their relationships within the field of vision or the picture
space. But as I looked, this purely aesthetic, Cubist's-eye
view gave place to what I can only describe as the sacramental vision of reality. I was back where I had been when
I was looking at the flowers—back in a world where everything shone with the Inner Light, and was infinite in its
significance. The legs, for example, of that chair—how miraculous their tubularity, how supernatural their polished smooth-

ness! I spent several minutes—or was it several centuries?—
not merely gazing at those bamboo legs, but actually *being*
them—or rather being myself in them; or, to be still more
accurate (for "I" was not involved in the case, nor in a certain sense were "they") being my Not-self in the Not-self
which was the chair.

Reflecting on my experience, I find myself agreeing with
the eminent Cambridge philosopher, Dr. C. D. Broad, "that
we should do well to consider much more seriously than we
have hitherto been inclined to do the type of theory which
Bergson put forward in connection with memory and sense
perception. The suggestion is that the function of the brain
and nervous system and sense organs is in the main *eliminative*
and not productive. Each person is at each moment capable
of remembering all that has ever happened to him and of
perceiving everything that is happening everywhere in the
universe. The function of the brain and nervous system is to
protect us from being overwhelmed and confused by this
mass of largely useless and irrelevant knowledge, by shutting
out most of what we should otherwise perceive or remember
at any moment, and leaving only that very small and special
selection which is likely to be practically useful." According
to such a theory, each one of us is potentially Mind at Large.
But in so far as we are animals, our business is at all costs
to survive. To make biological survival possible, Mind at
Large has to be funneled through the reducing valve of the
brain and nervous system. What comes out at the other end
is a measly trickle of the kind of consciousness which will
help us to stay alive on the surface of this particular planet. . . .

The effects of mescalin are the sort of effects you could
expect to follow the administration of a drug having the power
to impair the efficiency of the cerebral reducing valve. When
the brain runs out of sugar, the undernourished ego grows
weak, can't be bothered to undertake the necessary chores,
and loses all interest in those spatial and temporal relationships which mean so much to an organism bent on getting on in the world. As Mind at Large seeps past the no
longer watertight valve, all kinds of biologically useless things
start to happen. In some cases there may be extra-sensory
perceptions. Other persons discover a world of visionary
beauty. To others again is revealed the glory, the infinite
value and meaningfulness of naked existence, of the given,
unconceptualized event. . . .

"This is how one ought to see," I kept saying as I looked
down at my trousers, or glanced at the jeweled books in the
shelves, at the legs of my infinitely more than Van-Goghian
chair. "This is how one ought to see, how things really are."

And yet there were reservations. For if one always saw like this, one would never want to do anything else. Just looking, just being the divine Not-self of flower, of book, of chair, of flannel. That would be enough. But in that case what about other people? What about human relations? In the recording of that morning's conversations I find the question constantly repeated, "What about human relations?" How could one reconcile this timeless bliss of seeing as one ought to see with the temporal duties of doing what one ought to do and feeling as one ought to feel? "One ought to be able," I said, "to see these trousers as infinitely important and human beings as still more infinitely important." One ought—but in practice it seemed to be impossible. This participation in the manifest glory of things left no room, so to speak, for the ordinary, the necessary concerns of human existence, above all for concerns involving persons. For persons are selves and, in one respect at least, I was now a Not-self, simultaneously perceiving and being the Not-self of the things around me. To this new-born Not-self, the behavior, the appearance, the very thought of the self it had momentarily ceased to be, and of other selves, its one-time fellows, seemed not indeed distasteful (for distaste-fulness was not one of the categories in terms of which I was thinking), but enormously irrelevant. Compelled by the inves-tigator to analyze and report on what I was doing (and how I longed to be left alone with Eternity in a flower, Infinity in four chair legs and the Absolute in the folds of a pair of flannel trousers!), I realized that I was deliberately avoiding the eyes of those who were with me in the room, deliberately refraining from being too much aware of them. One was my wife, the other a man I respected and greatly liked; but both belonged to the world from which, for the moment, mescalin had delivered me—the world of selves, of time, of moral judgments and utilitarian considerations, the world (and it was this aspect of human life which I wished, above all else, to forget) of self-assertion, of cocksureness, of overvalued words and idolatrously worshiped notions.

At this stage of the proceedings I was handed a large colored reproduction of the well-known self-portrait by Cézanne—the head and shoulders of a man in a large straw hat, red-cheeked, red-lipped, with rich black whiskers and a dark unfriendly eye. It is a magnificent painting; but it was not as a painting that I now saw it. For the head promptly took on a third dimension and came to life as a small goblin-like man looking out through a window in the page before me. I started to laugh. And when they asked me why, "What pretensions!" I kept repeating. "Who on earth does he think he is?" The question was not addressed to Cézanne in particular, but to the human species at large. Who did they all think they were?

For relief I turned back to the folds in my trousers. "This is how one ought to see," I repeated yet again. And I might have added, "These are the sort of things one ought to look at." Things without pretensions, satisfied to be merely themselves, sufficient in their Suchness, not acting a part, not trying, insanely, to go it alone, in isolation from the Dharma-Body, in Luciferian defiance of the grace of God.

"The nearest approach to this," I said, "would be a Vermeer."

Yes, a Vermeer. For that mysterious artist was trebly gifted —with the vision that perceives the Dharma-Body as the hedge at the bottom of the garden, with the talent to render as much of that vision as the limitations of human capacity permit, and with the prudence to confine himself in his paintings to the more manageable aspects of reality; for though Vermeer represented human beings, he was always a painter of still life. Cézanne, who told his female sitters to do their best to look like apples, tried to paint portraits in the same spirit. But his pippin-like women are more nearly related to Plato's Ideas than to the Dharma-Body in the hedge. They are Eternity and Infinity seen, not in sand or flower, but in the abstractions of some very superior brand of geometry. Vermeer never asked his girls to look like apples. On the contrary, he insisted on their being girls to the very limit—but always with the proviso that they refrain from behaving girlishly. They might sit or quietly stand but never giggle, never display self-consciousness, never say their prayers or pine for absent sweethearts, never gossip, never gaze enviously at other women's babies, never flirt, never love or hate or work. In the act of doing any of these things they would doubtless become more intensely themselves, but would cease, for that very reason, to manifest their divine essential Not-self. In Blake's phrase, the doors of Vermeer's perception were only partially cleansed. A single panel had become almost perfectly transparent; the rest of the door was still muddy. The essential Not-self could be perceived very clearly in things and in living creatures on the hither side of good and evil. In human beings it was visible only when they were in repose, their minds untroubled, their bodies motionless. In these circumstances Vermeer could see Suchness in all its heavenly beauty—could see and, in some small measure, render it in a subtle and sumptuous still life. Vermeer is undoubtedly the greatest painter of human still lives. . . .

But meanwhile my question remained unanswered. How was this cleansed perception to be reconciled with a proper concern with human relations, with the necessary chores and duties, to say nothing of charity and practical compassion? The age-old debate between the actives and the contemplatives was being renewed—renewed, so far as I was concerned, with an unprecedented poignancy. For until this morning I had known contemplation only in its humbler, its more ordinary forms—as discursive thinking; as a rapt absorption in poetry or painting or music; as a patient waiting upon those inspirations, without which even the prosiest writer cannot hope to accomplish anything; as occasional glimpses, in Nature, of Wordsworth's "something far more deeply interfused"; as systematic silence leading, sometimes, to hints of an "obscure knowledge." But now I knew contemplation at its height. At its height, but not yet in its fullness. For in its fullness the way of Mary includes the way of Martha and raises it, so to speak, to its own higher power. Mescalin opens up the way of Mary, but shuts the door on that of Martha. It gives access to contemplation—but to a contemplation that is incompatible with action and even with the will to action, the very thought of action. In the intervals between his revelations the mescalin taker is apt to feel that, though in one way everything is supremely as it should be, in another there is something wrong. His problem is essentially the same as that which confronts the quietest, the *arhat* and, on another level, the landscape painter and the painter of human still lives. Mescalin can never solve that problem; it can only pose it, apocalyptically, for those to whom it had never before presented itself. The full and final solution can be found only by those who are prepared to implement the right kind of *Weltanschauung* by means of the right kind of behavior and the right kind of constant and unstrained alertness. Over against the quietist stands the active-contemplative, the saint, the man who, in Eckhart's phrase, is ready to come down from the seventh heaven in order to bring a cup of water to his sick brother. Over against the *arhat*, retreating from appearances into an entirely transcendental Nirvana, stands the Bodhisattva, for whom Suchness and the world of contingencies are one, and for whose boundless compassion every one of those contingencies is an occasion not only for transfiguring insight, but also for the most practical charity. And in the universe of art, over against Vermeer and the other painters of human still lives, over against the masters of Chinese and Japanese landscape painting, over against Constable and Turner, against Sisley and Seurat and Cézanne, stands the all-inclusive art of Rembrandt. These are enormous names, inaccessible eminences. For myself, on this memorable May morning, I could only be grateful for an experience which had shown me, more clearly than I had ever seen it before, the true nature of the challenge and the completely liberating response.

(From *The Doors of Perception*)

Drugs That Shape Men's Minds

In the course of history many more people have died for their drink and their dope than have died for their religion or their country. The craving for ethyl alcohol and the opiates has been stronger, in these millions, than the love of God, of home, of children; even of life. Their cry was not for liberty or death; it was for death preceded by enslavement. There is a paradox here, and a mystery. Why should such multitudes of men and women be so ready to sacrifice themselves for a cause so utterly hopeless and in ways so painful and so profoundly humiliating?

To this riddle there is, of course, no simple or single answer. Human beings are immensely complicated creatures, living simultaneously in a half dozen different worlds. Each individual is unique and, in a number of respects, unlike all the other members of the species. None of our motives is unmixed, none of our actions can be traced back to a single source and, in any group we care to study, behavior patterns that are observably similar may be the result of many constellations of dissimilar causes.

Thus, there are some alcoholics who seem to have been biochemically predestined to alcoholism. (Among rats, as Prof. Roger Williams, of the University of Texas, has shown, some are born drunkards; some are born teetotalers and will never touch the stuff.) Other alcoholics have been foredoomed not by some inherited defect in their biochemical make-up, but by their neurotic reactions to distressing events in their childhood or adolescence. Again, others embark upon their course of slow suicide as a result of mere imitation and good fellowship because they have made such an "excellent adjustment to their group"—a process which, if the group happens to be criminal, idiotic or merely ignorant, can bring only disaster to the well-adjusted individual. Nor must we forget that large class of addicts who have taken to drugs or drink in order to escape from physical pain. Aspirin, let us remember, is a very recent invention. Until late in the Victorian era, "poppy and mandragora," along with henbane and ethyl alcohol, were the only pain relievers available to civilized man. Toothache, arthritis and neuralgia could, and frequently did, drive men and women to become opium addicts.

De Quincey, for example, first resorted to opium in order to relieve "excruciating rheumatic pains of the head." He swallowed his poppy and, an hour later, "What a resurrection from the lowest depths of the inner spirit! What an apocalypse!" And it was not merely that he felt no more pain. "This negative effect was swallowed up in the immensity of those positive effects which had opened up before me, in the abyss of divine enjoyment thus suddenly revealed. . . . Here was the secret of happiness, about which the philosophers had disputed for so many ages, at once discovered."

"Resurrection, apocalypse, divine enjoyment, happiness. . . ." De Quincey's words lead us to the very heart of our paradoxical mystery. The problem of drug addiction and excessive drinking is not merely a matter of chemistry and psychopathology, of relief from pain and conformity with a bad society. It is also a problem in metaphysics—a problem, one might almost say, in theology. In The Varieties of Religious Experience, William James has touched on these metaphysical aspects of addiction:

The sway of alcohol over mankind is unquestionably due to its power to stimulate the mystical faculties in human nature, usually crushed to earth by the cold facts and dry criticisms of the sober hour. Sobriety diminishes, discriminates and says no. Drunkenness expands, unites and says yes. It is in fact the great exciter of the *Yes* function in man. It brings its votary from the chill periphery of things into the radiant core. It makes him for the moment one with truth. Not through mere perversity do men run after it. To the poor and the unlettered it stands in the place of symphony concerts and literature; and it is part of the deeper mystery and tragedy of life that whiffs and gleams of something that we immediately recognize as excellent should be vouchsafed to so many of us only through the fleeting earlier phases of what, in its totality, is so degrading a poison. The drunken consciousness is one bit of the mystic consciousness, and our total opinion of it must find its place in our opinion of that larger whole.

William James was not the first to detect a likeness between drunkenness and the mystical and premystical states. On the day of Pentecost there were people who explained the strange behavior of the disciples by saying, "These men are full of new wine."

Peter soon undeceived them: "These are not drunken, as ye suppose, seeing it is but the third hour of the day. But this is that which was spoken by the prophet Joel. And it shall come to pass in the last days, saith God, I will pour out of my Spirit upon all flesh."

And it is not only by "the dry critics of the sober hour" that the state of God-intoxication has been likened to drunkenness. In their efforts to express the inexpressible, the great mystics themselves have done the same. Thus, St. Theresa of Avila tells us that she "regards the center of our soul as a cellar, into which God admits us as and when it pleases Him, so as to intoxicate us with the delicious wine of His grace."

Every fully developed religion exists simultaneously on several different levels. It exists as a set of abstract concepts about the world and its governance. It exists as a set of rites and sacraments, as a traditional method for manipulating the symbols, by means of which beliefs about the cosmic order are expressed. It exists as the feelings of love, fear and devotion evoked by this manipulation of symbols.

And finally it exists as a special kind of feeling or intuition —a sense of the oneness of all things in their divine principle, a realization (to use the language of Hindu theology) that "thou art That," a mystical experience of what seems self-evidently to be union with God.

The ordinary waking consciousness is a very useful and, on most occasions, an indispensable state of mind; but it is by no means the only form of consciousness, nor in all circumstances the best. Insofar as he transcends his ordinary self and his ordinary mode of awareness, the mystic is able to enlarge his vision, to look more deeply into the unfathomable miracle of existence.

The mystical experience is doubly valuable; it is valuable because it gives the experiencer a better understanding of himself and the world and because it may help him to lead a less self-centered and more creative life.

In hell, a great religious poet has written, the punishment of the lost is to be "their sweating selves, but worse." On earth we are not worse than we are; we are merely our sweating selves, period.

Alas, that is quite bad enough. We love ourselves to the point of idolatry; but we also intensely dislike ourselves—we find ourselves unutterably boring. Correlated with this distaste for the idolatrously worshiped self, there is in all of us a desire, sometimes latent, sometimes conscious and passionately expressed, to escape from the prison of our individuality, an urge to self-transcendence. It is to this urge that we owe mystical theology, spiritual exercises and yoga—to this, too, that we owe alcoholism and drug addiction.

Modern pharmacology has given us a host of new synthetics, but in the field of the naturally occurring mind changers it has made no radical discoveries. All the botanical sedatives, stimulants, vision revealers, happiness promoters and cosmic-consciousness arousers were found out thousands of years ago, before the dawn of history.

In many societies at many levels of civilization attempts have been made to fuse drug intoxication with God intoxication. In ancient Greece, for example, ethyl alcohol had its place in the established religion. Dionysus, or Bacchus, as he was often called, was a true divinity. His worshipers addressed him as *Lusios*, "Liberator," or as *Theoinos*, "God-wine." The latter name telescopes fermented grape juice and the supernatural into a single pentecostal experience. "Born a god," writes Euripides, "Bacchus is poured out as a libation to the gods, and through him men receive good." Unfortunately they also receive harm. The blissful experience of self-transcendence which alcohol makes possible has to be paid for, and the price is exorbitantly high.

Complete prohibition of all chemical mind changers can be decreed, but cannot be enforced, and tends to create more evils than it cures. Even more unsatisfactory has been the policy of complete toleration and unrestricted availability. In England, during the first years of the eighteenth century, cheap untaxed gin—"drunk for a penny, dead drunk for two-pence"—threatened society with complete demoralization. A century later, opium, in the form of laudanum, was reconciling the victims of the Industrial Revolution to their lot—but at an appalling cost in terms of addiction, illness and early death. Today most civilized societies follow a course between the two extremes of total prohibition and total toleration. Certain mind-changing drugs, such as alcohol, are permitted and made available to the public on payment of a very high tax, which tends to restrict their consumption. Other mind changers are unobtainable except under doctors' orders—or illegally from a dope pusher. In this way the problem is kept within manageable bounds. It is most certainly not solved. In their ceaseless search for self-transcendence, millions of would-be mystics become addicts, commit scores of thousands of crimes and are involved in hundreds of thousands of avoidable accidents.

Do we have to go on in this dismal way indefinitely? Up until a few years ago, the answer to such a question would have been a rueful "Yes, we do." Today, thanks to recent developments in biochemistry and pharmacology, we are offered a workable alternative. We see that it may soon be possible for us to do something better in the way of chemical self-transcendence than what we have been doing so ineptly for the last seventy or eighty centuries.

Is it possible for a powerful drug to be completely harmless? Perhaps not. But the physiological cost can certainly be reduced to the point where it becomes negligible. There are powerful mind changers which do their work without damaging the taker's psychophysical organism and without inciting him to behave like a criminal or a lunatic. Biochemistry and pharmacology are just getting into their stride. Within a few years there will probably be dozens of powerful but—physiologically and socially speaking—very inexpensive mind changers on the market.

In view of what we already have in the way of powerful but nearly harmless drugs; in view, above all, of what unquestionably we are very soon going to have—we ought to start immediately to give some serious thought to the problem of the new mind changers. How ought they to be used? How can they be abused? Will human beings be better and happier for their discovery? Or worse and more miserable?

The matter requires to be examined from many points of view. It is simultaneously a question for biochemists and physicians, for psychologists and social anthropologists, for legislators and law-enforcement officers. And finally it is an ethical question and a religious question. Sooner or later—and the sooner, the better—the various specialists concerned will have to meet, discuss and then decide, in the light of the best available evidence and the most imaginative kind of foresight, what should be done. Meanwhile let us take a preliminary look at this many-faceted problem.

Last year American physicians wrote 48,000,000 prescriptions for tranquilizing drugs, many of which have been refilled, probably more than once. The tranquilizers are the best known of the new, nearly harmless mind changers. They can be used by most people, not indeed with complete impunity, but at a reasonably low physiological cost. Their enormous popularity bears witness to the fact that a great many people dislike both their environment and "their sweating selves." Under tranquilizers the degree of their self-transcendence is not very great; but it is enough to make all the difference, in many cases, between misery and contentment.

In theory, tranquilizers should be given only to persons suffering from rather severe forms of neurosis or psychosis. In practice, unfortunately, many physicians have been carried away by the current pharmacological fashion and are prescribing tranquilizers to all and sundry. The history of medical fashions, it may be remarked, is at least as grotesque as the history of fashions in women's hats—at least as grotesque and, since human lives are at stake, considerably more tragic. In the present case, millions of patients who had no real need of the tranquilizers have been given the pills by their doctors and have learned to resort to them in every predicament, however triflingly uncomfortable. This is very bad medicine and, from the pill taker's point of view, dubious morality and poor sense.

There are circumstances in which even the healthy are justified in resorting to the chemical control of negative emotions. If you really can't keep your temper, let a tranquilizer keep it for you. But for healthy people to resort to a chemical mind changer every time they feel annoyed or anxious or tense is neither sensible nor right. Too much tension and anxiety can reduce a man's efficiency—but so can too little. There are many occasions when it is entirely proper for us to feel concerned, when an excess of placidity might reduce our chances of dealing effectively with a ticklish situation. On these occasions, tension mitigated and directed from within by the psychological methods of self-control is preferable from every point of view to complacency imposed from without by the methods of chemical control.

And now let us consider the case—not, alas, a hypothetical case—of two societies competing with each other. In Society A, tranquilizers are available by prescription and at a rather stiff price—which means, in practice, that their use is confined to that rich and influential minority which provides the society with its leadership. This minority of leading citizens consumes several billions of the complacency-producing pills every year. In Society B, on the other hand, the tranquilizers are not so freely available, and the members of the influential minority do not resort, on the slightest provocation, to the chemical control of what may be necessary and productive tension. Which of these two competing societies is likely to win the race? A society whose leaders make an excessive use of soothing syrups is in danger of falling behind a society whose leaders are not overtranquilized.

Now let us consider another kind of drug—still undiscovered, but probably just around the corner—a drug capable of making people feel happy in situations where they would normally feel miserable. Such a drug would be a blessing, but a blessing fraught with grave political dangers. By making harmless chemical euphoria freely available, a dictator could reconcile an entire population to a state of affairs to which self-respecting human beings ought not to be reconciled. Despots have always found it necessary to supplement force by political or religious propaganda. In this sense the pen is mightier than the sword. But mightier than either the pen or the sword is the pill. In mental hospitals it has been found that chemical restraint is far more effective than strait jackets or psychiatry. The dictatorships of tomorrow will deprive men of their freedom, but will give them in exchange a happiness none the less real, as a subjective experience, for being chemically induced. The pursuit of happiness is one of the traditional rights of man; unfortunately, the achievement of happiness may turn out to be incompatible with another of man's rights—namely, liberty.

It is quite possible, however, that pharmacology will restore with one hand what it takes away with the other. Chemically induced euphoria could easily become a threat to individual liberty; but chemically induced vigor and chemically heightened intelligence could easily be liberty's strongest bulwark. Most of us function at about 15 per cent of capacity. How can we step up our lamentably low efficiency?

Two methods are available—the educational and the biochemical. We can take adults and children as they are and give them a much better training than we are giving them now. Or, by appropriate biochemical methods, we can transform them into superior individuals. If these superior individuals are given a superior education, the results will be revolutionary. They will be startling even if we continue to subject them to the rather poor educational methods at present in vogue.

Will it in fact be possible to produce superior individuals by biochemical means? The Russians certainly believe it. They are now halfway through a Five Year Plan to produce "pharmacological substances that normalize higher nervous activity and heighten human capacity for work." Precursors of these future mind improvers are already being experimented with. It has been found, for example, that when given in massive doses some of the vitamins—nicotinic acid and ascorbic acid for example—sometimes produce a certain heightening of psychic energy. A combination of two enzymes—ethylene disulphonate and adenosine triphosphate, which, when injected together, improve carbohydrate metabolism in nervous tissue —may also turn out to be effective.

Meanwhile good results are being claimed for various new synthetic, nearly harmless stimulants. There is iproniazid, which, according to some authorities, "appears to increase the total amount of psychic energy." Unfortunately, iproniazid in large doses has side effects which in some cases may be extremely serious! Another psychic energizer is an amino alcohol which is thought to increase the body's production of acetylcholine, a substance of prime importance in the functioning of the nervous system. In view of what has already been achieved, it seems quite possible that, within a few years, we may be able to lift ourselves up by our own biochemical bootstraps.

In the meantime let us all fervently wish the Russians every success in their current pharmacological venture. The discovery of a drug capable of increasing the average individual's psychic energy, and its wide distribution throughout the U.S.S.R., would probably mean the end of Russia's present form of government. Generalized intelligence and mental alertness are the most powerful enemies of dictatorship and at the same time the basic conditions of effective democracy. Even in the democratic West we could do with a bit of psychic energizing. Between them, education and pharmacology may do something to offset the effects of that deterioration of our biological material to which geneticists have frequently called attention.

From these political and ethical considerations let us now pass to the strictly religious problems that will be posed by some of the new mind changers. We can foresee the nature of these future problems by studying the effects of a natural mind changer, which has been used for centuries past in religious worship; I refer to the peyote cactus of Northern Mexico and the Southwestern United States. Peyote contains mescaline—which can now be produced synthetically—and mescaline, in William James' phrase, "stimulates the mystical faculties in human nature" far more powerfully and in a far more enlightening way than alcohol and, what is more, it does so at a physiological and social cost that is negligibly low. Peyote produces self-transcendence in two ways—it introduces the taker into the Other World of visionary experience, and it gives him a sense of solidarity with his fellow worshipers, with human beings at large and with the divine nature of things.

The effects of peyote can be duplicated by synthetic mescaline and by LSD (lysergic acid diethylamide), a derivative of ergot. Effective in incredibly small doses, LSD is now being used experimentally by psychotherapists in Europe, in South America, in Canada and the United States. It lowers the barrier between conscious and subconscious and permits the patient to look more deeply and understandingly into the recesses of his own mind. The deepening of self-knowledge takes place against a background of visionary and even mystical experience.

When administered in the right kind of psychological environment, these chemical mind changers make possible a genuine religious experience. Thus a person who takes LSD or mescaline may suddenly understand—not only intellectually but organically, experientially—the meaning of such tremendous religious affirmations as "God is love," or "Though He slay me, yet will I trust in Him."

It goes without saying that this kind of temporary self-transcendence is no guarantee of permanent enlightenment or a lasting improvement of conduct. It is a "gratuitous grace," which is neither necessary nor sufficient for salvation, but which if properly used, can be enormously helpful to those who have received it. And this is true of all such experiences, whether occurring spontaneously, or as the result of swallowing the right kind of chemical mind changer, or after undertaking a course of "spiritual exercises" or bodily mortification.

Those who are offended by the idea that the swallowing of a pill may contribute to a genuinely religious experience should remember that all the standard mortifications—fasting, voluntary sleeplessness and self-torture—inflicted upon themselves by the ascetics of every religion for the purpose of acquiring merit, are also, like the mind-changing drugs, powerful devices for altering the chemistry of the body in general and the nervous system in particular. Or consider the procedures generally known as spiritual exercises. The breathing techniques taught by the yogi of India result in prolonged suspensions of respiration. These in turn result in an increased concentration of carbon dioxide in the blood; and the psychological consequence of this is a change in the quality of consciousness. Again, meditations involving long, intense concentration upon a single idea or image may also result— for neurological reasons which I do not profess to understand —in a slowing down of respiration and even in prolonged suspensions of breathing.

Many ascetics and mystics have practiced their chemistry-changing mortifications and spiritual exercises while living, for longer or shorter periods, as hermits. Now, the life of a hermit, such as Saint Anthony, is a life in which there are very few external stimuli. But as Hebb, John Lilly and other experimental psychologists have recently shown in the laboratory, a person in a limited environment, which provides very few external stimuli, soon undergoes a change in the quality of his consciousness and may transcend his normal self to the point of hearing voices or seeing visions, often extremely unpleasant, like so many of Saint Anthony's visions, but sometimes beatific.

That men and women can, by physical and chemical means, transcend themselves in a genuinely spiritual way is something which, to the squeamish idealist, seems rather shocking. But, after all, the drug or the physical exercise is not the cause of the spiritual experience; it is only its occasion.

Writing of William James' experiments with nitrous oxide, Bergson has summed up the whole matter in a few lucid sentences. "The psychic disposition was there, potentially, only waiting a signal to express itself in action. It might have been evoked spiritually by an effort made on its own spiritual level. But it could just as well be brought about materially, by an inhibition of what inhibited it, by the removing of an obstacle; and this effect was the wholly negative one produced by the drug." Where, for any reason, physical or moral, the psychological dispositions are unsatisfactory, the removal of obstacles by a drug or by ascetic practices will result in a negative rather than a positive spiritual experience. Such an infernal experience is extremely distressing, but may also be extremely salutary. There are plenty of people to whom a few hours in hell—the hell that they themselves have done so much to create—could do a world of good.

Physiologically costless, or nearly costless, stimulators of the mystical faculties are now making their appearance, and many kinds of them will soon be on the market. We can be quite sure that, as and when they become available, they will be extensively used. The urge to self-transcendence is so strong and so general that it cannot be otherwise. In the past, very few people have had spontaneous experiences of a premystical or fully mystical nature; still fewer have been willing to undergo the psychophysical disciplines which prepare an insulated individual for this kind of self-transcendence. The powerful but nearly costless mind changers of the future will change all this completely. Instead of being rare, premystical and mystical experiences will become common. What was once the spiritual privilege of the few will be made available to the many. For the ministers of the world's organized religions, this will raise a number of unprecedented problems. For most people, religion has always been a matter of traditional symbols and of their own emotional, intellectual and ethical response to those symbols. To men and women who have had direct experience of self-transcendence into the mind's Other World of vision and union with the nature of things, a religion of mere symbols is not likely to be very satisfying. The perusal of a page from even the most beautifully written cookbook is no substitute for the eating of dinner. We are exhorted to "*taste* and see that the Lord is good."

In one way or another, the world's ecclesiastical authorities will have to come to terms with the new mind changers. They may come to terms with them negatively, by refusing to have anything to do with them. In that case, a psychological phenomenon, potentially of great spiritual value, will manifest itself outside the pale of organized religion. On the other hand, they may choose to come to terms with the mind

changers in some positive way—exactly how, I am not prepared to guess.

My own belief is that, though they may start by being
something of an embarrassment, these new mind changers will
tend in the long run to deepen the spiritual life of the communities in which they are available. That famous "revival
of religion," about which so many people have been talking
for so long, will not come about as the result of evangelistic
mass meetings or the television appearances of photogenic
clergymen. It will come about as the result of biochemical
discoveries that will make it possible for large numbers of
men and women to achieve a radical self-transcendence and
a deeper understanding of the nature of things. And this
revival of religion will be at the same time a revolution.
From being an activity mainly concerned with symbols,
religion will be transformed into an activity concerned mainly
with experience and intuition—an everyday mysticism underlying and giving significance to everyday rationality, everyday
tasks and duties, everyday human relationships.

(From *The Saturday Evening Post*)

WAY OF LIFE

Holy Face

Good Times are chronic nowadays. There is dancing every afternoon, a continuous performance at all the picture-palaces, a radio concert on tap, like gas or water, at any hour of the day or night. The fine point of seldom pleasure is duly blunted. Feasts must be solemn and rare, or else they cease to be feasts. "Like stones of worth they thinly placed are" (or, at any rate, they were in Shakespeare's day, which was the day of Merry England), "or captain jewels in the carconet." The ghosts of these grand occasional jollifications still haunt our modern year. But the stones of worth are indistinguishable from the loud imitation jewelry which now adorns the entire circlet of days. Gems, when they are too large and too numerous, lose all their precious significance; the treasure of an Indian prince is as unimpressive as Aladdin's cave at the pantomime. Set in the midst of the stage diamonds and rubies of modern pleasure, the old feasts are hardly visible. It is only among more or less completely rustic populations, lacking the means and the opportunity to indulge in the modern chronic Good Time, that the surviving feasts preserve something of their ancient glory. Me personally the unflagging pleasures of contemporary cities leave most lugubriously unamused. The prevailing boredom—for oh, how desperately bored, in spite of their grim determination to have a Good Time, the majority of pleasure-seekers really are!—the hopeless weariness, infect me. Among the lights, the alcohol, the hideous jazz noises, and the incessant movement I feel myself sinking into deeper and ever deeper despondency. By com-

347

parison with a night-club, churches are positively gay. If ever I want to make merry in public, I go where merry-making is occasional and the merriment, therefore, of genuine quality; I go where feasts come rarely.

For one who would frequent only the occasional festivities, the great difficulty is to be in the right place at the right time. I have traveled through Belgium and found, in little market towns, kermesses that were orgiastic like the merry-making in a Breughel picture. But how to remember the date? And how, remembering it, to be in Flanders again at the appointed time? The problem is almost insoluble. And then there is Frogmore. The nineteenth-century sculpture in the royal mausoleum is reputed to be the most amazing of its amazing kind. I should like to see Frogmore. But the anniversary of Queen Victoria's death is the only day in the year when the temple is open to the public. The old queen died, I believe, in January. But what was the precise date? And, if one enjoys the blessed liberty to be elsewhere, how shall one reconcile oneself to being in England at such a season? Frogmore, it seems, will have to remain unvisited. And there are many other places, many other dates and days, which, alas, I shall always miss. I must even be resignedly content with the few festivities whose times I can remember and whose scene coincides, more or less, with that of my existence in each particular portion of the year.

One of these rare and solemn dates which I happen never to forget is September the thirteenth. It is the feast of the Holy Face of Lucca. And since Lucca is within thirty miles of the seaside place where I spend the summer, and since the middle of September is still serenely and transparently summer by the shores of the Mediterranean, the feast of the Holy Face is counted among the captain jewels of my year. At the religious function and the ensuing fair I am, each September, a regular attendant.

"By the Holy Face of Lucca!" It was William the Conqueror's favorite oath. And if I were in the habit of cursing and swearing, I think it would also be mine. For it is a fine oath, admirable both in form and substance. "By the Holy Face of Lucca!" In whatever language you pronounce them, the words reverberate, they rumble with the rumbling of genuine poetry. And for any one who has ever seen the Holy Face, how pregnant they are with power and magical compulsion! For the Face, the Holy Face of Lucca, is certainly the strangest, the most impressive thing of its kind I have ever seen.

Imagine a huge wooden Christ, larger than life, not naked, as in later representations of the Crucifixion, but dressed in a long tunic, formally fluted with stiff Byzantine folds. The face is not the face of a dead, or dying, or even suffering man. It is the face of a man still violently alive, and the expression of its strong features is stern, is fierce, is even rather sinister. From the dark sockets of polished cedar wood two yellowish tawny eyes, made, apparently, of some precious stone, or perhaps of glass, stare out, slightly squinting, with an unsleeping balefulness. Such is the Holy Face. Tradition affirms it to be a true, contemporary portrait. History establishes the fact that it has been in Lucca for the best part of twelve hundred years. It is said that a rudderless and crewless ship miraculously brought it from Palestine to the beaches of Luni. The inhabitants of Sarzana claimed the sacred flotsam; but the Holy Face did not wish to go to Sarzana. The oxen harnessed to the wagon in which it had been placed were divinely inspired to take the road to Lucca. And at Lucca the Face has remained ever since, working miracles, drawing crowds of pilgrims, protecting and at intervals failing to protect the city of its adoption from harm. Twice a year, at Easter time and on the thirteenth of September, the doors of its little domed tabernacle in the cathedral are thrown open, the candles are lighted, and the dark and formidable image, dressed up for the occasion in a jeweled overall and with a glittering crown on its head, stares down—with who knows what mysterious menace in its bright squinting eyes?—on the throng of its worshipers.

The official act of worship is a most handsome function. A little after sunset a procession of clergy forms up in the church of San Frediano. In the ancient darkness of the basilica a few candles light up the liturgical ballet. The stiff embroidered vestments, worn by generations of priests and from which the heads and hands of the present occupants emerge with an air of almost total irrelevance (for it is the sacramental carapace that matters; the little man who momentarily fills it is without significance), move hieratically hither and thither through the rich light and the velvet shadows. Under his baldaquin the jeweled old archbishop is a museum specimen. There is a forest of silvery mitres, spear-shaped against the darkness (bishops seem to be plentiful in Lucca). The choir boys wear lace and scarlet. There is a guard of halberdiers in a gaudily-pied medieval uniform. The ritual charade is solemnly danced through. The procession emerges from the dark church into the twilight of the streets. The municipal band strikes up loud inappropriate music. We hurry off to the cathedral by a short cut to take our places for the function.

The Holy Face has always had a partiality for music. Yearly, through all these hundreds of years, it has been sung to and played at, it has been treated to symphonies, cantatas, solos on every instrument. During the eighteenth century the most celebrated *castrati* came from the ends of Italy to warble to it; the most eminent professors of the violin, the flute, the oboe, the trombone scraped and blew before its shrine. Paganini himself, when he was living in Lucca in the court of Elisa Bonaparte, performed at the annual concerts in honor of the Face. Times have changed, and the image must now be content with local talent and a lower standard of musical excellence. True, the good will is always there; the Lucchesi continue to do their musical best; but their best is generally no more nor less than just dully creditable. Not always, however. I shall never forget what happened during my first visit to the Face. The musical program that year was ambitious. There was to be a rendering, by choir and orchestra, of one of those vast oratorios which the clerical musician, Dom Perosi, composes in a strange and rather frightful mixture of the musical idioms of Palestrina, Wagner, and Verdi. The orchestra was enormous; the choir was numbered by the hundred; we waited in pleased anticipation for the music to begin. But when it did begin, what an astounding pandemonium! Everybody played and sang like mad, but without apparently any reference to the playing and singing of anybody else. Of all the musical performances I have ever listened to it was the most Manchester-Liberal, the most Victorian-democratic. The conductor stood in the midst of them waving his arms; but he was only a constitutional monarch—for show, not use. The performers had revolted against his despotism. Nor had they permitted themselves to be regimented into Prussian uniformity by any soul-destroying excess of rehearsal. Godwin's prophetic vision of a perfectly individualistic concert was here actually realized. The noise was hair-raising. But the performers were making it with so much gusto that, in the end, I was infected by their high spirits and enjoyed the hullabaloo almost as much as they did. That concert was symptomatic of the general anarchy of post-war Italy. Those times are now past. The Fascists have come, bringing order and discipline—even to the arts. When the Lucchesi play and sing to their Holy Face, they do it now with decorum, in a thoroughly professional and well-drilled manner. It is admirable, but dull. There are times, I must confess, when I regret the loud delirious blaring and bawling of the days of anarchy.

Almost more interesting than the official acts of worship are the unofficial, the private and individual acts. I have spent hours in the cathedral watching the crowd before the shrine. The great church is full from morning till night. Men and

women, young and old, they come in their thousands, from
the town, from all the country round, to gaze on the authentic
image of God. And the image is dark, threatening, and sinister. In the eyes of the worshipers I often detected a certain
meditative disquiet. Not unnaturally. For if the face of Providence should really and in truth be like the Holy Face, why,
then—then life is certainly no joke. Anxious to propitiate
this rather appalling image of Destiny, the worshipers come
pressing up to the shrine to deposit a little offering of silver
or nickel and kiss the reliquary proffered to every almsgiver
by the attendant priest. For two francs fifty perhaps Fate
will be kind. But the Holy Face continues, unmoved, to squint
inscrutable menace. Fixed by that sinister regard, and with
the smell of incense in his nostrils, the darkness of the church
around and above him, the most ordinary man begins to feel
himself obscurely a Pascal. Metaphysical gulfs open before
him. The mysteries of human destiny, of the future, of the
purpose of life oppress and terrify his soul. The church is
dark; but in the midst of the darkness is a little island of
candlelight. Oh, comfort! But from the heart of the comforting
light, incongruously jeweled, the dark face stares with squinting eyes, appalling, balefully mysterious.

But luckily, for those of us who are not Pascal, there is
always a remedy. We can always turn our back on the Face,
we can always leave the hollow darkness of the church. Outside, the sunlight pours down out of a flawless sky. The
streets are full of people in their holiday best. At one of the
gates of the city, in an open space beyond the walls, the
merry-go-rounds are turning, the steam organs are playing
the tunes that were popular four years ago on the other side
of the Atlantic, the fat woman's drawers hang unmoving, like
a huge forked pennon, in the windless air outside her booth.
There is a crowd, a smell, an unceasing noise—music and
shouting, roaring of circus lions, giggling of tickled girls,
squealing from the switchback of deliciously frightened girls,
laughing and whistling, tooting of cardboard trumpets, crack-
ing of guns in the rifle-range, breaking of crockery, howling
of babies, all blended together to form the huge and formless
sound of human happiness. Pascal was wise, but wise too
consciously, with too consistent a spirituality. For him the
Holy Face was always present, haunting him with its dark
menace, with the mystery of its baleful eyes. And if ever,
in a moment of distraction, he forgot the metaphysical horror
of the world and those abysses at his feet, it was with a pang
of remorse that he came again to himself, to the self of
spiritual consciousness. He thought it right to be haunted, he
refused to enjoy the pleasures of the created world, he liked

walking among the gulfs. In his excess of conscious wisdom
he was mad; for he sacrificed life to principles, to metaphysical abstractions, to the overmuch spirituality which is the
negation of existence. He preferred death to life. Incomparably
grosser and stupider than Pascal, almost immeasurably his
inferiors, the men and women who move with shouting and
laughter through the dusty heat of the fair are yet more wise
than the philosopher. They are wise with the unconscious
wisdom of the species, with the dumb, instinctive, physical
wisdom of life itself. For it is life itself that, in the interests
of living, commands them to be inconsistent. It is life itself
that, having made them obscurely aware of Pascal's gulfs and
horrors, bids them turn away from the baleful eyes of the
Holy Face, bids them walk out of the dark, hushed, incense-
smelling church into the sunlight, into the dust and whirling
motion, the sweaty smell and the vast chaotic noise of the
fair. It is life itself; and I, for one, have more confidence in
the rightness of life than in that of any individual man, even
if the man be Pascal.

(From Do What You Will)

Pascal

Life and the Routine of Living

It is worth remarking that the revelation of life confirms many
of the revelations of death.* The business and the distractions
which Pascal hated so much, because they made men forget
that they must die, are hateful to the life-worshiper because
they prevent men from fully living. Death makes these distractions seem trivial and silly; but equally so does life. It
was from pain and gradually approaching dissolution that
Ivan Ilyitch learned to understand the futility of his respectable bourgeois career. If he had ever met a genuinely living
man, if he had ever read a book, or looked at a picture, or
heard a piece of music by a living artist, he would have
learned the same lesson. But Pascal and the later Tolstoy
would not permit the revelation to come from life. Their aim
was to humiliate men by rolling them in the corruption of the
grave, to inflict a defiling punishment on them; they condemned, not only the distracting, life-destroying futilities with
which men fill their days, but also the life which these futilities

---

* I have borrowed the phrase from Shestov. 'La Révélation de la Mort' is
the title, in its French translation, of one of his most interesting books.

destroyed. The life-worshiper agrees with them in hating the
empty fooleries and sordidnesses of average human existence.
Incidentally the progress of science and industry has enormously increased the element of foolery and sordidness in
human life. The clerk and the taylorized workman leave their
imbecile tasks to spend their leisure under the influence of
such opiate distractions as are provided by the newspaper,
the cinema, the radio; they are given less and less opportunity
to do any active or creative living of their own. Pascal and
Tolstoy would have led them from silliness to despair by talking to them of death; but "memento vivere" is the life-worshiper's advice. If people remembered to live, they would
abstain from occupations which are mere substitutes for life.

The Life-Worshiper's Creed

The life-worshiper's philosophy is comprehensive. As a manifold and discontinuous being, he is in a position to accept all
the partial and apparently contradictory syntheses constructed
by other philosophers. He is at one moment a positivist and
at another a mystic: now haunted by the thought of death
(for the apocalypse of death is one of the incidents of living)
and now a Dionysian child of nature; now a pessimist and
now, with a change of lover or liver or even the weather, an
exuberant believer that God's in his heaven and all's right with
the world. He holds these different beliefs because he is many
different people. Each belief is the rationalization of the prevailing mood of one of these persons. There is really no
question of any of these philosophies being true or false. The
psychological state called joy is no truer than the psychological state called melancholy (it may be more valuable as an
aid to social or individual living—but that is another matter).
Each is a primary fact of experience. And since one psychological state cannot be truer than another, since all are equally
facts, it follows that the rationalization of one state cannot be
truer than the rationalization of another. What Hardy says
about the universe is no truer than what Meredith says; if the
majority of contemporary readers prefer the world-view
expressed in *Tess of the D'Urbervilles* to the optimism which
forms the background to *Beauchamp's Career*, that is simply
because they happen to live in a very depressing age and
consequently suffer from a more or less chronic melancholy.
Hardy seems to them truer than Meredith because the philosophy of "Tess" and "Jude" is more adequate as a rationalization
of their own prevailing mood than the philosophy of Richard
Feverel or Beauchamp. What applies to optimism and pessimism applies equally to other trends of philosophical thought.

Even the doctrines of "fixed fate, free will, foreknowledge absolute," for all the elaborateness of their form, are in substance only expression of emotional and physiological states. One feels free or one feels conditioned. Both feelings are equally facts of experience, so are the facts called "mystical ecstasy" and "reasonableness." Only a man whose life was rich in mystical experiences could have constructed a cosmogony like that of Boehme's; and the works of Voltaire could have been written only by one whose life was singularly poor in such experiences. People with strongly marked idiosyncrasies of character have their world-view almost forced upon them by their psychology. The only branches of philosophy in regard to which it is permissible to talk of truth and falsehood are logic and the theory of knowledge. For logic and the theory of knowledge are concerned with the necessities and the limitations of thought—that is to say, with mental habits so primordial that it is all but impossible for any human being to break them. When a man commits a paralogism or lays claim to a more than human knowledge of the nature of things, we are justified in saying that he is wrong. I may, for example, admit that all men are mortal and that Socrates is a man, but nevertheless feel impelled to conclude that Socrates is immortal. Am I not as well justified in this opinion as I am in my optimism or pessimism, whichever the case may be? The answer is: no. I may have a personal taste for Socrates's immortality; but, in the syllogistic circumstances, the taste is so outrageously bad, so universally condemned, that it would be madness to try to justify it. Moreover, I should discover that, if I put my paralogistic theories into practice, I should find myself in serious trouble, not only with other human beings, but even with things. The hero of Dostoievsky's *Notes from Underground* protests against the intolerable tyranny of two and two making four. He prefers that they shall make five, and insists that he has a right to his preference. And no doubt he has a right. But if an express train happens to be passing at a distance of two plus two yards, and he advances four yards and a half under the impression that he will still be eighteen inches on the hither side of destruction, this right of his will not save him from coming to a violent and bloody conclusion.

Scientific thought is true or false because science deals with sense impressions which are, if not identical for all human beings, at least sufficiently similar to make something like universal agreement possible. The difference between a scientific theory and a metaphysical world-view is that the first is a rationalization of psychological experiences which are more or less uniform for all men and for the same man at different times, while the second is a rationalization of experiences which are diverse, occasional, and contradictory. A man may be a pessimistic determinist before lunch and an optimistic believer in the will's freedom after it; but both before and after his meal he will observe that the color of the sky is blue, that stones are hard, that the sun gives light and warmth. It is for this reason that there are many philosophies, and only one science.

But even science demands that its votaries shall think, according to circumstances, in a variety of different ways. The mode of thinking which gives valid results when applied to objects of more than a certain size (in other words, to large numbers of objects; for anything big enough to be perceptible to our senses is built up, apparently, of enormous numbers of almost infinitesimal components) is found to be absolutely inapplicable to single objects of atomic or subatomic dimensions. About large agglomerations of atoms we can think in terms of "organized common sense." But when we come to consider individual atoms and their minuter components, common-sense gives results which do not square with the observed facts. (Nobody, of course, has ever actually observed an atom or an electron; but the nature of their behavior can be inferred, with more or less probability, from such happenings on a macroscopical scale as accompany their invisible activity.) In the sub-atomic world practically all our necessities of thought become not only unnecessary but misleading. A description of this universe reads like a page from Lewis Carroll or Edward Lear.

Seeing, then, that even sense impressions not only can but must be rationalized in irreconcilably different ways, according to the class of object with which they are supposed to be connected, we need not be troubled or surprised by the contradictions which we find in the rationalization of less uniform psychological experiences. Thus, the almost indefinitely numerous rationalizations of the aesthetic and the mystical experiences not only contradict one another, but agree in contradicting those rationalizations of sense experience known as scientific theories. This fact greatly disturbed our grandfathers, who kept on losing their faith, sacrificing their reason, striking attitudes of stoical despair, and, in general, performing the most extraordinary spiritual antics, because of it. Science is "true," they argued; therefore art and religion, therefore beauty and honor, love and ideals, must be "false." "Reality" has been "proved" by science to be an affair of space, time, mass, number, and cause; therefore all that makes life worth living is an "illusion." Or else they started from the other end. Art, religion, beauty, love, make life worth living;

therefore science, which disregards the existence of these things, must be false. It is unnecessary for us to take so tragic a view. Science, we have come to realize, takes no cognizance of the things that make life worth living, for the simple reason that beauty, love, and so on, are not measurable quantities, and science deals only with what can be measured. One psychological fact is as good as another. We perceive beauty as immediately as we perceive hardness; to say that one sensation is illusory and that the other corresponds with reality is a gratuitous piece of presumption.

Answers to the riddle of the universe often have a logical form and are expressed in such a way that they raise questions of epistemology and involve the acceptance or rejection of certain scientific theories. In substance, however, they are simply rationalizations of diverse and equally valid psychological states, and are therefore neither true nor false. (Incidentally, similar states are not necessarily or invariably rationalized in the same way. Mystical experiences which, in Europe, are explained in terms of a personal God are interpreted by the Buddhists in terms of an entirely godless order of things. Which is the truer rationalization? God, or not-God, whichever the case may be, knows.) The life-worshiper who adopts in turn all the solutions to the cosmic riddle is committing no crime against logic or the truth. He is simply admitting the obvious fact that he is a human being—that is to say, a series of distinct psychological states, a colony of diverse personalities. Each state demands its appropriate rationalizations; or, in other words, each personality has its own philosophies of life. Philosophical consistency had some justification so long as it could be imagined that the substance of one's world-view (as opposed to the logical trappings in which it was clothed and the problems of epistemology and science connected with it) was uniquely true. But if we admit, as I think we must, that one world-view cannot be truer than another, but that each is the expression in intellectual terms of some given and undeniable fact of experience, then consistency loses all philosophical merit. It is pointless to ignore all the occasions when you feel that the world is good, for the sake of being consistently a pessimist; it is pointless, for the sake of being consistently a positivist, to deny that your body is sometimes tenanted by a person who has mystical experiences. Pessimism is no truer than optimism, nor positivism than mysticism. Philosophically, there is no reason why a man should deny the thoughts of all but one of his potential selves. Each self on occasion exists; each has its feelings about the universe, its cosmic tastes—or, to put it in a different way, each inhabits its own universe. What relation these various private universes bear to the Universe in Itself, if such a thing exists, it is clearly impossible to say. We can believe, if we like, that each of them represents one aspect of the whole. "In my Father's house are many mansions." Nature has given to each individual the key to quite a number of these metaphysical mansions. The life-worshiper suggests that man shall make use of all his keys instead of throwing all but one of them away. He admits the fact of vital diversity and makes the best of it. In this he is unlike the general run of thinkers, who are very reluctant to admit diversity, and, if they do confess the fact, deplore it. They find diversity shocking, they desire at all costs to correct it. And even if it came to be universally admitted that no one world-view could possibly be true, these people would continue, none the less, to hold fast to one to the exclusion of all the rest. They would go on worshiping consistency, if not on philosophical, then on moral grounds. Or, in other words, they would practice and demand consistency through fear of inconsistency, through fear of being dangerously free, through fear of life. For morality is always the product of terror; its chains and strait-waistcoats are fashioned by those who dare not trust others, because they dare not trust themselves, to walk in liberty. By such poor terror-stricken creatures consistency in thought and conduct is prized among the highest virtues. In order to achieve this consistency they reject as untrue, or as immoral or antisocial (it matters not which; for any stick will serve to beat a dog), all the thoughts which do not harmonize with the particular system they have elected to defend; they do their best to repress all impulses and desires which cannot be fitted into their scheme of moral behavior. With what deplorable results!

Pascal, the Death-Worshiper

The consistent thinker, the consistently moral man, is either a walking mummy or else, if he has not succeeded in stifling all his vitality, a fanatical monomaniac. (By the admirers of consistency the mummies are called "serene" or "stoical," the monomaniacs "single-minded"—as though single-mindedness were a virtue in a being to whom bountiful nature has given a multiple mind! Single-mindedness is all very well in cows or baboons; in an animal claiming to belong to the same species as Shakespeare it is simply disgraceful.)

In spite of all his heroic efforts, Pascal never succeeded in entirely suppressing the life that was in him. It was not in his power to turn himself into a pious automaton. Vitality continued to flow out of him, but through only one channel. He became a monomaniac, a man with but one aim—to impose the death of Christian spirituality on himself and all his fellows. "What religion," he asks, "will teach us to cure pride and concupiscence?" In other words, what religion will cure us of living? For concupiscence, or desire, is the instrument of life, and "the pride of the peacock is the glory of God"— not of Pascal's God, of course, but of the God of Life. Christianity, he concludes, is the only religion which will cure men of living. Therefore all men must become Christians. Pascal expended all his extraordinary powers in trying, by persuasion, by argument, to convert his fellows to consistent death-worship. It was with the *Provincial Letters* that he opened the campaign. With what consummate generalship! The casuists were routed with terrific slaughter. Entranced by that marvelous prose, we find ourselves even now believing that their defeat was merited, that Pascal was in the right. But if we stop our ears to the charmer's music and consider only the substance of what he says, we shall realize that the rights were all on the side of the Jesuits and that Pascal was using his prodigious talents to make the worse appear the better cause. The casuists were often silly and pedantic. But their conception of morality was, from a life-worshiper's point of view, entirely sound. Recognizing the diversity of human beings, the infinite variety of circumstances, they perceived that every case should be considered on its own merits. Life was to be tethered, but with an elastic rope; it was to be permitted to do a little gamboling. To Pascal this libertarianism seemed horrible. There must be no compromise with life; the hideous thing must be ruthlessly suppressed. Men must be bound down by rigid commandments, coffined in categorical imperatives, paralyzed by the fear of hell and the incessant contemplation of death, buried under mounds of prohibitions. He said so with such exquisite felicity of phrase and cadence that people have gone on imagining, from that day to this, that he was upholding a noble cause, when in fact he was fighting for the powers of darkness.

After the *Letters* came the *Pensées*—the fragmentary materials of what was to have been a colossal work of Christian apology. Implacably the fight against life continued. "Admiration spoils everything from childhood onwards. Oh, isn't he clever! Isn't he good! The children of the Port Royal school, who are not urged on with this spur of envy and glory, sink into indifference." Pascal must have been delighted. A system of education which resulted in children sinking into "la nonchalance" was obviously, in his eyes, almost ideal. If the children had quietly withered up into mummies, it would have been absolutely perfect. The man was to be treated to the same deadening influences as the child. It was first to be

demonstrated that he lived in a state of hopeless wretched-
ness. This is a task which Pascal undertook with the greatest
satisfaction. All his remarks on the "misère de l'homme" are
magnificent. But what is this misery? When we examine
Pascal's arguments we find that man's misery consists in not
being something different from a man. In not being simple,
consistent, without desires, omniscient and dead, but on the
contrary alive and full of concupiscence, uncertain, inconsistent, multiple. But to blame a thing for not being something
else is childish. Sheep are not men; but that is no reason for
talking about the "misère du mouton." Let sheep make the
best of their sheepishness and men of their humanity. But
Pascal does not want men to make the best of their human
life; he wants them to make the worst of it, to throw it away.
After depressing them with his remarks about misery, he
brings them into paralyzing contact with death and infinity;
he demonstrates the nothingness, in the face of this darkness,
these immensities, of every thought, action, and desire. To
clinch the argument he invokes the Jansenist God, the Christian revelation. If it is man's true nature to be consistent and
undesiring, then (such is Pascal's argument) Jansenistic death-
worship is a psychological necessity. It is more than a psychological necessity; death-worship has been made obligatory
by the God of Death in person, has been decreed in a revelation which Pascal undertakes to prove indubitably historical.

Pascal's Universe

The spectacle of so much malignity, so much hatred, is
profoundly repulsive. Hate begets hate, and it is difficult not
to detest Pascal for his venomous detestation of everything
that is beautiful and noble in human existence. It is a detestation, however, which must be tempered with pity. If the man
sinned against the Holy Ghost—and surely few men have
sinned like Pascal, since few indeed have been endowed with
Pascal's extraordinary gifts—it was because he could not
help it.

His desires, in Blake's words, were weak enough to be
restrained. Feeble, a sick man, he was afraid of life, he dreaded
liberty. Acquainted only with the mystical states that are
associated with malady and deprivation, this ascetic had never
experienced those other, no less significant, states that accompany the fulfillment of desire. For if we admit the significance
of the mystical rapture, we must equally admit the significance
of the no less prodigious experiences associated with love in
all its forms, with the perception of sensuous beauty, with
intoxication, with rhythmic movement, with anger, with strife

and triumph, with all the positive manifestations of concupiscent life. Ascetic practices produce a condition of abnormality and so enable the ascetic to get out of the ordinary world into another and, as he feels, more significant and important universe. Anger, the feeling inspired by sensuous beauty, the orgasm of amorous desire, are abnormal states precisely analogous to the state of mystical ecstasy, states which permit the angry man, the aesthete, the lover, to become temporary inhabitants of non-Podsnapian universes which are immediately felt (just as the mystic's universe is immediately felt) to be of peculiar value and significance. Pascal was acquainted with only one abnormal universe—that which the ecstatic mystic briefly inhabits. Of all the rest he had no personal knowledge; his sickly body did not permit of his approaching them. We condemn easily that which we do not know, and with pleasure that which, like the fox who said the grapes were sour, we cannot enjoy.

To a sickly body Pascal joined an extraordinarily powerful analytical intellect. Too acute to be taken in by the gross illusions of rationalism, too subtle to imagine that a home-made abstraction could be a reality, he derided the academic philosophers. He perceived that the basis of reason is unreasonable; first principles come from "the heart," not from the mind. The discovery would have been of the first importance if Pascal had only made it with the right organ. But instead of discovering the heart with the heart, he discovered it with the head. It was abstractly that he rejected abstractions, and with the reason that he discovered unreason. His realism was only theoretical; he never lived it. His intelligence would not permit him to find satisfaction in the noumena and abstractions of rationalist philosophy. But for fixed noumena and simple unchanging abstractions he none the less longed. He was able to satisfy these longings of an invalid philosopher and at the same time to salve his intellectual conscience by choosing an irrational abstraction to believe in—the God of Christianity. Marooned on that static Rock of Ages, he felt himself safe—safe from the heaving flux of appearances, safe from diversity, safe from the responsibilities of freedom, safe from life. If he had allowed himself to have a heart to understand the heart with, if he had possessed a body with which to understand the body, and instincts and desires capable of interpreting the meaning of instinct and desire, Pascal might have been a life-worshiper instead of a devotee of death. But illness had strangled the life out of his body and made his desires so weak that to resist them was an easy virtue. Against his heart he struggled with all the force of his tense and focused will. The Moloch of religious principle demanded its sacrifice. Obediently, Pascal performed the rite of harakiri. Moloch, unsatisfied, demanded still more blood. Pascal offered his services; he would make other people do as he had done. Moloch should be glutted with entrails. All his writings are persuasive invitations to the world to come and commit suicide. It is the triumph of principle and consistency.

Musical Conclusion

And yet the life-worshiper is also, in his own way, a man of principles and consistency. To live intensely—that is his guiding principle. His diversity is a sign that he consistently tries to live up to his principles; for the harmony of life—of the single life that persists as a gradually changing unity through time—is a harmony built up of many elements. The unity is mutilated by the suppression of any part of the diversity. A fugue has need of all its voices. Even in the rich counterpoint of life each separate small melody plays its indispensable part. The diapason closes full in man. In *man*. But Pascal aspired to be more than a man. Among the interlaced melodies of the human counterpoint are love songs and anacreontics, marches and savage dance-rhythms, hymns of hate and loud hilarious chanties. Odious voices in the ears of one who wanted his music to be wholly celestial! Pascal commanded them to be still and they were silent. Bending toward his life, we listen expectantly for a strain of angelic singing. But across the centuries what harsh and painful sounds come creaking down to us!

(From "Pascal," *Do What You Will*)

Beliefs

No account of the scientific picture of the world and its history would be complete unless it contained a reminder of the fact, frequently forgotten by scientists themselves, that this picture does not even claim to be comprehensive. From the world we actually live in, the world that is given by our senses, our intuitions of beauty and goodness, our emotions and impulses, our moods and sentiments, the man of science abstracts a simplified private universe of things possessing only those qualities which used to be called "primary." Arbitrarily, because it happens to be convenient, because his methods do not allow him to deal with the immense com-

plexity of reality, he selects from the whole of experience
only those elements which can be weighed, measured, numbered, or which lend themselves in any other way to mathematical treatment. By using this technique of simplification
and abstraction, the scientist has succeeded to an astonishing degree in understanding and dominating the physical
environment. The success was intoxicating and, with an illogi-
cality which, in the circumstances, was doubtless pardonable,
many scientists and philosophers came to imagine that this
useful abstraction from reality was reality itself. Reality as
actually experienced contains intuitions of value and significance, contains love, beauty, mystical ecstasy, intimations
of godhead. Science did not and still does not possess intellectual instruments with which to deal with these aspects
of reality. Consequently it ignored them and concentrated its
attention upon such aspects of the world as it could deal with
by means of arithmetic, geometry and the various branches
of higher mathematics. Our conviction that the world is
meaningless is due in part to the fact (discussed in a later
paragraph) that the philosophy of meaninglessness lends itself
very effectively to furthering the ends of erotic or political
passion; in part to a genuine intellectual error—the error of
identifying the world of science, a world from which all
meaning and value has been deliberately excluded, with ultimate reality. It is worth while to quote in this context the
words with which Hume closes his *Enquiry*. "If we take in
our hand any volume; of divinity or school metaphysics, for
instance; let us ask, Does it contain any abstract reasoning
concerning quantity or number? No. Does it contain any experimental reasoning concerning matter of fact or evidence?
No. Commit it then to the flames; for it can contain nothing
but sophistry and illusion." Hume mentions only divinity and
school metaphysics; but his argument would apply just as
cogently to poetry, music, painting, sculpture and all ethical
and religious teaching. Hamlet contains no abstract reasoning
concerning quantity or number and no experimental reason
concerning evidence; nor does the Hammerklavier Sonata, nor
Donatello's David, nor the *Tao Te Ching*, nor the *Following
of Christ*. Commit them therefore to the flames: for they can
contain nothing but sophistry and illusion.

We are living now, not in the delicious intoxication induced by the early successes of science, but in a rather grisly
morning-after, when it has become apparent that what triumphant science has done hitherto is to improve the means for
achieving unimproved or actually deteriorated ends. In this
condition of apprehensive sobriety we are able to see that the
contents of literature, art, music—even in some measure of

divinity and school metaphysics—are not sophistry and illusion, but simply those elements of experience which scientists
chose to leave out of account, for the good reason that they
had no intellectual methods for dealing with them. In the arts,
in philosophy, in religion men are trying—doubtless, without
complete success—to describe and explain the non-measur-
able, purely qualitative aspects of reality. Since the time of
Galileo, scientists have admitted, sometimes explicitly but
much more often by implication, that they are incompetent
to discuss such matters. The scientific picture of the world is
what it is because men of science combine this incompetence
with certain special competences. They have no right to claim
that this product of incompetence and specialization is a
complete picture of reality. As a matter of historical fact,
however, this claim has constantly been made. The successive
steps in the process of identifying an arbitrary abstraction
from reality with reality itself have been described, very fully
and lucidly, in Burtt's excellent "Metaphysical Foundations
of Modern Science"; and it is therefore unnecessary for me
to develop the theme any further. All that I need add is the
fact that, in recent years, many men of science have come to
realize that the scientific picture of the world is a partial one
—the product of their special competence in mathematics
and their special incompetence to deal systematically with
aesthetic and moral values, religious experiences and intuitions of significance. Unhappily, novel ideas become acceptable to the less intelligent members of society only with a
very considerable time-lag. Sixty or seventy years ago the
majority of scientists believed—and the belief often caused
them considerable distress—that the product of their special
incompetence was identical with reality as a whole. Today
this belief has begun to give way, in scientific circles, to a
different and obviously truer conception of the relation between science and total experience. The masses, on the contrary, have just reached the point where the ancestors of
today's scientists were standing two generations back. They
are convinced that the scientific picture of an arbitrary abstraction from reality is a picture of reality as a whole and that
therefore the world is without meaning or value. But nobody
likes living in such a world. To satisfy their hunger for meaning and value, they turn to such doctrines as nationalism,
fascism and revolutionary communism. Philosophically and
scientifically, these doctrines are absurd; but for the masses
in every community, they have this great merit: they attribute
the meaning and value that have been taken away from the
world as a whole to the particular part of the world in which
the believers happen to be living.

These last considerations raise an important question, which must now be considered in some detail. Does the world as a whole possess the value and meaning that we constantly attribute to certain parts of it (such as human beings and their works); and, if so, what is the nature of that value and meaning? This is a question which, a few years ago, I should not even have posed. For, like so many of my contemporaries, I took it for granted that there was no meaning. This was partly due to the fact that I shared the common belief that the scientific picture of an abstraction from reality was a true picture of reality as a whole; partly also to other, non-intellectual reasons. I had motives for not wanting the world to have a meaning; consequently assumed that it had none, and was able without any difficulty to find satisfying reasons for this assumption.

Most ignorance is vincible ignorance. We don't know because we don't want to know. It is our will that decides how and upon what subjects we shall use our intelligence. Those who detect no meaning in the world generally do so because, for one reason or another, it suits their books that the world should be meaningless.

The behavior of the insane is merely sane behavior, a bit exaggerated and distorted. The abnormal casts a revealing light upon the normal. Hence the interest attaching, among other madmen, to the extravagant figure of the Marquis de Sade. The marquis prided himself upon being a thinker. His books, indeed, contain more philosophy than pornography. The hungry smut-hound must plough through long chapters of abstract speculation in order to find the cruelties and obscenities for which he hungers. De Sade's philosophy was the philosophy of meaninglessness carried to its logical conclusion. Life was without significance. Values were illusory and ideals merely the inventions of cunning priests and kings. Sensations and animal pleasures alone possessed reality and were alone worth living for. There was no reason why any one should have the slightest consideration for any one else. For those who found rape and murder amusing, rape and murder were fully legitimate activities. And so on.

Why was the Marquis unable to find any value or significance in the world? Was his intellect more piercing than that of other men? Was he forced by the acuity of his vision to look through the veils of prejudice and superstition to the hideous reality behind them? We may doubt it. The real reason why the Marquis could see no meaning or value in the world is to be found in those descriptions of fornications, sodomies and tortures which alternate with the philosophizings of *Justine* and *Juliette*. In the ordinary circumstances of life, the Marquis was not particularly cruel; indeed, he is said to have got into serious trouble during the Terror for his leniency toward those suspected of anti-revolutionary sentiments. His was a strictly sexual perversion. It was for flogging actresses, sticking pen-knives into shop girls, feeding prostitutes on sugar-plums impregnated with cantharides, that he got into trouble with the police. His philosophical disquisitions, which, like the pornographic day-dreams, were mostly written in prisons and asylums, were the theoretical justification of his erotic practices. Similarly his politics were dictated by the desire to avenge himself on those members of his family and his class who had, as he thought, unjustly persecuted him. He was enthusiastically a revolutionary—at any rate in theory; for, as we have seen, he was too gentle in practice to satisfy his fellow Jacobins. His books are of permanent interest and value because they contain a kind of *reductio ad absurdum* of revolutionary theory. Sade is not afraid to be a revolutionary to the bitter end. Not content with denying the particular system of values embodied in the *ancien régime,* he proceeds to deny the existence of any values, any idealism, any binding moral imperatives whatsoever. He preaches violent revolution not only in the field of politics and economics, but (logical with the appalling logicality of the maniac) also on that of personal relations, including the most intimate of all, the relations between lovers. And, after all, why not? If it is legitimate to torment and kill in one set of circumstances, it must be equally legitimate to torment and kill in all other circumstances. De Sade is the one completely consistent and thorough-going revolutionary of history.

If I have lingered so long over a maniac, it is because his madness illuminates the dark places of normal behavior. No philosophy is completely disinterested. The pure love of truth is always mingled to some extent with the need, consciously or unconsciously felt by even the noblest and the most intelligent philosophers, to justify a given form of personal or social behavior, to rationalize the traditional prejudices of a given class or community. The philosopher who finds meaning in the world is concerned, not only to elucidate that meaning, but also to prove that it is most clearly expressed in some established religion, some accepted code of morals. The philosopher who finds no meaning in the world is not concerned exclusively with a problem in pure metaphysics. He is also concerned to prove that there is no valid reason why he personally should not do as he wants to do, or why his friends should not seize political power and govern in the way that they find most advantageous to themselves. The voluntary, as opposed to the intellectual, reasons for holding the doctrines of materialism, for example, may be predominantly erotic, as they were in the case of Lamettrie (see his lyrical account of the pleasures of the bed in *La Volupté* and at the end of *L'Homme Machine*), or predominantly political, as they were in the case of Karl Marx. The desire to justify a particular form of political organization and, in some cases, of a personal will to power has played an equally large part in the formulation of philosophies postulating the existence of a meaning in the world. Christian philosophers have found no difficulty in justifying imperialism, war, the capitalistic system, the use of torture, the censorship of the press, and ecclesiastical tyrannies of every sort from the tyranny of Rome to the tyrannies of Geneva and New England. In all these cases they have shown that the meaning of the world was such as to be compatible with, or actually most completely expressed by, the iniquities I have mentioned above— iniquities which happened, of course, to serve the personal or sectarian interests of the philosophers concerned. In due course, there arose philosophers who denied not only the right of these Christian special pleaders to justify iniquity by an appeal to the meaning of the world, but even their right to find any such meaning whatsoever. In the circumstances, the fact was not surprising. One unscrupulous distortion of the truth tends to beget other and opposite distortions. Passions may be satisfied in the process; but the disinterested love of knowledge suffers eclipse.

For myself as, no doubt, for most of my contemporaries, the philosophy of meaninglessness was essentially an instrument of liberation. The liberation we desired was simultaneously liberation from a certain political and economic system and liberation from a certain system of morality. We objected to the morality because it interfered with our sexual freedom; we objected to the political and economic system because it was unjust. The supporters of these systems claimed that in some way they embodied the meaning (a Christian meaning, they insisted) of the world. There was one admirably simple method of confuting these people and at the same time justifying ourselves in our political and erotic revolt: we could deny that the world had any meaning whatsoever. Similar tactics had been adopted during the eighteenth century and for the same reasons. From the popular novelists of the period, such as Crébillon and Andréa de Nerciat, we learn that the chief reason for being "philosophical" was that one might be free from prejudices—above all prejudices of a sexual nature. More serious writers associated political with sexual prejudice and recommended philosophy (in practice, the philosophy of meaninglessness) as a preparation for social

reform or revolution. The early nineteenth century witnessed
a reaction toward meaningful philosophy of a kind that could,
unhappily, be used to justify political reaction. The men of
the new Enlightenment, which occurred in the middle years
of the nineteenth century, once again used meaninglessness
as a weapon against the reactionaries. The Victorian passion
for respectability was, however, so great that, during the
period when they were formulated, neither Positivism nor
Darwinism was used as a justification for sexual indulgence.
After the War the philosophy of meaninglessness came once
more triumphantly into fashion. As in the days of Lamettrie
and his successors the desire to justify a certain sexual loose-
ness played a part in the popularization of meaninglessness at
least as important as that played by the desire for liberation
from an unjust and inefficient form of social organization.
By the end of the twenties a reaction had begun to set in—
away from the easy-going philosophy of general meaninglessness toward the hard, ferocious theologies of nationalistic
and revolutionary idolatry. Meaning was reintroduced into
the world, but only in patches. The universe as a whole still
remained meaningless, but certain of its parts, such as the
nation, the state, the class, the party, were endowed with
significance and the highest value. The general acceptance of
a doctrine that denies meaning and value to the world as a
whole, while assigning them in a supreme degree to certain
arbitrarily selected parts of the totality, can have only evil
and disastrous results. "All that we are (and consequently all
that we do) is the result of what we have thought." We have
thought of ourselves as members of supremely meaningful
and valuable communities—deified nations, divine classes and
what not—existing within a meaningless universe. And because we have thought like this, rearmament is in full swing,
economic nationalism becomes ever more intense, the battle
of rival propagandas grows ever fiercer, and general war becomes increasingly more probable.

It was the manifestly poisonous nature of the fruits that
forced me to reconsider the philosophical tree on which they
had grown. It is certainly hard, perhaps impossible, to demonstrate any necessary connection between truth and practical
goodness. Indeed it was fashionable during the Enlightenment
of the middle nineteenth century to speak of the need for
supplying the masses with "vital lies" calculated to make those
who accepted them not only happy, but well behaved. The
truth—which was that there was no meaning or value in the
world—should be revealed only to the few who were strong
enough to stomach it. Now, it may be, of course, that the
nature of things has fixed a great gulf between truth about

the world on the one hand and practical goodness on the
other. Meanwhile, however, the nature of things seems to
have so constituted the human mind that it is extremely reluctant to accept such a conclusion, except under the pressure
of desire or self-interest. Furthermore those who, to be liber-
ated from political or sexual restraint, accept the doctrine
of absolute meaninglessness tend in a short time to become so
much dissatisfied with their philosophy (in spite of the services it renders) that they will exchange it for any dogma, however manifestly nonsensical, which restores meaning if only
to a part of the universe. Some people, it is true, can live
contentedly with a philosophy of meaninglessness for a very
long time. But in most cases it will be found that these people
possess some talent or accomplishment that permits them to
live a life which, to a limited extent, is profoundly meaningful and valuable. Thus an artist, or a man of science can
profess a philosophy of general meaninglessness and yet lead
a perfectly contented life. The reason for this must be sought
in the fact that artistic creation and scientific research are
absorbingly delightful occupations, possessing, moreover, a
certain special significance in virtue of their relation to truth
and beauty. Nevertheless, artistic creation and scientific research may be, and constantly are, used as devices for escap-
ing from the responsibilities of life. They are proclaimed to
be ends absolutely good in themselves—ends so admirable
that those who pursue them are excused from bothering about
anything else. This is particularly true of contemporary science. The mass of accumulated knowledge is so great that it
is now impossible for any individual to have a thorough grasp
of more than one small field of study. Meanwhile, no attempt
is made to produce a comprehensive synthesis of the general
results of scientific research. Our universities possess no chair
of synthesis. All endowments, moreover, go to special subjects—and almost always to subjects which have no need of
further endowment, such as physics, chemistry and mechanics.
In our institutions of higher learning about ten times as much
is spent on the natural sciences as on the sciences of man. All
our efforts are directed, as usual, to producing improved
means to unimproved ends. Meanwhile intensive specialization tends to reduce each branch of science to a condition
almost approaching meaninglessness. There are many men
of science who are actually proud of this state of things.
Specialized meaninglessness has come to be regarded, in certain circles, as a kind of hall mark of true science. Those who
attempt to relate the small particular results of specialization
with human life as a whole and its relation to the universe
at large are accused of being bad scientists, charlatans, self-

advertisers. The people who make such accusations do so, of course, because they do not wish to take any responsibility for anything, but merely to retire to their cloistered laboratories, and there amuse themselves by performing delightfully interesting researches. Science and art are only too often a superior kind of dope, possessing this advantage over booze and morphia: that they can be indulged in with a good conscience and with the conviction that, in the process of indulging, one is leading the "higher life." Up to a point, of course, this is true. The life of the scientist or the artist is a higher life. Unfortunately, when led in an irresponsible, one-sided way, the higher life is probably more harmful for the individual than the lower life of the average sensual man and certainly, in the case of the scientist, much worse for society at large. . . .

We are now at the point at which we discover that an obviously untrue philosophy of life leads in practice to disastrous results; the point where we realize the necessity of seeking an alternative philosophy that shall be true and therefore fruitful of good. A critical consideration of the classical arguments in favor of theism would reveal that some carry no conviction whatever, while the rest can only raise a presumption in favor of the theory that the world possesses some integrating principle that gives it significance and value. There is probably no argument by which the case for theism, or for deism, or for pantheism in either its pancosmic or acosmic form, can be convincingly proved. The most that "abstract reasoning" (to use Hume's phrase) can do is to create a presumption in favor of one or other hypothesis; and this presumption can be increased by means of "experimental reasoning concerning matter of fact or evidence." Final conviction can only come to those who make an act of faith. The idea is one which most of us find very distressing. But it may be doubted whether this particular act of faith is intrinsically more difficult than those which we have to make, for example, every time we frame a scientific hypothesis, every time that, from the consideration of a few phenomena, we draw inference concerning all phenomena, past, present and future. On very little evidence, but with no qualms of intellectual conscience, we assume that our craving for explanation has a real object in an explicable universe, that the aesthetic satisfaction we derive from certain arguments is a sign that they are true, that the laws of thought are also laws of things. There seems to be no reason why, having swallowed this camel, we should not swallow another, no larger really than the first. Once recognized, the reasons why we strain at the second camel cease to exist and we become free to consider on their merits the evidence and arguments that would reasonably justify us in making the final act of faith and assuming the truth of a hypothesis that we are unable fully to demonstrate.

"Abstract reasoning" must now give place to "experimental reasoning concerning matter of fact or evidence." Natural science, as we have seen, deals only with those aspects of reality that are amenable to mathematical treatment. The rest it merely ignores. But some of the experiences thus ignored by natural science—aesthetic experiences, for example, and religious experiences—throw much light upon the present problem. It is with the fact of such experiences and the evidence they furnish concerning the nature of the world that we have now to concern ourselves.

To discuss the nature and significance of aesthetic experience would take too long. It is enough, in this place, merely to suggest that the best works of literary, plastic and musical art give us more than mere pleasure; they furnish us with information about the nature of the world. The *Sanctus* in Beethoven's Mass in D, Seurat's *Grande Jatte, Macbeth*—works such as these tell us, by strange but certain implication, something significant about the ultimate reality behind appearances. Even from the perfection of minor masterpieces—certain sonnets of Mallarmé, for instance, certain Chinese ceramics—we can derive illuminating hints about the "something far more deeply interfused," about "the peace of God that passeth all understanding." But the subject of art is enormous and obscure, and my space is limited, I shall therefore confine myself to a discussion of certain religious experiences which bear more directly upon the present problem than do our experiences as creators and appreciators of art.

Meditation, in Babbitt's words, is a device for producing a "super-rational concentration of the will." But meditation is more than a method of self-education; it has also been used, in every part of the world and from the remotest periods, as a method for acquiring knowledge about the essential nature of things, a method for establishing communion between the soul and the integrating principle of the universe. Meditation, in other words, is the technique of mysticism. Properly practiced, with due preparation, physical, mental and moral, meditation may result in a state of what has been called "transcendental consciousness"—the direct intuition of, and union with, an ultimate spiritual reality that is perceived as simultaneously beyond the self and in some way within it. ("God in the depths of us," says Ruysbroeck, "receives God who comes to us; it is God contemplating God.") Non-mystics have denied the validity of the mystical experience, describing it as merely subjective and illusory. But it should be remembered that to those who have never actually had it, any direct intuition must seem subjective and illusory. It is impossible for the deaf to form any idea of the nature or significance of music. Nor is physical disability the only obstacle in the way of musical understanding. An Indian, for example, finds European orchestral music intolerably noisy, complicated, over-intellectual, inhuman. It seems incredible to him that any one should be able to perceive beauty and meaning, to recognize an expression of the deepest and subtlest emotions in this elaborate cacophony. And yet, if he has patience and listens to enough of it, he will come at last to realize, not only theoretically but also by direct, immediate intuition, that this music possesses all the qualities which Europeans claim for it. Of the significant and pleasurable experiences of life only the simplest are open indiscriminately to all. The rest cannot be had except by those who have undergone a suitable training. One must be trained even to enjoy the pleasures of alcohol and tobacco; first whiskies seem revolting, first pipes turn even the strongest of boyish stomachs. Similarly first Shakespeare sonnets seem meaningless; first Bach fugues, a bore; first differential equations, sheer torture. But training changes the nature of our spiritual experiences. In due course, contact with an obscurely beautiful poem, an elaborate piece of counterpoint or of mathematical reasoning, causes us to feel direct intuitions of beauty and significance. It is the same in the moral world. A man who has trained himself in goodness comes to have certain direct intuitions about character, about the relations between human beings, about his own position in the world—intuitions that are quite different from the intuitions of the average sensual man. Knowledge is always a function of being. What we perceive and understand depends upon what we are; and what we are depends partly on circumstances, partly, and more profoundly, on the nature of the efforts we have made to realize our ideal and the nature of the ideal we have tried to realize. The fact that knowing depends upon being leads, of course, to an immense amount of misunderstanding. The meaning of words, for example, changes profoundly according to the character and experiences of the user. Thus, to the saint, words like "love," "charity," "compassion" mean something quite different from what they mean to the ordinary man. Again, to the ordinary man, Spinoza's statement that "blessedness is not the reward of virtue, but is virtue itself" seems simply untrue. Being virtuous is, for him, a most tedious and distressing process. But it is clear that to some one who has trained himself in goodness, virtue really is blessedness, while the life of the ordinary man, with its petty vices and its long spells of animal thoughtlessness and insentience, seems a real torture. In view of the fact that knowing is conditioned by being and that being can be profoundly modified by training, we are justified in ignoring most of the arguments by which non-mystics have sought to discredit the experience of mystics. The being of a color-blind man is such that he is not competent to pass judgment on a painting. The color-blind man cannot be educated into seeing colors, and in this respect he is different from the Indian musician, who begins by finding European symphonies merely deafening and bewildering, but can be trained, if he so desires, to perceive the beauties of this kind of music. Similarly, the being of a non-mystical person is such that he cannot understand the nature of the mystic's intuitions. Like the Indian musician, however, he is at liberty, if he so chooses, to have some kind of direct experience of what at present he does not understand. This training is one which he will certainly find extremely tedious; for it involves, at first, the leading of a life of constant awareness and unremitting moral effort; second, steady practice in the technique of meditation, which is probably about as difficult as the technique of violin playing. But, however tedious, the training can be undertaken by any one who wishes to do so. Those who have not undertaken the training can have no knowledge of the kind of experiences open to those who have undertaken it and are as little justified in denying the validity of those direct intuitions of an ultimate spiritual reality, at once transcendent and immanent, as were the Pisan professors who denied, on *a priori* grounds, the validity of Galileo's direct intuition (made possible by the telescope) of the fact that Jupiter has several moons. . . .

Systematic training in recollection and meditation makes possible the mystical experience, which is a direct intuition of ultimate reality. At all times and in every part of the world, mystics of the first order have always agreed that this ultimate reality, apprehended in the process of meditation, is essentially impersonal. This direct intuition of an impersonal spiritual reality, underlying all being, is in accord with the findings of the majority of the world's philosophers.

"There is," writes Professor Whitehead, in *Religion in the Making,* "a large concurrence in the negative doctrine that the religious experience does not include any direct intuition of a definite person, or individual. . . . The evidence for the assertion of a general, though not universal, concurrence in the doctrine of no direct vision of a personal God, can only be found by a consideration of the religious thought of the civilized world. . . . Throughout India and China, religious thought, so far as it has been interpreted in precise form, disclaims the intuition of ultimate personality substantial to the universe. This is true of Confucian philosophy, Buddhist philosophy and Hindu philosophy. There may be personal embodiments, but the substratum is impersonal. Christian theology has also, in the main, adopted the position that there is no direct intuition of such a personal substratum for the world. It maintains the doctrine of a personal God as a truth, but holds that our belief in it is based upon inference." There seems, however, to be no cogent reason why, from the existing evidence, we should draw such an inference. Moreover, the practical results of drawing such an inference are good only up to a point; beyond that point they are very often extremely bad.

We are now in a position to draw a few tentative and fragmentary conclusions about the nature of the world and our relation to it and to one another. To the casual observer, the world seems to be made up of great numbers of independent existents, some of which possess life and some consciousness. From very early times philosophers suspected that this common-sense view was in part at least, illusory. More recently investigators, trained in the discipline of mathematical physics and equipped with instruments of precision, have made observations from which it could be inferred that all the apparently independent existents in the world were built up of a limited number of patterns of identical units of energy. An ultimate physical identity underlies the apparent physical diversity of the world. Moreover, all apparently independent existents are in fact interdependent. Meanwhile the mystics had shown that investigators, trained in the discipline of recollection and meditation, could obtain direct experience of a spiritual unity underlying the apparent diversity of independent consciousness. They made it clear that what seemed to be the ultimate fact of personality was in reality not an ultimate fact and that it was possible for individuals to transcend the limitations of personality and to merge their private consciousness into a greater, impersonal consciousness underlying the personal mind. . . .

The physical world of our daily experience is a private universe quarried out of a total reality which the physicists infer to be far greater than it. This private universe is different, not only from the real world, whose existence we are able to infer, even though we cannot directly apprehend it, but also from the private universe inhabited by other animals —universes which we can never penetrate, but concerning whose nature we can, as Von Uexkull has done, make interesting speculative guesses. Each type of living creature inhabits a universe whose nature is determined and whose boundaries are imposed by the special inadequacies of its sense organs and its intelligence. In man, intelligence has been so far developed that he is able to infer the existence and even, to some extent, the nature of the real world outside his private universe. The nature of the sense organs and intelligence of living beings is imposed by biological necessity or convenience. The instruments of knowledge are good enough to enable their owners to survive. Less inadequate instruments of knowledge might not only lead to no biological advantage but might actually constitute a biological handicap. Individual human beings have been able to transcend the limitations of man's private universe only to the extent that they are relieved from biological pressure. An individual is relieved from biological pressure in two ways: from without, thanks to the efforts of others, and from within, thanks to his own efforts. If he is to transcend the limitations of man's private universe he must be a member of a community which gives him protection against the inclemencies of the environment and makes it easy for him to supply his physical wants. But this is not enough. He must also train himself in the art of being dispassionate and disinterested, must cultivate intellectual curiosity for its own sake and not for what he, as an animal, can get out of it.

The modern conception of man's intellectual relationship to the universe was anticipated by the Buddhist doctrine that desire is the source of illusion. To the extent that it has overcome desire, a mind is free from illusion. This is true not only of the man of science, but also of the artist and the philosopher. Only the disinterested mind can transcend common-sense and pass beyond the boundaries of animal or average-sensual human life. The mystic exhibits disinterestedness in the highest degree possible to human beings and is therefore able to transcend ordinary limitations more completely than the man of science, the artist or the philosopher. That which he discovers beyond the frontiers of the average sensual man's universe is a spiritual reality underlying and uniting all apparently separate existents—a reality with which he can merge himself and from which he can draw moral and even physical powers which, by ordinary standards, can only be described as super-normal.

The ultimate reality discoverable by those who choose to modify their being, so that they can have direct knowledge of it, is not, as we have seen, a personality. Since it is not personal, it is illegitimate to attribute to it ethical qualities. "God is not good," said Eckhart. "I am good." Goodness is the means by which men and women can overcome the illusion of being completely independent existents and can raise themselves to a level of being upon which it becomes

possible, by recollection and meditation, to realize the fact of
their oneness with ultimate reality, to know and in some
measure actually associate themselves with it. The ultimate
reality is "the peace of God which passeth all understanding"; goodness is the way by which it can be approached.
"Finite beings," in the words of Royce, "are always such as
they are in virtue of an *inattention* which at present blinds
them to their actual relations to God and to one another."
That inattention is the fruit, in Buddhist language, of desire.
We fail to attend to our true relations with ultimate reality
and, through ultimate reality, with our fellow beings, because
we prefer to attend to our animal nature and to the business
of getting on in the world. That we can never completely
ignore the animal in us or its biological needs is obvious.
Our separateness is not wholly an illusion. The element of
specificity in things is a brute fact of experience. Diversity
cannot be reduced to complete identity even in scientific and
philosophical theory, still less in life which is lived with
bodies, that is to say, with particular patternings of the ultimately identical units of energy. It is impossible in the nature
of things, that no attention should be given to the animal in
us; but in the circumstances of civilized life, it is certainly
unnecessary to give all or most of our attention to it. Goodness is the method by which we divert our attention from
this singularly wearisome topic of our animality and our individual separateness. Recollection and meditation assist goodness in two ways: by producing, in Babbitt's words, "a supra-
rational concentration of will," and by making it possible for
the mind to realize, not only theoretically, but also by direct
intuition, that the private universe of the average sensual man
is not identical with the universe as a whole. Conversely, of
course, goodness aids meditation by giving detachment from
animality and so making it possible for the mind to pay
attention to its actual relationship with ultimate reality and to
other individuals. Goodness, meditation, the mystical experience and the ultimate impersonal reality discovered in mystical
experience are organically related. This fact disposes of the
fears expressed by Dr. Albert Schweitzer in his recent book
on Indian thought. Mysticism, he contends, is the correct
world view; but, though correct, it is unsatisfactory in ethical
content. The ultimate reality of the world is not moral ("God
is not good") and the mystic who unites himself with ultimate
reality is uniting himself with a non-moral being, therefore
is not himself moral. But this is mere verbalism and ignores
the actual facts of experience. It is impossible for the mystic
to pay attention to his real relation to God and to his fellows,
unless he has previously detached his attention from his ani-

mal nature and the business of being socially successful. But he cannot detach his attention from these things except by the consistent and conscious practice of the highest morality. God is not good; but if I want to have even the smallest knowledge of God, I must be good at least in some slight measure; and if I want as full a knowledge of God as it is possible for human beings to have, I must be as good as it is possible for human beings to be. Virtue is the essential preliminary to the mystical experience. And this is not all. There is not even any theoretical incompatibility between an ultimate reality, which is impersonal and therefore not moral, and the existence of a moral order on the human level. Scientific investigation has shown that the world is a diversity underlain by an identity of physical substance; the mystical experience testifies to the existence of a spiritual unity underlying the diversity of separate consciousnesses. Concerning the relation between the underlying physical unity and the underlying spiritual unity it is hard to express an opinion. Nor is it necessary, in the present context, that we should express one. For our present purposes the important fact is that it is possible to detect a physical and a spiritual unity underlying the independent existents (to some extent merely apparent, to some extent real, at any rate for beings on our plane of existence), of which our commonsense universe is composed. Now, it is a fact of experience that we can either emphasize our separateness from other beings and the ultimate reality of the world or emphasize our oneness with them and it. To some extent at least, our will is free in this matter. Human beings are creatures who, in so far as they are animals and persons tend to regard themselves as independent existents, connected at most by purely biological ties, but who, in so far as they rise above animality and personality, are able to perceive that they are interrelated parts of physical and spiritual wholes incomparably greater than themselves. For such beings the fundamental moral commandment is: You shall realize your unity with all being. But men cannot realize their unity with others and with ultimate reality unless they practice the virtue of love and understanding. Love, compassion and understanding or intelligence —these are the primary virtues in the ethical system, the virtues organically correlated with what may be called the scientific-mystical conception of the world. Ultimate reality is impersonal and non-ethical; but if we would realize our true relations with ultimate reality and our fellow beings, we must practice morality and (since no personality can learn to transcend itself unless it is reasonably free from external compulsion) respect the personality of others. Belief in a personal, moral God has led only too frequently to theoretical dogmatism and practical intolerance—to a consistent refusal to respect personality and to the commission in the name of the divinely moral person of every kind of iniquity.

"The fact of the instability of evil," in Professor Whitehead's words, "is the moral order of the world." Evil is that which makes for separateness; and that which makes for separateness is self-destructive. This self-destruction of evil may be sudden and violent, as when murderous hatred results in a conflict that leads to the death of the hater; it may be gradual, as when a degenerative process results in impotence or extinction; or it may be reformative, as when a long course of evil-doing results in all concerned becoming so sick of destruction and degeneration that they decide to change their ways, thus transforming evil into good.

The evolutionary history of life clearly illustrates the instability of evil in the sense in which it has been defined above. Biological specialization may be regarded as a tendency on the part of a species to insist on its separateness; and the result of specialization, as we have seen, is either negatively disastrous, in the sense that it precludes the possibility of further biological progress, or positively disastrous, in the sense that it leads to the extinction of the species. In the same way intra-specific competition may be regarded as the expression of a tendency on the part of related individuals to insist on their separateness and independence; the effects of intraspecific competition are, as we have seen, almost wholly bad. Conversely, the qualities which have led to biological progress are the qualities which make it possible for individual beings to escape from their separateness—intelligence and the tendency to co-operate. Love and understanding are valuable even on the biological level. Hatred, unawareness, stupidity and all that makes for increase of separateness are the qualities that, as a matter of historical fact, have led either to the extinction of a species, or to its becoming a living fossil, incapable of making further biological progress.

(From "Beliefs," *Ends and Means*)

Knowledge and Understanding

Knowledge is acquired when we succeed in fitting a new experience into the system of concepts based upon our old experiences. Understanding comes when we liberate ourselves from the old and so make possible a direct, unmediated contact with the new, the mystery, moment by moment, of our existence.

The new is the given on every level of experience—given perceptions, given emotions and thoughts, given states of unstructured awareness, given relationships with things and persons. The old is our home-made system of ideas and word patterns. It is the stock of finished articles fabricated out of the given mystery by memory and analytical reasoning, by habit and the automatic associations of accepted notions. Knowledge is primarily a knowledge of these finished articles. Understanding is primarily direct awareness of the raw material.

Knowledge is always in terms of concepts and can be passed on by means of words or other symbols. Understanding is not conceptual, and therefore cannot be passed on. It is an immediate experience, and immediate experience can only be talked about (very inadequately), never shared. Nobody can actually feel another's pain or grief, another's love or joy or hunger. And similarly nobody can experience another's understanding of a given event or situation. There can, of course, be knowledge of such an understanding, and this knowledge may be passed on in speech or writing, or by means of other symbols. Such communicable knowledge is useful as a reminder that there have been specific understandings in the past, and that understanding is at all times possible. But we must always remember that knowledge of understanding is not the same thing as the understanding, which is the raw material of that knowledge. It is as different from understanding as the doctor's prescription for penicillin is different from penicillin.

Understanding is not inherited, nor can it be laboriously acquired. It is something which, when circumstances are favorable, comes to us, so to say, of its own accord. All of us are knowers, all the time; it is only occasionally and in spite of ourselves that we directly understand the mystery of given reality. Consequently we are very seldom tempted to equate understanding with knowledge. Of the exceptional men and women, who have understanding in every situation, most are intelligent enough to see that understanding is different from knowledge and that conceptual systems based upon past experience are as necessary to the conduct of life as are spontaneous insights into new experiences. For these reasons the mistake of identifying understanding with knowledge is rarely perpetrated and therefore poses no serious problem.

How different is the case with the opposite mistake, the mistake of supposing that knowledge is the same as understanding and interchangeable with it! All adults possess vast stocks of knowledge. Some of it is correct knowledge, some of it is incorrect knowledge, and some of it only looks like knowledge and is neither correct nor incorrect; it is merely meaningless. That which gives meaning to a proposition is not (to use the words of an eminent contemporary philosopher, Rudolf Carnap) "the attendant images or thoughts, but the possibility of deducing from it perceptive propositions, in other words the possibility of verification. To give sense to a proposition, the presence of images is not sufficient, it is not even necessary. We have no image of the electro-magnetic field, nor even, I should say, of the gravitational field; nevertheless the proposition which physicists assert about these fields have a perfect sense, because perceptive propositions are deductible from them." Metaphysical doctrines are propositions which cannot be operationally verified, at least on the level of ordinary experience. They may be expressive of a state of mind, in the way that lyrical poetry is expressive; but they have no assignable meaning. The information they convey is only pseudo-knowledge. But the formulators of metaphysical doctrines and the believers in such doctrines have always mistaken this pseudo-knowledge for knowledge and have proceeded to modify their behavior accordingly. Meaningless pseudo-knowledge has at all times been one of the principal motivators of individual and collective action. And that is one of the reasons why the course of human history has been so tragic and at the same time so strangely grotesque. Action based upon meaningless pseudo-knowledge is always inappropriate, always beside the point, and consequently always results in the kind of mess mankind has always lived in —the kind of mess that makes the angels weep and the satirists laugh aloud.

Correct or incorrect, relevant or meaningless, knowledge and pseudo-knowledge are as common as dirt and are therefore taken for granted. Understanding, on the contrary, is as rare, very nearly, as emeralds, and so is highly prized. The knowers would dearly love to be understanders; but either their stock of knowledge does not include the knowledge of what to do in order to be understanders; or else they know theoretically what they ought to do, but go on doing the opposite all the same. In either case they cherish the comforting delusion that knowledge and, above all, pseudo-knowledge *are* understanding. Along with the closely related errors of over-abstraction, over-generalization and over-simplification, this is the commonest of all intellectual sins and the most dangerous.

Of the vast sum of human misery about one third, I would

guess, is unavoidable misery. This is the price we must pay for being embodied, and for inheriting genes which are subject to deleterious mutations. This is the rent extorted by Nature for the privilege of living on the surface of a planet, whose soil is mostly poor, whose climates are capricious and inclement, and whose inhabitants include a countless number of micro-organisms capable of causing in man himself, in his domestic animals and cultivated plants, an immense variety of deadly or debilitating diseases. To these miseries of cosmic origin must be added the much larger group of those avoidable disasters we bring upon ourselves. For at least two thirds of our miseries spring from human stupidity, human malice and those great motivators and justifiers of malice and stupidity, idealism, dogmatism and proselytizing zeal on behalf of religious or political idols. But zeal, dogmatism and idealism exist only because we are forever committing intellectual sins. We sin by attributing concrete significance to meaningless pseudo-knowledge; we sin in being too lazy to think in terms of multiple causation and indulging instead in over-simplification, over-generalization and over-abstraction; and we sin by cherishing the false but agreeable notion that conceptual knowledge and, above all, conceptual pseudo-knowledge are the same as understanding.

Consider a few obvious examples. The atrocities of organized religion (and organized religion, let us never forget, has done about as much harm as it has done good) are all due, in the last analysis, to "mistaking the pointing finger for the moon"—in other words to mistaking the verbalized notion for the given mystery to which it refers or, more often, only seems to refer. This, as I have said, is one of the original sins of the intellect, and it is a sin in which, with a rationalistic bumptiousness as grotesque as it is distasteful, theologians have systematically wallowed. From indulgence in this kind of delinquency there has arisen, in most of the great religious traditions of the world, a fantastic over-valuation of words. Over-valuation of words leads all too frequently to the fabrication and idolatrous worship of dogmas, to the insistence on uniformity of belief, the demand for assent by all and sundry to a set of propositions which, though meaningless, are to be regarded as sacred. Those who do not consent to this idolatrous worship of words are to be "converted" and, if that should prove impossible, either persecuted or, if the dogmatizers lack political power, ostracized and denounced. Immediate experience of reality unites men. Conceptualized beliefs, including even the belief in a God of love and righteousness, divide them and, as the dismal record of religious history bears witness, set them for centuries on end at each other's throats.

Over-simplification, over-generalization and over-abstraction are three other sins closely related to the sin of imagining that knowledge and pseudo-knowledge are the same as understanding. The over-generalizing over-simplifier is the man who asserts, without producing evidence, that "All X's are Y," or, "All A's have a single cause, which is B." The over-abstractor is the one who cannot be bothered to deal with Jones and Smith, with Jane and Mary, as individuals, but enjoys being eloquent on the subject of Humanity, of Progress, of God and History and the Future. This brand of intellectual delinquency is indulged in by every demagogue, every crusader. In the Middle Ages the favorite over-generalization was "All infidels are damned." (For the Moslems, "all infidels" meant "all Christians"; for the Christians, "all Moslems.") Almost as popular was the nonsensical proposition, "All heretics are inspired by the devil" and "All eccentric old women are witches." In the sixteenth and seventeenth centuries the wars and persecutions were justified by the luminously clear and simple belief that "All Roman Catholics (or, if you happened to be on the Pope's side, all Lutherans, Calvinists and Anglicans) are God's enemies." In our own day Hitler proclaimed that all the ills of the world had one cause, namely Jews, and that all Jews were sub-human enemies of mankind. For the Communists, all the ills of the world have one cause, namely capitalists, and all capitalists and their middle-class supporters are subhuman enemies of mankind. It is perfectly obvious, on the face of it, that none of these over-generalized statements can possibly be true. But the urge to intellectual sin is fearfully strong. All are subject to temptation and few are able to resist.

There are in the lives of human beings very many situations in which only knowledge, conceptualized, accumulated and passed on by means of words, if of any practical use. For example, if I want to manufacture sulphuric acid or to keep accounts for a banker, I do not start at the beginnings of chemistry or economics; I start at what is now the end of these sciences. In other words, I go to a school where the relevant knowledge is taught, I read books in which the accumulations of past experience in these particular fields are set forth. I can learn the functions of an accountant or a chemical engineer on the basis of knowledge alone. For this particular purpose it is not necessary for me to have much understanding of concrete situations as they arise, moment by moment, from the depths of the given mystery of our existence. What is important for me as a professional man is that I should be familiar with all the conceptual knowledge in my field. Ours is an industrial civilization, in which no society can prosper unless it possesses an elite of highly trained scientists and a considerable army of engineers and technicians. The possession and wide dissemination of a great deal of correct, specialized knowledge has become a prime condition of national survival. In the United States, during the last twenty or thirty years, this fact seems to have been forgotten. Professional educationists have taken John Dewey's theories of "learning through doing" and of "education as life-adjustment," and have applied them in such a way that, in many American schools, there is now doing without learning, along with courses in adjustment to everything except the basic twentieth-century fact that we live in a world where ignorance of science and its methods is the surest, shortest road to national disaster. During the past half century every other nation has made great efforts to impart more knowledge to more young people. In the United States professional educationists have chosen the opposite course. At the turn of the century fifty-six per cent of the pupils in American high schools studied algebra; today less than a quarter of them are so much as introduced to the subject. In 1955 eleven per cent of American boys and girls were studying geometry; fifty years ago the figure was twenty-seven per cent. Four per cent of them now take physics, as against nineteen per cent in 1900. Fifty per cent of American high schools offer no courses in chemistry, fifty-three per cent no course in physics. This headlong decline in knowledge has not been accompanied by any increase in understanding; for it goes without saying that high school courses in life adjustment do not teach understanding. They teach only conformity to current conventions of personal and collective behavior. There is no substitute for correct knowledge, and in the process of acquiring correct knowledge there is no substitute for concentration and prolonged practice. Except for the unusually gifted, learning, by whatever method, must always be hard work. Unfortunately there are many professional educationists who seem to think that children should never be required to work hard. Wherever educational methods are based on this assumption, children will not in fact acquire much knowledge; and if the methods are followed for a generation or two, the society which tolerates them will find itself in full decline.

In theory, deficiencies in knowledge can be made good simply by changing the curriculum. In practice, a change in the curriculum will do little good, unless there is a corresponding change in the point of view of professional educationists. For the trouble with American educationists, writes a distinguished member of their profession, Dr. H. L. Dodge, is that they "regard any subject from personal grooming to philosophy as equally important or interchangeable in furthering the process of self-realization. This anarchy of values has led to the displacement of the established disciplines of science and the humanities by these new subjects." Whether professional educationists can be induced to change their current attitudes is uncertain. Should it prove impossible, we must fall back on the comforting thought that time never stands still and that nobody is immortal. What persuasion and the threat of national decline fail to accomplish, retirement, high blood pressure and death will bring to pass, more slowly, it is true, but much more surely.

The dissemination of correct knowledge is one of the essential functions of education, and we neglect it at our peril. But, obviously, education should be more than a device for passing on correct knowledge. It should also teach what Dewey called life adjustment and self-realization. But precisely how should self-realization and life adjustment be promoted? To this question modern educators have given many answers. Most of these answers belong to one or other of two main educational families, the Progressive and the Classical. Answers of the Progressive type find expression in the provision of courses in such subject as "family living, consumer economics, job information, physical and mental health, training for world citizenship and statesmanship and last, and we are afraid least" (I quote again the words of Dr. Dodge) "training in fundamentals." Where answers of the Classical type are preferred, educators provide courses in Latin, Greek and modern European literature, in world history and in philosophy— exclusively, for some odd reason, of the Western brand. Shakespeare and Chaucer, Virgil and Homer—how far away they seem, how irrevocably dead! Why, then, should we bother to teach the classics? The reasons have been stated a thousand times, but seldom with more force and lucidity than by Albert Jay Nock in his *Memoirs of a Superfluous Man.* "The literatures of Greece and Rome provide the longest, the most complete and most nearly continuous record we have of what the strange creature Homo sapiens has been busy about in virtually every department of spiritual, intellectual and social activity. Hence the mind that has canvassed this record is much more than a disciplined mind; it is an experienced mind. It has come, as Emerson says, into a feeling of immense longevity, and it instinctively views contemporary man and his doings in the perspective set by this profound and weighty experience. Our studies were properly called formative, because, beyond all others, their effect was power-

fully maturing. Cicero told the unvarnished truth in saying
that those who have no knowledge of what has gone before
them must for ever remain children. And if one wished to
characterize the collective mind of this period, or indeed of
any period, the use it makes of its powers of observation,
reflection, logical inference, one would best do it by the word
'immaturity.' "

The Progressive and the Classical approaches to education
are not incompatible. It is perfectly possible to combine a
schooling in the local cultural tradition with a training, half
vocational, half psychological, in adaptation to the current
conventions of social life, and then to combine this combination with training in the sciences, in other words with the
inculcation of correct knowledge. But is this enough? Can
such an education result in the self-realization which is its
aim? The question deserves our closest scrutiny. Nobody, of
course, can doubt the importance of accumulated experience
as a guide for individual and social conduct. We are human
because, at a very early stage in the history of the species,
our ancestors discovered a way of preserving and disseminat-
ing the results of experience. They learned to speak and were
thus enabled to translate what they had perceived, what they
had inferred from given fact and home-grown phantasy, into
a set of concepts, which could be added to by each generation
and bequeathed, a treasure of mingled sense and nonsense,
to posterity. In Mr. Nock's words "the mind that has canvassed this record is an experienced mind." The only trouble,
so far as *we* are concerned, is that the vicarious experience
derived from a study of the classics is, in certain respects,
completely irrelevant to twentieth-century facts. In many ways,
of course, the modern world resembles the world inhabited
by the men of antiquity. In many other ways, however, it is
radically different. For example, in *their* world the rate of
change was exceedingly slow; in *ours* advancing technology
produces a state of chronic revolution. *They* took infanticide
for granted (Thebes was the only Greek city which forbade
the exposure of babies) and regarded slavery as not only
necessary to the Greek way of life, but as intrinsically natural
and right; *we* are the heirs of eighteenth- and nineteenth-
century humanitarianism and must solve *our* economic and
demographic problems by methods less dreadfully reminiscent
of recent totalitarian practice. Because all the dirty work was
done by slaves, *they* regarded every form of manual activity
as essentially unworthy of a gentleman and in consequence
never subjected their over-abstract, over-rational theories to
the test of experiment; *we* have learned, or at least are learning, to think operationally. *They* despised "barbarians," never

bothered to learn a foreign language and could therefore naively regard the rules of Greek grammar and syntax as the Laws of Thought; *we* have begun to understand the nature of language, the danger of taking words too seriously, the ever-present need for linguistic analysis. *They* knew nothing about the past and therefore, in Cicero's words, were like children. (Thucydides, the greatest historian of antiquity, prefaces his account of the Peloponnesian War by airily asserting that nothing of great importance had happened before his own time.) *We*, in the course of the last five generations, have acquired a knowledge of man's past extending back to more than half a million years and covering the activities of tribes and nations in every continent. *They* developed political institutions which, in the case of Greece, were hopelessly unstable and, in the case of Rome, were only too firmly fixed in a pattern of aggressiveness and brutality; but what *we* need is a few hints on the art of creating an entirely new kind of society, durable but adventurous, strong but humane, highly organized but liberty-loving, elastic and adaptable. In this matter Greece and Rome can teach us only negatively—by demonstrating, in their divergent ways, what *not* to do.

From all this it is clear that a classical education in the humanities of two thousand years ago requires to be supplemented by some kind of training in the humanities of today and tomorrow. The Progressives profess to give such a training; but surely we need something a little more informative, a little more useful in this vertiginously changing world of ours, than courses in present-day consumer economics and current job information. But even if a completely adequate schooling in the humanities of the past, the present and the foreseeable future could be devised and made available to all, would the aims of education, as distinct from factual and theoretical instruction, be thereby achieved? Would the recipients of such an education be any nearer to the goal of self-realization? The answer, I am afraid, is, No. For at this point we find ourselves confronted by one of those paradoxes which are of the very essence of our strange existence as amphibians inhabiting, without being completely at home in, half a dozen almost incommensurable worlds—the world of concepts and the world of data, the objective world and the subjective, the small, bright world of personal consciousness and the vast, mysterious world of the unconscious. Where education is concerned, the paradox may be expressed in the statement that the medium of education, which is language, is absolutely necessary, but also fatal; that the subject matter of education, which is the conceptualized accumulation of past experiences, is indispensable, but also an obstacle to be circumvented.

"Existence is prior to essence." Unlike most metaphysical propositions, this slogan of the existentialists can actually be verified. "Wolf children," adopted by animal mothers and brought up in animal surroundings, have the form of human beings, but are not human. The essence of humanity, it is evident, is not something we are born with; it is something we make or grow into. We learn to speak, we accumulate conceptualized knowledge and pseudo-knowledge, we imitate our elders, we build up fixed patterns of thought and feeling and behavior, and in the process we become human, we turn into persons. But the things which make us human are precisely the things which interfere with self-realization and prevent understanding. We are humanized by imitating others, by learning their speech and by acquiring the accumulated knowledge which language makes available. But we understand only when, by liberating ourselves from the tyranny of words, conditioned reflexes and social conventions, we establish direct, unmediated contact with experience. The greatest paradox of our existence consists in this: that, in order to understand, we must first encumber ourselves with all the intellectual and emotional baggage which is an impediment to understanding. Except in a dim, pre-conscious way, animals do not understand a situation, even though, by inherited instinct or by an *ad hoc* act of intelligence, they may be reacting to it with complete appropriateness, *as though* they understood it. Conscious understanding is the privilege of men and women, and it is a privilege which they have earned, strangely enough, by acquiring the useful or delinquent habits, the stereotypes of perception, thought and feeling, the rituals of behavior, the stock of second-hand knowledge and pseudo-knowledge, whose possession is the greatest obstacle to understanding. "Learning," says Lao-tsu, "consists in adding to one's stock day by day. The practice of the Tao consists in subtracting." This does not mean, of course, that we can live by subtraction alone. Learning is as necessary as unlearning. Wherever technical proficiency is needed, learning is indispensable. From youth to old age, from generation to generation, we must go on adding to our stock of useful and relevant knowledge. Only in this way can we hope to deal effectively with the physical environment, and with the abstract ideas which make it possible for men to find their way through the complexities of civilization and technology. But this is not the right way to deal with our personal reactions to ourselves or to other human beings. In such situations there must be an unlearning of accumulated concepts; we must respond to each new challenge not with our old conditioning, not in the light of conceptual knowledge based on the memory of past and different events, not by consulting the law of averages, but with a consciousness stripped naked and as though newborn. Once more we are confronted by the great paradox of human life. It is our conditioning which develops our consciousness; but in order to make full use of this developed consciousness, we must start by getting rid of the conditioning which developed it. By adding conceptual knowledge to conceptual knowledge, we make conscious understanding possible; but this potential understanding can be actualized only when we have subtracted all that we have added.

It is because we have memories that we are convinced of our self-identity as persons and as members of a given society.

> The child is father of the Man;
> And I could wish my days to be
> Bound each to each by natural piety.

What Wordsworth called "natural piety" a teacher of understanding would describe as indulgence in emotionally charged memories, associated with childhood and youth. Factual memory—the memory, for example, of the best way of making sulphuric acid or of casting up accounts—is an unmixed blessing. But psychological memory (to use Krishnamurti's term), memory carrying an emotional charge, whether positive or negative, is a source at the worst of neurosis and insanity (psychiatry is largely the art of ridding patients of the incubus of their negatively charged memories), at the best of distractions from the task of understanding—distractions which, though socially useful, are none the less obstacles to be climbed over or avoided. Emotionally charged memories cement the ties of family life (or sometimes make family life impossible!) and serve, when conceptualized and taught as a cultural tradition, to hold communities together. On the level of understanding, on the level of charity and on the level, to some extent, of artistic expression, an individual has it in his power to transcend his social tradition, to overstep the bounds of the culture in which he has been brought up. On the level of knowledge, manners and custom, he can never get very far away from the *persona* created for him by his family and his society. The culture within which he lives is a prison— but a prison which makes it possible for any prisoner who so desires to achieve freedom, a prison to which, for this and a host of other reasons, its inmates owe an enormous debt of gratitude and loyalty. But though it is our duty to "honor our father and our mother," it is also our duty "to hate our father and our mother, our brethren and our sisters, yea and our own life"—that socially conditioned life we take for granted. Though it is necessary for us to add to our cultural stock day by day, it is also necessary to subtract and subtract. There is, to quote the title of Simone Weil's posthumous essay, a great "Need for Roots"; but there is an equally urgent need, on occasion, for total rootlessness.

In our present context this book by Simone Weil and the preface which Mr. T. S. Eliot contributes to the English edition are particularly instructive. Simone Weil was a woman of great ability, heroic virtue and boundless spiritual aspiration. But unfortunately for herself, as well as for her readers, she was weighed down by a burden of knowledge and pseudo-knowledge, which her own almost maniacal over-valuation of words and notions rendered intolerably heavy. A clerical friend reports of her that he did not "ever remember Simone Weil, in spite of her virtuous desire for objectivity, give way in the course of a discussion." She was so deeply rooted in her culture that she came to believe that words were supremely important. Hence her love of argument and the obstinacy with which she clung to her opinions. Hence too her strange inability, on so many occasions, to distinguish the pointing finger from the indicated moon. "But why do you prate of God?" Meister Eckhart asked; and out of the depth of his understanding of given reality, he added "Whatever you say of Him is untrue." Necessarily so; for "the saving truth was never preached by the Buddha," or by anyone else.

Truth can be defined in many ways. But if you define it as understanding (and this is how all the masters of the spiritual life have defined it), then it is clear that "truth must be lived and there is nothing to argue about in this teaching; any arguing is sure to go against the intent of it." This was something which Emerson knew and consistently acted upon. To the almost frenzied exasperation of that pugnacious manipulator of religious notions, the elder Henry James, he refused to argue about anything. And the same was true of William Law. "Away, then, with the fiction and workings of discursive reason, either for or against Christianity! They are only the wanton spirit of the mind, whilst ignorant of God and insensible of its own nature and condition. . . . For neither God, nor heaven, nor hell, nor the devil, nor the flesh, can be any other way knowable in you or by you, but by their own existence and manifestation in you. And any pretended knowledge of any of those things, beyond and without this self-evident sensibility of their birth within you, is only such knowledge of them as the blind man hath of the light that has never entered into him." This does not mean, of course, that discursive reason and argument are without value. Where knowledge is concerned, they are not only valuable; they are indispensable. But knowledge is not the same thing as understanding. If we want to understand, we must uproot ourselves from our culture, by-pass language, get rid of emotionally charged memories, hate our fathers and mothers, subtract and subtract from our stock of notions. "Needs must it be a virgin," writes Meister Eckhart, "by whom Jesus is received. Virgin, in other words, is a person, void of alien images, free as he was when he existed not."

Simone Weil must have known, theoretically, about this need for cultural virginity, of total rootlessness. But, alas, she was too deeply embedded in her own and other people's ideas, too superstitious a believer in the magic of the words she handled with so much skill, to be able to act upon this knowledge. "The food," she wrote, "that a collectivity supplies to those who form part of it has no equivalent in the universe." (Thank God! we may add, after sniffing the spiritual nourishment provided by many of the vanished collectivies of the past.) Furthermore, the food provided by a collectivity is food "not only for the souls of the living, but also for souls yet unborn." Finally, "the collectivity constitutes the sole agency for preserving the spiritual treasures accumulated by the dead, the sole transmitting agency by means of which the dead can speak to the living. And the sole earthly reality which is connected with the eternal destiny of man is the irradiating light of those who have managed to become fully conscious of this destiny, transmitted from generation to generation." This last sentence could only have been penned by one who systematically mistook knowledge for understanding, home-made concepts for given reality. It is, of course, desirable that there should be knowledge of what men now dead have said about their understanding of reality. But to maintain that a knowledge of other people's understanding is the same, for us, as understanding, or can even directly lead us to understanding, is a mistake against which all the masters of the spiritual life have always warned us. The letter in St. Paul's phrase, is full of "oldness." It has therefore no relevance to the ever novel reality, which can be understood only in the "newness of the spirit." As for the dead, let them bury their dead. For even the most exalted of past seers and avatars "never taught the saving truth." We should not, it goes without saying, neglect the records of dead men's understandings. On the contrary, we ought to know all about them. But we must know all about them without taking them too seriously. We must know all about them, while remaining acutely aware that such knowledge is not the same as understanding and that understanding will come to us only when we have subtracted what we know and made ourselves void and virgin, free as we were when we were not.

Turning from the body of the book to the preface, we find an even more striking example of that literally preposterous over-valuation of words and notions to which the cultured and the learned are so fatally prone. "I do not know," Mr. Eliot writes, "whether she [Simone Weil] could read the Upanishads in Sanskrit—or, if so, how great was her mastery of what is not only a highly developed language, but a way of thought, the difficulties of which become more formidable to a European student the more diligently he applies himself to it." But like all the other great works of Oriental philosophy, the Upanishads are not systems of pure speculation, in which the niceties of language are all important. They were written by Transcendental Pragmatists, as we may call them, whose concern was to teach a doctrine which could be made to "work," a metaphysical theory which could be operationally tested, not through perception only, but by a direct experience of the whole man on every level of his being. To understand the meaning of *tat tvam asi,* "thou art That," it is not necessary to be a profound Sanskrit scholar. (Similarly, it is not necessary to be a profound Hebrew scholar in order to understand the meaning of "thou shalt not kill.") Understanding of the doctrine (as opposed to conceptualized knowledge about the doctrine) will come only to those who choose to perform the operations that permit *tat tvam asi* to become a given fact of direct, unmediated experience, or in Law's words "a self-evident sensibility of its birth within them." Did Simone Weil know Sanskrit, or didn't she? The question is entirely beside the point—is just a particularly smelly cultural red herring dragged across the trail that leads from selfhood to more-than-selfhood, from notionally conditioned ego to unconditioned spirit. In relation to the Upanishads or any other work of Hindu or Buddhist philosophy, only one question deserves to be taken with complete seriousness. It is this. How can a form of words, *tat tvam asi,* a metaphysical proposition such as *Nirvana and samsara are one,* be converted into the direct, unmediated experience of a given fact? How can language and the learned foolery of scholars (for, in this vital context, that is all it is) be circumvented, so that the individual soul may finally understand the *That* which, in spite of all its efforts to deny the primordial fact, is identical with the *thou*? Specifically, what methods should we follow? Those inculcated by Patanjali, or those of the Hinayana monks? Those of the Tantriks of northern India and Tibet, those of the Far Eastern Taoists, of the followers of Zen? Those described by St. John of the Cross and the author of *The Cloud of Unknowing*? If the European student wishes to remain shut up in the prison created by his private cravings and the thought patterns inherited from his predecessors, then by all means let him plunge, through Sanskrit, or Pali, or Chinese, or Tibetan, into the verbal study of "a way of thought, the difficulties of which become more formidable the more diligently he applies himself to it." If, on the other hand, he wishes to transcend himself by actually understanding the primordial fact described or hinted at in the Upanishads and the other scriptures of what, for lack of a better phrase, we will call "spiritual religion," then he must ignore the problems of language and speculative philosophy, or at least relegate them to a secondary position, and concentrate his attention on the practical means whereby the advance from knowledge to understanding may best be made.

From the positively charged collective memories, which are organized into a cultural or religious tradition, let us now return to the positively charged private memories, which individuals organize into a system of "natural piety." We have no more right to wallow in natural piety—that is to say, in emotionally charged memories of past happiness and vanished loves—than to bemoan earlier miseries and torment ourselves with remorse for old offenses. And we have no more right to waste the present instant in relishing future and entirely hypothetical pleasures than to waste it in the apprehension of possible disasters to come. "There is no greater pain," says Dante, "than, in misery, to remember happy times." "Then stop remembering happy times and accept the fact of your present misery," would be the seemingly unsympathetic answer to all those who have had understanding. The emptying of memory is classed by St. John of the Cross as a good second only to the state of union with God, and an indispensable condition of such union.

The word *Buddha* may be translated as "awakened." Those who merely know about things, or only think they know, live in a state of self-conditioned and culturally conditioned somnambulism. Those who understand given reality as it presents itself, moment by moment, are wide awake. Memory charged with pleasant emotions is a soporific or, more accurately, an inducer of trance. This was discovered empirically by an American hypnotist, Dr. W. B. Fahnestock, whose books *Statuvolism, or Artificial Somnambulism,* was published in 1871. "When persons are desirous of entering into this state [of artificial somnambulism] I place them in a chair, where they may be at perfect ease. They are next instructed to throw their minds to some familiar place it matters not where, so that they have been there before and seem desirous of going there again, even in thought. When they have thrown the mind to the place, or upon the desired object, I endeavor by speaking to them frequently to keep their mind upon it. . . . This must be persisted in for some time." In the end, "clairvoyancy will be induced." Anyone who has experimented with hypnosis, or who has watched an experienced operator inducing trance in a difficult subject, knows how effective Fahnestock's method can be. Incidentally, the relaxing power of positively charged memory was rediscovered, in another medical context, by an oculist, Dr. W. H. Bates, who used to make his patients cover their eyes and revisit in memory the scenes of their happiest experiences. By this means muscular and mental tensions were reduced and it became possible for the patients to use their eyes and minds in a relaxed and therefore efficient way. From all this it is clear that, while positively charged memories can and should be used for specific therapeutic purposes, there must be no indiscriminate indulgence in "natural piety"; for such indulgence may result in a condition akin to trance—a condition at the opposite pole from the wakefulness that is understanding. Those who live with unpleasant memories become neurotic and those who live with pleasant ones become somnambulistic; sufficient unto the day is the evil thereof—*and* the good thereof.

The Muses, in Greek mythology, were the daughters of Memory, and every writer is embarked, like Marcel Proust, on a hopeless search for time lost. But a good writer is one who knows how to *"donner un sens plus pur aux mots de la tribu."* Thanks to this purer sense, his readers will react tб his words with a degree of understanding much greater than they would have had, if they had reacted, in their ordinary self-conditioned or culture-conditioned way, to the events to which the words refer. A great poet must do too much remembering to be more than a sporadic understander; but he knows how to express himself in words which cause other people to understand. Time lost can never be regained; but in his search for it, he may reveal to his readers glimpses of timeless reality.

Unlike the poet, the mystic is "a son of time present." "Past and present veil God from our sight," says Jalal-ud din Rumi, who was a Sufi first and only secondarily a great poet. "Burn up both of them with fire. How long will you let yourself be partitioned by these segments like a reed? So long as it remains partitioned, a reed is not privy to secrets, neither is it vocal in response to lips or breathing." Along with its mirror image in anticipation, emotionally charged memory is a barrier that shuts us out from understanding.

Natural piety can very easily be transformed into artificial piety; for some emotionally charged memories are common to all the members of a given society and lend themselves to being organized into religious, political or cultural traditions.

These traditions are systematically drummed into the young
of each successive generation and play an important part in
the long drama of their conditioning for citizenship. Since the
memories common to one group are different from the memories shared by other groups, the social solidarity created by
tradition is always partial and exclusive. There is natural and
artificial piety in relation to everything belonging to *us*, coupled with suspicion, dislike and contempt in relation to everything belonging to *them*.

Artificial piety may be fabricated, organized and fostered
in two ways—by the repetition of verbal formulas of belief
and worship, and by the performance of symbolic acts and
rituals. As might be expected, the second is the more effective
method. What is the easiest way for a skeptic to achieve faith?
The question was answered three hundred years ago by Pascal. The unbeliever must act "as though he believed, take holy
water, have masses said etc. This will naturally cause you to
believe and will besot you." (*Cela vous abêtira*—literally, will
make you stupid.) We have to be made stupid, insists Professor Jacques Chevalier, defending his hero against the critics
who have been shocked by Pascal's blunt language; we have
to stultify our intelligence, because "intellectual pride deprives
us of God and debases us to the level of animals." Which is,
of course, perfectly true. But it does not follow from this truth
that we ought to besot ourselves in the manner prescribed
by Pascal and all the propagandists of all the religions. Intellectual pride can be cured only by devaluating pretentious
words, only by getting rid of conceptualized pseudo-knowledge and opening ourselves to reality. Artificial piety based
on conditioned reflexes merely transfers intellectual pride from
the bumptious individual to his even more bumptious Church.
At one remove, the pride remains intact. For the convinced
believer, understanding or direct contact with reality is exceedingly difficult. Moreover, the mere fact of having a strong
reverential feeling about some hallowed thing, person or
proposition is no guarantee of the existence of the thing, the
infallibility of the person or the truth of the proposition. In
this context, how instructive is the account of an experiment
undertaken by that most imaginative and versatile of the
Eminent Victorians, Sir Francis Galton! The aim of the
experiment, he writes in his *Autobiography*, was to "gain an
insight into the abject feelings of barbarians and others concerning the power of images which they know to be of human
handiwork. I wanted if possible to enter into these feelings. . . .
It was difficult to find a suitable object for trial, because it
ought to be in itself quite unfitted to arouse devout feelings.
I fixed on a comic picture, it was that of Punch, and made

believe in its possession of divine attributes. I addressed it
with much quasi-reverence as possessing a mighty power to
reward or punish the behavior of men toward it, and found
little difficulty in ignoring the impossibilities of what I professed. The experiment succeeded. I began to feel and long
retained for the picture a large share of the feelings that a
barbarian entertains toward his idols, and learned to appreciate the enormous potency they might have over him."

The nature of a conditioned reflex is such that, when the
bell rings, the dog salivates, when the much worshiped image
is seen, or the much repeated credo, litany or mantram is
pronounced, the heart of the believer is filled with reverence
and his mind with faith. And this happens regardless of the
content of the phrase repeated, the nature of the image to
which obeisance has been made. He is not responding spontaneously to given reality; he is responding to some thing, or
word, or gesture, which automatically brings into play a
previously installed post-hypnotic suggestion. Meister Eckhart,
that acutest of religious psychologists, clearly recognized this
fact. "He who fondly imagines to get more of God in thoughts,
prayers, pious offices and so forth than by the fireside or in
the stall in sooth he does but take God, as it were, and
swaddle His head in a cloak and hide Him under the table.
For he who seeks God in settled forms lays hold of the form,
while missing the God concealed in it. But he who seeks God
in no special guise lays hold of him as He is in Himself, and
such an one lives with the Son and is the life itself."

"If you look for the Buddha, you will not see the Buddha."
"If you deliberately try to become a Buddha, your Buddha
is samsara." "If a person seeks the Tao, that person loses the
Tao." "By intending to bring yourself into accord with Suchness, you instantly deviate." "Whosoever will save his life shall
lose it." There is a Law of Reversed Effort. The harder we try
with the conscious will to do something, the less we shall succeed. Proficiency and the results of proficiency come only to
those who have learned the paradoxical art of simultaneously
doing and not doing, of combining relaxation with activity, of
letting go as a person in order that the immanent and transcendent Unknown Quantity may take hold. We cannot make
ourselves understand; the most we can do is to foster a state
of mind, in which understanding may come to us. What is
this state? Clearly it is not any state of limited consciousness.
Reality as it is given moment by moment cannot be understood by a mind acting in obedience to post-hypnotic suggestion, or so conditioned by its emotionally charged memories
that it responds to the living *now* as though it were the dead
then. Nor is the mind that has been trained in concentration

any better equipped to understand reality. For concentration is merely systematic exclusion, the shutting away from consciousness of all but one thought, one ideal, one image, or one negation of all thoughts, ideals and images. But however true, however lofty, however holy, no thought or ideal or image can contain reality or lead to the understanding of reality. Nor can the negation of awareness result in that completer awareness necessary to understanding. At the best these things can lead only to a state of ecstatic dissociation, in which one particular aspect of reality, the so-called "spiritual" aspect, may be apprehended. If reality is to be understood in its fullness, as it is given moment by moment, there must be an awareness which is not limited, either deliberately by piety or concentration, or involuntarily by mere thoughtlessness and the force of habit. Understanding comes when we are totally aware—aware to the limits of our mental and physical potentialities. This, of course, is a very ancient doctrine. "Know thyself" is a piece of advice which is as old as civilization, and probably a great deal older. To follow that advice, a man must do more than indulge in introspection. If I would know myself, I must know my environment; for as a body, I am part of the environment, a natural object among other natural objects, and, as a mind, I consist to a great extent of my immediate reactions to the environment and of my secondary reactions to those primary reactions. In practice "know thyself" is a call to total awareness. To those who practice it, what does total awareness reveal? It reveals, first of all, the limitations of the thing which each of us calls "I," and the enormity, the utter absurdity of its pretensions. "I am the master of my fate," poor Henley wrote at the end of a celebrated morsel of rhetoric, "I am the captain of my soul." Nothing could be further from the truth. My fate cannot be mastered; it can only be collaborated with and thereby, to some extent, directed. Nor am I the captain of my soul; I am only its noisiest passenger—a passenger who is not sufficiently important to sit at the captain's table and does not know, even by report, what the soul-ship looks like, how it works or where it is going. Total awareness starts, in a word, with the realization of my ignorance and my impotence. How do electro-chemical events in my brain turn into the perception of a quartet by Haydn or a thought, let us say, of Joan of Arc? I haven't the faintest idea—nor has anyone else. Or consider a seemingly much simpler problem. Can I lift my right hand? The answer is, No, I can't. I can only give the order; the actual lifting is done by somebody else. Who? I don't know. How? I don't know. And when I have eaten, who digests the bread and cheese? When I have cut myself, who heals the wound? While I am sleeping, who restores the tired body to strength, the neurotic mind to sanity. All I can say is that "I" cannot do any of these things. The catalogue of what I do not know and am incapable of achieving could be lengthened almost indefinitely. Even my claim to think is only partially justified by the observable facts. Descartes's primal certainty, "I think, therefore I am," turns out, on closer examination, to be a most dubious proposition. In actual fact it is *I* who do the thinking? Would it not be truer to say, "Thoughts come into existence, and sometimes I am aware of them"? Language, that treasure house of fossil observations and latent philosophy, suggests that this is in fact what happens. Whenever I find myself thinking more than ordinarily well, I am apt to say, "An idea has occurred to me," or, "It came into my head," or, "I see it clearly." In each case the phrase implies that thoughts have their origin "out there," in something analogous, on the mental level, to the external world. Total awareness confirms the hints of idiomatic speech. In relation to the subjective "I," most of the mind is out there. My thoughts are a set of mental, but still external facts. I do not invent my best thoughts; I find them. Total awareness, then, reveals the following facts: that I am profoundly ignorant, that I am impotent to the point of helplessness and that the most valuable elements in my personality are unknown quantities existing "out there," as mental objects more or less completely independent of my control. This discovery may seem at first rather humiliating and even depressing. But if I wholeheartedly accept them, the facts become a source of peace, a reason for serenity and cheerfulness. I am ignorant and impotent and yet, somehow or other, here I am, unhappy, no doubt, profoundly dissatisfied, but alive and kicking. In spite of everything, I survive, I get by, sometimes I even get on. From these two sets of facts—my survival on the one hand and my ignorance and impotence on the other—I can only infer that the not-I, which looks after my body and gives me my best ideas, must be amazingly intelligent, knowledgeable and strong. As a self-centered ego, I do my best to interfere with the beneficent workings of this not-I. But in spite of my likes and dislikes, in spite of my malice, my infatuations, my gnawing anxieties, in spite of all my overvaluation of words, in spite of my self-stultifying insistence on living, not in present reality, but in memory and anticipation, this not-I, with whom I am associated, sustains me, preserves me, gives me a long succession of second chances. We know very little and can achieve very little; but we are at liberty, if we so choose, to co-operate with a greater power and a completer knowledge, an unknown quantity at once immanent and transcendent, at once physical and mental, at once subjective and objective. If we co-operate, we shall be all right, even if the worst should happen. If we refuse to co-operate, we shall be all wrong even in the most propitious of circumstances.

These conclusions are only the first-fruits of total awareness. Yet richer harvests are to follow. In my ignorance I am sure that I am eternally I. This conviction is rooted in emotionally charged memory. Only when, in the words of St. John of the Cross, the memory has been emptied, can I escape from the sense of my watertight separateness and so prepare myself for the understanding, moment by moment, of reality on all its levels. But the memory cannot be emptied by an act of will, or by systematic discipline or by concentration—even by concentration on the idea of emptiness. It can be emptied only by total awareness. Thus, if I am aware of my distractions— which are mostly emotionally charged memories or phantasies based upon such memories—the mental whirligig will automatically come to a stop and the memory will be emptied, at least for a moment or two. Again, if I become totally aware of my resentment, my uncharitableness, these feelings will be replaced, during the time of my awareness, by a more realistic reaction to the events taking place around me. My awareness, of course, must be uncontaminated by approval or condemnation. Value judgments are conditioned, verbalized reactions to primary reactions. Total awareness is a primary, choiceless, impartial response to the present situation as a whole. There are in it no limiting conditioned reactions to the primary reaction, to the pure cognitive apprehension of the situation. If memories of verbal formulas of praise or blame should make their appearance in consciousness, they are to be examined impartially as any other present datum is examined. Professional moralists have confidence in the surface will, believe in punishments and rewards and are adrenalin addicts who like nothing better than a good orgy of righteous indignation. The masters of the spiritual life have little faith in the surface will or the utility, for their particular purposes, of rewards or punishments, and do not indulge in righteous indignation. Experience has taught them that the highest good can never, in the very nature of things, be achieved by moralizing. "Judge not that ye be not judged" is their watchword and total awareness is their method.

Two or three thousand years behind the times, a few contemporary psychiatrists have now discovered this method. "Socrates," writes Professor Carl Rogers, "developed novel ideas, which have proven to be socially constructive." Why? Because he was "notably non-defensive and open to experi-

ence. The reasoning behind this is based primarily upon the
discovery in psychotherapy that if we can add to the sensory
and visceral experiencing, characteristic of the whole animal
kingdom, the gift of a free undirected awareness, of which
only the human animal seems fully capable, we have an
organism which is as aware of the demands of the culture as
it is of its own physiological demands for food and sex, which
is just as aware of its desire for friendly relationships as it is
aware of its desire to aggrandize itself; which is just as aware
of its delicate and sensitive tenderness toward others as it is
of its hostilities toward others. When man is less than fully
man, when he denies to awareness various aspects of his
experience, then indeed we have all too often reason to fear
him and his behavior, as the present world situation testifies.
But when he is most fully man, when he is his complete
organism, when awareness of experience, that peculiarly
human attribute, is fully operating, then his behavior is to be
trusted." Better late than never! It is comforting to find the
immemorial commonplaces of mystical wisdom turning up as
a brand-new discovery in psychotherapy. *Gnosce teipsum*—
know yourself. Know yourself in relation to your overt intentions and your hidden motives, in relation to your thinking,
your physical functioning and to those greater not-selves, who
see to it that, despite all the ego's attempts at sabotage, the
thinking shall be tolerably relevant and the functioning not
too abnormal. Be totally aware of what you do and think and
of the persons with whom you are in relationship, the events
which prompt you at every moment of your existence. Be
aware impartially, realistically, without judging, without reacting in terms of remembered words to your present cognitive
reactions. If you do this, the memory will be emptied, knowledge and pseudo-knowledge will be relegated to their proper
place, and you will have understanding—in other words, you
will be in direct contact with reality at every instant. Better
still, you will discover what Carl Rogers calls your "delicate
and sensitive tenderness toward others." And not only *your*
tenderness, the cosmic tenderness, the fundamental all-right-
ness of the universe—in spite of death, in spite of suffering.
"Though He slay me, yet will I trust Him." This is the utterance of someone who is totally aware. And another such utterance is, "God is love." From the standpoint of common sense,
the first is the raving of a lunatic, the second flies in the face
of all experience and is obviously untrue. But common sense
is not based on total awareness; it is a product of convention,
of organized memories of other people's words, of personal
experiences limited by passion and value judgments, of hallowed notions and naked self-interest. Total awareness opens

the way to understanding, and when any given situation is understood, the nature of all reality is made manifest, and the nonsensical utterances of the mystics are seen to be true, or at least as nearly true as it is possible for a verbal expression of the ineffable to be. One in all and all in One; samsara and nirvana are the same; multiplicity is unity, and unity is not so much one as not-two; all things are void, and yet all things are the Dharma-Body of the Buddha—and so on. So far as conceptual knowledge is concerned, such phrases are completely meaningless. It is only when there is understanding that they make sense. For when there is understanding, there is an experienced fusion of the End with the Means, of the Wisdom which is the timeless realization of Suchness with the Compassion which is Wisdom in action. Of all the worn, smudged, dog's-eared words in our vocabulary, "love" is surely the grubbiest, smelliest, slimiest. Bawled from a million pulpits, lasciviously crooned through hundreds of millions of loud-speakers, it has become an outrage to good taste and decent feeling, an obscenity which one hesitates to pronounce. And yet it has to be pronounced, for, after all, Love is the last word.

(From *Tomorrow and Tomorrow and Tomorrow*)

The essays in this collection have been selected from
the following volumes:

On the Margin, 1923
Along the Road, 1925
Jesting Pilate, 1926
Do What You Will, 1929
Music at Night, 1931
Beyond the Mexique Bay, 1934
The Olive Tree, 1937
Ends and Means, 1937
Grey Eminence, 1941
Science, Liberty and Peace, 1946
Themes and Variations, 1950
The Doors of Perception, 1954
Heaven and Hell, 1956
Tomorrow and Tomorrow and Tomorrow, 1956